Sporting Females

This book is an important piece of historical and sociological research. Based on extensive library research, the use of archival books and artefacts, original records and documents and media material, the book makes an outstanding contribution to the feminist study of sports. It provides a superb critical account of the development of female sports from the nineteenth century to the present day, examining theoretical ideas, historical material and topical issues. In doing so, it reveals the complex and paradoxical character of female sports. Both gender and class relations are analysed, as well as other aspects of life and culture which are intrinsic to the development of female sports. No other book is so comprehensive. Most histories and sociologies of sports focus on those of men, but this book places women at the centre of the discussion and thus fills an important gap in the market. It views sports as part of a battle for control of the body and, as such, as an important area for feminist intervention.

Jennifer Hargreaves is Reader in the Politics and Sociology of Sport at the Roehampton Institute, London.

Sporting Females

Critical issues in the history and sociology
of women's sports

Jennifer Hargreaves

London and New York

First published 1994
by Routledge
11 New Fetter Lane, London EC4P 4EE

Simultaneously published in the USA and Canada
by Routledge
29 West 35th Street, New York, NY 10001

Reprinted 1996, 1997, 2001

Routledge is an imprint of the Taylor & Francis Group

© 1994 Jennifer Hargreaves

Typeset in Garamond by LaserScript, Mitcham, Surrey
Printed and bound in Great Britain by
TJ International Ltd, Padstow, Cornwall

British Library Cataloguing in Publication Data
A catalogue record for this book is available from the British Library

Library of Congress Cataloguing in Publication Data
Hargreaves, Jennifer, 1937–
   Sporting females: critical issues in the history and sociology of
women's sports/Jennifer Hargreaves.
   p. cm.
   Includes bibliographical references and index.
   1. Sports for women – Great Britain – History. 2. Sports –
Sociological aspects. 3. Feminist theory. I. Title.
   GV709.18.G7G37   1994
   796'.0194 – dc20
                                          93-24575
                                             CIP

ISBN 0–415–07027–9 (hbk)
ISBN 0–415–070287 (pbk)

315357

To Campbell

Contents

Tables

Acknowledgements

During the years that I was collecting material and writing this book I received help from many friends and colleagues, some of whom read parts of it along the way and some of whom gave invaluable encouragement and stimulation when I was flagging – thanks go to Eric Dunning, Mary Evans, Tony Green, Sheila Miles, Peter Weston, Gary Whannel and Anita White. Jay Coakley and Margaret Talbot painstakingly read the completed manuscript for Routledge, but did much more than was required of them and provided insightful comments for which I am grateful. Jim Riordan very kindly spent many hours proof-reading the whole text and made helpful suggestions as well. Thanks also to Chris Rojek, my editor, who has been consistently supportive of my work and to the Roehampton Institute for allowing me some time for research.

My children, Carl and Jane, and my partner, Campbell, must be overjoyed that the book is finally completed because for such a long time they have seen me disappearing to be with my Amstrad instead of spending time with them. Their love and support have been indispensable.

Finally, and most importantly, the book would not exist without the women it is about. My enduring thanks go to all those who have so willingly and enthusiastically taken time and trouble to talk to me in person and on the telephone, and to write to me and give me material. Sporting females have been the inspiration for the book and it is written for them.

Jennifer Hargreaves

Introduction

If you go to your local library and look at the sports books, they will almost
certainly be predominantly about men. If you go to a university library, the
bulk of the writing in sports history and sociology assumes male standards.
Switch on your television to look at sports programmes and it's the same
story – you can be 90 per cent sure to see male rather than female performers; or go to a pub and listen to conversations about sports and they will
inevitably be conducted by men talking about male competitions. In spite of
the fact that more women are participating in more sports than ever before,
and in spite of a significant number of feminist interventions into sports
theory, much more attention is still given to the role of sports in the lives of
men than to the importance of sports to women. *Sporting Females: critical
issues in the history and sociology of women's sports* is therefore a political
intervention into the world of sports scholarship. It is an effort to bring
women's sports more centrally on to the agenda, to show the importance of
using gender as a fundamental category for analysis, and to explore some of
its complexities.

The twentieth century has seen tremendous changes in patterns of consumption and leisure, in relations between the sexes, and in the prominence
given to the body in western culture. These are some of the broad social
changes that make women's sports a fascinating topic for analysis. And
nineteenth-century women as well as twentieth-century women are the
subjects of this book, because they both have relevance to our understanding of sports today and to the relationship between sports, the body
and personal identity.

Sports are increasingly implicated in the social construction of womanhood, but the meanings attached to them vary tremendously according to a
person's individual biography. Most people only know about exceptional
sportswomen, however – those who have broken world records, been
labelled as 'unfeminine', or behaved bizarrely. Very little is known about the
various types of women who are involved in sports, and the values that they
bring to them. This book looks at sports in the lives of women with working-
class and middle-class backgrounds; single parents and those living with

partners; women with different ethnicities; the old and the young; the able-bodied and the disabled; and those with different sexual preferences. It is concerned with women who are sports professionals, administrators and coaches, as well as with those who participate at all levels of competition, and those who take part in other ways and for different reasons. There has been a strong tendency in the debate about women's sports to dwell on reductive categories (male vs female; masculinity vs femininity; nature vs culture; aggressive vs co-operative), which masks the multiple realities of women's lives. *Sporting Females* looks at *both* the lived experiences of women in sports *and* the structural forces influencing participation.

In its document *Women and Sport* (1991), the GB Sports Council adopts a definition of 'sport' which concurs with that given in the *Council of Europe Sport for All Charter*. It broadly embodies activities which are institutional-ized, strictly organized and highly competitive, as well as those which are freely arranged, recreative and aesthetic. A similarly extensive definition is employed in this book which includes references to mainstream activities and those that are less well known – for example, aerobics, body-building, croquet, cycling, hot-air ballooning, korfball, marathon running, punting, rambling, snooker, soccer, synchronized swimming, tennis, water-polo and wrestling. In addition, the early history of physical education is examined, as well as recent developments in the subject. The term 'sports' is used through the book rather than 'sport' in order to take account of the diverse and non-essentialist nature of the activities. The settings for women's sports are also varied, and references are made to a wide range of them – for example, sports-specific and non sports-specific organizations, clubs, leisure centres and recreative venues.

Although the main context of the book is the UK, there are numerous examples given of women's sports in other countries of the world – in particular, elsewhere in western Europe, and in North America.

The methodological approach is varied. It includes the use of archival books and artefacts, original records and documents, and media material, as well as data analyses and a variety of investigative techniques. For example, interviews have been carried out with hundreds of women from different social backgrounds involved in various ways in a variety of sports. Elderly women have been the subjects for oral history. A wealth of secondary source material has provided the necessary additional empirical evidence and the background for theoretical analysis. A pivotal procedure has been to link empirical material with theoretical ideas.

Sporting Females provides a critical account of the development of female sports from their formative years in the nineteenth century to the present day. But it is not an attempt to give a comprehensive history; that would be impossible. However, it is hoped that the examples included, and the critical and sometimes provocative discussions, will stimulate debate and understanding. There is a recognition that the problem of male power is fundamental, but also that sports do not produce a straightforward system of domination of men over women. The book analyses changes that have occurred, the conditions under which advances in women's sports have been made, and how we can make sense of what has happened in the past and what is happening today. The ways in which conventional gender relations have been built, reproduced and contested are examined, as well as examples of unexamined sexism. Time and time again, the evidence suggests that female sports have been riddled with complexities and contradictions throughout their history.

The particular issue of freedom and constraint is integrated into the text: it is examined as a theoretical problem in Chapters 1 and 2; it is embodied in the account of the historical development of women's sports in Chapters 3 to 6; and it is treated critically in the examples of contemporary sports in Chapters 7 to 11.

The purpose of theorizing is to help us understand the nature of sports in society. But Chapter 1 reveals the misleading implications of popular accounts of gender divisions in sports, and the general inability of different sociological perspectives to deal adequately with this problem. Although they represent different and sometimes conflicting theories of society, all the perspectives discussed, without exception, have marginalized gender in one way or another. In this respect they fail to provide a satisfactory analysis. Part of this failure is the strong tendency to treat gender as a variable, rather than as a relationship of power. Chapter 2 examines different feminist perspectives which have developed as a reaction to the general neglect of gender in 'mainstream' accounts. By placing women at the centre of the analysis, they provide an important challenge to the way in which male standards have become generalized standards in sports theory. Sports feminists have 'politicized' experience by drawing connections between ideas and practice. This highlights the complex and paradoxical character of female sports and exposes the need to understand better the complex link between capitalist relations and gender relations. Both Chapters 1 and 2 point to the impoverishment of separating and stereotyping the sexes. They also illustrate how gender oppression in sports can be understood as oppression of men as well as of women.

Chapters 3, 4, 5 and 6 provide a social history of the development of female sports and physical education in the UK from the late nineteenth century until the Second World War. Western culture has been profoundly influenced by the nature/culture dichotomy, and so have women's sports. Underpinning all these chapters are ideas about the 'nature of woman' and popular arguments about women's physical inferiority as biologically determined. It becomes clear that in the Victorian period the physical body was a fundamental symbol of power relations between men and women and moulded the development of women's sports for years to come. Patriarchal ideology had an important influence on the development of physical education (as well as sports), and the conservatizing influences of this subject, as well as the advances, are explored in Chapter 4. Historical evidence shows us how women had to struggle against popular definitions of their biologies in order to participate in physical activities; it also shows the link between other social factors and female physical education and sports, in particular the ways in which gender has interacted with social class. Even during the inter-war years, which represent a remarkable period of change when increasing numbers of women were actively flaunting old restrictions and participating in numerous and varied sports, in some contexts they faced harsh opposition which resulted in limited opportunities and slowed growth. These four chapters show how the whole of the history of women's sports embodies themes of continuity and change: although the movement of women into sports symbolizes emancipation, it was never without resistance. The history of women's sports also provides a basis for understanding sports today.

The second part of the book – Chapters 7–11 – is concerned mostly with contemporary sports. Chapter 7 discusses the nature of gender as an organizing principle, and explores ways in which sporting images of masculinity and femininity are linked to the creation of socially created gender identities in other spheres. It incorporates material which illustrates that current representations of the female sporting body show some collapse of conventional points of reference, some acceptance of values which have previously been marginalized, and the emergence of new, radicalized images of female physicality. Chapter 8 is to do with gender relations of power and institutionalized discrimination. It raises issues about some of the economic, practical and structural constraints which act as a material force upon women's participation in sports. It provides examples of women's lack of power and control in different national and international contexts. The internationalization of women's sports is also dealt with in a separate chapter about the Olympics. In Chapter 9 a gendered history of the modern Olympic Games accounts for the long-term resistance to women's full participation, but also shows how in recent years the globalization of Olympic sports has added new dimensions to the problem of female participation. This chapter illustrates the tremendous cultural power of international sports.

The final two chapters of *Sporting Females* focus on recent developments. They cover numerous sports and contexts, varied issues and controversies, and include references to women with different experiences and expectations. Chapters 10 and 11 are to do with the politicization of women's sports; with power and control; with sensitive issues such as homophobia and racism; and with morality and empowerment. What happens today will have inevitable repercussions for women in the next century.

Throughout the book we can see ways in which sports are related to other aspects of life and culture and how they are part of the battle for control of the physical body which is, of course, a social struggle. It is a critical analysis of women's sports which raises questions about the extent to which sports are radical activities for women, and how they might be viewed as a process of accommodation to existing structures of power and control, and to dominant ideologies. But sporting females symbolize freedom, and this book is also a celebration of women's achievements and their continuing determination to forge new definitions. It is clear that sports can be oppressive for both men and women, but that they also have the potential to be liberating for both sexes. Sports are therefore important contexts for feminist intervention. However, redefining relations of gender has important implications for men as well as women.

Chapter 1

Theories of sports
The neglect of gender

INTRODUCTION

Although for a century or more organized sports have occupied a central position in British cultural life, until comparatively recently they have been a neglected area of historical and sociological analysis. This is partly because mainstream ideas about sports are concerned with the physical body (something that appears as entirely 'natural' and unchangeable), and partly because sports are popularly believed to have a 'life of their own', essentially separate from 'important' aspects of the social world of work, politics and economics (something intrinsically innocent, playful and liberating). Not surprisingly, some of the earliest theorizing about sports during the 1960s was essentially uncritical and had a positivist orientation. It was assumed that sports are a feature of a common cultural heritage, embracing a central value system shared by all sections of society (see Chapters 1 and 2 in Hargreaves 1982). But during the 1970s and 1980s, as sports became more blatantly politicized and commercialized, and such problems as drugs and hooliganism became public issues, the significance of sports as *social* phenomena captured the imagination of theorists with a more critical orientation. Since that time the sociology of sports has expanded rapidly and is now a sophisticated field of social analysis.

THE PROBLEM OF SEXUAL DIFFERENCE

Analysing sports is an inherently controversial affair and the sociology of sports incorporates different and conflicting theories of society – those which in general support conventional ideas about sports, about the nature of society, and about masculine and feminine identities; and those which question them. The production of critical histories and sociologies of sports has been part of a wider theoretical movement focusing on 'culture' and on the significance of ideology and consciousness within it (Hall 1981). Part of this movement has been the attempt of sociologists to understand the organic relationships between sports and other cultural formations, to examine questions of agency and structure, and to look at the tensions between change and continuity. But although all these isssues are connected to relationships of power between different agents, and in particular to gender relations of power, a common characteristic of the various sports sociology perspectives is the marginalization of women's experiences and relationships of gender. In this respect, the history of sports sociology reflects the long history of male domination of modern sports and dominant ideas about sexual difference. Sports history and sociology reflect the male dominance of academic discourse.

It has been particularly difficult to transcend traditional assumptions that differences between the sexes are biological rather than cultural, and that feminine- and masculine-appropriate sports and male sporting superiority are in the 'natural' order of things (see Chapters 3 and 7). The notion that human behaviour is parallel in many ways to that of other primates underpins the argument that differing cultural behaviour between men and women is rooted in biology:

> we behave culturally because it is in our nature to behave culturally, because natural selection has produced an animal that has to behave culturally, that has to invent rules, make myths, speak languages, and form men's clubs, in the same way that the hamadryas baboon has to form harems, adopt infants, and bite its wives on the neck.
>
> (Tiger and Fox 1971: 20)

Although this extreme version of biological determinism is not prevalent in sports sociology, nevertheless biological determinism is influential in the general discourse of sports academia. For example, Desmond Morris's (1981) explanations of human aggression in sports as instinctive male behaviour are popular and influential; in the elite field of cultural analysis, the argument that sports are the 'natural' domains of men because of the innately different biological and psychological natures of men and women, has been given legitimacy (Carroll 1986); and the ideology of sexual difference is validated in the sports sciences (Hargreaves 1982: 2). To explain the cultural at the level of the biological encourages the exaggeration and approval of analyses based on distinctions between men and women, and masks the complex relationship between the biological and the cultural. As Paul Willis (1982: 119) points out, 'to know, more exactly, why it is that women can muster only 90% of a man's strength cannot help us to comprehend, explain, or change the massive feeling in our society that a woman has no business flexing her muscles anyway'.

Although sociologists of sport and leisure have provided a critique of biological determinism, at the same time they are implicated in the reproduction of ideas about sexual difference through the content and organization of their own work. There have been three main approaches: first, to disregard women by using the term 'sports' unproblematically, ignoring that what is really being examined is *male* sports from which generalizations are made about the experiences of all humans, and to refer to 'society' as if it is a single community in respect of men and women (Dunning 1971; Parker 1976). The second approach, which has been a reaction to the influence of feminism, is to devote some space to female sports and discussions of gender (usually a separate chapter or section) in an essentially male-oriented account (Coakley 1990; Elias and Dunning 1986; John Hargreaves 1986; Jarvie 1991). There is a tendency in both these approaches to fail to distinguish between sex and gender and implicitly to incorporate male-defined definitions and values. This book is characterized by the third, specifically feminist and minority perspective, which is a sociology exclusively of female sports (Boutilier and San Giovanni 1983; Lenskyj 1986; see next chapter). The last approach, unlike the other two, does not construct the female as 'the Other', but rather attempts to subvert dominant gender relations in sports sociology. However, because the whole of the history of modern sports has been based on gender divisions, even radical accounts of women's sports tend to focus on perceived *differences* between men and women, rather than on the less obvious *relations* of power between them. In general, therefore, sports sociology texts do not give equal treatment to male and female sports or integrate gender relations thoroughly into their analyses.

POPULAR IDEAS ABOUT SPORTS

Differences between men and women in sports are also a focus for sports providers, such as the GB Sports Council and local authorities. On the surface, however, their approach seems progressive: their policies are based on the premise that sports are beneficial to individuals and to society as a whole and that women should therefore participate in greater numbers, more in line with men's participation rates. The following statement made by the UK Sports Council (1992b: 75) reflects establishment ideas about sport being a harmonizing force which contributes to the well-being of society:

> We *know* that sport can make a positive contribution to national morale, health and the economy. We *believe* that it can enhance community spirit, equality of opportunity, personal development and social integration.

But these are not just the ideas of people in influential positions in sports, they are popular and powerful ideas in society at large. For example, a survey carried out by Mori in 1990 shows how highly the British public value sports:

> 90% agreed that most people who take part in sport get a great deal of pleasure from it;

> 83% agreed that people should be encouraged to take part in sport for health reasons;

79% agreed that taking part in sport gives people self-confidence and helps character development;

79% agreed that 'sport has a vital role to play in society today'.

(Sports Council 1992b: 15)

The way in which questions are structured and responses elicited in such a survey treats the nature of both sports and society uncritically. The orientation is unambiguously functionalist, in common with the 'mainstream tradition' of sports sociology which goes back to the 1960s (see, for example, Ball and Loy 1975; Loy and Kenyon 1969; Luschen 1970, 1988; Sage 1974). Put rather simply, the general idea in functionalist accounts is that sport helps individuals to develop stable personalities and contributes to their well-being and all-round development, thus functioning to benefit society as a whole. The representation of sports as 'affirmative culture' is associated with liberal democracy as a political system, and with the emergence of a pluralist society and the ideology that the interests of divergent groups have equal validity. Modern sport is viewed as a progressive movement in history reflecting the general enfranchisement of wider and wider sections of the population (including women), symbolized in the philosophy of 'Sport for All'.

POPULAR IDEAS ABOUT GENDER

Although such an uncomplex application of functionalism to a study of sports in society is no longer dominant in sports sociology, functionalist concepts remain influential. For example, 'socialization' is used widely in broadly different perspectives as a way of explaining how, through sports, individuals learn the dominant norms and values of society (Coakley 1990; Dyer 1982; McPherson, Curtis and Loy 1989). It is argued that girls are socialized to behave in 'feminine-appropriate' ways – a process which can be viewed as having beneficial or, less typically, negative effects. For example, Coakley (1990) argues that gender-role socialization results in inequalities between the sexes and discrimination against women. But there is a general failure with the concept of socialization to analyse adequately the extent of opposition to gender patterning, and a failure to analyse critically both traditional and newer images of femininity in sports. For example, the incompleteness of socialization results in the making of 'tomboys', in increasing numbers of young women playing traditional male team games, and in housewives demanding time away from the kitchen to participate in their favourite sports. But the tensions and conflicts between groups with opposing interests are minimized whenever the concept of socialization is used, whether or not it is seen as beneficial or detrimental. Changes, ambivalences and conflicts over gender divisions are marginalized, and the significance and shifting nature of gender relations often ignored.

A lot of official research also has a functionalist orientation. For example, implicit in the reports of the GB Sports Council and other policy documents (Sports Council 1982, 1988b, 1992b) is support of the basic structures, practices and values of mainstream sports and of the social system in general. They also neglect the interrelationships of power and gender. Such research reflects an empiricist orthodoxy, concentrating on statistical evidence and presenting results in a descriptive fashion as if they are unrelated to theories and meanings. The assumption that the theorist is neutral (someone who collects, presents and analyses the 'facts' of sport as value-free) does not take into account why, for example, certain surveys are financed and not others, and why certain questions are chosen and others left out (see the critique of Yiannakis [1989] by Ingham and Donnelly [1990]). The techniques used to analyse research data are often related to stereotyped ideas, and policies which reflect them. Empiricism assumes open-mindedness, but in practice tends to support established values and practices. For example, women's limited access to sports, by comparison with that of men, is looked at as a problem that can be corrected by social engineering of a piecemeal kind, and increased participation is seen to reflect the way in which organizations have responded to the changing needs of women as a group. The GB Sports Council (1992b: 27) claims that

> The gap between men's and women's participation has narrowed signifi- cantly over the last decade, and has shown signs of accelerating in recent years. Over 13 million adult women (57% [of women in the population]) participated in sport in the 4 weeks before interview in 1990, compared with 15.5 million adult men (73% [of men in the population]). (Walking is included as an activity in these statistics, and if it were left out the disparity between male and female participation would be much greater.)

The analysis of such data takes for granted the existing structures, arrange- ments and ideologies of sports for women, and as Liz Stanley (1980) argues:

> In brief, such an approach is one which takes the philosophy and prac- tical assumptions, ways of working, bases for defining problems within it as unproblematic. If women do not 'fit in' into the kind of provision that results from this approach, then the problem is *women*, not the approach.
> (Quoted in Talbot 1988: 33)

Increasing participation figures signify an improvement in the quality of life for large numbers of women, but they can be misleading. While some women have autonomy to participate in sports relatively freely, others face difficult constraints. It is essential that we treat critically the implication that women 'in general' have increased access to sport or even want increased access. Generalizations based upon women as a supposedly homogeneous group assume a spurious notion of consensus and ignore discriminatory practices and competing interests. They tend to mask the essentially historical nature of the 'needs of women', the varied and contradictory features of sports for women and the wielding of power, not only between men and women, but between different groups of women and different groups of men as well.

The GB Sports Council provides some evidence of different rates of sports participation according to certain subgroupings, such as age and disability, but not comprehensive data for all groups of women. And although in its publication on *Women and Sport* (1992a), the council looks at some of the factors which constrain women's participation, it seldom funds radical research of the sort which would analyse the unquantifiable underlying causes – for example, the evolution, legitimation and reproduction of systems of belief, cultural values and symbolic representations which affect women's participation in sports. It is also the case that the Sports Council has failed to consider the ethical dimensions of women's participation in 'patriarchal' and 'capitalist' sports, the nature and extent of opposition to existing arrangements, or the possibilities of alternatives. For example, the Sports Council's reference to education in its consultation document *Sport in the Nineties – New Horizons* (1992b: 21–3), makes no comment about the controversies surrounding the teaching of dance as an aspect of the National Curriculum for Physical Education (see Chapter 8). The National Curriculum Council took the decision not to implement the recommendations of the National Curriculum Physical Education Working Group to make dance compulsory for both sexes up to the age of 14 years (Department of Education and Science 1991), and the Minister for Sport and Her Majesty's inspectors condoned this decision. The opportunity to radicalize gender relations in school physical education has been lost, but in spite of the Sports Council's original support of equal opportunities for boys and girls in physical education, its silence on the issue since the National Curriculum has been implemented implicitly supports the position of the government.

ETHNOGRAPHIC RESEARCH

In attempts to acquire an authentic understanding of women's needs, desires, opportunities and constraints, feminists have tended to favour ethnographic research – in particular, participant observation and interviews. A number of studies of women and leisure fall into this category (for example, contributions to Wimbush and Talbot 1988), but there are remarkably few ethnographic studies of women's sports in Britain. Most examples are male enquiries about male sub-cultures around sports such as gambling, horse-racing, professional wrestling and soccer (Ashworth 1971; Fleming 1991; Goffman 1961; Marsh, Rosser and Harré 1978; Scott 1968). In these studies there is a general failure to examine reasons why the subcultures are (almost) exclusively male and to look at ways in which gender relations cohere with other features of the broader social context.

Participant observation and interview methodologies are part of the inter-actionist tradition which places the meaningfulness of social action at the centre of any kind of explanation (see Chapter 2 in Hargreaves 1982). Interactionism is concerned with the *problem of control* – how human beings can exert control over relationships, historical situations, activities and institutions. Culture is conceived of as a 'lived experience', constructed and changed through the interaction of men and women who make, resist and transform meanings, values and rules of behaviour. Whereas most research about women's sports treats gender as a variable, ethnographic research ensures that women are placed at the centre of any analysis. To apply such an approach to women's sports is an attractive idea, because we know so little about why women do or do not participate in sports, how they construct and change them, what meanings and values sports hold for them, the significance that some women attach to sports which are not those of the central value system, and what visions women might have about alternatives (see Chapters 10 and 11).

But it is possible to idealize the potential for autonomy in a way which is abstract and illusory. This has been the weakness of some interactionist sociology which gives an exaggerated emphasis to human subjectivity and fails to relate personal biographies to specific social structures and historical circumstances. It is important not to underestimate the ways in which cultural patterns and economic, political and ideological orders specific to the totality of social relations affect the participation of women in sports. If common patterns as well as differences are scrutinized, more could be understood about the realities of the dualism between agency and structure.

FIGURATIONAL SOCIOLOGY

The 'figurational' or 'process-sociological' study of sports, which derives from the work of Norbert Elias, would seem to have the answer because it claims to oppose 'false dichotomies' (agency from structure; individual from society), and to hold as centrally important the process, or interactive aspects of culture and relationships of power (see, for example, Dunning 1989; Dunning and Rojek 1992; Elias and Dunning 1986). Yet in spite of these claims, it is an approach which embodies epistomological problems. The following brief discussion derives from a fuller critique of figurational soci-ology (which makes special reference to its limitations in dealing with gender), and makes comments about Eric Dunning's riposte to it. Both are found in *Sport and Leisure in the Civilizing Process*, edited by Dunning and Rojek (1992).

The editors claim that the book was planned specifically to open up the debate for and against the application of the figurational perspective to sport and leisure. But because a disproportionately large amount of space is allocated to those papers that are generally in favour of the figurational approach, in comparison with those that criticize it, the overall effect is biased in its favour. And in spite of his avowed respect for 'detachment' and openness of debate (for an explanation of the notion of detachment, see Elias and Dunning 1986: 3–5), Dunning places himself, and Elias's approach to the social world of sports in which he so passionately believes, in a privileged and powerful position by writing a 'counter-critique'. This is a lengthy chapter which takes up 22.5 per cent of the total text (excluding the Preface and Introduction), where Dunning selectively attacks those authors who are critical of figurational sociology but who have no opportunity in the context of that publication to respond to his remarks. The book is a very clear example of male bias and gender neglect: there is one female and ten male contributors and, except for Dunning's response to the 'token feminist' chapter, the contributions reflect a general disregard for the significance of gender to the topics being discussed. The book justifies the criticism that sports sociology in general, and figurational sociology specifically, 'focuses on male experiences, marginalizes females and says very little about gender relations' (Hargreaves 1992a: 161). It is a good example of the institutionalization of gender relations of power in sports academia reproduced around men doing research about male sports. *Sport and Leisure in the Civilizing Process* is a celebration of the figurational approach which fits neatly into the conventional male-oriented pattern of sports sociology.

Elias describes the 'civilizing process' as a long-term trend towards 'an equalizing change in the balance of power between social classes and other groups' (Elias and Dunning 1986: 13), and he posits

> an equalizing of relationships between the sexes as a reflection of the lengthening of interdependency chains in social figurations. He proposes that societies with a more centralized, advanced and differentiated division of functions, and where social life is no longer exclusively tied to militarism and explicit expressions of violence, have complex and extensive chains of interdependence between people and a greater level of equality between the sexes.
>
> (Hargreaves 1992a: 167)

Elias also argues for a connection between the structure of relationships in society and the personality structure of individuals, and he introduces the state as an enabling mechanism of equality between the sexes which has monopolized the legitimate use of physical force. But empirical evidence connected to women in sports and leisure does not fit easily into this formulation. Positing a long-term 'narrowing of the gap between men and women' is a generalization which implies that women are a homologous group and fails to take account of the complexities and differences between different groups of women (Sports Council 1992a). There are just too many contradictions and complexities for the generalized framework of the figurational perspective to cope with. Furthermore, Elias's notion of equality is resistant to any moral or ethical position (1978: 153), and so it is unable to deal with the struggle in sports between individuals who believe in different forms of equality: for example, those who want women to 'catch up with the men'; those who want women to be 'equal but different'; and men and women who are fighting *together* to change the aggressively competitive, elitist and commodified models of sports to something more radical. The methodology of detachment disables figurational sociologists from answering such questions as 'Equality for what?'; 'Equality according to which criteria?'; 'Equality in whose interests?'; 'Equality at what cost?'. The notion of 'equality between the sexes' is empty and meaningless unless it is related to specific structures of power and placed in the context of specific economic, political and ideological forces.

Representations of the state in figurational sociology raise problems over gender as well. The term 'state', used descriptively, is characterized as an essentially neutral and benevolent institution which takes no account of the ways in which state power has emerged as male power and has become an organized and institutionalized form of social dominance. No reference is made to the complex gendered character of the state in modern capitalist countries (MacKinnon 1989). Dunning (1992), for example, makes no comment about the failure of sex equality legislation in Britain and in other western states to alter radically patterns of discrimination against women in leisure and sports, or the failure of most local government leisure policies to understand and deal with most forms of sex discrimination (see Chapter 8; Hargreaves 1992a; Yule 1990). As long as the power of men over women subtly permeates society, it is irrational to imagine that sex equality legislation will do much to change everyday examples of discrimination against women.

Even the collaborative work of Dunning, Murphy and Williams (1988; Williams, Dunning and Murphy 1989), which uncharacteristically considers the significance of gender in the context of football hooliganism, contains analytical problems. The authors discuss the propensity for physical violence among football hooligans, and the attitudes and relationships of these young men to and with women. The authors' research shows that the majority of hooligans come from lower-working-class backgrounds and that their construction and expression of a violent masculine style is a 'central life commitment'. It is argued that the hooligans' pleasure in perpetrating violence around football is reinforced at home, and that a common feature of their lives is a high level of violence against women. 'Many women in such communities', Williams, Dunning and Murphy reason (1989: xxix), 'grow up to be relatively violent themselves and to expect violent behaviour from their men. To the extent that this is so, the violent propensities of the men are reinforced.' Unfortunately, however, the analysis fails to consider how such dominance of and violence against women relates to other examples of male violence and to gender relations of power in the wider society (J. A. Hargreaves

1986). For example, it would be interesting to consider the links between violent acts carried out by football hooligans, violence against women in the home, violence and aggression encouraged in male sports generally, and the attitudes of women to sports, and their participation rates. But in spite of their own evidence of violence perpetrated by men against women, and that of numerous feminist researchers, the authors dismiss violent outbursts as counter-spurts in a generally more 'civilized' society.

Many of Dunning's criticisms are not backed up by documented evidence. For example, he is clutching at straws when he labels my work and that of other cultural theorists as economistic. He argues that 'Jenny Hargreaves remains content with a few one-dimensional, economistic assertions about patriarchy and capitalism' (1992: 256). To support his assertion, however, he cites only one paper which I wrote in 1984, which, he says, characterizes 'the more "scientific", as opposed to the critical, sides of [my] sociological work'. But this piece was written in a 'journalistic' style, for a specifically non-academic readership, and contains no references to or evidence of empirical work whatsoever; perversely, Dunning disregards all documented research which shows the link between gender power and cultural power. He shows a preference for generalized, unsubstantiated statements about gender and rejects analyses which position gender relations in sports in specific political/economic/ideological frameworks. Dunning makes no reference to other work of mine (or that of other sports feminists) which looks at the problems, complexities and contradictions of research and analyses of gender relations in sports (for example, Hargreaves 1986, 1989, 1990, 1992b, 1992c). Yet he creatively interprets what has been written and disregards the evidence upon which arguments are based – for example, he asks:

> How, independently of back-up from painstaking historical research, can Jenny Hargreaves maintain that women's concerns about their public safety have risen to *unprecedentedly* [Dunning's emphasis] high levels? How can she assert that the home has become *the most dangerous* place for women? What sort of time period does she have in mind? The last ten years? The last fifty? The last thousand?
>
> (Dunning 1992: 256)

In fact, I had written:

> Women's *reported* [emphasis not in original] concerns about personal safety in public have risen to unprecedentedly high levels and it is well documented that the home has become the most dangerous place for women.
>
> (1992a: 176)

The context in which this was written makes it clear that I am referring to the varied nature and extent of violence against women in contemporary western societies. The intention was to demonstrate that Dunning's assertion that the world has become a less violent and more civilized place for women is deeply problematic. Although I, personally, have not done 'painstaking historical research' into violence against women, I provide six references to the painstaking research of others in order to support my statement (ibid.: 177). Catharine MacKinnon (1989) provides additional empirical evidence of the nature of violent acts perpetrated by men against women and the problems of safety that women face in private spaces. She points out that male dominance is sexual (127), and gives over fifty references to recent feminist research, both interpretive and empirical, about different forms of sexual violence against women and children, including examples of rape, battery, sexual harassment, sexual abuse of children, prostitution and pornography (276–9). My claim, refuted by Eric Dunning, that 'public and private spaces in "civilized" societies are far from being "pacified" social spheres' is based upon the evidence of research of this kind. The concept of the 'civilizing process' does not take into account the extent and variety of violent acts perpetrated against women – including psychological, emotional and physical violence. It is clear that Dunning is unfamiliar with research on violence in the home, or with research about the inability of the state to deal with violence in private spheres, such as the family, and he provides no evidence for his assertion that the civilizing process brings with it greater equality between the sexes and a trend towards less violence against women. In characteristic fashion, however, he covers himself for all eventualities by claiming that 'it would not necessarily be inconsistent with that theory if a rise in violence against women . . . were currently occurring' (257). It is difficult not to object to Dunning's implication that, as a figurational sociologist, he has a more professional approach than the rest of us – the actual evidence is quite the opposite. He refuses to consider the wealth of excellent research carried out by those who work with 'passionate objectivity' rather than with a 'quest for detachment' (Hargreaves 1992a: 162–6). The problem for figurational sociology is not that many of us have *misunderstood* the theory, as Dunning would have it (257), but that we *disagree* with its claims and find the Marxist tradition of sports sociology more fruitful for understanding the social world of sports.

MARXISM

Some of the most stimulating developments in the sociology of sport have derived from a corpus of writing which has, broadly speaking, been based on the work of Karl Marx. However, in common with other perspectives, Marxist sports sociology is not a unified theory; it comprises a variety of approaches and the differences between them have produced controversy. They are all critical of the nature of capitalist sports; but some interpretations are determinist, and argue that the economic and ideological effects of sports are crucial in all situations, while others interpret Marxism as a humanist theory, and claim that it does not exclude the potential for resistance. Current developments have focused on questions of *autonomy and domination*; the relationship between creative and liberating forces in sports and cultural hegemony. But again, the bulk of the writing is about male sports, and, with few exceptions, the question of gender is dealt with in terms of antagonistic *divisions* and not by examining the complexities and contradictory features of gender relations.

NEO-MARXIST APPROACHES: ECONOMISM

From the 1970s, a number of books have been published which characterize sport as a mirror of capitalist society and which highlight the extent to which sports have become dominated on a global scale by commercialization (Beamish 1982, 1988; Brohm 1978; Hoch 1972; Rigauer 1981; Vinnai 1973). Some of these texts also draw attention to how important certain ruling groups consider sports to be and the ways in which they function to prop up the social relations intrinsic to a capitalist system of production. For example, it is argued that modern sports help to reproduce labour power by replicating features of industrial production and by inculcating the attitudes and values required for a docile and disciplined labour force. It is also stressed that modern sports are repositories for dominant ideology in their celebration of ruthless competition, aggression and violence and their embodiment of elitism, nationalism, racism, militarism, imperialism and sexism.

But the tendencies towards reductionism in economistic perspectives produce exaggerated accounts of a complete correspondence between sports and the mode of production, as if people are unavoidably trapped by the structural conditions of capitalist sports. Because the mode of production and class relations are given priority in the analysis, and the owners of capital are assumed to have virtually absolute control over culture, it is difficult to account for the different forms of sport that people participate in, the apparent autonomy from the economy that some of them enjoy, and culture-, class- and gender-based resistances. The focus in these approaches on paid labour provides a very partial view of the specific relationship between gender and the mode of production and, more specifically, ignores the significance of unpaid domestic labour.

Brohm, Hoch and Vinnai were three of the first theorists to look in some detail at the relationship between sports and sexuality. They argue that sexuality is mediated in sports; that sexual repression is necessary for the survival of capitalism; and that the machismo ethos of sports, by bonding men together, is a fundamental expression of male power and domination over women. Their arguments are supported by psychological explanations derived from Freudian theory and notions of sexual sublimation. Brohm (1978: 56), for example, states unequivocally that 'It is mainly through the sublimation of sexual drives that the practice of competitive sport contributes to the reproduction of the social relations of production'. The focus is upon males and the way that, through sports, their sexuality is sublimated to the needs of work discipline. In other words, sports are presented as a substitute – a way of regulating male sexuality and diverting young men from sexual problems. The celebration of sporting images of masculinity evokes contrasting images of the passive, unathletic female.

Although sexuality features as an important element of capitalist relations in the formulations of these authors, they simplify and distort its significance by implicitly reducing explanations to the level of some notion of 'normal' sexuality and 'normal' male and female behaviour. They also tend to imply that the relationships between gender relations and sports are static, and hence they fail to account for the ways in which images of sexuality have changed and are continuing to change. People are presented as if they are passive recipients of sexist ideology, which, in turn, is employed as if it is 'total' – containing no oppositional elements or variations of any sort. In this way sexism is presented as a straightforward product of capitalist sports, and there is a failure throughout this literature to explore in detail the ways in which gender relations have been undeniably and intimately bound up with economic and class determinants in *different and complex* ways, and how the interrelationships between these categories have varied historically. The general tendency has been to suggest that men's ability to dominate women pervades all sports in a mechanistic and uncomplicated way. This has produced an uncritical account of the extent and effects of sexism in sports which fails to acknowledge their contradictory features.

STRUCTURALIST MARXISM: THEORIES OF REPRODUCTION

Also during the 1970s theories of 'social reproduction', and in particular the writings of Althusser and Bourdieu, were applied to studies of culture and sports (see Chapters 1 and 2 in Hargreaves 1982). Although there are differences in the approaches of these two theorists, they have common features that identify them as 'reproduction theorists'. They both address themselves to the problem of explaining how the economies, dominant cultures and power relations of capitalist societies survive and are reproduced. Both Althusser and Bourdieu refer to sports in their analyses, but whereas economistic Marxists view them as a reflection of the totality, reproduction theorists argue that sports possess their own specific characteristics, making them relatively autonomous from other aspects of culture that also have their own unique dynamics. Nevertheless, it is argued that, however indirectly, different forms of culture function collectively so that the major features of capitalist society are reproduced. Theorists in this tradition assume that forces outside the economy have a reciprocal influence on it, which, although they work at different levels and in different ways, possess a logic about the way they are part of a total social formation. In other words, a major implication of theories of social reproduction is that social structures inevitably ensure that the dominant culture, class and power relations are reproduced and there is a 'structural causality' in the way the whole society works.

For Althusser, ruling-class ideology is the cohesive force on which the reproduction of the social relations of modern capitalist production depends. He describes a number of 'distinct and specialized institutions' as a *'plurality of Ideological State Apparatuses'* (ISAs) which '"function" massively and predominantly by ideology' (1971: 137–9). He identifies education as the dominant ISA in mature capitalist societies – particularly significant here because children in maintained schools participate in sports as part of the compulsory curriculum. He also cites the cultural ISA ('literature, the arts, sports, etc.'), the communications ISA ('press, radio and television, etc.') and the family ISA – through all of which we experience sports (ibid.: 137). According to Althusser, these are institutions where dominant ideology is concentrated and becomes a 'lived condition'. Althusser argues explicitly that it is ruling class ideology that unifies the diversity of the ISAs (ibid.: 139, 142). Although sports are said to have their own effective sphere of influence, or relative autonomy from other superstructural levels, it is argued that the ISAs are collectively and 'ultimately' determined by the economic base. Thus, the ideologies that Althusser says characterize modern sports, such as competitiveness, chauvinism, nationalism and sexism, function to reproduce existing patterns of domination. In sports, it is claimed, people learn rules and meanings *unconsciously* so that culture is *automatically* reproduced in a way which serves the needs of capitalism. Sports are conceived in this formulation, not as an area of free expression, of opposition, or of complexity, but essentially as an area of conformity.

The sphere of gender relations is barely discernible in Althusser's analysis. Patriarchy is assumed to be an ideological realm, and sexism in sports, as in other ISAs, is presented as an abstract and essentially ahistorical category which acts as a functional necessity of capitalist society (ibid.). It follows that both men and women are passive agents who are induced through sports to accept conventional gender divisions. In common with economistic Marxists, reproduction theorists imply a static relationship between sexuality and capitalism and fail to examine the unevenness of power relations between men and women. It would be difficult to use Althusser's theory to explain how some sports settings are havens for male chauvinism in ways that have shown little change since the nineteenth century, whereas, in others, gender relations have changed radically and are continuing to change in ways that would have been inconceivable even a decade ago.

Bourdieu (1978, 1984) incorporates sports more systematically into his theory of reproduction than does Althusser. In structuralist fashion, he posits cultural spheres, such as sports, as having unique features, tempos and crises which are not reflections of what is happening in other spheres, but which are 'homologous' with the capitalist economy and dominant social relations

(1978: 821). Bourdieu uses the term 'homologous' to argue that, 'in spite of the specific logic of the different *fields*', such as sports, there is an overall logic about the way these structures work together to reproduce the power relations between classes. 'Without any deliberate pursuit of coherence,' he says, 'there is, inevitably, class identity and harmony' (1984: 173).

Bourdieu employs the term 'habitus' to explain the process of reproduction. He argues that one's habitus is a set of beliefs, dispositions and behaviour patterns, 'characteristic of the different class and class fractions', and which is the product of upbringing and education (Garnham and Williams 1980: 213; Bourdieu 1984: 1–6). The habitus, he argues, 'is not only a structuring structure, which organizes practices and the perception of practices, but also a structured structure', because the principle of division into logical classes organizes people's perceptions of the social world (ibid.: 170). It is as if individuals are thus 'caged' in class-specific life-styles which encompass cultural tastes or preferences, such as sports. For example, Bourdieu observes that the working classes have an instrumental orientation and prefer sports demanding strength, endurance and the propensity to violence; whereas the 'privileged' classes regard the body as an end in itself for reasons of appearance or health, and participate in such activities as running – 'movements without any other aim than physical exercise and the symbolic appropriation of a world reduced to the status of a landscape' (1980: 252; 1984: 20–1, 212). He maintains that the relationship of the individual to his or her body is a fundamental aspect of the habitus which varies not only between classes, but between class fractions, defined through indices such as occupation, income or educational level, and also according to sex (1984: 102). He argues further that

> Sexual properties are as inseparable from class properties as the yellow-ness of a lemon is from its acidity: a class is defined by the place and value it gives to the two sexes and to their socially constituted dispositions. This is why there are as many ways of realizing femininity as there are classes and class fractions.
>
> (Bourdieu 1984: 107–8)

Bourdieu makes generalizations about differences between men and women – for example, he describes sports as 'physical capital', which is valued highly for men and boys and estimated low for women, in contrast with beauty contests and the occupations they lead to, which are 'physical capital' for girls and women. However, the focus of Bourdieu's analysis is class relations, under which gender relations are subsumed – for example, he argues that the working classes have a 'practical philosophy of the male body as a sort of power, big and strong, with enormous, imperative, brutal needs, which is asserted in every male posture' (ibid.: 193). He maintains that it is possible to 'map out a universe of class bodies' which 'tends to reproduce in its specific logic the universe of the social structure' (ibid.: 193), and he continues

We can hypothesize as a general law that a sport is more likely to be adopted by a social class if it does not contradict that class's relation to the body at its deepest and most unconscious level, i.e., the body schema, which is the depository of a whole world view and a whole philosophy of the person and the body.

(Bourdieu 1984: 217–18)

Employing a passive model of human behaviour, Bourdieu explicitly rejects the 'lived experience' (ibid.: 100) and what he describes as 'the subjectivist illusion' (ibid.: 244). He views social space as 'objective space' which determines people's interactions and experiences. According to Bourdieu, women's sports are determined by their class: he states, for example, that 'differences between the sexes in sports participation increase as one moves down the social hierarchy' (ibid.: 214), and that women from the dominant class are 'more at home with their bodies' (ibid.: 206). Petit-bourgeois women, Bourdieu says, are 'almost as dissatisfied with their bodies as working-class women' and sacrifice much time and effort to improve their appearance (ibid.: 206). He argues that the concern not to grow old and the interest in ascetic forms of exercise are part of a specifically bourgeois health cult (ibid.: 212), whereas the demand for 'a "liberated" body is characteristic of women in the new fractions of the bourgeoisie and petit bourgeoisie' (ibid.: 211).

But social classes and the relations between them are presented by Bourdieu as cultural 'facts' which have primacy over power relations between men and women. Class struggle is, for Bourdieu, 'a reproductive struggle, since those who enter the chase . . . are beaten from the start, as the constancy of the gap testifies' (ibid.: 165). Bourdieu tends to treat people as if they are properties of the system and fails to appreciate how cultural fields, such as sports, contain the capacity for people/women to resist and change social/gender relations.

Although Althusser gives primacy to theory, which discourages empirical research, whereas Bourdieu provides a wealth of empirical material concerned with how people make their own lives, they both presuppose a more or less homogeneous culture for each class. Such formulations ignore the serious conflicts, complexities and contradictions endemic to modern sports and, specifically, to gender relations in sports. Reproduction theory has a static and pessimistic quality which is silent on personal and sensitive aspects of sexuality, gender relations, struggles and change that are reactions to lived experiences and human interaction.

CULTURAL MARXISM: HEGEMONY THEORY

The economistic and reproduction theories described above are, in different ways, determinist. They stress the manipulative features of sports and fail to consider the extent to which individuals may be free to pursue activities that are creative and liberating. In an attempt to explain theoretically the complexities of the relationship between freedom and constraint in sports, theorists have turned to the work of Antonio Gramsci (1971; see also Anderson 1976), and specifically to the concept of 'hegemony'. Hegemony has been used to explain continuities *and* discontinuities in sports: the ways in which dominant meanings and interests which are inherited from past traditions engender opposition and have to be defended, while new meanings and different interests are constantly being worked out and struggled for (see Chapters 1 and 2 in Hargreaves 1982; Clarke and Critcher 1985; Gruneau 1983, 1988; John Hargreaves 1986). Hegemonic configurations of power are understood to be part of a continual process of change which incorporates negotiation and accommodation, a 'lived system of meanings and values – constitutive and constituting' (Williams 1977: 110).

Hegemony describes a form of control which is *persuasive*, rather than coercive. It is understood to be the result of people's positive reactions to values and beliefs, which, in specific social and historical situations, support established social relations and structures of power. This is very different from straightforward indoctrination. Hegemony resists the idea that people are passive recipients of culture and keeps intact what is arguably the inherent *humanism* of Marxism. Hegemony embodies a sense of culture as a way of life imbued with systems of meanings and values which are *actively* created by individuals and groups in different social settings, such as families, schools, the media, leisure contexts and sports. Culture is not assumed to be the 'whole of society', it is analytically distinct from political and economic processes, but, together with them, makes up the totality of social relations. Economic and cultural forces are assigned mutually constitutive roles, rather than the former having a determining effect upon the latter. The concept of hegemony proposes a dialectical relationship between individuals and society, accounting for ways in which individuals are both determined and determining, and it allows for cultural experiences such as sports to be understood as *both* exploitative *and* worthwhile (Gramsci 1971; Anderson 1976; Williams 1977).

Hegemony operates essentially as a result of the subtle effects of ideology – a material effect which is confirmed by the mundane realities of people's lives, through which it becomes 'commonsense' (Larrain 1979). Because sports are vastly popular, and can be compelling and enjoyable, they are important vehicles for the transmission of ideology. But hegemony is never total: although the specific task of ideology is to legitimize dominant power relations and produce cultural continuity, dominant ideas are not the only ones – there is always the potential for oppositional ideas to subvert dominant ones and lead to cultural change. Dominant and subordinate groups are not necessarily, therefore, unambiguously winners or losers.

Ideology is rooted in human 'praxis' – an essentially social activity in which ideas and meanings cannot be separated from action. New ideas about sports cannot *change* them, they can only, possibly, *lead* to change; to become real they have to be put into practice, and hence the key to change is the way people produce their lives in common. Ideas and meanings evolve, show continuity and undergo change, not because of their internal content, but because people interrelate with one another in particular social contexts. Sports are thus conceived as constitutive processes – parts of life that are structured by society and history, but also the result of actions and changing relationships. In this formulation, consciousness is not passive, but incomplete, inconsistent and transitory. Hegemony theorists do not view sports as 'all-or-nothing' phenomena, as determinist interpretations imply, but as areas of life which contain contradictions. In this formulation, it is argued that there is neither total incorporation into existing sports structures, nor absolute rejection of them.

Applying the concept of hegemony to the histories of sports enables them to be understood as a series of struggles for power between dominant and subordinate groups – the result of conflicting interests over unequal sports resources in specific social contexts. However, antagonistic class relations have provided the focus for such accounts, and although reference has been made to the relationship between class and gender, and even to the way that class and gender divisions are constructed *together*, there have been no attempts to explore this relationship rigorously or to look at the specific complexities of male hegemony (Clarke and Critcher 1985; Gruneau 1983, 1988; John Hargreaves 1986). Because of the relative silence on women's sports and gender divisions, there is an implication that class is the root cause of women's as well as men's oppression in sports, and that problems of gender are secondary. This is the position also of orthodox and structuralist Marxists and it has serious theoretical limitations because it does not deal with the complexities of the relationship between, as well as the relative independence of, capitalist relations and patriarchal relations.

However, it is possible to apply the concept of hegemony specifically to male leadership and domination of sports (J. A. Hargreaves 1986). Male interests predominate in most sports, and in many of them male hegemony has been more complete and more resistant to change than in other areas of culture. Nevertheless, male hegemony in sports has never been static and absolute, but is a constantly shifting process which incorporates *both* reactionary *and* liberating features of gender relations. The concept of male hegemony recognizes the advantages experienced by men, in general, in relation to women, but recognizes also the inability of men to gain total control. Some men and some women support, accommodate, or collude in existing patterns of discrimination in sports that are specific to capitalism and to male domination, while other men and women oppose them and struggle for change. Male hegemony is not a simple male vs female opposition, which is how it is often presented, but complex and changing.

Hegemony theory may provide a better framework for understanding how, in sports, as in other cultural activities, gender relations are part of a complex process specific to capitalist social relations. The complexities and contradictions of women's sports embody specific economic and political arrangements which intersect with such factors as class, age and ethnicity, as well as gender relations. The crux of feminist criticisms of all varieties of Marxism is that sexual categories are not intrinsic to Marxist concepts, but have only been appended to them. This was true of all sports sociology until the 1980s, when specifically feminist versions emerged which are discussed in the following chapter.

Chapter 2

Sports feminism
The importance of gender

FEMINIST PERSPECTIVES

Some of the first feminist interventions in sports sociology occurred in North America during the 1970s. A number of books were written about women's sports at that time which, although weakly theorized (Gerber, Felshin, Berlin and Wyrick 1974; Kaplan 1979; Klafs and Lyon 1978; Oglesby 1978; Parkhouse and Lapin 1980; Twin 1979), represented an important reaction to the forms of male dominance in sports sociology discussed in Chapter 1. Feminist sports sociology was an element of a more general sports feminism centring on the efforts of practising sportswomen to unmask discrimination and to equalize opportunities with men. Sports feminism was a late-comer to the women's movement which had tended to focus on questions of legal, political and ideological importance, rather than on cultural issues such as sports and leisure. But feminist interest in sports gained ground rapidly in North America and by the 1980s there were an increasing number of publications about women's sports with a more substantial theoretical content (*Arena Review* 1984; Birrell and Richter 1987; Boutilier and San Giovanni 1983; Greendorfer 1977; Hall 1985, 1988; Lenskyj 1986; Theberge 1985). There has also been a small but developing concern to take account of the effects of gender discrimination in sports against men, to assess the significance of homophobia, and for men and women to work together to look at the complexities of gender issues in sports (Griffin 1989; Kidd 1987; Messner and Sabo 1990; Pronger 1990; Sabo 1985; Sabo and Runfola 1980). Sports feminism has been spreading outside North America as well, notably in western Europe and Australia and New Zealand. In the UK, it has a particular character, having grown out of a more general concern with women's leisure and with the relationships between class, patriarchy and culture emanating from women's studies, cultural studies and social history (Deem 1986; Green, Hebron and Woodward 1987; Griffin, Hobson, MacIntosh and McCabe 1982; Hargreaves 1986, 1989, 1992; Scraton 1986; Talbot 1988; Willis 1982; Wimbush 1986; Wimbush and Talbot 1988).

The 1990s mark a period of developing theoretical sophistication in feminist sports sociology. But the general failure of the past to incorporate gender relations of power into analyses (including relations of power between men and women, and between different groups of women and different groups of men), to relate them to other structures of power in society, and to deal with conflict and change, needs now to be tackled thoroughly. One of the major problems is to take account of different circumstances, and most notably specific differences between various groups of men and women, without losing sight of widespread structures of control. The important impact of feminist intervention into sports sociology has been to uncover ways in which men's power over women in sports has been institutionalized; it has provided a practical and symbolic challenge to male privilege which has resulted in a general recognition of gender as a basic category of analysis, and it has raised consciousness about the complexities and contradictions of gender relations in sports theory and practice.

Sports feminists are both men and women who want discrimination in sports on account of gender to be eradicated. It is a desire for change. However, the major impetus of the 'sports feminist movement' has been a concern for *women's* rights and needs. Sports feminism is not a unified movement or idea, nor can its different forms easily be characterized as cultural, liberal, orthodox Marxist, radical, or socialist, so that they would tie in with categories of feminism found in the general debate about the causes of women's subordination. But this chapter points out the common ground between sports feminist approaches and those found in the general feminist literature since the 1970s. Although it is convenient to separate feminist theories and important to recognize differences, a good deal of overlap exists between them as well, and there should be resistance to the idea that somewhere, if only we can discover it, a definitive theory of female sports exists. Theoretical absolutism is not possible: theories are interpretations and they change as do the circumstances being analysed. However, this is not an argument for the sort of eclecticism that occurs when concepts from different and sometimes incompatible theories are put together as if they are coherent, without making clear the similarities, incompatibilities and different values underpinning them. Theorizing is to do with struggling over values which should be made explicit. The process of critical assessment can clarify problems and help to formulate alternatives.

EQUALITY OF OPPORTUNITY

The dominant pressure in sports feminism is the desire for equality of opportunity for women in comparison with men. It is an incentive which is based on the belief that, although male power in sports predominates, it is not inviolable. Sports feminism represents a struggle by women, and by men on their behalf, to get more of what men have always had. The growing concern to provide access for females to traditionally masculinized activities is a central feature of liberal democratic ideology, the intellectual and political framework of which is usually described as liberal-feminist. Liberal feminism is defined as 'an attempt to remove or compensate for the ascriptive and social impediments that prevent women from competing on equal terms with men, without otherwise challenging the hierarchical structures within which both sexes operate' (Miles and Middleton 1989: 189). Liberal sports feminism challenges historically acquired inequalities in sports between men and women, but it is not a challenge to the conventional character of modern sports or to the 'essential' nature of modern capitalism and patriarchy (Dyer 1982; Gerber, Felshin, Berlin and Wyrick 1974; Klafs and Lyon 1978; Parkhouse and Lapin 1980; Twin 1979).

Liberal ideology embraces the notion that throughout the history of industrial society women have been approaching nearer to equality with men in all aspects of life and culture. In sports this supposedly progressive process started during the late nineteenth and early twentieth centuries, continued during the inter-war and post-war periods, and then accelerated in recent years. Liberalism is based upon the belief that, by implementing legal and social reforms, society upholds the principles of democracy, which embodies the philosophy of equality between the sexes. Equality of opportunity in sports is influenced by the generalized effects of government legislation and by more specific strategies aimed at sports. For example, government legislation in Britain and the USA (Sex Discrimination Act [1975] and Title IX [1972], respectively) was intended to tackle and outlaw discrimination against women in public and educational contexts (see Chapter 8), and the GB Sports Council aims to equalize opportunities between the sexes as part of its general 'Sport for All' campaign (Sports Council 1982, 1988, 1992b). Sports liberalism is associated with the roles of organizations which hold power in the provision of sports resources – for example, the central government and other public bodies, such as local authorities; and sports organizations, such as the governing bodies. For those who, like women, are characterized as deprived, the practical implication of the philosophy of equality is to provide additional resources for them. Such policies cohere with those of sports feminists who want easier access and better facilities for women in sports, improved funding and rewards, equal rights with men under the law, top quality coaching on a par with men, and an equivalent voice with men in decision-making. Their demands are supported by empirical evidence – the fact that, for example, far more men than women participate in sports in Britain, and in a greater number of activities and with greater frequency than women (Sports Council 1988, 1992a, 1992b).

Liberal feminism is essentially pragmatic. Sports activists have struggled to put the theory of equal opportunity into practice, and they have achieved tremendous successes, especially in the last decade. There is no doubt that in advanced industrial countries such as Britain, *more* sports are now *more* accessible to *more* women than ever before. Liberal feminism also implicitly rejects biological explanations for non-participation and embraces the belief that if women are given the opportunity they can participate in the full range of sports that men enjoy (Dyer 1982; Ferris 1981). These implications are important because the most consistent justification for opposition to women's equality with men has been articulated in terms of the supposed limitations inherent in female biology. The assumption underpinning liberal intervention is that culture and not nature is the reason why so few women have been involved in sports, and that any barriers that still prevent women from participating can be removed by rational intervention.

There are, however, contradictory implications in the liberal feminist position. The conception of equal opportunities, symbolized by the phrase 'Catching up the men' (Dyer 1982), is a limited one, concerned more with quantitative than qualitative change. It suggests a structure for women's sports which is modelled on men's sports and which works according to the established principles of intense competition. An idealized vision is presented to us, as if the trend is an inevitably improving one with few ethical problems. Parkhouse and Lapin (1980: 31), referring to the USA, typify this position when they say:

> Equality is a right, not a privilege. However, it has become apparent in this 'land of opportunity' that equal opportunity becomes a reality only if we act if that right is denied.

But such an articulation masks the weaknesses of the concept of equality. Questions about where the values come from that perpetuate inequalities and in whose particular interests they work are left unanswered. Questions such as, 'Equality for which particular women?', 'Equality for what purpose?', and 'Equality according to which criteria?' are left unexplored. In liberal sports feminism there is a general tendency to accept the values of mainstream sports and a failure to relate the concept of equality to wider social, economic, ideological and political issues.

Furthermore, 'equal rights for women' implies that they are a homogeneous group and misleadingly assumes that an overall increase in participation is an improvement for women *in general* (see Chapter 1, p. 10–11). In reality, the increase in women's participation is not the same for all groups of women, and there are no statistics which provide a comprehensive guide to the variable rates of participation of women from different backgrounds. Nor can the particularly difficult and sometimes unique problems faced by certain groups of women – those who are single parents, low paid, from Asian communities, or disabled, for example – be dealt with in numerical form. Women from different backgrounds do not experience patriarchal culture in identical ways, and they have different opportunities and expectations about sports. Blanket statements also mask the smaller range of sports in which women participate, in comparison with men, and the excessively low participation rates in some specific sports and contexts; and they say nothing about the nature and frequency of participation. Generalized statistics also mask the large discrepancy between the participation rates of women 'in general' and the proportionately tiny number of women in powerful decision-making positions in comparison with men (see Chapter 8).

Liberal feminism also tends to overlook the limitations of legal reform and to underestimate the strength of entrenched resistance to changing attitudes and behaviour (Banks 1981). It is implausible to imagine that genuine equality will result from legal reforms when the power of men over women subtly permeates society, or to think that sport could be changed fundamentally by legislation which embodies gender as an organizing principle (Hargreaves 1992). Theoretically, liberal feminism fails to examine the extent and nature of male power in sports in the specific context of capitalism, and fails to incorporate the ideological and symbolic dimensions of gender oppression. It takes for granted the distinctly masculine modes of thought and practice in sports, so that it seems 'commonsense' for women to follow in the steps of men. Such an implication embodies a failure, in theory and in practice, to recognize the complexities of gender relations of power in sports – in particular, those based on unequal divisions of power between different groups of men and different groups of women, as well as between men and women. The notion of equality for women in sports fails to specify which women want to be equal with which men. Far from challenging male sports, liberalism endorses them.

There is a powerful tendency in this perspective to divert attention away from the gender-linked value system of mainstream sports and to accept the dominant ideologies that support them. Liberal feminists fail to question and examine the 'moral and human consequences of the structures and procedures which have been created by patriarchal society' (Talbot 1988: 32). Margaret Talbot is alluding here to the endemic features of modern sports which render them harmful rather than enriching, such as aggressive competition, chauvinism, sexism, racism, xenophobia, physical and psychological abuse of athletes, violence, and the commodification of sports. Liberalism incorrectly embodies the popular idea that the allocation of increased resources for women's sports reflects a broad political and ideological consensus, and in doing so fails to examine oppositional values which relate to broader structures of power. Nevertheless, equal opportunities is by far the most popular approach, accepted as 'commonsense' by the majority of people pioneering for improvements for women in sports. Because liberal strategies have been successful, they may pave the way for more radical changes in the future.

SEPARATISM

The issue of separatism is not new to women's sports. It has a history going back to its formative years in the late nineteenth century, since which time a number of separatist positions have evolved, based on different experiences and values. Most separatist sports philosophies have been a reaction, in one way or another, to dominant ideas about the biological and psychological predispositions of men and women, supposedly rendering men 'naturally' suited to sports, and women, by comparison, essentially less suited; they have also been a strategy for dealing with the cultural power that men wield in sports.

The early forms of organized sports and physical education for females were established in the late nineteenth century. They were marked by their insular, separatist nature, developing mostly in the private spheres of schools, colleges and clubs. Because organized sports for women were for the most part separated from men's sports, it was easy to define them as qualitatively different, in tune with conventional ideas about 'femininity' and 'masculinity'. In order to survive, organized female sports tended to accommodate to traditional biological assumptions, rather than openly challenging them (Hargreaves 1979, 1987; see Chapters 3, 4 and 5.) But after the turn of the century, sports feminists in North America advocated separate sports for men and women for ethical reasons. In common with some female physical education specialists in Europe, they opposed men's sports because they believed they concentrated too much on competition and were over-specialized and corrupted by commercialization (Hargreaves 1984; Theberge 1985). But although for different reasons, both these models of separate sports for women provided the historical basis for the idea that there should be 'feminine-appropriate' sports and 'masculine-appropriate' sports, and a pattern of sex-role stereotyping was established. The early history of separate sports for men and women throughout Europe and North America provided a practical and ideological foundation for separate sports to continue.

Better articulated and more forceful forms of separatism have developed in recent years, to a large extent as a reaction to the powerlessness, frustration and anger experienced by sportswomen who have suffered serious discrimination and experienced blatant male chauvinism. The fiercest struggles have tended to occur in traditional male sports and, not surprisingly, women who have experienced harsh discrimination by men on account of their sex often become vehemently opposed to men in these settings. Opposition to men's control of sports, rather than to their violent and aggressively competitive character, is the resulting separatist position. It espouses the belief that women should be able to participate in sports that are associated with conventional images of masculinity and fiercely controlled by men's organizations, such as boxing, golf, motor-racing, rowing, rugby, speed-skating, snooker and weight-lifting. And it is argued that to be separate is the first step towards wresting control from men and putting more sports for women 'on the map'. This form of separatism is not necessarily incompatible with the ideology of equal opportunity – it is seen as a way of balancing the advantages that men have had for so long. Separate organizations give women access to masculinized sports, create wider definitions of sporting femininity and provide women with opportunities to administer and control their own activities.

However, the argument also prevails among some feminist sports groups that the characteristics of male sports are reactionary and undesirable and they argue, like their predecessors, that women should not emulate men's sports, but should build instead alternative models which are intrinsically more humane and liberating. The following quotation from Twin's book (1979: 164), exemplifies this position: 'Sports should not become for women what they have been for men: a display of aggression, a proof of toughness, and a kind of primitive communication that replaces emotional intimacy.' These expressions of separatism focus on the male/female distinction; the assumption is that conventional gender relations seriously inhibit women's development. Those women who argue for separate sports for themselves do so because they feel their oppression *as women*; they believe that their common interests transcend differences and that independence from men is self-realization (Birrell and Richter 1987: Theberge 1985).

The philosophy of separate development has characteristics in common with radical feminism which has been an important influence in theoretical debates about women's liberation. Radical feminists do not share a single doctrine, but they share in an opposition to patriarchy which, they argue, is the basis of other forms of oppression rather than a by-product of them (Daly 1978; Firestone 1979; Millett 1971). Patriarchy is defined as a system of power relations by which men dominate women. Radical feminists allege that the ability of men to dominate women is the most basic form of oppression because it is rooted in essential physical and psychological differences between the sexes. Characteristics normally ascribed to men, and associated with sports, such as strength, competitiveness, aggression and assertiveness, are rejected, and characteristics popularly classified as female, such as co-operativeness, grace and tenderness, are celebrated. This is a 'pro-woman' and 'anti-male' stance which asserts not only women's difference from men, but their superiority over men (Weir and Wilson 1984).

In common with this essentialist position, sometimes the argument for separate development of sports for men and women is based on biologist assumptions. Ironically, if it is claimed that women have uniquely different characteristics from men, there is implicit support of the image of power invested in the male body. Male domination in sports is thus reducible to the distinctive biological natures of males and females which are treated as if they are culturally and historically universal. It is as if patriarchy is a biological system with an underlying uniformity. The idea of 'feminine-appropriate' and 'masculine-appropriate' sports locks people into a fixed concept of the 'natural' which is blind to history and ignores changing feminine and masculine identities and different gender relations. It also inaccurately presents all men and all men's sports as having similar characteristics. There is a strong tendency in this perspective to invoke a rigid system of male domination, which is, invariably, an exaggeration.

POSITIVE ACTION

But there is a strong cultural dimension which favours the argument for separate development. Because organized sports have always been dominated by men and permeated by sexist attitudes and behaviour, many women recognize the limitations of equal opportunity programmes. There is growing evidence in North America and in western Europe that in sports teaching, coaching and administration, women have more scope and better prospects in single-sex organizations than when they have to compete with men in open competition in mixed organizations (White and Brackenridge 1985). In common with women working in other fields, sports feminists recognize that positive action in favour of women can help to balance the advantages that men have had for so long. In view of the historical evidence, the argument that to place women's experiences at the centre of any practical or theoretical intervention is the best way to be sensitive to the specific needs of women, is very powerful. This is the reason why some women's sports groups have adopted an exclusionist policy and refused membership even to men who are sympathetic and supportive of women's interests. (This occurred when the British Women's Sports Foundation was inaugurated in 1985.) Separatist strategies of this sort recognize the long history of men's structural domination of women in institutional contexts. They also reflect the wish of increasing numbers of sports feminists to avoid the dangers of assimilating women's sports to male structures (Birrell and Richter 1987).

Separatism provides particular benefits to women in practical ways as well. The provision of closed space for women in the form of women-only sports sessions is increasingly popular. The opportunity to be in an area with other members of their own sex is a 'luxury' which many women seldom enjoy. It provides important opportunities for female bonding, frees women from the discrimination and sexism which they experience on a day-to-day basis, and provides them with a sense of control and autonomy which they otherwise lack (Clarke 1988). For many women closed space removes the fear of harassment, ridicule and inhibition which they would experience in mixed groups and provides the only setting for them to gain confidence and enjoyment in their sporting bodies. And it is the only condition under which some women will participate in physical activities, for religious or cultural reasons. When women take practical action for themselves, the relationship between theory and practice becomes clear and the feminist slogan 'The personal is political' comes alive.

UNNECESSARY DIVISIONS

However, separate development for men and women embodies further complexities, contradictions and problems. It re-creates social divisions, specifically those between men and women, but also between different groups of women and different groups of men. The major division is between heterosexual males and females, reproducing and confirming dominant gender divisions in society; but pejorative attitudes to 'deviant sexuality' have resulted in further divisions in sports – for example, some situations highlight sexual preference because lesbians and gay men bond together in their own clubs and organizations as a reaction to the homophobia they experience in mainstream sports (see Chapter 10).

Although in sports women are constantly being exploited and unequal gender divisions are constantly being reaffirmed, nevertheless, by ignoring non-sexist attitudes and non-sexist sports, the philosophy of separate development tends to exaggerate the overall extent of sexism. In sports, as in other areas of life, there are numerous, different male/female relationships and there are situations where sex and sexuality, as well as, for example, age, ability, ethnicity, or class are unimportant. In some sports women are un-equivocally subordinated in their relationships with men; in other situations women collude in apparently subordinate roles; in some spheres women share power with men and have greater autonomy than in the past; and in a limited number of situations women wield power over men. Similarly, men's attitudes to women are numerous and varied: some men are reactionary and sexist in their dealings with women and resist women's claims for equality; but not all men oppress women and some seek equality with women while others even seek forms of subordination. Although it is impossible to assess the extent to which changing gender relations may alter the 'global pattern' of male domination in sports (Connell 1983), nevertheless radical feminist claims for separate development invariably exaggerate the extent of male domination and ignore ways in which gender relations have changed historically and are changing now. Separatist ideology carries the implication that only women can bring about changes in favour of women and that there are fixed limitations to the social changes which women might seek in sports. But, as bell hooks claims:

> Since men are the primary agents maintaining and supporting sexism and sexist oppression, they can only be successfully eradicated if men are compelled to assume responsibility for transforming their consciousness and the consciousness of society as a whole.

(Quoted in Hearn 1984: 24)

If the opposite of domination is sharing, then it could be argued that a distinctly female culture is not progressive. Clarke and Critcher (1985: 24), for example, say that 'For all the signs of change, sport remains largely an area where existing gender roles are re-established and confirmed. Segregation is its ultimate form'. Paul Willis (1982: 134) suggests a radical alternative. His ideas coincide with those of feminists who want reciprocal relations between the sexes and who seek qualitatively different sports for *men and women*:

> Sport could be presented as a form of activity which emphasises human similarity and not dissimilarity, a form of activity which isn't competitive and measured, a form of activity which expresses values which are indeed unmeasurable, a form of activity which is concerned with individual well-being and satisfaction rather than with comparison. In such a view of sport, differences between the sexes would be unimportant, unnoticed.

Such a vision directs us to be less concerned about the biological gap between the sexes than about the meanings attached to it. The relationships between sex and gender, and nature and culture, raise theoretical questions about the ideological and symbolic means of perpetuating discrimination. Rigid separatism exaggerates sexism by focusing on sexuality rather than on culture; it is incompatible with the development of mixed sports and with the potential for direct power-sharing between men and women or between individuals with different sexual identities. It tends to be advocated dogmatically and in a way which celebrates exclusionist policies and differences between people. Separatism can exclude not only men, but many women as well, and in its aggressive form celebrates rigid divisions and stereotypes which limit both sexes. Explanations of women's oppression which emphasize biological differences make a number of theoretical omissions. Opposing men to women seriously underestimates, or even ignores, other dimensions of female oppression connected with such factors as class, economics, politics and ideology. Such constructions tend to be resistant to the idea that men may also be oppressed and that gender relates in various ways to features of the social totality. It neglects ways in which men and women are exploited *together* in sports, and how gender relations articulate with capitalist relations.

CAPITALIST RELATIONS AND GENDER RELATIONS

In recent years the debate in feminist sports literature has taken account of the articulation between gender relations and capitalist relations. It has characteristics in common with the general debate between radical feminists and Marxist feminists. The focus is on whether patriarchy or capitalism is the primary reason for women's oppression. In the case of radical feminism, it is argued that if it is patriarchal ideology that produces systems of cultural, social, economic and political control, then a transformation of capitalism would not necessarily do anything to change such structures of power (Eisenstein 1979: 28). Examples of women in communist states who were seen to be still subordinated to men were used to support this claim (ibid.). In contrast, Marxist feminism challenges essentialist notions of human nature, asserting that class is the root cause of women's oppression, and that problems of anything to do with sexuality are secondary (Hartmann 1979). Whereas radical feminists claim that male domination and female subordination are universal because sexism has its roots in the prior facts of human biology and not in capitalism, Marxist feminists say that ideas about gender and sexual difference are socially constructed, that the causes and effects of oppression differ in different societies, and that the character and extent of female oppression have changed historically. Marxist feminists claim that positing the major social division to be between men and women obscures the specific forms of exploitation of women in capitalist societies and, in particular, class differences between women. In their view, sexism in sports is perceived to be a component of bourgeois ideology which underpins the sexual division of labour, essential to the stability of capitalism. Traditional Marxists do not believe that equality between the sexes in sports can ever be achieved under capitalism.

GENDER AND CLASS

An increasing volume of feminist research in Britain shows how women's access to leisure, in general, and to sports, specifically, is mediated by social class (Deem 1986; Green, Hebron and Woodward 1987; Griffin, Hobson, MacIntosh and McCabe 1982; Hargreaves 1989; Talbot 1988; Wimbush 1986). This research is linked to the more general feminist critique of the family and to the domestic labour debate, which has focused on the economic significance of housework and the way in which it reproduces labour-power. It shows how the oppressive characteristics of the private sphere of the home and the demands of domestic labour and mothering limit women's leisure, in general, but affect working-class women to a greater extent than their middle-class counterparts. Not surprisingly, although more working-class females are participating in sports than ever before, it is still the case that they do so in smaller numbers than middle-class women and that active participation plays no part whatsoever in the lives of huge numbers of working-class women. In addition, most of those who actively campaign for the rights of women in sports are middle-class, as are the majority of those women who hold positions of responsibility and power in sports, in common with those who theorize about it. The middle-class character of women's sports leads to criticisms that the sports feminist movement does not represent the needs of all women, and there is evidence that there are conflicts in women's sports along class lines (see Chapter 10). But we need to know more about the specific ways in which class inequalities accentuate gender inequalities in sports. We also need a more complex theoretical analysis which can deal with the connections between class, gender and cultural power (power to control sports resources) than either radical feminism or orthodox Marxist feminism provides. This is an issue with which socialist feminism has been concerned. Socialist feminism developed out of a desire to reassess orthodox Marxist theory on the position of women, in order to understand the complexities of the relationship between, and the relative independence of, capitalist relations and gender relations (Banks 1981; Barrett 1982; Page 1978; Weir and Wilson 1984). But the opposition that has been posed between patriarchy and capitalism has tended to mask the significance of other variables, such as ethnicity, which themselves have a relationship to gender and class.

MAKING WOMEN'S SPORTS POLITICAL

Socialism and feminism are concerned with liberation. Class oppression and sexual oppression have been two major forms of oppression in human history and socialist feminists want to abolish both and are seeking a theory which does not subordinate one to the other. Michele Barrett (1982: 41) explains:

> The contemporary Women's Liberation Movement has, by and large, rejected the possibility that our oppression is caused by either naturally given sex differences or economic factors alone. We have asserted the importance of consciousness, ideology, imagery and symbolism for our battles. Definitions of femininity and masculinity, as well as the social meaning of family life and the sexual division of labour, are constructed on this ground. Feminism has politicized everyday life – culture in the anthropological sense of the lived practices of a society – to an un-parallelled degree. Feminism has also politicized the various forms of artistic and imaginative expression that are more popularly known as culture, reassessing and transforming film, art, the theatre and so on.

The concern with *meanings* which this quotation articulates is intrinsic to cultural politics, but has been almost entirely absent from feminist theories of sports. For example, very little is known about the specific configurations which maintain, or break down, male hegemony in sports, or the ways in which meanings in sports are produced, reproduced, resisted and changed. Sportswomen as a whole have not been enthusiastic feminists, and feminist intervention in sports has lagged behind feminist attempts to 'politicize' other areas of culture. But this is changing, and sports are becoming part of a larger movement for female autonomy. The most dynamic feminism arises from personal experience and the most radical challenges for women's sports have been practical ones. Women are taking action and producing new versions of sports for themselves, which supports the view of sports as constitutive, creative processes, and presents an optimistic vision of the potential of women to transcend practical and symbolic forms of oppression in sports. But it is a struggle. Advances are not inevitable – there is incorporation, opposition and failure. Sports are loci for freedom and for constraint: they produce new opportunities and meanings for women and they reproduce prejudices and oppression.

Freedom for women in sports is visionary, and constraint looks back to the past. The history of women's sports can provide an understanding of the origins and causes of women's subordination in sports, and of the nature of resistance to change and struggles for change. A historical perspective is essential to understand how residual forms of sport for women coexist with dominant and emergent ones. By looking at the experience of women historically, we can better understand male experience and the whole of the history of sports. The concern in this book is to produce an account of women's sports which incorporates experience, history and social arrangements.

AGENCY AND CONSTRAINT

This is the concern also of other sports feminists. Resisting reductionist perspectives and taking into account the complexities of the various forms of domination relevant to sports in advanced capitalist countries – for example, 'gender, race, class, and sexuality' – is a central interest of the contributors to Messner and Sabo's (1990) edited book, *Sport, Men, and the Gender Order: Critical Feminist Perspectives.* The editors argue that no form of domination should be privileged so that others are distorted or ignored, and they posit a 'wheel model', explained as follows:

> At the hub, constantly keeping the wheel in motion, is the historical dynamic of structural constraint (which includes structural, ideological, and characterological oppression) and human agency (which includes critical thought and resistant, transformative action). The spokes of the wheel represent varied forms of oppression: class, race, gender, age, and sexual preference (others certainly can be added). The rim of the wheel represents social theories of liberation, whose role is to link the spokes in such a way that the hub can move the wheel.
>
> (Messner and Sabo 1990: 10–11)

The image of a constantly moving wheel which symbolizes the ongoing process between agency and constraint seems remarkably similar to the concept of hegemony discussed in the previous chapter. But there is a major conceptual problem in the separation of what Messner and Sabo characterize as 'structural constraints' from their description of 'oppressions' (for example, gender, ethnic and class oppressions), which could equally well be characterized as structural constraints. And the level of generality recalls the problems of structuralist analyses (discussed in Chapter 1). The writers also say nothing about the nature of the constraints or oppressions in relation to the specific political and economic conditions of capitalism. However, the contributors to this book reflect the concern to understand gender as a relational concept in all its complexities and to search out the interrelationships of all the factors of analysis. Their ideas confirm the moving nature of theory which is part of the struggle for change. The book also reflects the importance of the contribution of men to sports feminism.

DAMAGED MEN

Men have been described as both 'guarantors' and 'victims' of patriarchy, and recent work on men and masculinities has been written by men who reject dominant ideas about their sex because, in their own words: 'Our power in society as men not only oppresses women but also imprisons us in a deadening masculinity which cripples our relationships – with each other, with women, with ourselves' (quoted in Segal 1990: 287). In modern, western societies, men are victims in the sense that they are forced in a very brutal way to subjugate their sensitivities in favour of aggressive displays of masculinity. Messner (1987: 54) argues that sports have become central to this process in a society (USA) where traditional male roles are in crisis:

> Both on a personal/existential level for athletes and on a symbolic/ideological level for spectators and fans, sport has become one of the 'last bastions' of male power and superiority over – and separation from – the feminization of society.

Messner and Sabo are examples of the increasing number of men who have sensed the brutalization of their own subjectivities through their participation in aggressive, competitive sports. Messner became aware of how the narrow definitions of success and failure in basketball 'limited the foundation upon which his self-image was constructed . . . [and] he became aware of how competition, homophobia, and misogyny in the sports world limited his ability to develop truly intimate relationships with women and with other men' (Messner and Sabo 1990: 14). Sabo rejected the hypermasculine and brutal aspects of American football. 'Six years of chronic back pain and a resulting lower lumbar, double-level spinal fusion also prompted him to rethink the beliefs and practices that inform traditional men's sports' (ibid.). And many other men have been humiliated and have suffered a sense of failure of manliness by being incapable of meeting the demands of traditional male sports and have thus excluded themselves from them altogether. Such experiences highlight the importance of the suggestion that

> since the sports world is an important arena that serves partly to socialize boys and young men to hierarchical, competitive, and aggressive values, it is also an important context within which to confront the need for the humanization of men.
>
> (Messner 1987: 65–6)

However, Oglesby (1990: 242) argues that although men are writing about 'their own alienation from self' in sports, they continue to use the term sport in the conventionally male sense, and they fail to acknowledge the importance of the 'traditional feminine', thus reproducing the ways in which specifically feminine characteristics are undervalued. Their renouncing of the 'masculine' in sports, she continues, leaves a great space which they fail to fill and which leaves her to ask, 'But where is the celebration of the feminine in feminism?'

Sex-role stereotyping in sports impoverishes both men and women: few of either sex have a wide and fulfilling range of movement experiences – those that are energetic, powerful, skilful and dynamic, as well as those that are expressive and sensuous and which use the body flexibly and sensitively. There is a need to examine more closely the lived complexities of men's as well as women's sporting experiences and the changing forms of masculinities and femininities in sports which are linked to changing values. Although many men may be agents of oppression, they are not inherently oppressive and they have a primary role to play, with women, in the elimination of gender oppression in sports. bell hooks writes that

> [men] should share equally in resistance struggles. In particular men have a tremendous contribution to make to feminist struggle in the area of exposing, confronting, opposing, and transforming the sexism of their male peers.
>
> (Quoted in Hearn 1984: 24)

STRATEGIES FOR CHANGE

Every form of sports feminism is implicated in the elimination of gender oppression, yet until recently there has been only a weak connection between feminist theory and practice. Now that link is being forged and the experiences of sportswomen (performers, administrators, coaches, etc.) are helping theoretical development, and theory is influencing change. From the 1950s, male standards in sports sociology became generalized standards, and women were evaluated by men, and evaluated themselves according to criteria created by men. Taking a critical stance now by placing women at the centre gives theory a new direction, enabling men and women to deconstruct popular ideas and stereotypes which have been taken for granted and which have limited people for generations. Both theory and practice are contested spheres and are constantly changing; the unity between them is essential for the 'politicization' of experience. This is different from liberal reformism. But gaining power is necessary for those who seek change, and power comes from organization. For women to become a political force in sports, there must be organizations to attract them to the movement and to gain support to fight and win campaigns. The US and UK Women's Sports

Foundations, founded in 1974 and 1985 respectively, are examples of national associations which, in part, fulfil this role. They work to politicize women's sports and to unite theory and practice in order to subvert male domination (see Chapter 11).

Although sports feminists share experiences and meanings which unite them as a group, there are also a great many differences between them. In addition to gender and class, other factors such as age, disability, ethnicity, marital status, occupation and sexual orientation affect women's involvement in sports and point to ways in which women's sports derive meaning from the totality of social relations. All these categories are important to a proper analysis of women's sports which will facilitate change. Although the sports feminist movement in the UK does not appear at present authentically to represent the needs of all women, there is growing concern to develop a broad base of women's sports which will incorporate the interests of women with diverse needs and varied backgrounds. Black sports feminists and lesbian sports feminists, for example, argue that power and oppression in sports derive from race and sexuality, as well as class and gender, and that their specific needs should be taken into account. The Women's Sports Foundation has the potential to co-ordinate the efforts of feminist theorists and those involved in sports practice in order to understand the limits and possibilities of female sports, based on actual social practices.

The essence of sports feminism is the belief that sports can be an enriching, sensuous experience with the potential for women to gain physical confidence and a sense of enjoyment and fulfilment. Sports feminism embodies the belief, therefore, that women should be mobilized to participate in sports. But such a philosophy relates to definitions of oppression and freedom which are highly complex; they are to do with the values which people hold, with the contexts which they are in, and with larger structures of power. The choices facing sports feminists are similar to those facing feminists involved in other aspects of culture:

1 co-option into a male sphere of activity
2 a separatist all-female strategy
3 a co-operative venture with men for qualitatively new models in which differences between the sexes would be unimportant.

If the third option were encouraged and resources were concentrated on participatory, co-operative activities, including regulating and controlling sports competition in order to maximize its 'valuable' elements and minimize its 'destructive' ones, there would be a shift away from the conventionally aggressive, male-dominated, competitive model of sports. However, the greatest power to control sports is still vested in men who hold traditional attitudes and who are involved in traditional activities, and it is unrealistic to argue that entrenched practices which are underpinned by political and economic power can easily be changed. Since each of the strategies outlined above can help to break down male privilege and open the way to greater autonomy for women, it may be more radical and expedient to encourage the development of women's sports in all these ways than to assert that only one approach is worthwhile. Such a philosophy embodies a creative tension. It recognizes the problems of change, but it does not pretend to be neutral.

Chapter 3

Nature and culture
Introducing Victorian and Edwardian sports for women

INTRODUCTION

Female emancipation has been characterized as 'one of the most striking aspects of the industrial phase of social development' (McGregor 1955: 48), and nineteenth-century feminism has been described as an essentially middle-class phenomenon, mainly concerned from the mid-century onwards with remedying injustices in education and employment (Kanner 1973; Klein 1971). Although most nineteenth-century feminists disregarded sports in their efforts to improve the status of women, nevertheless, because sports are intimately connected with the physical body – the most conspicuous symbol of difference between the sexes – their development represented a new and important form of freedom. But advances in sports, as in other spheres, were uneven: although the last two decades of the nineteenth century marked a period of accelerated improvement in women's lives, working-class women achieved considerably less than their middle-class counterparts. And it is misleading to imagine that even middle-class women experienced a metamorphosis to emerge dramatically as 'new women'. They enjoyed radical forms of freedom, such as sports, but they also suffered prejudice, opposition and setbacks, and were themselves sometimes ambivalent and contradictory about their new roles. Although the first women's suffrage movement in England was set up in 1866, no real step forward in political emancipation for women was achieved during the nineteenth century (Duffin 1978a), and feminism did not reach its peak until the early twentieth century. It was at this time that women's sports expanded rapidly and when there were increasing opportunities for working-class as well as for middle-class women. However, the balance of power between men and women in sports was always desperately uneven. Victorian and Edwardian sports were major male preserves which generated and reproduced patriarchal assumptions.

CONSTRUCTING DIFFERENCES

The Victorian period gave rise to modern sports, and the British boys' public schools provided the setting for their 'modernization' when games became organized activities with rules and regulations characteristic of sports today (Dunning and Sheard 1979; Gathorne-Hardy 1977; McIntosh 1968). The 'cult of athleticism' aptly describes the exaggerated status given to games in these schools, and the close association with specifically Victorian images of masculinity, embodying physical prowess, gentlemanly conduct, moral manliness and character-training. Games-playing in the boys' public schools provided the dominant image of masculine identity in sports and a model for their future development in Britain and throughout the world. Sports constituted a unique form of cultural life; they were overwhelmingly symbols of masculinity and chauvinism, embodying aggressive displays of physical power and competitiveness. In the nineteenth century there was no question that sports were the 'natural' domain of men and that to be good at them was to be essentially 'masculine'.

Whereas men were identified with Culture, and with their roles at work and in other spheres outside the home, women were symbolically aligned to Nature and to their reproductive roles and positions as wives and mothers in the home. Men were characterized as naturally aggressive, competitive and incisive – well suited to the rigours of the games field; in contrast, it was a popular idea that women were inherently emotional, co-operative and passive and therefore unsuited to take part in strenuous physical activities and competitive sports (Delamont and Duffin 1978; Ortner 1974; Vertinsky 1990). The belief in innate biological and psychological differences between the sexes constituted a powerful and pervasive form of sexism – experienced as 'unproblematic commonsense behaviour' – which systematically subordinated women in sports for years to come.

The most significant biological differences between men and women are connected with procreation. Women menstruate, bear children, suckle them, and go through the menopause; men do not. However, although these essential biological differences need not prevent healthy women from exercising (except for short periods during a pregnancy and following the birth of a child), they have provided the major justification for limiting women's participation at all times of their life-cycle (Atkinson 1978; Vertinsky 1990). The Victorians maximized cultural differences between the sexes and used biological explanations to justify them. This is the essence of biological reductionism. Biological ideas were used specifically to construct social ideas about gender and to defend inequalities between men and women in sports. Because large numbers of men and boys were seen to play sports, and women generally were not – the evidence confirmed that this was in the 'natural' order of things. However, although these popular images exerted tremendous pressure on nineteenth-century women to conform to them, it was nevertheless possible for some women to construct alternatives. The body is the fundamental symbol of power relations between men and women in sports and, since the nineteenth century, the female body has been a locus of struggle to control and resist dominant images of sports and femininity.

THE NATURE OF WOMAN

Nineteenth-century attitudes to women's participation in sports were consolidated by attitudes to women that were pervasive throughout society. By the second half of the nineteenth century science was characteristically applied to social situations and, when women were characterized as a 'problem' in response to changes in their lives with the growth of industrial capitalism, they became the subject matter of investigation (Klein 1971). Science provided a supposedly 'factual' or 'objective', but in effect conservative, legitimation of patriarchal relations or male domination, and scientific method was viewed as a rational replacement for previously held emotional and uncritical theories about the role of women (ibid.). Numbers of influential social theorists, politicians, medical practitioners and educationalists used scientific arguments to depict women as passive victims of their biology. For example, early forms of positivism were used as a justification for anti-feminism by attempting to apply laws, analogous to those established in the natural sciences, to social situations. Auguste Comte's positivism reinforced established ideas about women as functional to the 'needs' of society, which were viewed as synonymous with the 'needs' of men and rested upon constitutionally defined characteristics of men and women. Positivism incorporated fixed notions of human nature – that is, male nature, and female nature – an idea which constituted the very essence of the problem of change for women. Frances Power Cobbe (1869: 15–20) described Comte's positivism as 'essentially evil', because, she said, it 'affirms the principle that man should provide for woman', and with the exception of 'active and friendly discourse', she argued that it was expected for women to be kept 'in entire idleness'.

Social Darwinism and its key notion of the 'survival of the fittest' became fashionable towards the end of the century. In the debate about women, Darwin's evolutionary theory was employed to justify 'maternity as the "highest function" of womanhood' – essential to the healthy progress of the nation (Dyhouse 1976: 41–2). In common with positivism, it equated social with natural processes, and defined 'problems of society' from the point of view of those in control. The medical profession in Europe and North America extended and refined arguments about female 'nature' and applied them, in the main, to oppose middle-class women and girls who were seeking an education in any way equivalent to that available to boys. Dr Edward Clarke in the United States and Dr Henry Maudsley in England became the classic proponents of the 'scientific' principle that the physiology of the female sex was governed by a fixed degree of energy for all physical, mental and social actions (Dyhouse 1978). They argued that too much brain activity would sap the absolutely fixed and limited energy resources of the female body to such an extent that pathological conditions would result. The nub of the problem, as they expounded it, was related to the excessive energy expended in procreative functions, which left a minimum available for other physical, psychic and intellectual ones. Their contention was that particular demands are made upon the female body by its accelerated development during puberty, and that menstruation, childbirth and suckling are so debilitating that at those times, whenever possible, alternative activities should be terminated altogether. Dr Robert Barnes (1873) articulated the predominant view of the medical profession at the time: 'The functions of ovulation, gestation, labour, lactation, the menopause, in turn all dominate over the entire organism of woman.' In 1887, the chairman of the British Medical Association proposed that in the interests of social progress, national efficiency and the 'progressive improvement of the human race', women should be denied education and other activities which would cause constitutional overstrain and inability to produce healthy offspring (Pfeiffer 1888; Maudsley 1874).

There were vigorous and well-articulated protests against these claims of the medical profession – the most notable was Dr Elizabeth Garrett Anderson's published attack on Maudsley's theory in 1874. But the view of the physically limited female, institutionalized in the scientific and medical establishments, outweighed oppositional ideas. Throughout Europe and North America, there were influential authority figures who adopted an intractable 'scientific' viewpoint about women's 'fixed' and inferior natures, and there were numerous publications which served to sustain the conservation of female energy thesis right into the first three decades of the twentieth century (Dyhouse 1976).

Theorists who were apparently more liberal in their attitudes also appropriated the biological approach and added to the general climate of 'establishment' opinion. Havelock Ellis, for example, argued that the only reasonable way to study the 'problem' of women was to treat them as objects of natural science. He was strongly influenced by Darwinism and the 'Law of Nature', and although he argued for equality between the sexes, it was in the idealist sense that:

> Man and woman are . . . complementary opposites; two aspects of one essence. . . . So long as women are unlike in the primary sexual characters and in reproductive function, they can never be absolutely alike even in the highest psychic processes.
>
> (Cited in Dyhouse 1978: 7)

In 1894 he reasoned that there was a causal relationship between the different physiological characteristics of men and women and resultant behavioural and psychological predispositions. For example, he argued that the female vasomotor system was unstable and highly sensitive to stimuli, causing women to be mentally and physically more irritable than men. According to this logic, women's practical and homely abilities, and apparent dislike of intellectual pursuits and of activities such as sports, had an organic origin.

Herbert Spencer, often interpreted as liberal in his views on women, was in reality also conservative. In 1861 he argued that sexual differences could best be understood by assuming a somewhat earlier arrest of individual evolution in women than in men, causing women to be unsuited to important social and political activities. In his publication *The Principles of Biology* (1867), he defended the supposed incontrovertibility of biological science and argued that excessive mental labour for women had a detrimental effect on their physiques and reproductive functions. By applying Darwinian concepts to social sciences, 'he tried to connect mental, moral and social development directly with evolution, and identified evolution with progress' (Thomson 1950: 103). Spencer strongly supported the monogamous nuclear family, and argued that women should be relieved of duties outside the home so that all their energies could be devoted to child-bearing and rearing, this being the most 'progressive' and 'efficient' form of human organization.

Throughout the nineteenth century biological accounts of women's behaviour were dominant, and alternative social interpretations were unusual. The extreme positions were exemplified in the debate between John Ruskin and John Stuart Mill (Mill 1970; Millett 1972). The term 'Nature', which was employed by Ruskin as the ultimate determinant of women's position, had emotional and persuasive overtones. It represented an idealized view of women and their innate qualities, and its use implied not only its 'obvious' existence, but also that it was recognized by everyone to be the same thing. On the other hand, Mill's 'rational', but minority, view of women's status, was that women were products of their domestic and social circumstances, and hence their subjugation was politically and culturally created. Both formal and informal education he believed to be the most oppressive factors which socialized girls into an acceptance of, and belief in, the notion of their innate inferiority. In contrast to Ruskin, for Mill the 'basic fact about human nature was its infinite malleability'. He acknowledged the ideological character of the 'nature of women' which he claimed was an 'eminently artificial thing . . . the result of forced repression in some directions, unnatural stimulation in others', making everything which is usual appear natural (Mill 1970).

Reducing explanations of women's social behaviour to the level of biology diminished the effectiveness of the nineteenth-century feminist challenge to the established system of patriarchy, and affected attitudes to women's participation in sports in a fundamental way. Any account of human behaviour which is rooted in the body is the most difficult to disclaim because the attempt to do so threatens a person's self-identity or very 'sense of being'. The body is vulnerable to the invasion of ideology because it exhibits apparent autonomy, as if it is self-determined and immune from manipulation. Throughout the nineteenth century, the concept of the 'nature of woman' was integrated into people's attitudes and behaviour so that it became a material reality – a part of everyday, commonsense consciousness, sustained by the practices and attitudes of women themselves. Sufficient numbers of middle-class women followed the dictates of fashion and wore restricting clothes, ate little and took no exercise, so that, not surprisingly, they would often faint, become ill and behave submissively, thus confirming the medical stereotype of the 'delicate' female. The acceptance by women of their own incapacitation gave both a humane and a moral weighting to the established scientific 'facts'. Many women believed in their own inferiority and hence supplied further 'proof' of the 'rational' validity of the belief. There were insufficient women who were visibly healthy and energetic, or who participated in sports, to provide a substantially different image.

THERAPEUTIC EXERCISE

Doctors legitimated popular ideas about the inherent sickness of middle-class women by diagnosing them as constitutionally weak. The chief pre-scription for ailing middle-class women was enforced passivity and the elimination of all mental excitement. Cures proliferated for the treatment of 'nervous disorders' and other fashionable diseases which, it was argued, were linked to the reproductive system (Atkinson 1978, 1987; Vertinsky 1987, 1990). They became integrated into a fast-developing 'medical-business-complex':

> Sickness filled the gap of inactivity so effectively that it came to invade middle-class culture. . . . In time the perfect lady became the image of the disabled lady, the female invalid – the 'conspicuous consumptive'.
>
> (Duffin 1978b: 26)

It has been argued that the oppression of women arose from the acquisition of private property under capitalist production, which made possible the exploitation of biological differences (Hamilton 1978). Without doubt, the stereotype of the frail middle-class lady, which was encouraged by the medical profession throughout the 1880s, supported male domination economically as well as ideologically (Duffin 1978b). The middle-class lady with the delicate nature supplied the dominant image of femininity, was institutionalized in the family setting, and provided a backward-looking scenario for the 'new woman' to enter. Yet at the very time that women's behaviour in its most conservative form became explicitly stereotyped, and the burden of ill-health caused the dominant image of femininity to be an essentially negative concept, the germ of a more positive attitude to the female body was developing, linked to the idea of health and fitness through exercise. The theory of constitutional overstrain was not used as an argument against *all* types of exercise for women – during the nineteenth century increasing numbers of physicians took the view that *gentle* forms of physical exercise, if taken in reasonable amounts, would aid women's health and ability to bear healthy children. Activities were censored if they were excessively energetic, or because of the behaviour they invoked, whereas medical gymnastics and massage became established treatments for those with health problems, as well as popular forms of exercise for fit women.

Gymnastics is a form of activity which lends itself readily to scientific principles of classification. Swedish gymnastics, devised by Per Henrik Ling, was a system of free-standing exercises, based upon physiological principles. The system attracted interest amongst doctors who saw its potential for medical practice. Ling promoted his exercise system as a positive aid to health, and as a form of therapy, and he applied it to the specific needs of women whom he viewed as innately different from men:

> women need health as men do, nay, still more, since within her own life she is to nourish another. . . . Woman's anatomical characteristics are analogous with man's, but her physiological predisposition demands less vigorous treatment. The law of beauty is based purely on the conception of life and must not be abused. The rounded forms of woman must not be transformed into angularity or nodosity such as in man.

(Cited in Webb 1967 and quoted from the Lingiad, Stockholm 1939)

Medical gymnastics had been used as a form of therapy for middle-class women from as early as the 1830s, from which time doctors who subscribed to Ling's theories opened private institutions in London, and then in other urban centres. They set themselves up as practitioners of medical gymnastics and made comfortable livings from their invalid middle-class clients. Middle-class women also took up gymnastics as a social and leisure activity in health clubs. For example, from the time of its foundation in 1857, the Ladies Sanitary Association held regular classes in Swedish gymnastics – the association was largely the creation of Mrs Mathias Roth, whose doctor husband was an advocate of Swedish gymnastics in English schools (Armytage 1955a). The Ling system comprised just one of a vast number of exercise systems commercially exploited at this time (Crunden 1975). Increasing numbers of private gymnasia were springing up and became well-organized and lucrative ventures and, by 1886, the National Physical Recreation Society was inaugurated as a co-ordinating body. However, although its stated aim was 'the promotion of physical recreation among the working classes', evidence suggests that almost everyone involved until after the turn of the century was middle-class. Medical gymnastics became fashionable and increasingly popular – for example, 1886 marks the year of a 'Calisthenic Converzazione' held at the Portman Rooms in Baker Street, in the heart of fashionable

London, and classes for ladies became a special feature at the London Orion Gymnasium at this time. During the next two or three years there was a vast increase in the numbers of gymnastic classes held for women throughout the country (Webb 1967).

The 'raison d'être' of Ling's system of exercise was health. In so far as it had a hard core of theory, it was formed by the anatomical and physiological principles largely 'borrowed' from medical science. Swedish gymnastics was further popularized through the work of the first women specialists of physical education who were trained at the college opened by Madame Bergman Österberg in 1885 (later called Dartford College), and at the other colleges of physical education which followed (Fletcher 1984; Hargreaves 1979; McIntosh 1968; see also Chapter 4). These colleges did not confine themselves to teacher education; they also became absorbed into the lucrative business of body therapy. During the 1880s the use of massage had become popular in England, prompted by the influx of trained masseuses and remedial gymnasts from Sweden, and students were trained in both massage and remedial gymnastics. The colleges accrued a steady income from remedial provision – for example, Rhoda Anstey, the principal of Anstey College, combined her business acumen with her professional training and set up a 'Hygienic Home for Ladies' which was a sort of health clinic run alongside the teacher-training college (Crunden 1974). The college training was recognized by the medical profession, and graduates were entitled to become members of the Society of Trained Masseuses, established in 1894, and were able to take the examination of the Chartered Society of Massage (Crunden 1973). After graduating, they often worked with doctors in medical practices, or set themselves up in private clinics, or worked in the hospital system. They provided gymnastic classes for women and children in normal health, and medical gymnastics and massage for those with pathological conditions. In 1895, a former student from Dartford College, whose work was chiefly medical, wrote about her patients:

> One lady had suffered from sciatica for six weeks. I attended her daily for one week and worked a complete cure. An old lady of seventy-six occasionally takes massage to prevent a return of synovitis in the knee. How I wish others would understand they need not suffer so much if only they would give Swedish gymnastics a chance before their diseases become chronic.
>
> (Boyle 1895)

Towards the end of the century there was a boom in the numbers of clinics, gymnasia, health spas and seaside holidays, all subscribed to by the middle classes. There was also a proliferation in the numbers and types of personnel employed to deal with the 'health problems' of clients, including a new range of medical semi-specialists such as dietitians, masseuses and remedial gymnasts (Duffin 1978a). The variety of treatments available extended a choice to middle-class women and provided expensive antidotes for their 'sickness' and boredom.

CAPITALISM AND BOURGEOIS PROSPERITY

Throughout the nineteenth century the 'nature of woman' was a powerful and persuasive concept integral to capitalist social relations. Although industrial expansion was on a small scale by contemporary standards, Britain was undoubtedly the leading, and by far the wealthiest, nation of the world (Briggs 1959: Cole and Postgate 1966; Hobsbawm 1977). The period after the middle of the nineteenth century marks a time of relative stability, although changes in living and work patterns associated with burgeoning urbanization and industrialization materially affected the position of women throughout society (ibid.; Best 1971). However, the technological developments which revolutionized industrial methods of production affected middle-class women in a qualitatively different way from their working-class counterparts. The increasing specialization of labour created a multitude of new jobs at low wages for working-class women, for whom paid work was an economic necessity, whilst middle-class women became increasingly affluent, abundantly leisured, and, in general, robbed of economic usefulness (Klein 1971; Sharpe 1976). There was unprecedented acceleration of bourgeois prosperity, and the newly consolidated bourgeoisie, together with the expanding intellectual, professional and commercial middle classes, formed a large social bloc whose living standards and patterns of behaviour became entrenched and apparently inviolable.

However, the middle classes were expanding more rapidly than the rest of the population, and with a surplus of women estimated at between 26 and 28 per cent, the number of middle-class women in need of employment grew (Banks 1968; Banks and Banks 1964; Best 1971; Cole and Postgate 1966; Kanner 1973; Peterson 1973). The steady expansion of women's employment before the First World War was the most concrete reflection of the redefinition of their social position and of their increasing independence. However, although it is commonplace to describe the war as 'the great liberator of women', the events of 1914–18 accelerated a trend in the pattern of women's work which had already been established (Roberts 1971; Rowbotham 1973). The extent of the breakthrough of women into diverse occupational fields has often been exaggerated, but there was a significant increase in the numbers of middle-class girls taking up a professional training or some form of employment, not only as a precautionary measure to safeguard their futures, but increasingly as a means of achieving some degree of personal fulfilment, or with a commitment to leading a worthwhile life. The pay and work conditions of most middle-class employees were poor, and genteel female destitution was treated as a serious problem. But there was no comparison with the long and exhausting labour and the extent of poverty and degradation of the mass of working-class women in Britain who survived at subsistence level only and who contradicted the 'conventional wisdom' of the fragile, weak female. Middle-class women whose families had fallen on hard times were in a relatively privileged position in relation to most working-class women: they identified with more fortunate women from their own class and, together with them, constituted an elite with the bourgeois values and ideologies of that class.

VICTORIAN FAMILISM

The character of the family directly affected the position of middle-class women. The consolidation, most notably of the bourgeois family, developed concomitantly with the consolidation of industrial capitalism (Best 1971; Hamilton 1978; Vicinus 1973; Young 1937). The idealized model of the respectable family centred on the man as the 'head of the house' and its dominant authority figure who operated primarily in the economic sphere. The relationship between the man and woman was viewed as a reciprocal one in that the woman's dependent role as wife, housekeeper and child-bearer, which confined her to 'the interior world of the family . . . left the bourgeois man "free" to accumulate capital' (Rowbotham 1973: 3). The woman was expected to set an impeccable moral example for the family: it was from the 'saintly mother' in the home that children learned first about the sexual division of labour and associated attitudes of odedience, hard work, honesty and loyalty (Vicinus 1937).

The model of the Victorian family may have been a reality for the affluent middle classes, but 'working-class men's wages were rarely sufficient to support families, and women's earnings in the nineteenth century were characteristically essential, not supplementary' (Baxandall, Ewen and Gordon 1976: 3). Nevertheless, in the public image, the woman's work-role was always secondary to her role in the family as wife, mother and housekeeper, which constituted the Victorian ideal of the sexual division of labour. The idealization of the 'gentle sex' became a self-conscious, yet taken-for-granted response of the middle classes.

To what extent this vision of family life was a reality is less important than the way it was integrated with dominant medical opinions about the female body and elevated as a concept which permeated social consciousness, affecting women's participation in physical activities. Victorian familism became a form of institutionalized sexism which dominated social relations, giving them a material base at work and in the family, and also in the leisure and educational contexts. The ideology of domesticity did not exclude women totally from participation in activities which can broadly be defined as sports, but it militated against female involvement in vigorous and diverse forms of physical activities.

CONSPICUOUS RECREATION

The life-styles of the middle classes reflected acquisitiveness. Garden suburbs flourished from the mid-century onwards as middle-class families moved in large numbers into detached, semi-detached and terraced houses in the newly developed areas (Best 1971). The insular, self-contained nature of these modern homes made the family a spatially segregated recreation unit where the women publicized the spending power of their husbands and fathers in the form of 'conspicuous consumption', 'conspicuous leisure' and 'conspicuous waste' (Veblen 1899). Homes grew more palatial and gardens became part of the improved amenities of domestic life for the middle classes. By the mid-Victorian period the bourgeois family had reached a plateau of prosperity, sufficient for domestic duties to be taken care of by a growing army of servants. Even when growth and prosperity seemed to suffer a more general contraction from the mid-1870s, the Victorian bourgeoisie was able to resist any serious curtailment of expenditure and consumption, and this was reflected in all forms of women's leisure, most of which occurred within the ambit of the family. Middle-class recreation reflected the closeness of family relationships and promoted the image of family life.

The idleness of the bourgeois 'lady' became symbolic of her husband's or her father's material success – her finery reflected his affluence, and the way in which she organized her leisure defined his social standing (Wymer 1949). Generally speaking, the middle classes had more leisure time to enjoy than previously and a 'consumer-amusement-market' for the family developed (Bailey 1978). The material circumstances of middle-class women improved with the growing power in society of their men, but conspicuous displays of affluence were also symbolic of the economic dependence of middle-class women on men, and the virtual stranglehold of patriarchal relations, viewed by most women as a universal state (Rowbotham 1973).

Lavish, extravagant and restrictive clothes were tangible symbols of a life of leisure, but caused women discomfort and sometimes illness, and restrained them from performing any but the smallest and meanest of movements. Thorstein Veblen writes about the crippling effects of the corset on American women:

> The corset is, in economic theory, substantially a mutilation, undergone for the purpose of lowering the subject's vitality and rendering her permanently and obviously unfit for work. It is true, the corset impairs the personal attractions of the wearer, but the loss suffered on that score is offset by the gain in reputability which comes of her visibly increased expensiveness and infirmity. It may broadly be set down that the womanliness of woman's apparel revolves itself in point of substantial fact, into the more effective hindrance to useful exertion offered by the garments peculiar to women.
>
> (Veblen 1899: 181)

Even after the turn of the century, in America and Britain many middle-class women remained expensive, unhealthy and immobile showpieces, and all forms of female 'sports' or 'physical recreation' complemented the middle-class conception of ladylike behaviour. The emphasis was on family-centred entertainment, characterized as 'conspicuous recreation', in which women played prescribed roles which coexisted with, and had a similar function to, their roles as 'conspicuous consumptives'. Women's participation in conspicuous recreation embodied the characteristics of passivity and subordination, with little hint of energy or independence. They played 'gentle', respectable games, exemplified by croquet and its indoor derivatives like 'Parlour Croquet', 'Carpet Croquet' or 'Table Croquet' (Jewell 1977), or quoits or skittles, or gentle forms of tennis and badminton. And women reinforced the sporting superiority of men by watching them compete in horse-racing or at regattas or cricket matches.

Croquet derived from an Irish peasant game, adopted in England about the middle of the nineteenth century. In its original converted form, known as 'Tight Croquet', it featured the most pronounced manifestations of bourgeois conspicuous recreation – less to do with physical activity than social ostentation:

Nobody could have called it a good game played, as it was, with only one hand in order that womenfolk might be able to hold up their parasols to guard their complexions from the sun . . . a game of frills and fancies, of petticoats, giggles and maidenly blushes.

(Wymer 1949: 226)

The early success of croquet was its appeal to the 'fair sex'. By the mid-nineteenth century it was a highly fashionable pastime and became something of a craze. It was said that 'hardly a house with a lawn was without a croquet set' (Jewell 1977: 96). Croquet provided a new model for sport: it was a social game which could be played by both sexes in a suburban garden.

Engravings, prints and photographs provide some of the scant evidence available that the model of the conspicuous sporting lady prevailed into the twentieth century. Women from the middle and upper classes would be seen in flamboyant wasp-waisted dresses, displaying themselves as ornamental, inactive players, or at the race-track or the cricket ground sitting in the stands or mingling in the crowds. 'Real' sports were uncomplicatedly symbolically male. For example, Brian Dobbs's book entitled *Edwardians at Play* contains fifty illustrations, but there is only one depicting a female participant – a decorative lady partnering the Prince of Wales at lawn tennis. She is undoubtedly wearing a corset, has a most fashionable pair of shoes, a pretty hat perched on her head, and even with a racket in her hand looks unable to move more than an inch or two in any direction (Dobbs 1973: 80)! Even on the tennis court she was a physically incapacitated player, inhibited and subdued by convention and 'bound by a code of behaviour as tight as the stays she was compelled to wear' (Margetson 1969: 99). Such middle-class women represented the embellishment of man with no apparent connection to the sort of vigorous action that epitomizes female sports today. Well past the turn of the century large numbers of middle-class women continued to be conspicuous players, as well as conspicuous spectators and socializers at male sports competitions. They were defined always as subordinate to sportsmen (McGregor 1955), reproducing dominant images of masculinity and femininity. For example, in 1919, the sports correspondent of *The Times* wrote:

> Athletic meetings . . . always attract a large number of women, perhaps it is the gay colours of the runners, perhaps it is their youth and splendid physical condition, whatever the reason they come in their thousands and bring brightness and colour to the scene even if their appreciation is not always particularly intelligent.
>
> (Cited in Winter 1979: Part III: 4)

Middle-class recreation was an unambiguously 'conspicuous' event. Although the middle classes were indulging more openly in social pleasure and imitating the opulent pastimes of the upper classes (Margetson 1969), in sports, as in other spheres, their women were at all times required to show restraint and to acknowledge the 'ladylike' modes of behaviour prescribed for them.

For example, tennis started off as a decorous game of pat-ball, characteristic of conspicuous recreation. Private courts denoted social ambition and status, and tennis became a mania for the affluent. Playing games was a new and enjoyable way for middle-class women to display their talents as 'cultured' ladies, and since the chief objective of most daughters was to find a husband, playing games in the family setting gave them opportunities to display themselves to the opposite sex in a seemingly innocent and acceptable way. The game was said to have 'swept like a wind of change through the quiet countryside [bringing] the sexes together on the courts in a wave of exciting activity', and in Cambridge, for example, tennis parties were described as 'the highlight of society in the 80s and 90s' (Margetson 1969: 211). By this time, increasing numbers of women were playing the game more actively and developing some pride in their physical skills:

> The ladies tied their long dresses back with an apron with pockets in it for spare tennis balls and ran about with little straw hats firmly pinned on their hair, determined to show off their athletic abilities.
>
> (Margetson 1969: 211)

Tennis became a more active game for women but could survive only in a form which implicitly assumed that women were inferior to men. Mixed tennis was an ideal setting for the reproduction of conventional gender roles:

needless to say, when men and women found themselves playing together it was deemed only honourable for the males to give [women]
every possible advantage, such as allowing the lady to stand as near as she
liked to the net when serving. On no account would any man hit the ball
too fiercely in the direction of a woman or, if perchance he did so by
mistake, he would certainly allow her another shot.

(Wymer 1949: 251)

The more women played, however, the more they got a 'feel' for the physical
potential of the game. Although they were limited by conventions, they
began to play more energetically and to force a shift in the definitions of
legitimate female physical activity. As argued in the previous chapter, women's
sports can be understood as processes of struggles and contradictions, and
women were active agents in those processes. In sports, generally, and in
tennis, specifically, women were *determined* and *determining*.

In the context of the home, the 'playing of games' became an important,
fashionable accomplishment for middle-class women, in the same category
as those much admired genteel activities such as playing the piano, singing,
drawing, painting, reciting poetry and doing needlework. From the beginning of the nineteenth century until about 1850, the 'accomplishments' were
given primacy in the education of the vast majority of middle-class girls who
went to private schools, and they remained a feature of the curriculum,
though in a decreasing number of schools, for around fifty more years (Borer
1976; Gathorne-Hardy 1977). Although shallow and pretentious by modern
standards, such an education was sufficient for girls to learn all the features
of conspicuous living and conspicuous recreation. It was in order to enhance
their ladylike images and dispositions that they went on crocodile walks,
marched for deportment, did calisthenics, played croquet and danced. The
physiological benefits of exercise were ignored: rude health was considered
to be vulgar, whereas frailty and lack of appetite were viewed as attractive
and normal. Exercise was undertaken in a self-conscious manner and in the
restrictive clothing of the time. It invoked an attitude – a way of thinking and
feeling – about what it was to be 'feminine' which became internalized and
hence 'real'. Images of femininity embodied in conspicuous recreation in the
home and in private girls' schools mutually reinforced one another.

FEMALE EDUCATION AND EXERCISE FOR GIRLS

At the same time there were changes going on in other contexts. The
demand for an education for girls that was better than that available in the
established private schools, or through private tuition at home, became
closely linked to advances in female sports and physical education.
Developments in female education during the last third of the nineteenth

century probably did more to legitimate more active forms of sport and exercise for women than any other factor.

Education was one of the main and most urgent of the feminist causes, and a central issue in the debate was the concern for economic emancipation:

> The practical exclusion of girls from the highest educational advantages offered to this class is in very many cases equivalent to a sentence of lifelong pauperism and dependence. It is to the last degree indecent that women should be dependent on marriage for a professional maintenance.
>
> (Wolstenholme 1869: 318)

Although exceptional, colleges for women were established quite early in the century – notably Queens College in 1848, and Bedford College the following year: they were the first landmarks in the development of higher education for women, and became affiliated to London University in 1869 (Dent 1970). The provision of university education expanded from the late 1860s with the opening of colleges for women at Cambridge, then at Oxford, and then at the newest provincial universities (Armytage 1964; Partington 1976; Pedersen 1975). There was a parallel, and spectacular, development of education for middle-class girls, dating from the early efforts of Misses Buss and Beale, who were the first headmistresses of the North London Collegiate School (1850) and Cheltenham Ladies' College (1858), respectively. The movement for female education developed momentum with the founding of the Girls' Public Day School Company in 1872 and the Church Schools Company in 1883, followed by the establishment of increasing numbers of new schools including the first residential girls' public schools – St Leonards (1877), Roedean (1885), and Wycombe Abbey (1898) (Dent 1970; Delamont and Duffin 1978). There also developed a concern for well-educated and competent teachers – many of the early women university graduates became teachers, teacher-training annexes to the schools were set up, and specialist teacher-training colleges were established. Teaching changed from being a refuge for destitute middle-class girls to being a respectable and even prestigious form of employment with rigorous intellectual and 'professional' standards and a strong service ethic. Intrinsic to this development was the opening of the specialist colleges of physical education – Dartford College in 1885, Anstey College in 1897 and Bedford College in 1903 (see the following chapter).

Although in most accounts of educational movements physical education and sports have remained peripheral topics, all forms of schooling and teacher training incorporated some form of physical education, and the formative phase of women's sports was closely associated with the development of higher education for women, in particular with the colleges of physical education and Oxford and Cambridge universities (Fletcher 1984; McCrone 1988). The schools and universities for the education of upper- and middle-class women provided the first institutional settings for female physical education and sports.

From the start, the new elite schools for middle-class girls acquired a reputation for a high level of scholarship, with comprehensive curricula ranging from Greek to gymnastics (Dent 1970). By the last decade of the century most of them had an established physical education curriculum which included a range of activities – quite radical by comparison with physical education in the boys' public schools where for the most part only games were played. The women who were running the new girls' schools held avant-garde ideas about the benefits of exercise for young women. They were in touch with the latest educational philosophies of the time (in North America and Europe) that advocated a properly constructed programme of physical education for both sexes.

Herbert Spencer (1861: 147) had noted a growing opinion that existing methods of bringing up children did not sufficiently regard the welfare of the body, and believed there was an 'awakening of interest in physical training'. He observed that by comparison with boys, girls had no opportunities to enjoy spontaneous, playful exercise but, instead, were given a contrived system of 'factitious exercise' – gymnastics. Spencer was referring to the calisthenics which took place in private girls' schools:

> the sportive activities to which the instincts impel are essential to bodily welfare. Whoever forbids them, forbids the divinely appointed means to physical development.
>
> (Spencer 1861: 168)

A similar criticism of the forms of exercise for girls was made by Miss Beale in evidence submitted to the Schools' Inquiry Commission on the Education of Girls in private schools (1868: 41):

> A walk during which books may be read or French spoken, does little or nothing for recreation. The game of croquet, which is much practised in schools, is compatible with a good deal of listless idling, and hardly deserves the name of physical exercise . . . a professor of calisthenics has been engaged to give set lessons; but the whole object of those exercises is to give the pupils a better style of walking and to show them how to deport themselves. They do not supply the vigour and joyousness which belong to the free and healthy play of boys. If the professors of calisthenics would devise some games which would do for girls what cricket and football do for boys they would render a public service. For the habit of playing with zest at some game which brings all the limbs into free exercise is not without an important reflex effect on the intellectual work. It is because girls do not play with sufficient abandon and self-forgetfulness, that their lessons are apt to be done in a superficial way. If their play were more bracing and recreative, their mental improvement would be sounder and more rapid than it is.

A further look into girls' education in private schools, this time in the Metropolitan London area, was commissioned as a result of the Taunton Report in 1868, and concern was expressed about the prevalence of failures in girls' health, attributed in large part to the neglect of physical training. The analysis of the returns from one hundred private schools for girls showed that sixty provided no form of exercise other than 'walking abroad and croquet', while thirty provided nothing but a form of calisthenics (McIntosh 1968: 128).

Medical opinion was shifting in support of more energetic forms of exercise for girls and some doctors were arguing that physical education should be a compulsory component of the curriculum. The absence of any reasonable amount and quality of exercise, together with long sedentary periods, was described as an error 'of attitude and training' and said to interfere seriously with physical development by delaying the processes of ossification, for example. 'Freedom, not restraint of posture', doctors affirmed, 'must rule the carriage of growing girls, especially at school' (Smith 1885).

From the 1850s, Ling's system of gymnastics which, as we have seen, was a popular therapeutic form of exercise for affluent middle-class women, was said to be particularly suitable for young girls:

> Ling's Exercises, provided they are well and scientifically conducted, form a most valuable branch of female education . . . such exercises are especially called for in the education of girls who should not be wasp-shaped and indolent with tender or twisted spines, but should be able to run races and 'hold their own' in the course of life.
>
> (Chapman 1856: 16)

Mathias Roth campaigned for thirty years for Ling's system to be used as the basis of a national programme of exercise in schools, similar to those in Germany and Scandinavia (McIntosh 1968: 131). He worked indefatigably to convince the education bureaucrats that gymnastics had relevance to healthy as well as infirm people, and he used the following analogy repeatedly to colour his argument:

> Many parents, tutors and principals of educational institutions think it enough to engage a drill sergeant, or a teacher of calisthenic movements. . . . It is very singular that we would not confine the care of a horse to a man who had not a knowledge of the animal's anatomy and physiology; while the man who is entrusted to the development and strengthening of the human body is not expected to possess so much science as is deemed absolutely necessary in the trainer of our horses.
>
> (Roth 1851: cited in McIntosh 1968: 99–100)

Herbert Spencer reflected the more general ideas of increasing numbers of educators and liberal reformers. He argued vehemently that an over-rigorous intellectual curriculum – 'this prolonged exercise of brain and deficient exercise of limbs' (1861: 179) – had a pernicious effect, especially on girls, producing sickness and malformations:

> Being in great measure debarred from those vigorous and enjoyable exercises of body by which boys mitigate the evils of excessive study, girls feel these evils in their full intensity. Hence, the much smaller proportion of them who grow up well-made and healthy. In the pale, angular, flat-chested young ladies, so abundant in London drawing-rooms, we see the effect of merciless application, unrelieved by youthful sports; and this physical degeneracy hinders their welfare far more than their acccomplishments aid it.
>
> (Spencer 1861: 186–7)

These ideas of Spencer's on the surface seem very radical and would have aided the development of physical education for girls. However, the evolutionary principle of Spencer's later writing about women was already present in his educational philosophy. His belief that 'Nature' required a balanced use of the physical and intellectual energy available to boys and girls confirmed his acceptance of the ultimate benefit of 'Nature'. He described children in analogous terms to animals in respect of their physiological needs for exercise which, he said, if satisfied, would have evolutionary benefits for the human race:

> The first success in life is 'to be a good animal', and to be a nation of good animals is the first condition to national prosperity.
>
> (Spencer 1861: 146)

The fixed degree of energy and constitutional overstrain theory was not in any way incompatible with the encouragement of girls' physical education. Allowing girls to 'run wild' was, for Spencer, a healthy preparation for the time when women needed their strength for bearing children and he argued that girls stood no risk of becoming unladylike if they did so:

> Rough as may have been their playground frolics, youths who have left school do not indulge in leapfrog in the street, or marbles in the drawing-room. . . . If now, on arriving at the due age, this feeling of masculine dignity puts so efficient a restraint on the sports of boyhood, will not the feeling of feminine modesty gradually strengthening as maturity is approached, put an efficient restraint on the like sports of girlhood? . . . How absurd is the supposition that the womanly instincts would not assert themselves but for the rigorous discipline of school mistresses!
>
> (Spencer 1861: 171)

By the 1860s, it was believed that the sentiment '*mens sana in corpore sano*' (a sound mind in a sound body) had a scientific foundation (Haley 1968). It was developing into a major educational and social theme, nurtured throughout the late Victorian period, and epitomized by the ideal of manliness, particularly in the form of Muscular Christianity in the boys' public schools (McIntosh 1968: Gathorne-Hardy 1977). The idea that strength of character was interdependent with sturdiness of body gave a moral gloss to organized games for boys. When Charles Kingsley (author of the popular children's story, *The Water Babies*) declared, 'there has always seemed to me something impious in the neglect of health, strength and beauty' (1877: 2), he did much to dispel the suspicions of the body as a source of sin, with the view that to cultivate the health of the body was a personal responsibility to God, and a duty to one's country.

The ideal of a nation of strong and beautiful women was Kingsley's concern also. He argued that if the education of girls was to be patterned after that of boys then 'the public school games, not the public school learning should provide the model'. Kingsley visualized 'educated' girls possessing a Hellenic 'healthfulness', combined with virtues 'which no books can give them' – courage, self-reliance, honour, and a preparation for the 'give and take of life' (cited in Haley 1968). Kingsley denounced 'stillness, silence and stays' for causing severe and unnatural restriction of the movement of females, resulting in the degeneration of the 'nation's stock' (Armytage 1955a: 73).

Matthew Arnold (son of Thomas Arnold [headmaster of Rugby School] and inspector of schools between 1851 and 1886) added the weight of his opinion in support of the argument for physical exercise as a necessary constituent of the educative process. He attacked the 'barbaric' and excessive aspects of athleticism in favour of forms of activity which enhanced physically and morally healthy attitudes (Armytage 1955b; Haley 1968). In the educational context the equating of moral rectitude with physical well-being had become firmly established, and both boys' and girls' physical education fitted into the drive for national efficiency which was a major concern of liberal reformers.

The education of middle-class girls trained them to fit into the social character or pattern of culture. However, the social character is not static, or a single experience, and the second half of the nineteenth century was a time of rapid social transformation, part of which was the changing experience of being a woman. Physical education in schools and colleges, like other aspects of education, was affected by popular ideas about the social position of women and, at the same time, was a force for changing them.

The middle classes who had displayed a general lack of interest in female education in the 1850s, had become almost obsessed about their daughters' schooling by the 1870s. But the fight to improve women's education was fraught with difficulties. Although there was conflict within the medical profession, it was the discourse of doctors who used the theory of constitutional overstrain to fiercely oppose female education that remained dominant (Dyhouse 1976, 1978). It had to be shown that girls were not innately inferior to boys, so that both sexes could have the same education.

The notion of 'double conformity' aptly describes the way women dealt with the contradictory demands imposed upon them – 'a strict adherence on the part of both educators and educated to [two] sets of rigid standards: those of ladylike behaviour at all times and those of the dominant male cultural and educational system' (Delamont 1978). The schools and colleges managed to resolve the ambiguous position that girls and young women were in by preparing them for a vocation *and* for marriage. The development of physical education was an integral aspect of this process – it represented an advance for women and was at the same time an activity which incorporated conservative ideas about discipline, high moral standards and 'ladylike' behaviour.

The development of education for women was a prerequisite for the development of sports. The majority of women's sports, in their institutionalized forms, occurred in the education system and particularly in the specialist colleges of physical education and in the universities. Teachers of physical education employed their energies and expertise to open up sports in the girls' schools and to inaugurate inter-school, local and regional competitions. Many of the first sports clubs were started by former college and university students and the majority of the members of the first national teams were from the schools, colleges and universities.

Female physical education and sports were influenced by a combination of factors including the changing position of women in society, the general debate about exercise for girls and women, what was happening in physical education in boys' schools, and the opinions of educators, physical educators, doctors, the Muscular Christians and liberal reformers. Physical education was becoming more typically an integral and important aspect of curricula in girls' secondary schools and increasing numbers of sports and leisure pursuits were becoming available to women outside the education sphere. However, there was no dramatic transformation to a new overall programme of physical education – ideas and emphases varied from school to school and there was a certain continuity of traditional work at the same time as new patterns of exercise were emerging. Not surprisingly, as Elizabeth Garrett Anderson observed, it was those people who had the closest concern for a general advance in girls' education who pioneered most vigorously for reforms and improvements in physical education:

> the same people who during recent years have been trying to improve the mental training of girls, have continually been protesting in favour also of physical development, and to a great extent their protests have been successful. The school-mistresses who asked that girls might share in the Oxford and Cambridge Local Examinations, were the first to introduce gymnastics, active games, daily baths and many other hygienic reforms sorely needed in girls' schools.
>
> (Garrett Anderson 1874: 62)

Although dominant bourgeois ideology had been effective in sustaining existing gender relations for many years, it was not a fixed, abstracted system of beliefs and values, and biological reductionism was not a static idea or set of ideas. Gender relations incorporated an ensemble of ideas and values which constituted a central component of social consciousness, dialectically related to material social processes. But ideology is never total; it is an intricate and changing amalgam of conceptions and meanings which are part of a 'process' of legitimation. So dominant ideas exist alongside emergent ones which can grow and gain power and legitimacy. And it is in the nature of ideology, as a non-coercive agent, that it is used more rigorously to maintain dominant ideas at times when those ideas are most threatened. So, as women took more action and made increasing demands after the turn of the century, arguments about their inferior biologies gained in intensity and women had to find strategies to overcome them. The following chapter deals with the rapid growth of physical education and looks further at the complexities and contradictions which it embodied.

Chapter 4

The legitimation of female exercise
The case of physical education

ELITE DAY SCHOOLS

Physical education became an integral feature of the curriculum in increasing numbers of elite girls' schools from the middle of the nineteenth century. Although individual headmistresses enjoyed considerable autonomy, and in some respects their opinions and programmes differed, they were all influenced by the report of the government-sponsored Schools' Inquiry Commission on the Education of Girls (1868), mentioned in the previous chapter. The report led in 1874 to the establishment of the 'Association of Headmistresses of Endowed and Proprietary Schools', which provided an important forum for the exchange of ideas. It was through this association that two of the early pioneers of female education influenced the general pattern of physical education in other schools – Dorothea Beale, headmistress of Cheltenham Ladies' College from 1858, and Frances Mary Buss, headmistress of the North London Collegiate School from 1850. Schools and colleges in other parts of Europe and in North America were also influenced by the ideas of Misses Beale and Buss, while at the same time ideas from the Continent and from North America were filtering across to Britain. (See Mangan and Park (eds) 1987 – in particular, Atkinson and Park's contributions.)

Miss Beale worked in a piecemeal fashion to improve facilities for exercise in her school, continuing the calisthenic exercises that were included in the school's first prospectus, providing a large room for calisthenics in 1876, and abolishing croquet because, she said, it encouraged physical deformity and idleness. Later, she employed a teacher trained in Swedish gymnastics and provided a room filled with swings, and a gymnasium 'specially fitted with all the needful appliances' (McCrone 1987: 108). But Miss Beale was always concerned to project an image of ladylike involvement in exercise which was acceptable to the high-class clientele of 'noblemen and gentlemen' at Cheltenham Ladies' College (Glenday and Price 1974: 13). She held conventional ideas that competitive games enhanced masculinity and were incompatible with essential feminine characteristics, and although she was persuaded to provide quite extensive games facilities in her school by the last decade of the century, she continued to oppose 'athletic rivalries' and prohibited prizes and matches against other schools (McCrone 1987).

At the London Collegiate School Miss Buss advocated a range of activities which, together, constituted a programme of physical education. In common with another twenty girls' schools in London, she included the musical gymnastics of the American Dio Lewis. A detailed account of Lewis's work appeared as an appendix to the Schools' Inquiry Commission report, recommended by Miss Buss in her submission:

> no school ought to omit Physical Training, that is, Callisthenics, or something equivalent. This we have of late enforced among the elder girls. Our system, an American idea, called Musical Gymnastics, is excellent. Easy, graceful and not too fatiguing, gently calling every part of the body into play by bright, spirited music, which cultivates rhythm of movement, it has become popular, and has wonderfully improved the figure and carriage of the girls. Our exercises last for 20 minutes to half an hour almost daily – as much as we can manage, always 4 days out of 5.
>
> (Cited in Webb 1967: 18)

Miss Buss built and equipped a gymnasium with an unusual range of apparatus including a 'giant stride', parallel bars and a wall-mounted ladder; and she appointed a teacher of gymnastics. She made provision for her pupils to attend the Public Swimming Pool at St Pancras and provided dancing as an extra. Elizabeth Garrett Anderson, a governor of the school at the time, encouraged Miss Buss to include organized outdoor games during a lengthened lunch interval and, by 1885, the games club was a regular feature of the lunch-break. The girls were able to participate in a fairly informal and spontaneous manner in games that they were familiar with as aspects of bourgeois home recreation – ninepins, badminton, fives, battledore and shuttlecock. By the end of the 1890s, the games played at the North London Collegiate School included hockey, netball and tennis, and, from that time, Sports Day became an annual event at the school (McCrone 1988).

From the 1860s, throughout the expanding sector of elite day schools for girls, there was a remarkably rapid development of a curricular programme of physical education, following the general pattern established by Misses Beale and Buss. Most schools included forms of gymnastics as well as calisthenics, some games, and other activities such as swimming and dancing. All these forms of exercise were justified by the headmistresses on the grounds of health. Their sensitivity to health was a way of dealing with medical opposition to female education, and helped to alleviate anxiety about the undue strain of academic work upon the female constitution. Miss Buss reflected the general view when she said, 'It may be well to state that the health of the pupils is the first consideration of this school' (Scrimgeour 1950: 46). She considered that good sanitation, ventilation, hygiene and health teaching were necessary complements to physical education, and she arranged for her pupils to have regular physical examinations by a qualified doctor who prescribed treatment by exercise to cure postural defects (Webb 1967: 20). The practice of medical inspections was taken up in other schools, and by the turn of the century it had become a regular feature of the work of the newly evolving specialist teacher of physical education (Burstall 1911). The physical education teachers, in co-operation with the school doctors, had become caretakers of the pupils' physical well-being. By the turn of the century, throughout these girls' schools, physical education was considered to be a vital element of development and it was a formal and supervised aspect of the timetable. Making physical education compulsory gave the school greater control over the whole range of pupils' activities.

The teaching of physical education in elite girls' schools had a radical character. What the headmistresses set up in their schools was different in content and ideology from the models of physical education in the boys' public schools. Edward Thring, who was the headmaster of Uppingham Public School for Boys, pointed out to the headmistresses at their conference in 1887 that they had a greater potential for change than the headmasters of the boys' public schools:

> you are fresh, enthusiastic, and comparatively untrammelled whilst we are weighed down by tradition, cast like iron in the rigid moulds of the past . . . the hope of teaching lies in you.
>
> (Glenday and Price 1974: 21)

PUBLIC BOARDING SCHOOLS

A number of the public boarding schools for girls modelled themselves closely on the boys' public schools. In many ways they came closest to achieving the wishes of feminist pioneers who wanted an education for girls almost identical to that of boys. There were some similarities in the academic curriculum, but, ironically, it was in the emphasis on games where the imitation of boys' public schools became most slavish (Dures 1971; Gathorne-Hardy 1977). St Leonards, Roedean and Wycombe Abbey were exemplars of games-oriented girls' schools. They also copied other features of boys' public school life that were concerned with uniformity and attitude or 'spirit' – like the house system and the prefect system (Dures 1971; Gathorne-Hardy 1977; McIntosh 1968). The original prospectus of Roedean (1885) prioritized physical education and characterized it, quite explicitly, as a palliative to academic work:

> Special pains will be taken to guard against overwork, and from 2 to 3 hours daily will be allotted to outdoors exercises and games. Opportunities will be given for Swimming, Riding and Gymnastics.
>
> (Zouche 1955)

The games played at Roedean were hockey, tennis and cricket; additional activities included running, fencing and dancing (McIntosh 1968). An even broader physical education syllabus was recommended by Jane Frances Dove who was headmistress at St Leonards School and later at Wycombe Abbey School. It included team games (hockey, lacrosse, basketball, cricket, rounders), 'games for smaller numbers' (lawn tennis, fives, bowls, croquet, quoits, golf, hailes), and individual sports (swimming, skating, archery, tobogganing) (Dove 1891: 400–2).

But it was the team games that were most fiercely promoted and achieved pride of place in many of these schools: and there was a rapid proliferation of inter-form, -house and -school matches, including the associated paraphernalia of competition – cups, colours and uniforms (Gathorne-Hardy 1977). Games-playing became a serious business – for example, at Roedean and Wycombe Abbey the girls underwent rigorous training in the gymnasium in preparation for the demands of the games field: in 1898, the headmistress of Roedean proudly reported that half the girls could show their heads above the horizontal bar from a hanging position, and nearly every girl could go hand over hand up the 16-foot rope (McIntosh 1968: 133). Middle-class girls were now able to participate in forms of exercise which would have been unimaginable for them only a few decades before, and which were still inaccessible to most girls in British society. In many ways, games-playing in the girls' boarding schools had taken on the characteristics of what used to be an exclusively male phenomenon and one which just as fiercely continued to embody an idealized image of masculinity. Because of their radical significance, team games for girls had to be justified and defended.

HEALTH AND MORALITY

The justification for physical education was different in emphasis between the two broad groups of girls' schools – the day schools, including those in the Girls' Public Day School Trust (GPDST), and the public boarding schools. Underpinning the arguments of the former group was a notion about the scientific relationship between the mental and the physical. Primacy was assigned to exercise for health – the provision of a fit body to enhance intellectual growth. It was never argued that girls were physically as capable as boys, but simply that girls required some suitable form of exercise to encourage healthy development and to provide a 'balance' to classroom work. This belief in the 'harmonious development of the powers' was shared with the latter group, but for them, the moral value of games was of paramount importance – a position articulated clearly by Miss Dove (1891: 396–7), headmistress of St Leonards School:

We do not desire the girls to be brainless athletes any more than we wish that they should be delicate or stunted blue-stockings, and either of these exaggerated types is made doubly deplorable if, as sometimes happens, there is a deficiency of moral power.

The point of convergence between the games of boys and girls was not in the type of games played or the physical prowess of the players, but in the idea that games could develop the moral qualities required for responsible leadership. The idea that public schools were training grounds for leaders, and that games could develop important character traits and team loyalty, was applied to girls in public schools as well as to boys. Again, Miss Dove makes the argument explicit:

> I think I do not speak too strongly when I say that games . . . are essential to a healthy existence, and that most of the qualities, if not all, that conduce to the supremacy of our country in so many quarters of the globe, are fostered, if not solely developed, by means of games.
>
> (Dove 1891: 398)

This was written in 1891, at the height of the era when notions of empire-building were an entrenched part of British ruling-class ideology. The essence of the ideology, *esprit de corps* – 'a power of corporate action' – was to be internalized in the girls' schools nowhere more completely than in organized team games such as cricket, hockey and lacrosse:

> Here is a splendid field for the development of powers of organization, of good temper under trying circumstances, courage and determination to play up and do your best even in a losing game, rapidity of thought and action, judgement and self-reliance, and, above all things, unselfishness, and a knowledge of corporate action, learning to sink individual preferences in the effort of loyally working with others for the common good.
>
> (Dove 1891: 400–2)

Games-playing provided the setting for girls to emulate certain physical and moral characteristics previously ascribed exclusively to males, and it was an undisguised assertion that women were not too weak to be educated. However, although 'glorification of sport as the training-ground of character . . . always implies a certain anti-intellectualism' (Bourdieu 1978: 826; Musgrave 1970: 60–1), at no time did the same degree of philistinism take hold in the girls' schools as in the boys' schools. Games-playing in the girls' schools was an extension of women's entry into the intellectual context of the university world; the supervision of girls' games was undertaken by members of the academic staff who were young graduates, predominantly from Oxbridge, and who had themselves played at university (AEWHA 1954: 4). These women, and now their pupils, had managed to some extent to resist discrimination both of the mind and of the body.

However, games-playing in girls' schools was a practice of contradictions.

Because of the glaring chauvinist trappings of male sports, it must have appeared to be a breakthrough into the staunchest of male domains. But the breakthrough was an essentially symbolic one. Since the girls were not educated with the boys and they did not play games with them, the male sporting role was not directly challenged. Furthermore, as soon as the 'stumps were drawn', the young female games-players assumed once more their stereotyped and public images of femininity. The ambivalence of, and irony in, the way women accommodated to their roles in sports is unwittingly, but perfectly, encapsulated in the compliment paid to a headmistress about the behaviour of her cricket team:

Your girls play like gentlemen, and behave like ladies.

(Dove 1891: 407)

Surprisingly early in the history of girls' education there had unfolded, as increasingly characteristic, a remarkably comprehensive 'programme' of physical education and therapy. Some form of gymnastics, together with organized games, became the core components of the curriculum and from the 1880s became consolidated into a formalized system common to the majority of elite girls' schools by the turn of the century. This trend was established before 1885 – the date that the first specialist college of physical education was opened. After that time, the main agents of the proliferation of the subject were the newly trained teachers of physical education. The subject became formalized and attitudes to it entrenched, leading to claims that the 'physical training mistress became a power in the land' and 'the games mistress could over-rule the head' (Gathorne-Hardy 1977: 250–1). Such claims may appear exaggerated, but nevertheless they signify an intrepid character. Certainly headmistresses welcomed the new specialist physical education teachers: not only did they bring to the schools a knowledge of games, health and hygiene, but also a high concept of discipline and responsibility which fitted in well with the contemporary ideology of elite female education (Glenday and Price 1974: 73–4).

EXERCISE FOR WORKING-CLASS GIRLS

Throughout the nineteenth century there was no equivalent form of physical activity in schools for working-class girls. Prior to Forster's Education Act of 1870, military drill for boys, supervised by army sergeants, was the only organized form of physical activity for working-class children. Military drill became established in state elementary schools as an effective device to inculcate 'mechanical obedience', viewed as necessary to provide an industrial and paramilitary training for workers and soldiers. Drill required precision, an unquestioning response to authority, controlled use of the body, and movements in time and space identical to those of every other member of the class (Hughes 1975).

In certain areas, there was concern to provide something equivalent for girls. For example, the London School Board showed an early keenness for some form of exercise for girls in London elementary schools. Mathias Roth's persistent advocacy of Ling's system (discussed in Chapter 3) was rewarded when the London School Board agreed that 'the only way to develop a scientific system of physical training was to introduce an expert who would organize the subject by instructing teachers in all girls' schools' (Deasey 1972: 38). In 1879, Miss Concordia Löfving from Sweden, a trained exponent of Ling's system of gymnastics, was appointed by the London School Board as the 'Lady Superintendent of Physical Education' in girls' and infants' schools (McIntosh 1968: 113). This event effectively marks the start of organized physical education for girls in state schools, and stimulated the dissemination of knowledge about Swedish gymnastics to practising teachers in elementary schools throughout the London area, and then in other parts of the country.

Miss Löfving's work was well received – within a year of her appointment there had been applications from 600 schoolmistresses for her course, which comprised practical and theoretical Swedish gymnastics, anatomy, physiology and teaching method. But even more influential was her successor, Martina Bergman – later Madame Bergman Österberg – who worked for the London School Board from 1882 to 1887. During that time she trained 1,312 women teachers in Swedish gymnastics and introduced the system into nearly 300 schools. By the spring of 1888, the Swedish method was being taught by certificated teachers in all the girls' and infants' departments of the London School Board (Deasey 1972: 38; McIntosh 1968: 113–15; Smith 1974: 95; Webb 1967: 55–76).

There were many advocates of physical education for the poor who came from different interest groups – doctors, teachers, military men, industrialists, philanthropists and social reformers. They showed interest in physical education for varied reasons – to promote health, to encourage military preparedness, to improve industrial efficiency and to foster social order. If any one system of physical education were to be adopted on a wide scale, or as a national programme, it needed to be flexible in order to satisfy all those requirements. Swedish gymnastics was probably better able than any other system to be adapted for these diverse objectives.

The Swedish system was theoretically formulated on 'scientific' principles which afforded it immediate status and credibility as a healthy activity. The underpinning concept was the 'harmonious development of the whole body', in the sense that the body was viewed as an organism of differentiated parts, all of which should be equally exercised according to physiological laws, aimed to produce in each individual, according to age, strength and sex, 'the highest degree of health and physical culture'. It was claimed that if the exercises were correctly performed they would develop the chest, straighten the back, effect co-ordination of movement, correct round shoulders, strengthen the abdominals, improve digestion, quicken circulation and activity of the liver, develop elasticity of thought and quickness of thought and action, produce courage, and quieten the heart-beat.

(Unpublished synopsis of Ling's system issued to [Dartford] students)

Ling's theory was useful because, although not derived directly from Darwinism, it fitted readily into the Social Darwinist concern for national fitness, and had no previous association in Britain with the crudities of military drill. Drill had a non-scientific and more pragmatic history, and there was general unease about exercise for girls which had military connotations. Swedish gymnastics represented an advance for working-class girls who had no other opportunities for physical activity in school. It had a certain aesthetic 'feel' and appeal that was a qualitatively new experience for them, though there was, as in drill, demand for exact placement of body parts and accurate timing. A pamphlet entitled 'Ling's Swedish System – Gymnastic Tables (Without Apparatus)', written by Madame Österberg and published by the London School Board in 1887, opened with the words, 'Joy and brightness combined with strict discipline are essential to a good gymnastic lesson' (Wickstead 1937: 2). However, the notion of 'joy and brightness' was a very limited one, and in no way at odds with a compliance with work discipline. The potential for natural, spontaneous movement was denied by the nature of the system and the parameters of behaviour laid down. In practice, the Swedish system was remarkably similar to military drill in its capacity to invoke a high level of discipline: and although it had originally been devised to deal with the needs of individuals, this was never its function in working-class contexts. Swedish gymnastics was taught to huge classes where the teacher assumed absolute authority, close attention being paid to effort, exactness, detail of action, and perfection of style, so that all movements were executed in precise unison:

The first Table, 'especially arranged to meet the requirements of the 7-year-old children' consists of 6 exercises:
 (1) Hips firm
 (2) Feet closing and opening
 (3) Trunk bending forward and raising (hips firm)
 (4) Foot placing sideways (hips firm)
 (5) Marching
 (6) Arm bending upwards
Each movement is preceded by the command 'Po-sition' and followed by 'Re-pose'.

(Wickstead 1937: 2–3)

Like drill, Swedish gymnastics was cheap, safe and easily learned; it was a suitable method of controlling large numbers of children, and its ritual nature made it a unifying experience. Although doctors, educators and military personnel argued over the philosophy of physical education, they shared ruling-class anxiety about social unrest associated with the economic depression, a widening of class differentials and radical working-class activity. And they shared the concern in ruling circles to regulate aspects of working-class life as a means of retaining control and influence (see, for example, Bailey 1978; Johnson 1970). The advocates of Swedish gymnastics also shared these concerns – Mathias Roth, for example, argued for a highly organized form of gymnastics which would prevent 'vicious practices . . . promote feelings of fellowship through concerted exercise and . . . produce habits of sharp obedience, smartness, order and cleanliness' (McIntosh 1968: 100, 111). He campaigned for a national system of gymnastics as a means of increasing work and military power by teaching people the means of preserving health, and in order to decrease the mortality rate, to keep the working classes out of gin palaces, and to counteract the effects of the occupational injuries of men and women workers. He addressed his arguments to the army, to the Board of Health and to the Poor Law Board, as well as to the Education Department (ibid.: 100–1, 107).

The upsurge of interest in Swedish gymnastics was intensified by ruling-class approval and patronage which ensured its consequent survival. Madame Österberg promoted the image of Swedish gymnastics by organizing public displays and by forging links with influential people to gain support. In 1883, a display of Swedish gymnastics performed by about 100 poor London girls became an auspicious event, attended by numerous dignitaries including the Prince and Princess of Wales, lords and ladies, bishops and clergy, military personages, politicians, mayors, sheriffs and educationalists (May 1967: 114). This prestigious occasion gave Swedish gymnastics a nationally important dimension illustrated by approbation in numerous press reports. This is an extract from *The Standard*, 25 July 1883:

> With a sharp military tone, that any commanding officer might have envied, Miss Bergman faced her company and counter-marched them, the girls moving with perfect steadiness and precision to their own voices singing 'The Minstrel Boy' though the little ones on the right flank had to take an abnormally long stride and even then lost a little distance. The girls were afterwards put through a series of flexion and extension motions, by which the neck and spine, the joints, and every muscle in their bodies were brought into active and harmonious exercise, the lungs being exercised by singing and counting.
>
> (Cited in May 1967: 115)

This demonstration of Swedish gymnastics symbolized and consolidated class divisions. It was performed by very young, impressionable working-class girls from poor districts in the East End of London – Islington,

Limehouse, The Borough, Bermondsey, Poplar and Ratcliffe – and under the auspices of prestigious members of the upper class. It was a patriotic ritual which provided a moving, visual impact and a symbolic consolidation of the different social positions of those taking part and those in the audience. In such a ritual, there was implicit acceptance of the existing set of social relations as a normal and universal arrangement.

The Swedish system received legitimacy through the support of ruling-class figures, but the hidden reality was that the Swedish system was a means of social control which had an ideologically subordinating function: it was no accident that Swedish gymnnastics, rather than freer, more spontaneous forms of movement, became the accepted form of exercise for working-class girls. There was opposition, for example, to the methods of Archibald MacLaren who recommended the use of apparatus as a component of a national system of exercise. Mathias Roth complained that 'MacLaren and his like seemed to think that climbing poles, ascending ropes, leaping, flinging the body around a bar and other *tours de force* constituted gymastics' (cited in McIntosh 1968: 92–8). MacLaren wanted gymnastics to be combined with 'swimming, country pursuits, riding, walking and other "agents of health"'. He was antagonistic to the absence of apparatus in the Swedish system which he considered was inadequate for healthy men and women and 'suitable to the invalid only' (ibid.). However, MacLaren's ideas, which he shared with other opponents of Swedish gymnastics, and the arguments of increasing numbers of doctors and educators that 'natural' movement was a basic need of young children, did not stop increasingly systematic and effective legislation against the traditional, non-official sports of children (Gillis 1975), or the preference for Swedish gymnastics as a method of directing and controlling, in an institutionalized setting, the spontaneous and natural activities of children.

Since the early 1880s, an eminent ruling-class figure, Reginald, Earl of Brabazon, twelfth Earl of Meath, had urged the case for state promotion of games and gymnastics 'to halt the degeneration of the masses'. His vigorous advocacy of physical activities reflects his overpowering concern for social control – 'to combat rowdyism and riotous behaviour in the streets'. In his capacity as president of the Metropolitan Association of Open Air Spaces, he provided £500 to open a Swedish gymnasium in a board school in a poor area of East London, 'with a view to the establishment of gymnasia through-out the metropolis' (Meath 1905). The Earl of Meath is usually portrayed as thoroughly well-meaning in his enthusiasm for Swedish gymnastics but, as Springall has pointed out, 'his social and political attitudes reflected those of the Tory imperialist with a military background' (Springall 1970: 97). In general, the concern to develop an exercise system to monitor behaviour was applied to young working-class males, but Lord Meath was concerned about the relevance to girls, as well. He wrote a letter to Madame Österberg, praising a display of Swedish gymnastics she had organized, performed by working-class girls, in the presence of Her Royal Highness, Princess Louise:

> The British nation owes a great .debt of gratitude to you for having practically introduced the Swedish system of physical training into the London elementary girls' schools, and through your college at Dartford you are bringing up a splendid army of well-formed and well-trained women to carry on your beneficent work. If there were more Colleges like yours, and more thorough systematic training of physical exercises in all schools, a long step would have been taken to solve the problem which puzzles our statesmen in the matter of the physical condition of the masses of the people.
>
> (Meath 1905)

Lord Meath's consuming interest in physical exercise reflected his belief that 'the body had to be dealt with before the mind would be receptive to improving thoughts of the Empire' (Springall 1970: 99). On this basis he advocated a system of exercise for both sexes. At the same time he held conventional ideas about gender divisions, arguing for a differentiated curriculum for working-class boys and girls – boys to be educated as war recruits and girls to be educated for domestic labour and for their future duties as wives and mothers (Dyhouse 1976: 46–7).

Swedish gymnastics was a part of the structure of ruling-class hegemony – that is, the direction or leadership obtained by ruling-class elements over a society (Hall, Lumley and McLennon 1977; Anderson 1976-7). How the processes of consent and control actually work at the level of the individual is a complex issue, but an important factor of ruling-class hegemony in the nineteenth century seems to have been the ability to define and control the legitimate use of the body. Madame Österberg gained recognition as the leading exponent in Britain of the Swedish system, and in that capacity she gave numerous interviews, public lectures and demonstrations. In 1887 she was asked to give evidence to the Cross Commission, which was investigating state schooling, and when Swedish work was sponsored as a national system in schools from 1904, Madame Österberg's tables of exercises formed the basis of the new syllabuses (Österberg 1887; Smith 1974).

In the same way that the form and content of the total educative process varied with class, so too did the form and content of physical education. Swedish gymnastics, with its strong association with discipline, was the only form of exercise on the curriculum for girls in most state elementary schools (Smith 1974), whereas in private schools for middle-class girls Swedish gymnastics was treated as part of a wider range of activities, and therefore commanded a less central position in the physical education programme. In addition, differences in the numbers of those taking part meant that the experience of gymnastics was normally dissimilar for working-class and middle-class girls. In elementary schools the size of classes averaged around sixty, so that the fundamental issue was one of order and discipline; for girls in elite schools where classes were small there was a greater focus on the body as a mechanism for health, on its relationship to intellectual skills, and ultimately to the social position of the girls in society. The Swedish system of gymnastics provides an example of the way ideology is inscribed in social practice, lending itself to different interpretations in different contexts.

THE LEGEND OF MADAME ÖSTERBERG

In 1885, while continuing her work for the London School Board, Madame Österberg opened a college in Hampstead for the training of teachers of physical education, which moved to Dartford ten years later. The establishment of Dartford College, as it came to be known, signalled an historic accomplishment. It offered the first full-time specialist course in the theory and practice of physical education in England and served as an exemplar for the specialist training of physical education teachers in other colleges – Anstey College (founded 1897), Chelsea College (1898), Bedford College (1903) and Liverpool College (1904).

Madame Österberg's contribution to the early development of physical education in England has become legendary. She achieved public acclaim during her lifetime and her indomitable spirit and exceptional energy appear to characterize her life's work. Sir George Newman, in his capacity as Chief Medical Officer of Health to the Board of Education, provides a poetic interpretation of her role as the 'morning star of the reformation' whose work, he said, 'we intend to see . . . is not lost in years to come but is made – as far as we can make it – of permanent value to the nation' (Newman 1915). Madame Österberg's work has been characterized as unique in its contribution to the feminist cause, and her name has been linked with those of other prime movers in the education of women:

> To Madame Bergman Österberg undoubtedly belongs the honour of having shared in the development of the new type of womanhood, now showing its grit, charm and power in directions which astonish the world. It can scarcely be doubted that the liberation of women's bodily powers, which we owe largely to her influence, has a direct association with the present manifestation of women's capacity and energy in the general work of the world, just as has that feeling of their mental powers which we associate with the honoured names of Miss Buss and Miss Beale.
>
> (Greene 1915–17)

Undoubtedly Madame Österberg's personal determination was a key factor in the establishment of the Swedish system as the official paradigm for the teaching of physical education in English elementary schools and in elite girls' schools. However, the nature of her work, which tends to be celebrated uncritically, needs to be more precisely specified. The social conditions which led to the favourable reception of Swedish gymnastics and the ideology surrounding the new profession of teachers of female physical education are of particular interest here.

Madame Österberg's specific intention was to establish a new physical education profession for young middle-class English women. In an unpublished undated manuscript entitled 'The Training of Teachers of Physical Education', she identifies the core components of the practical work to be Swedish gymnastics and games which, she argued, complemented one another perfectly:

> English out of door games combined with Swedish gymnastics form a safe and rational basis for physical education. . . . Games develop health, vigour, endurance, skill, character – but sometimes foster a one-sided development. Without National Gymnastics these bad positions acquired at home, in school as well as in the playground, may become habitual. Applied with knowledge and intelligence, Swedish gymnastics exactly supplement the English Games.

Madame Österberg's concern for a national system of gymnastics, and her passion for the moral connotations of playing games in order to stimulate 'brave deeds and noble thoughts' (ibid.), became assimilated in British nationalism. The professional paradigm for the physical educator was based on an ideology of moral endeavour and spartan uprightness, inextricably linked with the most rigorous, austere and exemplary forms of behaviour. Madame Österberg was an uncompromising disciplinarian who imposed upon her students the sternest of regimes. She expected them to dress impeccably, to be smart, clean, tidy, punctilious in manners, studious and punctual, and to respect authority. She was an autocrat who, in common with other college principals of the time, monitored students' activities in every practical detail, forbidding them to visit each other's rooms, enforcing an early lights-out rule, imposing cold baths and refusing weekend leave (*Kingsfield Book of Remembrance*). She demanded from her students an unquestioning and total commitment – physically, intellectually and ideologically, which was a whole 'way of life'.

The ideology which became associated with female physical education and sports, and which diffused into the schools and other colleges, became synonymous with regimented standards of behaviour. The first principal of Bedford College, who had been trained by Madame Österberg, was described by an old student as 'a sort of moral yardstick' who firmly believed that 'the discipline of the school emanates from the gymnasium' (Squire 1964). An old student of Anstey College said:

> the great idea was always to look SMART! We were buzzed before a gym or drill class to see that hair was tidy, stockings without a wrinkle,

everything correct; tunic girdles with the same length ends – all immacu-
late. This idea was carried throughout and in mass drill never a mistake
was to be made, or anyone a fraction out of time!

(Cited in Crunden 1974: 17)

Students of physical education came from the expanding middle classes:
they were in general inspired by the idea of work as a vocation. Girls were
handpicked because they were healthy and intelligent, with 'energy, zest,
tact and devotion', characteristics which, Madame Österberg (1896) said, 'are
the sine qua non of all successful teachers – those are the qualifications
necessary for this profession'. She articulated her philosophy more fully two
years later:

> Parents need to be dispossessed of the idea that girls with feeble intellects –
> those in fact who are unfit for other callings – can take up this work of
> physical training. . . . My girls are destined to become pioneers in all that
> relates to hygiene and a more rational method of life for the sex. To carry out
> this great work effectively they must possess not less but more than average
> intelligence. I need girls with brains and character. None others will do.
>
> (Physical Training College Report 1898, Osterberg 1895–8)

She decried slackness of any sort, lack of effort, and complacency, and she
did not hesitate to demand withdrawal of students from the course if they fell
short of her requirements. Her highly critical bearing and the general absence
of praise were intentional devices to equip students for their professional,
pioneering roles. 'How can you keep your children in order if you cannot
keep your hair tidy?' she demanded; and 'If you cannot control your legs,
how can you control your class?' She urged a sense of community and pride
which had a strong elitist ring – 'No student of mine', she explained, 'ever
says "I cannot". The day may come when you are nervous. Remember that
you are one of Madame Österberg's students, and it will be enough to carry
you through any situation' (cited in May 1969: 110–11).

FEMINIST CONCERNS AND LIMITATIONS

A powerful ideology was inscribed in women's specialist physical education
courses: the colleges aimed 'to send out women trained in mind and character
as well as in body' (Crunden 1974: 14). This attitude, which provided the
day-to-day impetus and broad overriding philosophy for the new physical
education profession, also constituted a particular version of feminism. In a
special commemoration, Madame Österberg's niece wrote about her aunt's
conviction that a 'freer, sounder and more responsible womanhood was
essential to the well-being of any country'. Madame Österberg's objective,
she wrote, 'was not Swedish gymnastics, nor even physical education . . .
her life's work was dedicated to the social, economic, and spiritual freedom

of women' (Broman 1937). This was the sentiment that linked Madame Österberg's name with women's emancipation in Britain, Sweden, and the USA. The following account of her ideas was written in June 1891 by a reporter for the Women's Herald – the 'Women's Penny Paper . . . Conducted, Written and Published by Women':

> Madame Bergman Osterberg is a sound liberal and naturally thinks that women should have the vote. She is a warm supporter of her own sex and hopes to see all professions and trades open to women equally with men. She maintains that women's economical independence will be of the very greatest importance in the question of her general emancipation. Such independence can, however, only be gained by efficient work, and for such work a healthy physique is the indispensable foundation.

Although this forceful feminist sentiment would seem to be incompatible with popular stereotypes about women's roles, Madame Österberg's radicalism also embodied conventional ideas about women. Her feminism was essentially a form of nationalism, supportive of the popular Social Darwinist view that an improvement of the human race was conditional upon raising the level of health, intellect and morality of its womanhood. This is made clear in the following extract from *The Sidcot Quarterly* in 1892:

> I try to train my girls to help to raise their own sex, and so to accelerate the progress of the race; for, unless the *women* are strong, healthy, pure, and true, how can the race progress?
>
> (Bradley 1892: 144)

She shared with many other feminists a passion about the vital importance of motherhood in evolution, and a belief that female education should be geared to the role of women as mothers (Dyhouse 1976). Victorian familism, discussed in Chapter 3, was incorporated into the rhetoric, ideology and practical arrangements of life in all the specialist colleges of physical education. Madame Österberg described the course of training in her college as an education for a future life as a wife and mother:

> Nothing is taught here which a woman can afford to ignore. One cannot but think what an immense boon it would be to many girls, after leaving school, to spend one or two years at College. The outdoor exercise and the training here would fit them far better for the battle of life . . . to become the organiser of the perfect home, or the trainer of a vigorous and beautiful new generation.
>
> (Österberg 1896: 7)

Justifications for female exercise idealized the woman's body and her ability to bear healthy children. The conception of the physical capacities of women encapsulated in the rhetoric about Swedish gymnastics illustrates this point:

It is the best training for motherhood . . . it is moulding and reshaping and reforming the most beautiful and plastic material in the world, the human body itself.

(Österberg, cited by Webb 1967: 200)

The idealization of the role of the woman in the family was a central feature of the version of feminism associated with the women's physical education profession. The colleges reproduced the structure and ideologies of the 'perfect' Victorian home, thus reinforcing conventional sexual divisions in society. However, this idea was not applied to working-class girls performing Swedish gymnastics and had no practical relevance to the lives or needs of proletarian women, the majority of whom laboured for long hours and for low wages. Madame Österberg believed that working-class women were essentially inferior and, as a former student reported, '[she] felt she could never have laid the foundations of a healthy womanhood in Great Britain by training the working classes, and for that reason made me ashamed for my country' (Crump undated).

Specialist courses in physical education were exclusively middle-class affairs. Students were accepted only if they were healthy, refined, intelligent, well educated, and could afford £100 per annum for the two-year course. They came from affluent middle-class families, having attended fee-paying schools or finishing schools, or having had a private tutor or governess (Crunden 1974; Dartford College archives; Fletcher 1984). The colleges provided a training which qualified the students to teach as well as to work as remedial gymnasts and masseuses. Most graduates worked with people from their own class, either in private health clinics or in the hospital service, as we have seen in the previous chapter, or in elite girls schools, colleges and universities. They also taught in elementary schools, and did voluntary work in clubs for poor children or for working women. Only six years after Madame Österberg opened her college, it was reported that the 'old students have found good positions in some of the most important schools and colleges in England. The Ling system is adopted at Girton, Newnham, Cheltenham, Bedford, and elsewhere' (*Women's Herald* 1891). And the training allowed graduates an unusual sort of economic independence to combine their qualifications in varied ways, illustrated in the Dartford College Report of 1895 (pp. 23, 26):

Miss G.M. Hosken, 1 Gordon Road, Cardiff, has considerable variety in her work. She conducts classes in the normal department of the University of South Wales and Monmouthshire, and also takes gymnastics at the Cardiff High School for Girls. . . . At the time of writing, she had joined the High School Games Committee, and was hoping to introduce hockey and other games. 'I am forgetting to mention a free class which I give to dressmakers, shop assistants, women telegraphists, and cashiers. Coming straight from work, they are often tired, but they enjoy the exercise, do their best, and I must say I enjoy it too.'

(Österberg 1895–8)

Miss F. Buckland, Hill View, High Road, Sidcup, still continues her class in Ladbroke Grove, in connection with the North Kensington High School, the members of which have increased considerably during the last year. A class has been started in Sidcup which bids fair to become a great success. With several voluntary classes for poor children, with private lessons and with further engagements for next term, we should hardly think that Miss Buckland has much idle time on her hands.

CLASS RELATIONS

The relationship between the college personnel and the working classes confirmed their respective class positions. The staff and students who taught Swedish gymnastics to working-class girls and women were part of a general movement of middle-class women into voluntary organizations concerned with social control. Although most sporting and recreational clubs in working-class areas were for boys and men, and there was limited provision for girls and women (Dawes 1975), the new female physical education specialists played an important role in this sphere. The Dartford College Report for 1895 shows that eight out of thirty-one former students were involved in voluntary youth work, giving free gymnastic classes to working-class girls and 'working women' in clubs and training homes. At Chelsea College, helping in London girls' clubs was an integral part of every student's training; and Dorette Wilkie, the principal, became famous for introducing games for children into London parks (Crump undated). Students training at Anstey College maintained a close association with the factory girls' clubs in the Birmingham area, taught classes of children from elementary schools and local orphanages, gave displays for local charities and, as employees of Messrs Cadbury Bros, taught gymnastics and swimming to factory hands at Bourneville. In 1910, after an annual factory club competition, the Countess of Grosvenor drew attention to the plight of factory girls, and went on to suggest that it was a beautiful task for women to provide evenings of recreation and instruction to brighten their lives (Crunden 1974: 11, 16, 18). But in all these contexts a most stringent and explicit brand of self-discipline was demanded of working-class girls and women: regular attendance, good behaviour, smart appearance, care of the body, good posture, attention to the word of command, perfection of performance and absolute self-control all accorded with factory discipline and embodied an ascetic rather than a sensuous use of the body (ibid.).

Clubs for working-class girls were part of an overall movement to rational-ize working-class leisure using, in this instance, the energies of idealist, 'do-gooding', middle-class women. At a time when most middle-class girls remained within their own class structures in their conspicuous attempts to find husbands, students of physical education appeared to be 'filled with the highest ideals to do some good to the Community, apart from being independent' (ibid.). The ideology of service to society – the notion of personal responsibility to a general cause, or *'noblesse oblige'* – was emphasized, and the new and partially liberated army of middle-class physical education teachers provided a good deal of the required staffing. Voluntary social work of this sort was an indicator of a particular kind of attempt to control working-class people in an institutionalized setting. In the contexts of drill and Swedish gymnastics in the elementary schools the body was being used consciously and compulsorily, under the aegis of the state: in the philanthropic sphere of the youth club, the voluntary use of the body assumed a remarkably similar symbol of control. In both these settings, the superior status of the specialist teacher or instructor exerted pressure to conform: it represented authority, hierarchy and social distance, and thus implicitly consolidated relations between the dominant and subordinate classes. Although the provision of clubs and facilities represented some sort of material and cultural advance for working-class girls, it was clearly of a very limited kind and served as a mechanism of control to deflect attention away from wider social issues. In the context of the girls' clubs, the feminism of the early physical education specialists was an aspect of bourgeois ideology – the concept of the new physically and morally invigorated woman was incorporated into the ruling-class concern for social order.

The functional relationship between the specialist women physical educators and the ritual use of the human body for control purposes was extended and strengthened around the turn of the century. From this time the number of clubs and recreational activities for working-class girls and women increased, as did the number of trained physical education specialists involved in those contexts (Österberg 1898). Physical education graduates took up appointments with the prison service and as superintendents of physical education with the county councils and the school boards (*Register of Gymnastic Teachers and Medical Gymnasts* 1908, 1913), and they were involved in the teaching of the Swedish system to elementary teachers in the expanding sector of teacher-training (Barnes 1891). In 1887, in evidence to the Cross Commission, Madame Österberg had anticipated, and argued for, the introduction of the Swedish system, by specialists, into government training colleges, and for the subsequent inspection of the work by trained specialists on a national scale. Madame Österberg's theory of physical education provides a good illustration of the contradictory nature of ideology: the Swedish system was flexible enough to be considered suitable as a mechanism of working-class control, as well as being interpreted as appropriate to the needs of middle-class girls, whilst presenting itself as a neutral, scientific body of knowledge.

THE GROWTH OF A NEW PROFESSION

The 'health-through-science' concept provided a link between these different types of movement and formed the basis of a body of theoretical knowledge which legitimated the physical education profession. This was a necessary procedure to enable the new teachers of physical education to develop a 'professional' identity. If professionalism is viewed as a strategy for controlling an occupation (Parry and Parry 1974: 161), then the requirements of the physical education specialists to possess this form of knowledge was a device which, together with entry restrictions, regulation of training and testing procedures, and the strict command of 'professional' conduct, was a cohesive force and a method of maintaining power and control and dictating the profession's ethos. The ideal of altruistic service to the community was also a central tenet of the professional values of the physical education women and provided them with occupational solidarity and further legitimation in the community.

The association with 'science' signalled the professional identity and professional competence of the physical education specialist, as the occupational descriptions 'teacher of scientific physical education' and 'health mistress' indicate (Montefiore 1896: 285). Physical education graduates played a fundamental role in relating the argument that good health enhances intellectual potential to the practical situation – in middle-class girls' schools they were in effect mediators of both the physical well-being and the academic achievement of pupils. If the schools took possession of their pupils' health and physical development, it was easier to establish that fitness actually did improve academic work, and the process could even be controlled. Systematic medical inspections became a standard feature of girls' education, and the physical education teachers worked closely with the school doctors as expert agents of body control. Therapeutic exercises were prescribed by school doctors for numerous physical defects and weaknesses, and were carried out in the schools by the physical education teachers (Atkinson 1978, 1987). The knowledge and skill to perform remedial work became a clearly defined and essential component of the composite expertise required of the physical education specialists, as the following advertisement illustrates:

> Physical Mistress wanted to teach Swedish Drill, Games (Cricket and Hockey), Medical movements and massage if required . . . Gymnasium fitted with Heath and George's Apparatus.
>
> (Cited in Crunden 1973: 56)

Those who promoted exercise for schoolgirls were not denying the relationship between the body and the mind, but they replaced the idea that intellectual activity depleted essential energy reserves with the assumption that the body had a store of vigour which, with care and exercise, was sufficient for the intellect to flower. Hence, good health was the conditional starting point for the education of middle-class girls, and the physical education mistress became established as the schools' supreme caretaker of girls' bodies.

The model of the bourgeois lady as 'conspicuous consumptive', discussed in the previous chapter, was replaced in the educational context by a qualitatively different image connected with the notion of 'positive health'. In practical and instrumental terms, as well as ideologically, the medical profession was implicated in the diffusion of both these images, which shared in common a heightened female self-consciousness of women's bodies.

The social definition of the legitimate female body and the legitimate use of the female body in physical education were, as Bourdieu suggests, part of a larger field of struggles for monopolistic power over the body (Bourdieu 1978: 826–7). In the case of the physical education specialists at the end of the nineteenth century, the struggles were between fractions of the dominant class – for example, 'moralists, doctors (especially health specialists), educators, and pacemakers in the matters of fashion and taste' (ibid.). In the case of the early development of women's physical education, any potential professional opposition to the definition of legitimate exercise in the context of education was countered by a clever synthesis of the interests of the pedagogical and medical authorities.

For twelve years Madame Österberg monopolized the training of women physical education specialists: her college remained the only women's college until 1897, and there was no equivalent training for men until the 1930s. It was exceptional for so much power to be wielded by one individual in the development of a profession: during thirty years Madame Österberg laid the foundation for the progress of physical education for years after her death. But she had a remarkably parochial and inflexible attitude, jealously guarding her position of control: she even opposed two of her own protégées, when, for example, they opened Anstey College in 1897 and Bedford College in 1903; and she unrelentingly refused to co-operate with her former students in the founding of the first professional organization in 1899 – the Ling Association. She supported instead the rival, and insular organization – the Bergman Österberg Union, founded in 1900 (Ling Association 1899–1909: 2–9; May 1967: 103). However, the early efforts of the Ling Association bore fruit and by 1904 the association was conducting its own examinations and issuing a Diploma in Physical Training. The antagonisms were resolved only after Madame Österberg died in 1915, when a single, professional organization re-entitled the 'Ling Association and Affiliated Gymnastic Societies' was formed so that 'the teachers of Swedish Gymnastics in England [could] now go forward as a united body to advance the cause of Swedish Gymnastics in the country' (Ling Association 1919: 9). The early phase of occupational organization followed a pattern similar to that of other professions: a centralized body had emerged in response to the perceived need to protect its members and to promote their interests. It replaced the dissipated efforts of different interest groups within the incipient profession. However, unlike those cases of women attempting to enter other professions, such as medicine and law, the physical education women did not have to compete with men to be treated on equal terms and did not threaten in any way an entrenched, dominant male position. The physical education colleges were tightly integrated institutions and in the early days the women who were involved in shaping the new profession enjoyed an unusual degree of autonomy as a group.

The growth of the physical education profession can be seen as part of the general process of professionalization – a large-scale phenomenon which was a peculiar historical product. It was characteristic of a specific stage in the development of industrial capitalism and of an expanding middle class, and in particular of the absolute increase in middle-class women's employment (Johnson 1972). But this only partially explains the emergence of a self-styled 'profession', and does not in itself account for the ability of one individual woman to realize her idealism in a practical form and to dominate the training of a specific group of women for over thirty years. Madame Österberg's charisma, innovatory capacity and powerful connections explain why she, personally, was successful. But her success was possible only because there was a manifest demand for specialist teaching and therapeutic work and her physical education paradigm was perfectly suited to the needs of girls' schools and health clinics and did not offend the dominant social consensus about women's bodies.

A PROCESS OF STRUGGLE

Nevertheless, advocates of physical education had to withstand criticism and censure from the medical authorities who applied the 'conservation of energy' principle, and from the more conservative wing of Social Darwinism. Yet once physical education had become established in schools and colleges, the debate centred on the amount and type of exercise allowed. There is no evidence of opposition to Swedish gymnastics – which had the well-argued 'science-for-health' defence – and so games appeared to take the brunt of the attack. Critics expressed fears about obsessional games-playing evidenced in girls' schools, and about the supposed fetish of exercise which had developed in a way that was comparable to the cult of athleticism in the boys' schools:

> The pendulum has probably swung too far in the direction of over-exertion. . . . This is especially true of the wealthier girls, who belong to the social classes in which men and boys care so much for games and sport.
>
> (Burstall 1907: 99)

Powerful criticism came from the eugenists who claimed that the adolescent games-player would suffer irreparable damage, which, in the most extreme cases, would induce severe hormonal imbalances. Specific attacks directed at the colleges of physical education became particularly vociferous after the turn of the century:

> there is a well-known Girls' College [Dartford] which makes pre-eminently for the cult of mannishness. And here are seen, absorbed in fierce contest during the exhausting heat of summer afternoons, grim-visaged maidens of sinewy build, hard and tough and set as working women in the '40's, some with brawny throats, square shoulders and stern loins that would do credit to a prize ring. All of which masculine developments are stigmata of abnormal sex-transformation, precisely similar in origin to male antlers in female deer; namely, deterioration of important sex-glands, with consequent obliteration of the secondary sex-characteristics arising normally out of the functional efficiency of these.
>
> (Kenealy 1920: 139)

The struggle over the legitimate female body in games centred on connotations of impropriety and mannishness and involved a wider public, including parents and the press. Emily Davies had stopped the Girton pioneers playing football on the lawn because she said, 'it would certainly shock the world if it were known' (cited in Atkinson 1978: 149). Games, more than other physical activities, offended the bourgeois standards expected of girls and young women and shocked the sensitivities of those people with an idealized notion of the 'ladylike' wife and daughter. In 1881, a local newspaper report of a cricket match between two respectable girls' schools in Birmingham describes the hitting as 'very spirited on both sides'. A hostile report in another paper states:

> We can only hope that when these muscular maidens come to be married no similar entry will have to be made in this chronicle of their connubial felicity . . . we may assume that the feminine character [of the costume] must have been greatly modified. If the exhibition was in any sense public, we must confess to a preference for those less pretentious places of education where English lasses used to be taught modesty, if little science.
>
> (Cited in Atkinson 1978: 148–9)

To a large extent the physical activities of pupils and students were contained within the educational setting and somewhat insulated from the public's view. By the end of the century the innovatory gymslip (a pleated tunic designed by one of Madame Österberg's students) was being worn in the colleges and in several schools, and notions of bodily freedom and more natural forms of movement were becoming prevalent. However, although advances were achieved, they tended to be gradual and cautious because of sustained opposition. For example, in 1910 a Dartford student caused public disquiet and shocked the sporting press when she played for Kent in a tunic, while all the other players wore regulation skirts, 'not less than six inches off the ground' (AEWHA 1954: 10). Off the pitch, students conformed to a model of well-bred, bourgeois conformity, to compensate for their perceived departures from this norm on the field. All vestiges of masculinity were instantly converted to an image of stereotyped propriety and femininity. The entertaining of visiting players after a match was an extension of the family-household ideal, when bourgeois social etiquette was demanded of the erstwhile games-player-turned-hostess. This was one way in which the ambivalent position of the female games-player could be resolved.

The expansion of physical education for women was internally related to the concomitant struggle of middle-class women to achieve social and economic status via education and professionalization and, in contrast to the general repression of women at the time, the establishment of a physical education profession for women was, in a sense, a remarkable achievement, and a material advance, in both educational and economic terms. However, physical education was marked by its insular, separatist nature. The women involved were already in a privileged social position and they were concerned mainly with acquiring equal rights with men under the existing social order. Rhoda Anstey was an ardent campaigner for the franchise and was one of the original members of the Gymnastic Suffrage Society who marched with her staff and students together with 'mill girls and sweated women workers from London's East End' (Crunden 1974: 9). She was one of the most radical figures from the women's physical education profession, but even so she reflected the dominant middle-class feminist position at that time and showed no concern for a more complete social transformation. The physical education specialists challenged some features of dominant ideology – notably attitudes to the female body – but were in general conservative about wider social and political issues.

The struggle over the physical body was important for women because control over its use was the issue central to their subordination: the repression of women's bodies symbolized powerfully their repression in society. The physical education women gained considerable ground by widening the definitions of how they could legitimately use their bodies, but although relative freedom was gained in relation to what went on before, they were still seriously restricted in a number of ways. The early development of female physical education embodies conflict: a tightly defined paradigm of legitimate physical education had been established and alternatives had been opposed. For example, a smattering of German gymnastics which incorporated the use of apparatus had been introduced by Rudolph Oberhölzer into London schools (Hargreaves 1979: 80), in opposition to Madame Österberg, with whom he disagreed about the respective effects of the two systems of gymnastics on bodily development. Madame Österberg believed that German gymnastics would develop characteristics that were too manly – her notion of freedom to move rested upon assumptions about the different, innate characteristics and needs of men and women, so that, as she put it, gymnastics 'develop body, mind and morals simultaneously . . . a vital factor in making manly men and womanly women' (Swinerdon 1895). She used her powerful influence as inspector of schools with the London School Board to ban all apparatus from schools in the London area (Johnson 1973: 20), thus preventing the growth of an alternative, freer gymnastic form. Other freer forms of movement, which had no connotations of masculinizing females, were opposed by Madame Österberg as well. Even after her death, the Ling Association sustained a virtual monopoly of female gymnastics in the educational context, and barred the entry of Margaret Morris into the state sector of education. Margaret Morris is often regarded as the British equivalent of Isadora Duncan, with a highly creative and artistic, but none-theless methodically formulated, system of movement. Margaret Morris's approach was vehemently opposed by those who had a vested interest in Swedish gymnastics on the grounds that it was moving too far in the direction of spontaneity with a consequent lack of discipline (White 1977).

There was little evidence of voluntarism in the Swedish system or in the way games and other sports were taught in the colleges of physical education. All types of exercise were highly regulated and serious – in significant ways the very antithesis of play. In this case, Huizinga's (1971) thesis that modern industrial civilization has driven the play element out of sports and games seems to be applicable. Madame Österberg justified the lack of spontaneity and play-like quality in her system as a necessary safety precaution to ensure healthy growth:

> The recreative element should not decide the choice of movements, nor the more or less pleasing characters of the performance. The choice left to the child itself may be injurious. Continued climbing, jumping, vaulting, during the whole lesson would abnormally accelerate the action of the heart.
>
> (Österberg 1896: 286)

The model of the legitimate use of the female body in physical education in the late Victorian period took an 'ascetic' form, emphasizing rectitude and effort, in opposition to an alternative 'hedonistic' use of the body emphasizing physical freedom and expression. In the specific social and historical context, Madame Österberg triumphed over other more artistic and aesthetic forms of movement which had a greater potential to change the social consciousness of women about their bodies.

The dominant model of physical education was a particularly influential ideology. Towards the end of the nineteenth century and, more typically, after the turn of the century, middle-class girls and increasing numbers of working-class girls gained their experience of all forms of physical activity through their schooling. Ideas and meanings attached to gymnastics, games, athletics, swimming and dancing have been mediated in schools and have had a lasting effect upon how women think about their bodies. The history of competitive sports for women in sports clubs has also been closely associated with the expansion of the physical education profession and with the development of sports in the university sector (McCrone 1988). Graduates from higher education, but in particular from the colleges of physical education, constituted the core of the membership of competitive sports teams at national and international levels and they had control of the organizing bodies of sports for women. Female sports were inextricably bound up with and influenced in a fundamental way by the development of the women's physical education profession.

Chapter 5

Recreative and competitive sports
Expansion and containment

INTRODUCTION

By the first decades of the twentieth century, increasing numbers of girls and women were participating in more various and vigorous forms of sport and physical exercise. This chapter is concerned with the expansion of women's leisure and with the development of competitive sports for women. Like the activities described in the previous two chapters – conspicuous recreation, therapeutic exercise and physical education – recreative and competitive sports were also circumscribed by the most powerful and pervasive feature of the dominant ideology concerning women – biological determinism. They also developed their own unique characteristics.

ELITE SPORTS

Throughout the nineteenth century, even amongst the upper classes for whom leisure was the 'rule of life', sports were predominantly the prerogative of the male. When women did participate, they did so in the main for social reasons and seldom in competition (Margetson 1969: 52). However, from the beginning of the nineteenth century, archery was a popular sport for aristocratic ladies which, unusually, incorporated keen competition into a social event. The following quotation is taken from a journal account of an archery competition in 1830:

> The ladies were dressed all in the same costume – white and green satin, with white hat and green feathers, green shoes, etc., and their bows and quivers full of arrows slung in an elegant position on their shoulders. . . . The elegance and superior feats of the ladies were the theme of universal admiration. The company consisted of the principal families in the county and the members of the Archery Club.
> (Wymer 1949: 212. See also Ensor 1949 [1936]: 164)

Early in the century rigorous country sports, like riding to hounds, were not in general accessible to upper-class women who, for 'decency', still rode side-saddle and wore flowing dresses and beplumed hats. Although hounds were bred to run faster than ever before, it was impossible for women to enjoy the new fashion of 'galloping at the fences' (Margetson 1969: 55). To ride astride (or have the legs apart) was considered to be provocative and to symbolize sexual abandonment. For a young unmarried woman it was believed to carry the risk of breaking the hymen, signalling the loss of virginity and rendering her less marriageable. Nevertheless, elite female sports, like the sports of other social groups, were growing and changing – not abruptly and dramatically – but as a process of adjustment and accommodation. New, more radical forms of exercise were being formulated alongside established conservative activities and, towards the end of the century, sports and games were becoming increasingly popular among women with aristocratic connections. Public disapproval was encountered, and to a large extent transcended, because women anticipated much of the criticism and responded to it in the way they took part in new activities. Patriarchal ideology was the most consistent and sustaining set of values which women had to deal with, although there is no reason to suspect that the new sportswomen did not believe its basic premises anyway. Although aristocratic women were more insulated from the public eye than middle-class and working-class women, nevertheless, they were also impelled by convention to demonstrate that their sports had a utilitarian function, that there was no immodesty or impropriety associated with them, and that the level of physical activity was moderate. In this way, upper-class women extended their physical horizons without threatening their existing set of social relationships with men.

A book which was published in 1894, entitled *Ladies in the Field: Sketches of Sport*, is characteristic of other similar publications. This book was written by and for upper-class women – it is edited by Lady Greville and contains contributions by the Duchess of Newcastle and Lady Boynton and a copy was donated to the Fawcett Library by Lady Astor. Not surprisingly, it reflects dominant ideas of the time about elite female sports. There are articles on an unusually diverse assortment of activities – riding, hunting, team- and tandem-riding, tiger-shooting, rifle-shooting, deer-stalking and driving, covert-shooting, kangaroo-hunting, cycling and punting – all of which are described as desirable pastimes for women, with the potential to enrich their lives, strengthen their health and improve moral welfare. For example, we read that riding tends greatly to enhance moral and physical well-being and improves the temper, the spirit and the appetite (Greville 1894: 3). Above all, every contribution assumes that female sports should not undermine in any way a woman's essential 'femininity'. This is especially significant in those sports normally associated with 'male' characteristics – it is stated, for example, that a lady who is fond of shooting need lose nothing in grace, charm or refinement. She does not necessarily become masculine either in manner or conversation!

(Greville 1894: 200)

Elite sportswomen adopted a characteristically contradictory position – on the one hand, they were lessening inequalities between themselves and men, but at the same time they accepted the notion of innate differences between the sexes:

It is scarcely necessary nowadays to offer an apology for sport. . . . Women cheerfully share with men, hardships, toil and endurance, climb mountains, sail on the seas, face wind and rain and the chill gusts of winter as unconcernedly as they once followed their quiet occupations by their firesides. . . . Women who prefer exercise and liberty, who revel in the cool sea breeze and love to feel the fresh mountain air fanning their cheeks, who are afraid neither of a little fatigue nor of a little exertion, are the better, the truer, and the healthier, and can yet remain *essentially feminine in their thoughts and manners*.

(Greville 1894: 22; emphases added)

In all elite sports differences in behaviour between men and women are highlighted. Lady Greville's account rests upon the implicit assumption that, characteristically, women possess an improving ethical disposition which can be employed in sports to 'refine the coarser ways of men', 'contribute to the disuse of bad language' and 'lead the way to habits of courtesy and kindness' (ibid.: iii, iv). Hunting in the shires is claimed to provide a healthy way of training a man's character, whilst the woman is depicted as his moral exemplar as she rides with him through the countryside. In addition, it is claimed that a woman's 'tact, kindness . . . courtesy and politeness . . . part of our ideal lady's nature . . . go a long way towards what is called "keeping the country together"' (ibid.: 31, 76–7).

In her role as sportswoman, as in her role as wife and mother, a woman was expected to behave in an exemplary fashion and to display her feminine traits. In sports, as in the family, it was argued that the influence of a woman's innate superior morality would, through her influence on others, improve the condition of the nation. Sports were thus idealized: they were claimed to be of great benefit to individual women and to contribute to the evolution of society.

The topical Social Darwinist ideas of the late nineteenth century, discussed in Chapter 3, had manifestly infiltrated the world of elite female sports. References to the physical and mental benefits of exercise, its capacity for generating self-discipline, the high moral gains derived from participation, the inculcation of 'finest feminine qualities', and the imparting of traits such as courage and leadership are commonplace. All this is combined with the contemporary, popular scientific approach to the learning of skills and techniques, involving the application of the laws of mechanics and physiology in order to resist fatigue or over-exertion and to perfect sporting performance (see, for example, Hayes 1893; Sheddon and Apsley n.d.; Slaughter 1898; Ward 1896). Punting, for example, is described as a very graceful art, exemplified by the aesthetically pleasing image of a slim girl punter who makes no apparent effort, it is explained, because of the efficient distribution of muscular effort throughout her whole body so that she benefits from the physiological effects of exercise (Greville 1894: 269–72).

The ultimate stamp of approval, and a factor which is given primacy in literature about female sports, is the exemplary model provided by Queen Victoria. In a journal entitled *The Sportwoman's Library*, it is claimed that women had 'come to be reckoned as a power in the land in the matter of sport' and that 'Her Majesty's example has probably had not a little to do with the increased love of sport among women of the present day' (Slaughter 1898: 8).

It is argued that Victoria's conduct of distinction on the throne and in her private life provided a stimulus to women to 'take the share in the sports as well as in the more serious duties of our national life' (ibid.). The influence of the patrician element especially set the cultural tone of women's sports and complemented the severe restrictions imposed by the more conservative exponents of Social Darwinism.

SPORTING SENSUALITY

The evidence of history shows how women's sports are 'lived cultures' which embody tensions, conflict and contradictions. It also shows us that even for different fractions of the same class there are differences, and that neither women, nor sports, can be treated as homogeneous. Women's sports are invested with meanings which are imposed on women, but which women also create for themselves. Victorian and Edwardian women acknowledged the emancipatory potential of sports because the qualitatively new physical experiences were a contrast to the severe constraints of the past, but they did so in different ways. For example, in the literature on elite female sports, there are a few cases which are out of character with its overall respectable, cultured image and with the general tone and moral stance of the publications. Some women appeared to be making radical claims which were opposed to the views about the limited constitutional capacities of women at the time and touched upon the sensuous and hedonistic potential of exercise. Hunting is described as an experience akin to that of music and dance, or the delirium of battle, which enhances emotions 'deeply seated in the joy of exercise when the body is brought into play, and masses move in concert of which the subject is but half conscious' (Greville 1894: 31). Cycling is characterized as 'the youngest of women's sports' and graphically claimed to be a pleasure in itself and to possess elements of excitement –

assertions which could be construed as having somewhat risqué connotations for the time:

> Hers is all the joy of motion, not to be under-estimated, and the long days
> in the open air; all the joy of adventure and change. Hers is the delightful
> sense of independence and power. . . . And, above all, cycling day after
> day, and all day long will speedily reduce or elevate her to that perfect
> state of physical well-being, to that healthy animal condition, which in
> itself is one of the greatest pleasures in life.
>
> (Greville 1894: 264)

The ability to experience the sensuous joy of movement depended upon
dress reform. The delicate, absolutely 'ladylike', perfect moral exemplar of
womanhood was gradually acquiring a new perspective associated with a
more vigorous and uncluttered image. Women's clothes best symbolized this
development – the severe restrictions of stays, corsets and hobble skirts were
being replaced by looser-fitting and lighter clothing. After the turn of the
century the female form was being released from the 'distortions and disten-
sions' of the Victorian era:

> no longer did women insist, with what seems to our more modest gaze an
> extreme salaciousness, upon the erotic attractions of her hips and her
> buttocks, thrusting these portions of herself, well padded and be-
> ribboned, into the eye of the yearning male. By 1910 the womanly body
> had begun to look like a womanly body.
>
> (Dangerfield 1970: 135)

Dress reform accelerated the development of female sports, and female
sports, in turn, stimulated changes in sportswear. If any one event best
characterized the emancipatory tendency of women's sports, it was the
advent of the safety bicycle. 'Suffrage, dress reform and liberty' – these were
the most common demands of the British and American feminists, and the
evidence suggests that the invention and subsequent popularity, from 1885,
of the safety bicycle advanced the cause of female dress reform. It was
claimed by Dr Elizabeth Mitchell, writing in Canada in 1896, that bicycling in
Europe influenced female reforms in North America:

> I am quite sure, that had it not been for the extraordinary great vogue
> which bicycling has had for the past two years in London and Paris, we
> should still be wearing hoops.
>
> (Cited in Hall 1971: 245)

The bicycle liberated women from their 'actual and symbolic encumbrances
of long skirts and tight lacing' (Roberts 1977: 569). The new forms of dress
designed for the bicycle – shortened skirts, divided skirts, knickerbockers,
skirts with elastic insets, and bloomers or 'rational dress', allowed women a new
physical independence and symbolized their revolt against restrictions. With

the bicycle, women appropriated two unprecedented forms of freedom – bodily and spatial mobility.

Dress reform gave women greater scope for movement, extending the range of activities available to them, and as they ventured into more varied spheres of action, so further changes in sportswear inevitably resulted. However, this seemingly radical acceleration of bodily freedom did not represent as broad-minded an attitude to the body as one might suppose. An important feature of late Victorian and Edwardian mores, which had its roots in seventeenth-century puritanism, was a de-emphasis of the sensuous nature of women and a predominance given to their actions, missions, qualities of character, and home life (Roberts 1973: 45). Their conscience or soul, duty and reason, were expressions of the highest part of their nature, whereas the body or appetite, or animalism – in reality the sexual instinct or desire – represented the lowest part of human nature (Cominus 1937: 156). Young middle-class girls were undoubtedly brought up to be perfectly innocent and sexually ignorant – a condition linked to their economic dependence upon their fathers and husbands. Moral purity continued to be embraced by better-off middle-class families whose reputation rested upon their daughters' chastity. Not unexpectedly, sports which symbolized freedom and spontaneity and which could be associated, however spuriously, with sexuality, were opposed on moral as well as scientific grounds. Cycling, for example, was claimed to be an indolent and indecent activity which tended to destroy the sweet simplicity of a girl's nature and which might cause her to fall into the arms of a strange man! The worst fear was that cycling might even transport a girl to prostitution (Hall 1971).

So middle-class women, in particular, took to cycling with caution and propriety. They went to great lengths with safety hooks and eyes, lengths of like-coloured elastic or weights sewn into their skirt hems, to devise ways of making long gowns quickly and efficiently convertible to short ones for safety when cycling, but possible to change instantly back to cover the ankles as soon they dismounted (Pennell 1894: 260–1). Attitudes to the sexuality of the female body, exemplified in sports, changed over the years – the eroticism of the flamboyant dresses worn for conspicuous recreation was replaced by the sexless character of the clothes that were easier to move in, but covered all possible parts of the body from sight. For example, the skirts and petticoats of the early hockey era covered the ankles, the blouses were high-necked and long-sleeved and the hockey players wore gloves and hats. As games were played more vigorously, sporting attire for ladies became distinctly shapeless – the dark blue serge box-pleated gymslip, with tights sewn into knickers, or black and brown woollen stockings with laced shoes were worn by increasing numbers of lady gymnasts towards the end of the century. The introduction of splashes of colour added a 'feminine' touch to the proceedings, but did little to affect the sense of strict uniformity and depersonalization. This is a description of a gymnastics display reported in the *Daily News* in 1890:

Their costume consists of a dark blue tunic and knickerbockers with a red
sash with falling ends tied at the side. A knot of blue ribbon ties the bodice
in front and the stockings are dark blue with red ribbons.

(Cited in Winter 1979b Pt I: 35)

Sporting activities sought to desensualize sportswomen and it was not infrequently argued that sports should be used to reduce sexual desire. In *The
Handbook for Girl Guides*, written in 1912, cold baths and healthy exercises
are recommended as an antidote to the dreadful consequences of what it
seems reasonable to assume are implied to be masturbation and lesbianism:

All secret habits are evil and dangerous, lead to hysteria and lunatic
asylums, and serious illness is the result. . . . Evil practices dare not face
an honest person; they lead you on to blindness, paralysis and loss of
memory.

(Middlemass 1977: 146)

A great number of female sports encapsulated ascetic attitudes which
women seemed to accept and reproduce unquestioningly. Sportswomen
were keen to get on with their sports, but tended to be conservative about
the general politics of women's position in society and in particular about
their sexuality. And they had no leadership from the late Victorian feminists
who focused on the economic and social liberation of women at the expense
of their sexual liberation (Vicinus 1973: ix–x).

DEALING WITH OPPOSITION

Like other sports, cycling illustrates the contradictory features of the development of female sports – moral and scientific arguments were employed
both to support and to oppose its development. Unlike other sports, cycling
rapidly achieved phenomenal popularity which, at its height, far surpassed
the earlier croquet and tennis crazes and resulted in the rapid formation of a
large number of clubs with excursions and meetings on a widespread scale
(Pennell 1894: 261). As early as 1880 the Cyclists Touring Club (CTC)
admitted women members, and other clubs with special ladies' sections and
ladies' cycling clubs and associations, as well as specialist journals, developed from that time. Individual tastes were catered for; most participants
cycled through the town and countryside as a leisurely social recreation,
though a few, it was observed in 1894, 'have turned the high-way into a
race-course, and occasionally, have broken records and done other
wonders' (ibid.). However, there was a resistance to organized racing for
women and it was not until 1916 that the CTC sponsored its first ladies' rally
(McCrone 1988: 182). However, although cycling became a fashionable,
consumer-oriented sport, popularized in cycling papers and women's journals,

such as *Lady Cyclist Magazine* and *Wheelwoman*, its public acceptance as a female recreation depended upon women participating in as unobtrusive a manner as possible. Cycling for women became respectable in large part because most of those who participated consented to their roles as 'inconspicuous cyclists'. Nevertheless, cycling symbolized physical freedom and excitement and, through the hiring of bicycles, was more widely accessible to working women than other sports. Even the sudden demise of the bicycle after 1900, when sales fell dramatically, did not detract from the new concepts of female liberation of which women had taken possession. Cycling had accelerated the ongoing revolution in social relationships which was consummated in the new century with the advent of the automobile and motor-cycle; it had accelerated also a process of reappraisal of women's potential for physical and bodily freedom which various forms of games-playing and sports carried forward into the twentieth century.

However, because there was general awareness and uneasiness about the puritan conception that the body was a source of sin, free, sensuous movement, which could be defined as erotic and sexually provocative, posed an additional problem for women. Swimming and athletics and, to a lesser extent, more rhythmic forms of gymnastics, demanded a new quality of physical freedom embodying a greater range of movement and fluid actions. These sports were freer, less tense and rigid, and defined as more aesthetic than other sports, and clothing for them was, necessarily, minimized, exposing more of the female body. The shape of the 'real' woman suddenly became conspicuous, in contrast to the distorted one. When women started to participate in these activities for the first time, there was some scope for them to be self-indulgent and to celebrate their newfound physical enjoyment; but as greater numbers of women became involved, there was powerful opposition, requiring the most careful justifications in response.

As early as 1858, when 'St Marylebone Public Baths was thrown open to the feminine public', the occasion was reported in a reputable woman's journal entitled *Work and Leisure*. The building was described as 'a very respectable edifice', with 'the purity of new-laid paint of fairest tint . . . the water of crystal clearness, [and] the temperature most agreeable' (Elleret 1858: 413). Female swimming was eulogized:

> And oh! what a delight for the dweller in city confines, just passing from the hot and dusty streets, to leap into this clear flood, and feel that sense of exhilaration which free exercise in the water always bestows, and which before could only be gained at the cost of a country journey, or at least was unattainable for aught of womankind, within the bounds of this vast metropolis. How different from the only bath hitherto within their reach, the solitary stepping into a narrow box of water merely to lie prone a few minutes in listless inaction, is this dash of sparkling drops over the

head, this expanse of ambient fluid buoying up the frame, with space for the free play of every limb, and with pleased friends and companions around, sharing and heightening the enjoyment.

(Elleret 1858: 413)

However, indulgence in the intoxicating effects of swimming was quickly put into sober perspective: it was necessary for 'respectable' women to be assured that the context was in no way morally or socially corrupting. First, female sports were strictly class-specific: working-class women used municipal facilities for washing themselves, but the cost of swimming was beyond their pockets. Middle-class women were therefore 'protected' from those of a lower social class or of 'doubtful virtue':

> though the cost of admission is very moderate, being only 8 pence, this is a higher price than is charged for any other bath in the establishment, and therefore quite sufficient to keep it select.

(Elleret 1858: 413)

The practical arrangements in public swimming pools also assured that women were separated from the opposite sex:

> we have certainly no wish that St Marylebone should ever present such a scene as was customary, not so very long since, at Bath, where, as Anstey describes it –
> 'Twas a glorious sight to see the fair sex
> All wading with gentlemen up to their necks.'

(Elleret 1858: 413)

'Public' swimming was available to London women for the first time, but in reality it was the province of middle-class ladies only and remained so for many years. It was a novel enterprise which was the result of the energy and initiatives of women who lived in the area and who campaigned to gain access to a leisure activity previously monopolized by men. These women were fiercely opposed by the all-male committee who organized and controlled the facility, yet eventually persuaded them to make the pool at Marylebone available for the 'exclusive use of womankind' on a trial basis for one day in the week. To begin with, this concession was accepted as a privilege rather than as a right, but it provided the motivation for women to make similar demands in other locations and for women to demand more and more swimming time. Gradually swimming became established as a morally acceptable recreation for the 'fair sex' and arguments were made to promote it as a functional activity, a 'life-preserving art', and as a form of exercise beneficial to women's health (ibid.). Implacable masculine opposition was ineffective in halting the steady advances in the development of women's sports which obtained their momentum from the determination of individual women and groups of women to take part in an increasing number of activities with greater bodily freedom and physical competence than ever before. This example of female swimming illustrates how women were dependent upon men to grant them opportunities and how gaining access to various sports was a process of struggle by women to undermine male hegemony.

Some middle-class recreations had become mixed social events, but it was inconceivable that public swimming could come into this category. Although early swimming costumes covered as much of the body as was reasonable for safety, nevertheless, the shape of the woman's body was visible, and the closeness of male and female bodies in the water smacked of depravity and was anathema to middle-class ethics. Separate public swimming was rigidly adhered to until the 1920s, and even then, in some regions, mixed participation was only possible in the guise of family bathing. There were separate entrances for men and women, and strict rules of procedure disallowed men from getting out of the water on the 'women's side' of the pool, and vice versa (Rawlinson 1979). Even as a feature of the seaside family holiday, respectable families organized bathing with propriety to avoid embarrassment and to ensure absolute modesty and morality (Whitelaw 1965: 8). And there were conventions and devices which evolved to ensure decency and sensitivity – the 'changing tent', for example, was a structure which swimmers could remain inside as they walked to the edge of the water and in which they could hide their bodies when they re-emerged.

Female sports acquired a moral legitimacy if they encapsulated conventional, respectable ideas about femininity: it was not the actual involvement in exercise as much as the method of participation that was problematic – a position explicitly articulated by the author of a book, written in 1896, entitled *Bicycling for Ladies*:

> I have found that in bicycling, as in other sports essayed by them, women and girls bring upon themselves censure from many sources. I have also found that this censure, though almost invariably deserved, is called forth not so much by what they do as the way they do it.
>
> (Ward 1896: ix)

The continual criticisms and opposition handed out by men were a way for them to maintain power and monopolize resources. Not surprisingly, when women did secure new opportunities for themselves, they never questioned the conventions of participation and the standards of behaviour expected of them. On the one hand this appears to be an example of accommodation and compromise, but there is no evidence to suggest that women demanded or desired changes in etiquette as well.

RATIONALIZED SPORTS

By rationalized forms of sport is meant activities in their less spontaneous, and more organized, regularized forms, including competitive team games with codified rules and bureaucratic procedures. Men's sports provided a model for the rationalization of women's sports and games. But although for both sexes organized sports and games were, in their early days, predominantly middle-class phenomena, whereas men's sports had previously gone through a 'bourgeoisifying' process, most women's sports took a 'bourgeoisified' form straightaway. There were few remnants of folk sports or rough, 'uncivilized' women's or girls' games to undergo transformation (Bailey 1978; Dunning and Sheard 1979). The boys' public schools played a key role in the rationalization of sports for males which took place from the mid-nineteenth century onwards, whereas the equivalent function for women's sports was shared between girls' schools, universities, the colleges of physical education and private clubs, and occurred later – from the last decade of the century. The development of female sports in schools and colleges was discussed in the previous chapter: the following brief résumé gives other examples of the increasing range of activities available to girls and women.

During the 1860s women became involved in competitive sports, but to a very limited degree. Some games were popular with women, but unique to one locality, like bandy – a type of hockey on ice, originating in the Fens:

> Not even the women could resist any longer the lure of bandy. Using a rather thinner stick and lighter ball, they now arranged matches of their own.
>
> (Wymer 1949: 195)

Cricket was probably played by women as well, because in 1864 when the overarm bowling action was allowed for the first time in the men's game, it was suggested that it was a style previously 'adopted by women who found it more convenient than underarm because of the voluminous skirts of the period' (Jewell 1977: 57). But these are spasmodic examples, and there is no evidence to suggest that bandy or cricket or other team games were extensively or regularly played by women at the time.

It was the game of croquet which directed the trend of women's sports into new and lasting forms of organization, with competition on a more formalized basis. Although it originated as a social activity, characterized in Chapter 3 as 'conspicuous recreation', croquet was easily adapted for competition. Its change of name to 'Loose Croquet', when two hands were permitted on the mallet, heralded its transition to a tournament sport, and in 1867 the All-England Croquet Club was inaugurated. From then on croquet clubs proliferated country-wide and large numbers of middle-class women took part in organized competitions. Because croquet required little physical exertion, and provided a setting where conventional images of femininity could be displayed, men and women competed together. Archery was another sport which in no way threatened conventional images of femininity, and the men's association (Grand National Archery Association) supported the women's game and organized ladies' national championships for the first time in 1880. However, dominant images of femininity were shifting, and by 1882 when croquet, quite unexpectedly, went out of fashion, and archery was losing its limited popularity, other, more vigorous sports became favoured by women.

Unlike archery and croquet, sports which incorporated a more active image of the female body were mostly played separately by men and women, and there was a delay between the sexes in the establishment of competitive play. For example, rules for men's tennis had been drawn up in 1875 by a modified committee of the Marylebone Cricket Club, just one year after the 'invention' of the modern game of tennis. Then, in 1877, the committee of the Wimbledon All-England Croquet and Lawn Tennis Club took over the organization of the sport and made rule changes which lasted some years. A milestone in the history of tennis occurred in 1879; women's events were included on the first programme of the newly instituted Oxford University Tennis Championship (Marshall 1898: 314). However, outside the relatively insulated spheres of the universities and schools, and most particularly at Wimbledon – the most prestigious tennis venue – there was vehement opposition to women's competitions. Men had been playing at Wimbledon since 1877, but it was argued that 'tournament play was all too tiring for the weaker sex' (Wymer 1949: 250), and a ladies' singles championship was not allowed at Wimbledon until 1884. Maud Watson won this event wearing a bustle, a hat and high-heeled shoes. The event was described as

> a leisurely affair, the more so as the distinguished charmers participating were weighed down by heavy dresses over multi-petticoats, and were permitted to simper or take a rest if their service broke down . . . in a final which provided more titters than jitters.
>
> (Revie 1972: 18)

Nevertheless, women's tennis gained impetus. In 1888, the Lawn Tennis Association was established as the governing body for the game and the rules were revised and officially codified, incorporating women's events, and introducing the mixed doubles (Marshall 1898). However, although in many club and tournament competitions women were playing ladies' doubles and mixed doubles, there was fierce resistance to their inclusion during the Wimbledon fortnight. It was only in 1913, after continual controversy and struggle, that these two doubles events became permanent Wimbledon fixtures. All events in which women played lasted for three sets, in contrast to five sets for the men, setting a precedent for the future development of the game.

The replacement of bustles, corsets, stiff petticoats and ankle boots with looser dresses and sports shoes, enabled players to move more freely and become more skilful. However, in 1887, when Lottie Dod, who was only 15 years old, won the ladies' singles title, she was the only player who could volley and smash effectively, and it was not until the second decade of the twentieth century that significant numbers of women had mastered these skills and were playing in tournaments all over the country with more power and agility than ever before (Wymer 1949: 251; Revie 1972: 19). The new abilities of female tennis players to use their bodies with more speed, control and vigour than previously were, however, less important in the public promotion of female tennis than the demands that they conform to strict standards of behaviour and discipline – 'to start at once, to arrive in time, never to be in a hurry and never to relax good style by slovenly play' (Marshall 1898). In tennis, as in other sports, women continued to be judged according to traditional norms of femininity which in part continued to restrict their development.

Tennis was ahead of many other sports in its international development. Aristocrats and affluent middle-class people throughout Britain, in other parts of Europe, and in North America and the colonies played tennis. They could afford their own courts and the fees to join clubs and they could travel to competitions at home and abroad. The International Lawn Tennis Federation was founded in 1912 which accelerated the growth of the game so that it became perhaps '*the* most international of all games' (Revie 1972: 37), and was given a stamp of approval by royal patronage. However, female players still suffered discrimination, and although English female players of the period were admired abroad, it was also fashionable to decry their efforts (ibid.: 36–7).

Golf is another game with a surprisingly long history of female involvement, but only among small numbers of privileged women (Lowerson 1982). Men monopolized resources for golf throughout the country, and for most of the nineteenth century golf clubs had no female members. But during the 1860s women started taking action for themselves, playing on vacant ground and then forming their own clubs, and men's associations responded by allowing women limited access to their facilities. The women's game could only expand after permission was given for them to play on some main links for the first time from 1885 (Ensor 1949: 166). Independent all-female clubs were rare and most women accepted the very restricted arrangements offered by male-controlled clubs (McCrone 1988). But the increase in the number of female players resulted in the founding of the Ladies' Golf Union in 1890 from which time the women's game was consolidated. At the same time punting, badminton and skating were expanding as popular sports for women and followed similar processes of rationalization: in the late 1880s the first Ladies' Punting Championship took place at Maidenhead; in 1900 women took part in organized badminton competitions; and in 1906 competitive skating events for women were inaugurated (Salaman 1894; Slaughter 1898; Dobbs 1973). Women had played these sports informally in previous years, but as soon as they were organized into competitive events increasing numbers of clubs opened up, paralleled by a rapid increase in competitive opportunities.

It is difficult to be precise about when hockey was first played since 'Victorian prejudices form a shroud for the secret activities of the early players' (AEWHA 1954: 1). Like croquet and tennis, it was originally an aspect of home-made entertainment and had become fashionable as a country-house and holiday game. Female players were influenced by the men's game through their family connections. For example, a majority of the members of the All-England Team in 1898 had learned the game by watching men's matches for years, by playing informally with their brothers and friends, and by competing in informal mixed matches (Österberg 1896–8: 47). Hockey (in common with cricket) is an example of a sport which was originally played informally by both sexes together, but which, as it developed on a larger scale and became institutionalized in schools, colleges and clubs, took on less spontaneous features embodying the rigid separation of the sexes.

As more middle-class women gained access to formal education, they took part in organized sports in increasing numbers. Women's hockey quickly developed a firm affiliation to the sphere of education because the universities, schools and colleges could provide sufficient players in the right age-groups to make it a viable activity. Women's hockey was being played in universities from the 1870s, and became established in girls' schools and then in the specialist colleges of physical education from the 1880s, and later spread out to clubs and other institutions. The year 1887 marks the date when the first-known private club was formed, called Molesey Ladies, followed in quick succession by clubs at Ealing (1888) and Wimbledon (1889). The early rationalization of the women's game occurred almost exclusively within the university sector by 'educated women' who had a monopoly of control and a vested interest in the development of the sport (Margetson 1969: 208). This liaison facilitated the rapid expansion of women's hockey, the proliferation of competition, and the establishment of hockey as the major national team game for women. The men's Hockey Association was formed in 1886, and in spite of hostility from this association, it provided the organizational model for the women's game (AEWHA 1954: 4). From the mid-1890s games between English and Irish university teams were played – the first English team to go on tour was composed of past and present students from Newnham College, Cambridge who played a team from Alexandra College, Dublin (ibid.). To enable a full English squad to be formed for future international matches, some of the most enthusiastic players organized the inaugural meeting of the Women's Hockey Association (WHA). Further development was speedy: in 1895 the formation of county associations occurred and territorial matches were played. Within four years, fifty-two clubs had affiliated to the Women's Hockey Association, and in 1901 a paper called *The Hockey Field*, although a private enterprise, became the official organ of the Association and crystallized the rationalization of the modern game (ibid.: 5).

Hockey is a potentially fast, vigorous, aggressive and 'dirty' game, and the early female hockey players were some of the most physically adventurous women of their time. Nevertheless, like other sportswomen, they went to great lengths to protect their public image of respectability upon which they placed a higher premium than personal safety when they voted *against* a resolution in the early days of rule-making that 'no player shall wear hatpins, or sailor or hard-brim hats' (ibid.: 4–5)! In 1898, a resolution was passed at the Annual General Meeting of the WHA to allow entry only to ticket-holders at matches. This was a move 'to protect the game from "roughs" and other undesirable spectators' who had demonstrated against the players on previous occasions as 'unsexed creatures' (ibid.). Alongside advancement and enthusiasm, there continued to be constant and hostile opposition to women's sports, which encouraged the adoption of strict rules of etiquette and the continuation of single-sex spheres. Although there was a slight, but favourable shift in attitude to women's participation in physical and sporting activities after the turn of the century (Dobbs 1973: 176–7), there was renewed antagonism to hockey, in particular, from doctors and spectators. So, it remained imperative for women players to be as ladylike in their play as possible – to tackle each other gently and fairly, to behave with respectable demeanour on and off the hockey pitch, and to dress inoffensively. Hockey provided an example for the pattern of development of other team games. During the 1890s other competitive games for females which were taken up in schools, colleges and clubs included lacrosse, rounders, basketball, netball and, finally, in the closing years of the century, cricket. However, the official governing bodies of these women's games were formed much later – lacrosse in 1912; rounders in 1923; netball in 1926; cricket in 1926.

Competitive swimming was an almost exclusively male preserve for a very long time. The Amateur Swimming Association (ASA) was formed in 1869 and races for men were regular events from that time (Sports Council 1977); but competitive swimming for women started much later. The tragedy of the *Princess Alice*, a pleasure boat which sank in the Irish Sea in 1878, was decried as an unnecessary horror, and provides an index of the low swimming ability among women: of the 399 women on board, only one could swim the short distance to safety – all the others drowned (Thomas 1904). The Life-Saving Association was inaugurated in 1893, as a breakaway group of the ASA, and it is likely that women took part in life-saving activities from that time (Sinclair and Henry 1893). There were still few opportunities for organized or competitive swimming except in schools and colleges. Some exhibition events occurred just before the turn of the century – the most notable was the 20-mile demonstration swim completed in 6 hours 20 minutes by Miss Agnes Beckwith at the Royal Westminster Baths in 1878 – an event which was patronized by Her Royal Highness the Princess of Wales, the Duke of Clarence and the Duke of York. Miss Beckwith, whose father was a professional swimming champion, is described as the original pioneer of women's swimming (ibid.: 20). But although a minority of early sporting heroines were given official and 'royal' approval, their performances were exceptional and it is difficult to assess the extent to which they influenced a more general trend in women's sport. In swimming, no formalized races for women took place before 1900 and women were not admitted to the National Championships until 1901. This marked the first time women were allowed in the company of men in a major competitive event. Women were precluded from Olympic competition until 1912 when, after negotiation and struggle, they were allowed to participate in two events only (Rawlinson 1979).

THE POLY CLUBS

London was the leading centre for the growth of organized sports outside schools and universities, and the history of activities in the London poly-technics provides an interesting illustration of women's recreation in the big urban centres. The Women's Institute of the Regent Street Polytechnic opened in 1888, and within two years the swimming pool was made available one night a week for the exclusive use of women members. The Swimming Club was the first women's sports club at Regent Street – founded in 1890 – and during the same year women's clubs for tennis, golf, hockey, gymnastics and netball were formed. These clubs flourished and became popularly known as the 'Poly' clubs. By the end of 1894 there were additional clubs with active memberships for cricket, roller-skating, fencing, badminton and basketball. To begin with, traditional attitudes about gender divisions affected the ways the clubs were run – all of them were all-female groups and only female spectators were admitted to the Ladies' Swimming Gala and to the Ladies' Gymnastic and Calisthenic Displays. But over a period of time, and in line with other public venues, increasing numbers of mixed organizations and competitions evolved at the Regent Street Polytechnic.

There were so few organized sports for women that the teams from Regent Street Polytechnic were supreme in many events and experienced difficulty in finding other teams to compete against. This changed somewhat in 1896, when the Northampton Polytechnic Institute (also in London) was opened (Lesley 1979; Winter 1979a Pt II, 1979b). After that time, similar institutes which organized women's sports were springing up in the greater London area and in other conurbations throughout the country. Rudolph Oberhölzer, a world champion gymnast from Zurich, introduced German gymnastics at the Northampton Polytechnic and he was the major advocate of the German system in Britain. This system of gymnastics had been pioneered by Jahn in Germany and popularized in various countries in Europe and North America (McIntosh 1957). German gymnastics included work on apparatus and became the basis of competitive, Olympic gymnastics, whereas the Swedish system was restricted to free-standing floor-exercises, sometimes with small equipment like dumb-bells, and was concentrated in the educational and medical contexts. German gymnastics was opposed by proponents of the Swedish system with 'scientific' arguments, and the controversy between the advocates of these two systems (see Chapter 4) affected the development of female gymnastics in a fundamental way. Because Swedish gymnastics was the preferred model for girls in schools, and those in power in educational circles ensured its continued monopoly in educational contexts, there was very little German gymnastic equipment available in the country, very few teachers of the system, and a tiny number of clubs which promoted it as a competitive sport. The 'foundations of (Women's) British Olympic Gymnastics were laid' at the Northampton Institute, and by the turn of the century, the lady gymnasts from this polytechnic were the leaders in their field, and the polytechnic remained a stronghold of the sport for thirty years (Johnson 1973: 20–1).

Summer 1890 marked a significant breakthrough in Victorian attitudes towards women taking part in sports in public. In that year women's sports in Britain became public entertainment when the 'Poly Gymnasium Squad' was invited to give a display at the Royal Military Exhibition (Lesley 1979). The exhibition was promoted by patrons and sponsors from the world of business and commerce and the audience was elite and ostentatious. The event, opened by His Royal Highness the Prince of Wales, was one of the highlights of the London social season. The gymnastic display was reported widely in the press with praise for performance and propriety – a reflection of public attitudes to women's sports. One account that the display was carried off with military 'precision and eclat' so that 'there was nothing that even the most fastidious could object to' typifies this approach (Winter 1979a Pt I: 36).

Women's gymnastics was quickly patronized by members of the ruling class for whom it was a way of gaining publicity and kudos, of displaying and reinforcing their values, and of having a controlling interest in an increasingly popular activity. Gymnastic displays involved free-standing exercises, marching and calisthenics, and work with small apparatus, such as hoops and balls. They incorporated a great deal of symbolism and ritual and, with large numbers of bodies moving in identical ways, they created a moving and unifying effect on performers and spectators alike. The 'Poly Girls' gave many demonstrations and exhibitions where important dignitaries, politicians and members of the royal family were present. For example, in 1908, at the Franco-British Exhibition opened by His Royal Highness the Prince of Wales and attended by King Edward, Queen Alexandra and the President of the French Republic, there was an impressive display of female gymnastics (Winter 1979a Pt II: 11, 14, 23). By 1908 gymnasts from the polytechnics had become the '"pin-ups" of the London sporting world', and they gained publicity in the national and sporting press, most particularly in *The Times*, the *Daily Telegraph*, the *News of the World*, and *Sporting Life* (ibid.: 12). All the reports stressed the efficiency of those taking part, their precision and consistency, the attention to detail, and the uniformity of their work. Above all, 'the smart appearance of members was always a matter of comment' (Winter 1979a Pt II: 8, 14; Pt III: 4). As female sports became increasingly popular, the public image of the 'new sportswomen' seemed to embody the values of the British ruling class: they represented important disciplinary and even military ideas, and their sporting performances exemplified the emerging ideals of a changing image of femininity which personified energy and positive health. In their capacity as public figures, the early twentieth-century sportswomen were able to promote a national image of womanhood at home, and they were able also to enhance the image of British women abroad.

The early organization of women's sports was crude. Arrangements for competitions were made in an ad hoc fashion and there were no governing bodies to provide a system of control. On this basis the 'Poly Girls' made up the bulk of the first 'national' women's gymnastic team whose members took part in the 1908 Olympics in London (Winter 1979a Pt II: 14). The prominent position of the polytechnics in women's sports continued, but always stamped with respectability and a cautious use of the body.

THE CONSTANT FOCUS ON BIOLOGY

Medical opinions for and against female exercise, apparent from the beginning of the nineteenth century, were central to the legitimation of female sports. They reflect some of the complexities, contradictions and struggles which were part of the early development of women's sports, and provide part of a history of ideas about women's bodies, aspects of which are still relevant today. Accounts of the apparently detrimental effects of female exercise were published throughout the nineteenth century and continued to have credibility and a powerful effect on female participation in sports well into the twentieth century. For example, in 1837 in a book entitled *Exercises for Women*, riding is condemned because it is claimed to produce 'unnatural consolidation of the bones of the lower part of the body, ensuring a frightful impediment to future functions' (Walker 1837: 8). Over seventy years later, in *Eugenics Review*, it is argued that an emphasis on games and athletics is likely to do irreparable damage to the growing adolescent girl and that hockey, specifically, could disable a woman from breastfeeding (Murray 1910–11, cited in Dyhouse 1976: 45–6).

However, whilst the medical argument opposing exercise for women was that it was *damaging* to health, there were also medical arguments in support of exercise for women on the grounds that it *promoted* positive health. In 1858 two papers, published in the *English Woman's Journal*, and supported by medical opinion, recommended exercise for women and argued that the subtle processes of early socialization preclude girls from taking part in physical activities:

> almost insensibly at first, but more markedly year by year, a different system is pursued with the boy and girl; the boys are 'made hardy', and many are the baths and rides and the tumbles, constituting the difference between the training of papa's little lad and mamma's little lady. . . . Who thinks of nice large playgrounds for her? She must not slide on the way to school, nor are snowballs or mud pies a becoming recreation.
>
> (*English Woman's Journal* 1858: 149)

In this formulation, lack of exercise is condemned as the cause of general bodily atrophy, deformity, dysfunctioning of muscles and organs, 'delicacy' and various manifestations of ill-health including the 'ravages of scrofulous disease' and even premature death. Cleanliness, sufficient sleep, good food and, above all, *ample exercise in the open air*, are stipulated as the basic requirements of health, especially relevant to girls from 'higher in the social scale', those leading sedentary occupations, and those in urban areas (ibid.). With regular exercise, it is claimed, the human body becomes as a 'divine image . . . a varied and powerful instrument for the expression of the soul':

> Bodies that can move in dignity, in grace, in airy lightness, or conscious strength, bodies erect, firm, energetic and active – bodies that are truly sovereign in their presence, the expressions of a sovereign nature.
>
> (Blackwell 1858: 189–90)

Although these positions for and against exercise for women appeared to be in opposition, they were both underpinned by a belief in Social Darwinism and a concern for the national good as well as for the future of the human race. They both transposed the 'laws' of nature to social phenomena. Arguments for and against female exercise were related to women's procreative functions and the point of convergence of these apparently opposite approaches was that women could take part in 'reasonable' forms of exercise, in 'reasonable' amounts, and in a 'reasonable' manner, articulated by a doctor in 1892 in an article in the *Lancet*, which was the most prestigious British medical journal:

> Lawn tennis, gymnastics, swimming . . . and cricket even, all come in for a share of commendation. Let us add but one caution . . . namely that while there is little need of restriction as to the kind of athletic play, there is real occasion for its limitation as to time and degree. The healthy growth of both sexes depends upon the same conditions supplied to each in its own measure.
>
> (Cited in Dyhouse 1976: 45–6)

Some doctors, like Dr W. Richardson, who wrote an article entitled 'Physical Exercises for Women', which was published in *The Young Woman* in 1892, viewed exercise as a natural remedy for the socially defined infirmities of the past, resulting in

> less bloodnessness, less . . . swooning; less of lassitude, less of nervousness, less of hysteria, and much less of that general debility to which, for want of a better term, the words 'malaise' and 'languor' have been applied.
>
> (Richardson 1892: 15)

He also claimed that the effects of unimpeded movement on the woman's body would counter the pernicious results of the dictates of fashion:

> She has become less distortioned. The curved back, the pigeon chest, the disproportioned limb, the narrow feeble trunk, the small and often distorted eyeball, the myopic eye, the puny ill-shaped external ear – all these parts are becoming of better and more natural *contour.*
>
> (Richardson 1892: 15)

In common with increasing numbers of the medical establishment, Dr Richardson was in favour of varied forms of activities for women – he mentions 'croquet, cycling, lawn tennis, "stool-ball", cricket, swimming and dancing':

> In our days we have learned with comparative rapidity that women with every advantage practise physical exercises as well as men, and become excellent competitors with men in many exercises from which the last generation would have kept them distinctly apart . . . and now there is scarcely an athletic sport or exercise of any kind in which the young woman does not take her share as well as the young man.
>
> (Richardson 1892: 15)

Arguments of this sort were gaining ground and becoming more representative and influential so that, from the beginning of the twentieth century, most doctors were in favour of exercise for women. Medical opinion was embedded in a society debating changes in women's status and it was subject to numerous views, including those of women themselves. The women in question were mostly from the middle and upper classes, and many doctors would have been familiar with their arguments. The increased participation of middle-class women in sports was a practical way of confirming theoretical arguments in favour of female exercise. The struggle over women's bodies was confined mostly to those from the middle classes, although sports were an aspect of traditional culture for working women in some specific regions of the country and were accessible to increasing numbers of women in waged work. But in general working-class women were required to work in long and exhausting labour and, until later in the twentieth century, few of them had the time, money or energy to participate.

PROBLEMS OF DEMOCRATIZATION

In 1870, the feminist Frances P. Cobbe wrote that women would never participate in sports and amusements until they had begun to participate in meaningful work. 'Not one lady in 500 past girlhood' she claimed, 'cares for any game or sport . . . as men care for these things' (1870: 7). And as she predicted, women's involvement in sports did not occur to any extent until they had gained access to paid employment. The development of female sports was part of a general movement: the entry of women into spheres that men had previously dominated was no longer just a function of work, it was also a function of leisure and, of course, of education. These three spheres were closely connected in the expansion of organized sports for women. The sports clubs which sprang up, like those associated with the Regent Street Polytechnic, attracted middle-class 'working girls' who were employed in the vicinity in schools, offices, shops and journalism (Lesley 1979). The following extract comes from a report in the *Daily Mirror* (1911), describing women's sports at Regent Street Polytechnic:

> The members are young women whose sedentary occupations keep them employed indoors all day and their ages range from 16 to 25 . . . Many of whom worked long hours in the great stores around Oxford Street.
>
> (Winter 1979a Pt I: 35)

The lady gymnasts from the Northampton Polytechnic were 'solidly middle-class', and they had employment in London as milliners, court dressmakers, a secretary of the Labour Party, a teacher, shop assistants, and commercial secretaries (Desmond 1979).

However, it would be a mistake to exaggerate the extent of women's involvement. By 1890 'outdoor sport for women was in most quarters an "unheard of event"', and even at the beginning of the twentieth century, conventional attitudes were slow to shift. Sporting accomplishments became fashionable, but only for a tiny, elite sector of the female population:

> the glamour of the names of these ladies should not conceal the very real prejudice which existed at the time against women. . . . For such illustrious women, indulgence in sport could be seen as a kind of charming foible, but it would be a disaster if the ordinary wife and mother were to mimic them.
>
> (Dobbs 1973: 177)

Sports were still overwhelmingly a symbol of masculinity – the core manly virtues of courage, aggression and the competitive instinct were still intimately associated with them. The cult of athleticism was in essence a cult of manliness and so if women were to join in on an equal footing, they could hardly be simultaneously projected as sexual objects by men. The reactionary position, articulated in the *Badminton Magazine* in 1900, makes this position clear:

beauty of face and form is one of the chief essentials [for women], but unlimited indulgence in violent, outdoor sports, cricket, bicycling, beagling, otter-hunting, paper-chasing, and – most odious of all games for women – hockey, cannot but have an unwomanly effect on a young girl's mind, no less than her appearance. . . . Let young girls ride, skate, dance and play lawn tennis and other games in moderation, but let them leave field sports to those for whom they are intended – men.

(Cited in Dobbs 1973: 177)

Sports which were considered to be intrinsically more suited to woman's 'nature' – or *feminine-appropriate* sports – were challenged less as time progressed. Mixed sports, when allowed, were acceptable if the women played supportive, ladylike roles as men's partners. However, it was much more of a problem for women to participate in team games and traditional male sports which encouraged those 'manly' codes of behaviour that obtained normally in all-male settings. Men could prove their superiority by beating other men in competition, but the power of men's sports to define masculinity was reduced if women participated in them, and if women played men's sports, dominant images of femininity were threatened, too. By a separation of the sexes, men and women never opposed one another in open competition, and hence the newly learned female 'aggressiveness' and 'competitiveness' could be defined as qualitatively different from men's. Even so, a woman's participation in traditional male sports was symbolic of her competition with men and she faced ridicule about their desexing characteristics.

Because women's sports had a strong middle-class character, and because they were overshadowed by the sporting status of men, the material gain for women overall was limited. Women's sports reinforced *and* undermined dominant attitudes to women in society: in some forms they were the stark embodiment of inequalities between men and women, but for those who took part, they were some sort of concrete gain, and expressed, *par excellence*, a 'feeling' of emancipatory potential for the female sex.

THE PROBLEM OF LEISURE

The notions of freedom associated with women's sports posed a problem intrinsic to the nature of bourgeois culture. In the work-oriented value-system of industrial capitalism, leisure was a potentially corrupting influence which threatened the disciplines of the middle-class world. Leisure smacked of indolence and wastefulness, presenting a contrast to the well-ordered conditions of the home and workplace. So the Victorian bourgeoisie was ambivalent about leisure: sports were easy to justify as a criterion for physical and moral improvement, but if they were indulged in primarily for pleasure, cautious appraisal was required because they existed in somewhat uneasy tension with the prevailing middle-class work ethic. Leisure, therefore, took on a utilitarian orientation – it was viewed as an adjunct to work, necessary to refresh the body for the 'business of life' – a position expounded in an article written in a historical journal in 1879:

> Recreation is, or ought to be, not a pastime entered upon for the sake of pleasure which it affords, but an act of duty undertaken for the sake of the subsequent power which it generates, and the subsequent profit which it ensures.

(Cited in Bailey 1978: 67)

Towards the end of the nineteenth century sports became accessible to working-class girls and women, as well as to their middle-class counterparts, and the idea that they were forms of leisure which had recuperative qualities and were thus functional to work was central to their legitimation. The belief that leisure should have some manifest moral or improving content penetrated women's sports as they became democratized, just as it had justified the involvement of middle-class women in voluntary philanthropic activities (Klein 1971: 17), necessitating a shift from their stereotypically static wifely roles to a less insular social position of increasing participation in public life. However, their benevolence was confirmation of a deeply moralistic attitude extending from the home into the community and provided an opportunity for enlightened women to escape from the confines of domesticity without undermining their prior duty to home and family. Philanthropy was by no means a new phenomenon in the Victorian period, but it increased with remarkable intensity in the last decade or so of the century when attention was directed towards programmes for youth. Youth work was a socially acceptable extension of the traditional female role at a time when other kinds of female emancipation were much more controversial – it has been suggested that the work of middle-class women with young people was an important method of bringing bourgeois ideology into working-class spheres of life (Rowbotham 1975: 113). Welfare work was part of a conscious attempt to control working-class free time and collective group behaviour, including the games and pastimes of young people. Many clubs and organizations were instituted, patronized by members of the upper class, and monitored and staffed by middle-class personnel. They all segregated the sexes, and those for females opened their doors to increasing numbers of working-class girls and women as the twentieth century progressed (Meller 1976: 177). The National Association of Working Girls' Clubs was instituted in the 1880s, and its associate members included clubs organized by the Church of England, the Girls' Friendly Society and Mothers' Unions, and there were other associations such as the Girls' Guild, the YWCA, various factory and church clubs, and the Girl Guides. The institutionalized setting provided the opportunity for establishing codes of conduct and a corporate identity with a firm disciplinary, religious and educational orientation. In her book *Clubs for Working Girls*, published in 1890, Maude Stanley, who devoted her life to the girls' club movement, wrote, 'We have not wished to take our girls out of their class but we have wished to see them ennoble the class to which they belong. The tone will soon become free from vulgar boisterousness if the ladies will take part in the evenings of recreation' (cited in Dawes 1975: 106). Almost all these 'socio-religious' organizations included some form of sport or physical activity on their programmes, such as hockey, swimming or gymnastics, chosen for their 'improving' qualities (Meller 1976: 177). These openings supplemented those available to women in sports and social clubs, schools and colleges and the polytechnics.

Sports were an excellent purveyor of values, and organized sports for women embodied rigid bourgeois values. Women's sports given moral legitimation, characteristic of bourgeois leisure generally, projecting a pre-ferred image of women. This image had nothing in common with the one portrayed by poor girls and women who took part in foot-races and pede-strian races during the eighteenth and early nineteenth centuries, as a way of making a meagre living. Not surprisingly, these events did not survive the Victorian era (Radford 1993). Physical prowess, courage, strength, endur-ance and aggression were traits associated exclusively with men's sports, but were positively discouraged, or underplayed, in most female sports. Loyalty, co-operation, smartness, cleanliness, fairness, exemplary manners and a strict inner discipline of moderation, self-control and respect for authority were celebrated in sports as female virtues. Penetrated as they were by bourgeois morality, and supported by medical opinion, female sports be-came integral to dominant ideology. The uniting of medical and moral opinions was a way both of legitimating and popularizing them.

The story of women's sports comprises themes of continuity as well as of change. Ideas about the female body become internalized – a part of 'com-monsense' reality which is difficult to challenge. But ideology is not just something which occurs in consciousness as a static set of ideas – it is part of a process of reproduction and of change which is inscribed in social practice. At the same time as women had to accommodate to conservative ideas about their physical capabilities, by their actions in sports they were effecting a change in public opinion about their physical image and the meanings associated with it. Bourgeois women used physical activity creatively to reinterpret Social Darwinism in a way which legitimated a freer, more positive mode of physical expression, arguing persuasively that healthier women were more feminine and were also more functional for national well-being. The biologically determined stereotype of the 'delicate' female came to coexist with the more vigorous model of the sporting woman – by the twentieth century the former image was fading and becoming residual and the latter image was increasing in popularity and becoming dominant.

Chapter 6

The inter-war years
Limitations and possibilities

INTRODUCTION

The First World War had been especially costly for Britain, and the ensuing social and economic problems seemed hardly likely to benefit the development of sports. Although there was an immediate post-war economic boom, it was only temporary. In the 1920s rising unemployment and strikes reflected class tensions; and throughout the depression of the 1930s the quality of life deteriorated for increasing numbers of people, in particular those from poor working-class families in the industrial areas of high unemployment in the Midlands and the North. Problems were magnified for women – for example, they were dismissed from their wartime jobs which were restored to men on such a scale that in the spring of 1919 more than half a million women were registered as unemployed (Beddoe 1983: 34). The labour of women who did work was cheap – in industry they earned half the wages of men, they did outwork for meagre amounts, and many of them were forced back into domestic service simply to survive. Feminism seemed to be in retreat: the image of the domesticated housewife became dominant in the 1920s, disseminated through advertising, posters, the radio, women's magazines, and films (ibid.). But, as Howkins and Lowerson (1979: 4) point out, this period simultaneously produced conditions which stimulated the growth of sports and recreation:

> The dominant image of the interwar period in Britain is that of the hungry thirties – of mass unemployment and extremist politics. In recent years this view has been challenged by historians who stress the rise of the motor car, the growth of consumerism, house building and the relative stability of parliamentary government.

During the first decade after the First World War – characterized as one of hedonism – substantial numbers of people from different social backgrounds were embracing new pleasures, made possible by the increase in availablility of leisure goods and services which were shifting to a more central place in the economy as a result of the decline of heavy industry. In contrast to the horrors and hardships of war, sports, together with other forms of recreation, provided a seductive vision of the 'good life'. But there were underlying patterns of inequality: it was mostly those from relatively affluent regions and privileged social classes, young people rather than adults, and men rather than women who were able to enjoy sports. The picture was similar in other parts of Europe and in North America. Social unrest and poverty for some did not seem to stifle a popular public demand for more leisure and an expansion of opportunities to participate in sports and to watch them.

However, because most research has focused on *male* participation, we only have a hazy idea of the extent to which women were part of the general growth of sports and recreation. As more evidence emerges it seems likely that, although men benefited most from increased opportunities, the inter-war years represent a remarkable period in the development of women's sports. The Great War had been a unique and liberating experience for many women, leaving them with confidence to flout old restrictions and re-create cultural meanings. But the uneven pattern of poverty and prosperity left by the Depression made it easier for middle-class women, and working-class women who were relatively affluent or young and single, to participate in sports, than for the masses of poorer working-class women. And although women in general were subject to the effects of traditional ideologies of sexuality, it was more difficult for poor working-class women to battle against the powerful idea that men, but not women, deserved access to leisure outside the home. Not surprisingly, also, the survival of reactionary attitudes about the limitations of female biology continued to influence the type and extent of women's involvement. Women *were* making choices about sports, but within structures of constraint.

EXCITEMENT AND SPECTACLE

Whereas Britain had been the greatest influence on world sports prior to the Great War, during the 1920s and 1930s the maturation of capitalism in the United States began increasingly to influence their global development. Sports became integral to the commercialization of popular culture: together with the cinema, dance-hall, gramophone, motoring, travel, communications and eating out, they were part of the mass entertainment industry, closely linked to the mechanisms of the market. Technological advances improved transport networks, professionalism boomed, large stadia were built, and sporting spectacles and international events gained in popularity. The commercialization of sports stimulated new needs and expectations – they had become firmly established as dramatic entertainment.

Sports events attracted record crowds, and the inter-war years saw a rise in certain forms of female spectatorship. For example, in an account of recreational cricket in Bolton, Jack Williams (1990: 116–17) writes that, although women were a minority of spectators at men's matches, they provided an essential financial support to the semi-professional clubs. They formed ladies' committees and took responsibility for refreshments, fund-raising and social activities, and 'sums raised by ladies' committees were often the third largest source of club income after gate receipts and members' subscriptions'. Some working-class women took their babies to sports events in their prams, and a few entrepreneurs encouraged female spectators and gamblers by reducing admission for them at speedway and greyhound tracks and providing makeshift baby-minding facilities (Jones 1990). But Margery Spring-Rice's classic study (1939) testifies to the harsh realities of the lives of large numbers of married women who were physically debilitated as a result of multiple pregnancies, lack of medical attention and having overall responsibility for domestic labour and child-care. Sports were irrelevant to their lives – they had neither the energy and time nor the money to participate or even to watch.

Although in far fewer numbers, better-off women as well as men attended sports spectacles, and they had more choice of what they watched than ever before. In Britain the 1930s marked the 'Golden Age' of soccer and cricket attendances, and in the United States baseball, American football and basketball were flourishing businesses. But a diversity of other sports established themselves as popular spectator events as well. For example, at the Empire Stadium, Empire Pool and Sports Arena at Wembley, which comprised the largest sports complex in the world at the time, a fantastic variety of events was organized. From 1923, when the first facilities were opened, a number of sports that had originated in other countries, such as ice-hockey, greyhound-racing and speedway, were put on the Wembley programme, as well as athletics, basketball, bicycle-racing, boxing, darts, lawn tennis, rugby league, skating, snooker, soccer, swimming and diving, table tennis, TT motor-cycle-racing, water-polo, and wrestling. There were national and international meetings, and amateur and professional matches. Whilst most of the performers were men, in some of the sports, like ice-skating, swimming and diving, table tennis and tennis, women participated as well. Surprisingly, there were women speedway riders who competed in open competitions with men (Low: 1953).

The sports events at Wembley were combined with other forms of spectacle and entertainment – there were interval diversions, circuses, cultural displays, dog-shows, exhibitions, parades, a massive amusement park, bars, restaurants, lounges, shops and a dance floor. And there were female professionals in several of the 'sporting' entertainments such as ice-pantomimes and water carnivals. The American influence was apparent in the aquatic shows which were modelled on the swimming and diving spectaculars of Annette Kellerman, and American performers like Gloria Nord, the ice-ballerina, were employed. These entertainments were new and exciting, and they produced an alluring world of fantasy, fun and spectacle. For women in particular, sports spectacles were suggestive of a much freer, more provocative use of the body than ever before, quite in contrast to the traditional attitudes to the sporting female institutionalized in clubs, schools and colleges. Women were being caught up in what New York sportswriter Paul Gallico describes as 'the wildest, maddest, and most glamorous period in all the history of sport':

> It was an incredible period, this dizzy, spinning, sports reel of athletes, events, records, personalities, drama and speed, a geared-up, whirling, golden world in which a lifetime was lived in five years, or sometimes even overnight, as heroes and heroines, champions and challengers burst upon the scene, shone like exploding star shells, and often vanished as quickly.
>
> (1988: 3–4)

Writing on sports proliferated in the press and in the numerous specialist magazines of the time. But it was the advent of the radio which made the greatest impact on people's knowledge and interest. The radio brought distant events directly into the sitting-room and sports became 'home-based entertainment' for families of armchair listeners. Achievements were celebrated, and the making and breaking of records dramatized. The exciting immediacy of the radio transformed sportsmen and sportswomen into folk heroes and heroines and figures of national and international stature. They were being systematically 'packaged' and 'sold' as commodities for consumption – a process which has become increasingly widespread and sophisticated since the advent of television and with increased intensity of competition.

Although sportsmen predominated as well-known personalities, there were famous sportswomen in this period as well. Outstanding performers from Europe, North America and the colonies were known and admired – and Britain's exceptional sportswomen were known and admired there. For example, across the world people celebrated the American swimmer Gertrude Ederle's courage and achievement when she became the first woman to swim the English Channel in 1926; and also in the 1920s the American Helen Wills was treated as a child prodigy when she burst upon the tennis scene with pigtails, and the Norwegian Sonja Henie was an international star with the reputation of being the most skilful and exciting female figure-skater ever. At this time the 'natural athlete' and the 'all-rounder' seemed authentic concepts because it was not uncommon for keen athletes to participate in more than one sport and in different events. 'Babe' Didrikson, for example, was one of the most versatile female athletes in the history of sports. In 1930 she broke the world javelin record at the age of 16, and two years later she competed in eight athletic events in the US Athletic Championships, winning five of them. In the same year she won two gold medals and one silver medal at the Los Angeles Olympics. Didrikson was formidable in running, jumping and throwing events, but she was also outstanding in other sports – notably first as an amateur and then as a professional golfer, and also in baseball, basketball, tennis, swimming, diving and billiards.

Male hegemony has never been absolute in sports. In spite of the historic subordination of women, it has always been possible for outstanding female athletes to assert themselves and to disrupt conventional images of femininity. Suzanne Lenglen did so in tennis. She dominated the women's game from the first time she won Wimbledon in 1919 at the age of 20, playing in the final against Mrs Lambert Chambers who was twice her age. The contest was not a simple test of skill, but a symbolic battle between the old and the new – in terms of styles of play, styles of dress and attitudes to the role of women. Mrs Chambers was conventional. She played solidly from the base-line, corseted in a long and heavy dress; off the court she remained staid and respectable, wearing a sports blazer. In contrast, Suzanne Lenglen was a glamorous Frenchwoman who played with agility and dressed radically, leaping and stretching for shots in a sleeveless, white silk dress which came just below the knee, wearing white shoes and stockings and a bright-coloured bandeau. Off the court she was equally flamboyant, with bobbed hair, vivid make-up, fashionable and expensive clothes, sparkling jewellery, and exotic accoutrements. This was a match between a player who masked her sexuality and one who was seen to behave, by comparison, in a provocative manner. Mrs Chambers was reproducing a respectable image of femininity, whereas Suzanne Lenglen was actively redefining female sports and social skills. The conventional image coexisted with the radical one: the former was becoming increasingly residual, the latter was emerging to become acceptable in the future (Clerici 1976; Revie 1972).

But there was continuous resistance to change, and individual sports-women were often forced to flout tradition and confront officialdom for new conventions to be considered. For example, at the British Ladies' Golf Championships in 1933, instead of the stipulated skirt, sleeved upper clothing and hat or bandeau, Gloria Minoprio wore 'a complete dark-blue outfit beginning with a turban-like woollen hat, descending to a high-necked close-fitting sweater and ending in a pair of exquisitely tailored trousers with knife-edge creases' (Cousins 1975: 79). Her appearance prompted rebukes, not only from powerful men in the world of golf, but from the Ladies' Golf Union itself – the women's representative association. Her behaviour was deemed rebellious and her outfit improper – tight sweaters were considered provocative and trousers unseemly for ladies. The stance taken was an essentially moral one – the suitability of these clothes on the grounds of comfort and freedom of movement was not discussed. Nevertheless, Gloria Minoprio had made the first step towards more practical clothing for female golfers which became accepted in future years. Suzanne Lenglen was also labelled as a rebel (Revie 1972: 41). The process of change in women's sports has never been straightforward, but associated with unevenness and struggle, challenge and resistance. Whereas athleticism has always been a popular symbol of masculinity, sportswomen have had to deal with the constant tension between freer uses of the body and acceptable images of femininity. The focus of opposition to Suzanne Lenglen was her sexuality – opposition to her tennis dresses which made possible an image of the 'real' body underneath and which allowed her to move energetically so that people caught glimpses of parts that 'respectable' ladies never made visible in public. Some Wimbledon spectators were excited by her radical image; others walked out on account of her 'indecency'. But Suzanne Lenglen embodied a popular male-defined image of femininity as well as being hugely successful, winning six Wimbledon Championships and six French Championships – a combination which enabled her to turn professional in 1926 for a reported sum of $100,000 (ibid.). She had become, in modern terms, a superstar.

The story of Kitty Godfree (McKane) is more typical of the emerging competitive sportswoman. The games curricula in girls' schools and colleges of physical education stimulated a love of sports in many women and provided opportunities for competition. With this background Kitty Godfree went on to become a British badminton and tennis player, best known for her sucesses at tennis. She travelled widely all over Europe, to South Africa, and to North America, playing singles, women's doubles and mixed doubles. She played for Britain in the Wightman Cup and reached the finals of the singles in the French and US championships, winning the singles title at Wimbledon in 1924 and 1926, and the mixed doubles title with her husband in 1927 (Arlott 1975). Unlike Suzanne Lenglen, Kitty Godfree retained amateur status throughout her competitive career – she had no coaching and had to work as well as play, receiving small prizes such as £5 vouchers to be spent in department stores or jewellers. Kitty Godfree was typical of most top female athletes – they came from middle-class backgrounds and relied upon the support of their families and the goodwill of their employers to be able to find the time and money required to compete in numerous events at far-flung venues. Kitty Godfree was an exemplar of the female amateur sports tradition – with no thoughts of 'big money'; to her, tennis was fun and she enjoyed the travel and social benefits.

In spite of the strict amateur codes of competition, however, the market was becoming increasingly central to the construction of spectator sport. And although there were infinitely fewer female sports stars in comparison with the number of males, those who had become popular entertainers enhanced the profitability of their sports and in some cases could expect 'hospitality' payments. For example, in 1926 when Helen Wills travelled to Paris to play a challenge match against Suzanne Lenglen, she and her mother were resident in the luxurious Carlton Hotel and Helen Wills was given a wardrobe designed by a Paris couturier (Tinling 1983: 40–1). There was also a small amount of sponsorship for top performers and events that were considered to be 'newsworthy' – for example, after Gertrude Ederle's channel swim, the *News of the World* put up £1,000 for the first British woman to break her record. Although in very small numbers, some leading sportswomen turned professional.

FEMALE SPORTS AND CLASS

It is difficult to assess the extent to which successful sportswomen influenced ideas about female athleticism. Their feats were well known – publicized in the national press, on radio and in popular women's magazines – and all reactions, whether of admiration or shock, fed a changing popular consciousness about women in sports. There is no doubt that the idea amongst women that sports were fun was infectious – increasing numbers were participating in various events and experiencing obvious pleasure from doing so. However, throughout the inter-war years many sports remained specific to upper- and middle-class women, and since that time have remained resistant to democratization. Sports such as golf and tennis come into this category, but also 'adventure' sports, such as climbing, sailing and skiing provided settings for displays of affluence and social standing, allowing middle-class women to enjoy the growing penchant for travel in Britain and abroad. These women were also the pioneers of competition in elite sports – for example, Evie Pinching was one of a group of British women who campaigned throughout the 1920s and 1930s for female ski-racing. In common with better-known sports, national and international skiing competitions were established during the inter-war years – for example, the first women's world skiing championship took place in 1931.

New sports increased the range of those characterized as 'elite' in Chapter 3. Only wealthy women or those with rich patrons were able to take part in car-racing and aviation which were potent symbols of female liberation. American Amelia Earhart is legendary – she set a women's altitude record of 14,000 feet in 1922 and flew solo across the Atlantic in 1932 (Cadogan 1990; Modman 1981). Amy Johnson, an Englishwoman, made solo flights from England to Australia, India and Tokyo in 1930 and 1931, and to Cape Town and back in 1932. Then she made new records – in 1933, with her husband, for the flight across the North Atlantic, and in 1936 for return flights between England and India, and England and Cape Town (Arlott 1975: 541). Both these aviatrixes were celebrated for the sort of heroism usually reserved for men – Amelia Earhart disappeared on a round-the-world flight and Amy Johnson in the Thames estuary (Cadogan 1990). The Honorary Mrs Victor Bruce, although less well known, made her fortune through sports during the 1920s and 1930s. She progressed from motor-biking to car-racing (she raced at Brooklands and drove solo in the Monte Carlo Rally), to speed-boat racing (she set a record for a two-way English Channel crossing), to flying (she successfully completed a round-the-world solo flight). The press were interested in her exploits and the publicity brought her sponsorship.

It was relatively easy for women from privileged backgrounds to take part in exotic and adventurous sports and to make inroads into sports which had been traditionally monopolized by men, in comparison with those who lacked time and money. Yet although there was a growing public consciousness about women's sporting achievements, few sportswomen worked in an organized and politicized way to acquire more power. Stimulated by a love of participation and a liberal belief that they should have greater equality with men, most sportswomen worked in an individual and ad hoc manner to improve their own position. There were some notable exceptions – for example, those who could be characterized as separatist feminists because they pioneered to set up, organize and control their own sports organizations. A group of women who formed the Pinnacle Club in 1921 had a specific vision that it was possible and preferable to have guideless mountaineering for women, completely without male intervention of any sort. Their club was described by one of its founder members as

the result of a 'long conspiracy', prompted by the feeling we many of us shared that a rock-climbing club for women would give us a better chance of climbing independently of men, both as to leadership and general mountaineering.

(Pilley 1989: 84)

The Pinnacle Club's use of the expression 'sans homme' symbolizes the way in which women have understood the advantages of all-female contexts and have been prepared to fight to take power for themselves. By 1934 the club had eighty members which reflected the steady growth in popularity of climbing for women and also the way in which these women were actively extending ideas about female physical ability and leadership skills; they were guiding and participating in climbs which, they claimed, 'ten years ago were thought of as suited only to the strongest parties of men' (ibid.).

In the world of horse-racing women were also taking positive action and breaking barriers – most particularly in breeding and training, and to some extent in riding. Their struggle was for equal recognition with men in a very popular and public sport which was a bastion of male power. Women involved with equestrian sports were usually born or married into wealthy families with horse-breeding and horse-racing traditions. But although they might own and breed racehorses, as well as train and ride them, the all-male Jockey Club refused to give licences to female trainers and jockeys. Only since the second decade of the century has the Jockey Club recognized women as owners and have horses been entered in races such as the Derby and the Grand National as the official property of women. Throughout this period, although a number of women had become well-known and respected trainers, nevertheless they were still forced to use a male pseudonym (usually the name of one of their employees). And although women had a tradition of working horses and competing as non-licensed jockeys in special ladies' races and a very limited number of open races, they were excluded from riding in major meetings, such as the Derby and the Grand National (Ramsden 1973; Martin 1979). Because the Jockey Club was the official decision-making body for horse-racing, the men who composed it had the power to decide the rules and procedures and resist change. But because women were taking action for themselves, there developed an interesting discrepancy between the official position and actual practice.

A handful of women also held prestigious positions in other areas of horse-racing. For example, in 1928 Mrs Vernet became a partner in the bookmakers Ladbrokes (Ramsden 1973: 128), and in 1938 Rita Cannon was appointed racing correspondent to the *Daily Mail* (ibid.: 139). But the major actors in this most popular sport, and those who held the formal power, were men. The few women who broke into horse-racing were exceptional and from middle- or upper-class backgrounds. Lower-class women only held supporting, subservient roles such as 'stable girls, cloakroom attendants, payers-out at the Tote windows, barmaids, trainers' wives, daughters and sisters' (ibid.: 184). Contrasts between men and women, though diminishing in certain ways, remained consistent in others, and as in some other sports, differences between women from different social groups remained stark. It is clear from this example that the intersection of class and gender is central to an analysis of female sports. Although in different ways, problems of class and gender *together* also influenced the development of female sports in other parts of Europe and in North America.

SPORTS IN SCHOOLS

Class-related sports participation in adulthood was the result, to a large extent, of experiences at school. The class divisions in physical education for girls in Britain which were established at the end of the nineteenth century (discussed in Chapter 4), were reproduced in the twentieth century. In most schools for middle-class girls and in the colleges and universities there was a flourishing and expanding physical education curriculum, but the situation in state schools was very different (Fletcher 1984; McIntosh 1981). Although there was official advocacy of the therapeutic value of physical education throughout the 1920s and 1930s – partly because the war had stimulated a concern for national fitness – in practice, facilities and teaching in many state schools remained poor. In elite girls' schools gymnastics was a core subject, but many elementary schools still lacked an equipped gymnasium, and even in the 1930s, because posture had become the 'yardstick of gymnastics', the approach tended to stress a very limited range of movement. In the case of games, class differences were more marked. The games curriculum in girls' public schools, endowed schools and grammar schools was well established and included cricket, hockey, lacrosse, netball, rounders and tennis. But for working-class girls the picture was very different. Although there had been official recommendations about games provision for girls in secondary schools – the 1919 Syllabus of Physical Education included suggestions about games; in 1921 the Board of Education's Chief Medical Officer wrote about the value of games in girls' secondary schools; and in 1926, the Hadow Report stipulating that all children should have secondary education from the age of 11 years stated that the new 'modern' schools should have their own facilities for physical education and games (ibid.) – in practice, facilities in the state sector were limited and unevenly distributed. Even by 1933, when the *Syllabus of Physical Training for Schools* was published by the Board of Education recommending a comprehensive curriculum of physical education for children in the state sector, to include athletics, dancing, games and swimming, in many schools a shortage of money, space and qualified teachers militated against its implementation. Small-side games were popular because they could take place in the limited spaces of the yards and playgrounds of urban schools, and it was for this reason that netball became established as the major team sport for working-class girls: '*Netball* has proved itelf a remarkably suitable game for playgrounds' (ibid.: 39). Rounders was the favoured summer game for working-class girls, and in a very limited number of schools there was athletics, hockey or swimming. The 1933 syllabus explained to teachers that the choice of games for girls depended largely on the 'facilities offered in the district and the standard of training in ball games the school can show as a whole'. It referred to the difficulties of introducing to girls in elementary schools those games played in private girls' schools:

> *Cricket* presents considerable difficulties owing to the cost of good pitches. It may be possible in certain schools to secure both the services of a teacher who is a first-class coach and the right facilities for play, but unless suitable conditions are available, the game should not be attempted. *Lacrosse* with its difficult preliminary technique and expensive equipment does not yet come within the scope of elementary schools. *Hockey* is being played with increasing success in certain districts where sufficient level pitches can be secured. *Lawn Tennis*, owing to the problem of securing sufficient courts for classes of 40, is not a game for the in-school games period, though some schools may be in a position to provide opportunities for a certain number of girls to play out of school hours.
>
> (Board of Education 1933: 39)

The reminiscences of six elderly women who came from working-class families and left school between 1924 and 1931 confirm the class-specific nature of participation. They talked with regret about the limited opportunities they had for sports while at school. 'Drill, throwing the cricket ball, running and swimming was all we had a chance to do,' one woman recounted.

'I was good at swimming and I joined a club after I left school. Then I gave it up when I got married – my husband didn't like me being out.' Another woman remembered travelling from school to a nearby gymnasium once a week where she had a chance to climb ropes and 'play on the apparatus'. 'We didn't do any real sports,' she said, 'just running races on sports day and sometimes a bit of dancing.' 'We couldn't afford proper dress for sports,' it was recalled, 'but we tucked our skirts into our knickers and in the summer we'd jump over ropes and roll across mats in the playground. We had running races, too.' Only one of the women played a little netball and they all claimed that the boys had a better time of it – 'They played football and had teams and matches against other schools, and cricket, too,' was a typical remark. Two women from the industrial North of England recounted the pleasure of playing their own games in the playground because they had no opportunities for organized sports. They played with wooden hoops, and straw ropes which were given to them by local greengrocers, and they played hop-scotch and tag and a game called 'Checkers and Bobbers' (an object was thrown into the air and pieces of old pottery had to be picked up before it landed).

Middle-class girls, in contrast, had many more opportunities and aspirations. This report from a woman who was one of the original pupils at a grammar school which opened in 1918 in the suburbs of the south-east of London is typical of other middle-class secondary schoolgirls in the 1920s:

> We did gymnastics all the year through, in a really well-equipped gym, with wall bars and ropes and boxes and springboards. In the winter we played hockey and lacrosse – that was my favourite sport – and in the summer we played cricket and some rounders and tennis. I was in most of the teams and we played in different tournaments and against other 'good' schools in the area. Some of us joined clubs after we left school and played in matches and socially. . . . My husband's family had a tennis court in the garden and . . . we played a lot with friends. It was great fun.

Inter-school competition consolidated class differences because matches were played between teams from similar schools, and clubs for school-leavers were composed of players with similar class backgrounds.

ORGANIZATION AND GROWTH

Not surprisingly, the organization and growth of the women's games movement in England was closely associated with the elite girls' schools, colleges and universities. Although after the First World War increasing numbers of working-class women were participating in an increasing number of sports, the organizing bodies were set up and controlled by middle-class women, most of whom had a college or university education. National associations for hockey and lacrosse were formed at the end of the last century, and for other games they were formed during the 1920s. These organizations were the prerequisites for increased competition, enabling regular county and territorial matches to be played. A similar pattern of development was occurring in other parts of Britain and Europe, and in North America and the colonies, which made possible the inauguration of international associations. Sheila Fletcher describes the specialist colleges of physical education as 'nurseries for internationals' (1985: 34). However, the growing strength of the female games movement was no protection against hostility. Although becoming increasingly residual, opposition to women's participation in all sports still came from prestigious people in the educational and medical establishments and was articulated according to nineteenth-century ideologies about the limitations of the female constitution. For example, letters from a London headmistress and a Harley Street doctor were published in the *Lancet* in 1921, both claiming that girls were both psychologically and physically damaged, as well as essentially de-sexed through playing games (Fletcher 1984: 75–6). Those who were promoting games-playing for girls were forced to take seriously such challenges and set up their own research to show that vigorous physical exercise did nothing to destroy a young woman's ability to have healthy children (ibid.). Arguments in support of girls' games, reproduced from the earlier period, also focused on female sexuality – games were seen to be a moral safeguard, delaying maturity and keeping girls away from the opposite sex (ibid.: 29). But in spite of opposition, by the 1930s the acceleration of competitive games for women was unstoppable.

The founding of the British Women's Cricket Association (WCA) in 1926 was the result of the deliberations and determination of a group of hockey and lacrosse players who met at the elite Malvern College. The WCA was a co-ordinating body for women's cricket – its aims, according to Pollard (1934), were 'simple, brief and to the point' – to arrange fixtures and tours between the scattered colleges and public schools where cricket was already established and to encourage the formation of clubs from which county teams might be built. The association was immediately successful – after just one year, ten clubs, twenty-eight schools and two business houses had affiliated to the WCA, with a total membership of 347; forty-nine matches were arranged, and a 'Cricket Week' was organized which subsequently became an annual event. In 1929, the first county match was organized and by 1938, membership had doubled, the number of affiliated clubs had increased to 138, and twenty county associations were established. The first international matches were played during the English team's tour to Australasia in 1924-5 and the first test match took place in England in 1937 (Heyhoe Flint and Rheinberg 1976; Pollard 1934; Williams 1989).

Cricket was a traditional bastion of male chauvinism, but because most female cricket at this time was institutionalized in the private spheres of clubs, schools, colleges and universities, it was relatively easy for women to determine their own progress. But there was a culture of female cricket outside the education context as well, and a growing interest in serious competition – for example, girls and boys played street cricket together, traditional inter-village matches continued in some regions, private clubs were established, and factory teams grew in number. In the 1930s there was a notable growth of interest among working-class women in the industrial regions of the North of England. Williams (in Holt 1990b: 117) describes the situation in the Bolton area: 'Bolton Ladies' CC was formed in 1931 and played for the rest of the decade whilst in 1935 there were press reports of at least four other women's teams playing occasionally.' But women's cricket did not grow without opposition – as the game became more public, antagonists became more vociferous. Even tolerant comment was often synonymous with condescension and patronizing humour – in short, the women's game was seldom treated seriously. For example, the year 1929 saw the first women's public cricket match, described in the press as the 'Northern Lovelies' versus the 'Southern Sweeties' (ibid.).

Netball was a specifically English and 'feminized' version of American basketball. It was devised by female students of physical education at the end of the last century, in rejection of basketball, which was considered to be 'too physical' for young women. Unlike other team games, it was not a 'male' sport, copied by women, nor was it ever played by men. Netball was, therefore, immediately characterized as a 'feminine-appropriate' sport and was never opposed to the extent that other team games were. Its growth as an organized, competitive sport was pioneered by enthusiasts in colleges and polytechnics, but it developed less of a middle-class character as it became the most popular female team game in working-class schools and clubs. Netball spread from England to other parts of Britain and Europe – France, Sweden and Denmark – and when ex-public schoolgirls and graduates from colleges and universities went to the colonies, they took it with them. The game became particularly popular in the USA, Canada, South Africa, India, Burma, Cape Colony and New Zealand, and later, during the 1930s, in the West Indies. The All-England Netball Association (AENA) was set up in 1926, followed by the establishment of similar organizations in other countries, and, although there were no agreed international rules at that time, ad hoc arrangements were made for a few fixtures between teams from those countries with national associations (AENA 1976).

There is less information available about other organized, but less widely-played sports for women. Stoolball, for example, which had been a traditional sport, played mostly in the rural south-eastern counties of England by local women under the patronage of upper-class women (Lowerson 1993), was revived during the First World War. W.W. Grantham – a volunteer soldier with the rank of major – used stoolball as a form of therapy for recuperating soldiers and organized games with members of the gentry, nurses and patients. Lowerson (ibid.) writes that 'Many ordinary women players and their gentry patronesses felt a growing resentment at this arrogant male incursion into an already restricted area of female sporting hegemony.' Nevertheless, a national organization was inaugurated, standardized rules were drawn up and it was estimated that by the mid-1930s there were as many as 1,000 stoolball clubs. The game was played by different classes of women throughout the 1920s and 1930s – in teams associated with church and factory clubs, and in schools and colleges.

STRUGGLING FOR RESOURCES

When women played in separate spheres from the men, it was relatively easy for them to determine their own progress, but when they required the same facilities as men, they were inevitably discriminated against. In numerous sports contexts, men held the power to stop women's progress because they monopolized resources and held controlling and decision-making positions. For example, at universities with a strong rowing tradition, like Oxford and Cambridge, female students had fewer boats, far less river time, inferior coaching, and poor finance in comparison with their male counterparts. The first official women's rowing race in England took place in 1919, between eights from Newnham College, Cambridge and the London School of Medicine – arguably because so many young men had been away during the First World War and it had become easier for women to borrow racing boats (Cooper 1989). From that time, rowing became established as a female sport and gained momentum during the next decade. The Women's Amateur Rowing Association (WARA) was founded in 1926 and the first Oxford v Cambridge boat race took place the following year – over a century after the men. However, the advance of women's rowing did not go uncontested – continually between 1919 and 1939 women were harassed, were barred from competitions, and had to struggle for resources. Biological arguments were used to oppose their participation and in many situations they were disallowed from rowing on the grounds that it was 'much too unladylike' (Cooper 1989; Dodd 1989).

In general, women faced many more difficulties outside the education context. Golf provides a good example. Although women had established their own golf association at the end of the nineteenth century – the Ladies' Golf Union (LGU) – harsh discrimination against them continued unabated throughout the inter-war period. Some women played on the limited number of municipal courses – in Scotland it was possible to pay as little as 6d for eighteen holes (Jones 1986) – but although some working-class women played golf, it was mostly men who benefited from the expansion of public facilities. Most English women golfers were middle-class – the wives of doctors and other professionals, bank managers and industrialists. Many women golfers had developed an interest in games while at school and university – they found that golf was a game that could be fitted in to married life, especially during term-time if their children were sent away to boarding school. But most golf clubs were private clubs where women were denied full membership, had no voting power, had limited access to club facilities, had much less playing time than men and were usually barred from weekend play and local tournaments. This militated against any but well-off, leisured women being able to take up competitive golf seriously. This was the case also in other parts of Britain and in Ireland, and it was privileged lady golfers from these countries who played against a team from the USA in the Curtis Cup tournament, started in 1932.

Similar inequalities were commonplace in bowls where men monopolized the greens for themselves during the evenings and relegated women to afternoon play (Mason 1989). On angling, Lowerson (1989: 31) writes that, 'Rarely were women found on the banks . . . [they] were generally seen as a threat to the significant male bonding rituals of club and riverbank'. Although women made unprecedented changes in a great range of sports between the two world wars, the reality was that gender relations remained, in the main, markedly uneven. Many sportswomen were still treated in a subordinate and often patronizing fashion and had to overcome tremendous practical and ideological resistance. Throughout the inter-war years sportswomen gained advances as a result of negotiation and struggle.

FOLLOWING THE MEN

The most common form of women's struggle in sports was trying to get equality of opportunity with men. This was the case in swimming and other aquatic events. Swimming was dominated by men in a number of different ways. Men in general had more leisure time than women and therefore swam in greater numbers, but they also held a monopoly of administrative power in swimming pools, clubs and organizations and allocated for themselves much more pool time and many more events in competitions than they allowed for women. However, after the First World War women had begun to expect, and to demand, greater equality. Swimming was still dominated by the middle classes but was not exclusive to them. The provision of municipal pools and the relatively low entrance fees and club subscriptions had made swimming accessible to girls and women from different social classes. Increasing numbers of swimming clubs opened, and female competitive swimming flourished. Most clubs had separate men's and women's sections, and organized training was done during those limited times when the pools were available for women only. But there was pressure for more mixed public swimming and there were increasing numbers of mixed swimming galas, without the restrictions of men and women being separated on the poolside. There were, therefore, more opportunities for men and women to watch one another compete and train together outside scheduled club times. As a result, in a number of swimming pools where men's water polo was popular, women started to practise the game in-formally with the men, and then when enough of them were interested, they organized their own teams and matches.

A number of women's sports started informally in this way. However, it was never straightforward for women to get what they wanted and water-polo players, in common with other sportswomen, had to struggle for resources against uneven odds. The greatest problem was getting pool time, and women often had to travel long distances to practise or play matches because men had priority in their local pool. Nevertheless, by 1923 there were enough teams who played competitively to warrant the formations of county and regional associations, such as the Southern Counties Ladies' Water-Polo Association which affiliated to the Southern Counties Amateur Swimming Association. The year 1928 marked the start of junior cup com-petitions, and during the 1930s annual inter-county competitions took place and selected teams played international matches.

The example of water-polo illustrates how women were grasping oppor-tunities that previously had been ascribed only to men and how they were active agents in this process. Following the rules and competitive procedures of men's water-polo, they organized their own associations, competitions, training and judging arangements. Some media accounts continued to deni-grate women's sports, but by the 1930s many local and national newspapers were treating them seriously. This account of the first inter-county water-polo match between Kent and Sussex records this shift and illustrates how sports-women were displaying a new and powerful muscularity, actively redefining acceptable physical images of women:

> The standard of play was a revelation. If the ladies lacked the speed and strength of the throw which the men possess, they have nothing to learn in gameness and sticking to their job. It was a hard fight all the time and the girls went at it with vigour, worrying their marks with commendable tenacity. Kent had a telling advantage with . . . their captain, playing centre forward. Her fast swimming, strong throws and general experience of the game, put her streets ahead of any other player in the water. . . . She it was who scored all four goals, one of them following that rare exploit when the centre goes straight up the bath from the swim-up and scores from a purely solo effort.
>
> (*Beckenham Advertiser* 1930)

Amateur sportswomen of this period were often 'all-rounders' – for example, it was not unusual for young women to be top-level swimmers in different strokes and in sprints and long-distance events, as well as being divers, water-polo players, and members of the ornamental swimming or figure-floating squads (the precursors of sychronized swimming).

Throughout the inter-war years, before the advent of television and the rupturing of community culture, amateur sports were popular forms of local entertainment. Galas, for example, attracted sizeable audiences – in 1930 it was reported that there were 700 people watching a floodlit gala at an open-air baths in the suburbs of West London (*Chiswick Times* 1930). Galas were mixed affairs, including aquatic tricks, swimming, diving and water-polo matches. Described as 'spectacular and humorous', 'skilful and entertaining', they were a mixture of slapstick and skill and were some of the few sporting occasions when men and women performed in public together:

> Miss Coppard imitated a porpoise, and a submarine, besides waltzing in the water. Mr Wilkinson imitated a torpedo, a turtle having a sun bath, and a monkey on a stick.
>
> (*Beckenham Advertiser* 1930)

The stars of the shows were usually women who were top-level swimmers and divers, billed, for example, as 'champion of Kent and Surrey', 'winner of the five mile Thames race', 'Southern Counties champion', 'British record holder', 'Olympic swimmer', or 'international water-polo player'. They were mostly middle-class, but in regular employment and so able to train only in the evenings and at weekends. Nevertheless, they became well-known amateur performers, travelling to venues throughout the country where they provided cheap entertainment with a wide and recognizable range of skills:

> The ladies entertained the large crowd to a wonderful display of swimming, embracing in their extensive repertoire porpoising, swimming backwards on the breast, propelling, diamond cross, waltzing, marching, and water-wheel, and a score of other delightfully executed movements, and in diving they also entertained with some great feats, which included back 'somersaulting', twin-diving, ladies' dive, learners' dive, 'naughty boy' dive – very amusing dives – swallow diving, and the highly entertaining Charley's Aunt.
>
> (*Anglian Daily Times* 1933)

Sunny Lowry, who had gained publicity when she swam the English Channel in 1933 doing the new crawl stroke, became a great attraction at seaside resorts during the 1930s. She was asked to give demonstration swims in different parts of the country and, as a promotion for Eugene Permanent Waves, she trained a troupe of girls in water-ballet and for water-cabaret.

The female sporting body was now unequivocally public. Aquatic sports, in common with others, provided legitimate opportunities for a woman to display her sparsely clad body for open viewing, producing an energetic and powerful image of the female body. But aquatic events were highly respectable as well as pleasurable and diversionary. Swimmers, divers and figure-floaters wore identical, loose-fitting, regulation thick black costumes, low and square-cut around the thighs, and with wide shoulder straps. They also wore thick white rubber swimming hats, with the club or association crest on the front. Costumes for organized swimming were symbols of respectability, in obvious contrast to the glamorous silky costumes of the showbiz Hollywood-style swimmers and divers, and, like their predecessors, amateur swimmers of the inter-war years were strictly disciplined and expected to behave in a seemly and ladylike way once out of the water. But although the new image of physicality was always coupled with respectability, there was not inevitable acceptance. For example, as well as being celebrated as an English Channel swimmer, Sunny Lowry was also rebuked as 'a harlot for revealing her knees' (Reed 1990: 48).

FURTHER EXPANSION

The Polytechnic Sports Clubs, discussed in the previous chapter, became active again after the First World War and also played a key role in the rapid expansion of competitive sports for women in Britain. The Northampton Polytechnic Institute (NPI) had what was considered to be the finest gymnasium in the country, fully equipped with Olympic apparatus. It was there that evening classes for women took place twice a week when Rudolph Oberholzer, a former world gymnastic champion, worked with teachers who were members of the Gymnastic Teachers Institute. Similar evening institutes, including the YMCAs, provided gymnastic classes and teaching courses for women. NPI became a training ground for some of the best female gymnasts in the country who competed in the first national competition in 1924 and in the 1928 Olympics. Before that time there were no international competitions, only gymnastic displays organized in Britain and in Europe. Some of the best gymnasts were sponsored by the *Daily Mirror* and became known as 'The Daily Mirror Eight'. Women's gymnastics were respectable as well as entertaining, with a middle-class character and a surprisingly old clientele by comparison with today – the ages of the 1928 Olympic team ranged from the mid-twenties to over 40. Discipline was strict, elders were addressed formally, and gymnasts still wore shapeless uniforms, even though by the 1930s short-sleeved shirts were allowed and gym slips had risen to 4 inches from the ground when kneeling (Desmond 1973).

But there was continuing opposition to Olympic gymnastics for women, on the grounds that apparatus work was unsuitable for the female physique. This dated back to the earlier conflicts between Oberholzer and Madame Osterberg, advocates of the Olympic and Swedish systems, respectively (discussed in Chapters 4 and 5). Those who recommended Swedish gymnastics had a monopoly of power in the educational context, and when in the early 1930s the London County Council banned all apparatus from its schools, gymnastic apparatus classes held on their premises had to close (Desmond 1973). From that time the struggle to advance women's Olympic gymnastics in England intensified. Some teachers organized private classes, and together with the Polytechnic clubs (who were outside the jurisdiction of the local authorities) and some church clubs, they provided the only opportunities for Olympic gymnastics to continue. Therefore, unlike other female sports, the development of competitive gymnastics occurred outside the education context.

Women from Regent Street Polytechnic made up the majority of the English running and netball teams, as well as the demonstration team for physical drill sent to the Women's Olympiads in Monte Carlo in 1921 and Paris in 1922 (Eliott-Lynn 1925: xi; Winter 1979 Pt 111: 12–13). On their return, some of these women grouped together and held a meeting to form the London Olympiads Athletic Club – the first women's athletic club in England. Later that year, with the active support of Major Marchant, Director of Physical Exercise at the Polytechnic, it blossomed into the Women's Athletic Association (WAA). These women believed that the inauguration of a national organization for women's athletics was necessary if the English team was to maintain its pre-eminence, and they set up the necessary arrangements and structures to make it successful (ibid.).

These events tell us something about the complex character of gender relations in the development of female sports. Female athletes, in common with other sportswomen, were active agents in the development of their sports, flouting traditional restrictions and fighting against hostility from men in powerful positions, as well as from women who stuck to reactionary ideas. But female sports could not develop in an insular fashion. Forming their own sports organizations gave women a potentially powerful vehicle for progress, but they still depended on the support of men who were sympathetic to their cause. For example, we have seen how Major Marchant and Rudolph Oberhölzer openly identified with the cause of women's sports. They were active promoters of the feminist cause in the sense that they ran classes for women, coached their teams and campaigned for public support. They knew that in most sports men had a monopoly of experience and resources, so if they supported the development of women's sports, then institutions which had previously been absolute male preserves could be opened up to women. In the case of fencing, for example, the army's facilities and coaches were opened to women during the inter-war period, and working in the armed forces provided a new context for women to participate in athletics. In golf, allowing women a handicap gave them the opportunity to play with men who could give them instruction. As in tennis, all the professionally paid coaches were men and so aspiring women players went to them to improve their skills. It is not surprising that the tendency for women's sports was to copy the ways in which men's sports had developed.

Roller-skating provides an interesting exception to this general pattern – men and women had traditionally skated together for recreation, they practised together, had the same coaches and competed against one another in open competition. Ironically, this was to change in 1939 when separate men's and women's championships were inaugurated.

STRUGGLING FOR WOMEN'S ATHLETICS

The establishment of female athletics was fraught with difficulties. Because of the intrinsically vigorous nature of running, jumping and throwing events, female athletes were particularly vulnerable to reactionary medical arguments. Athleticism is to do with action, power, speed and strength, suggestive of a qualitatively new notion of womanhood. Whereas the bicycle had symbolized the freedom of women to escape by mechanical means to a new form of independence, the new freedom for women experienced through participation in athletics was at the level of their own bodies. But exposure of working muscles has always provoked hostile claims that muscularity causes masculinization of the female body and detracts from essential femaleness. In addition, athletes seldom had exclusive use of facilities and often had difficulty negotiating with men for time and space. It is not surprising, therefore, that women did not participate in athletics to any extent until after the First World War and that there was a 40-year gap between the date when men's athletics was first organized for competition and when athletics for women was formally instituted – the Amateur Athletic Association (AAA) for men was founded in 1880, and the Women's Athletic Association (WAA) in 1922. But a member of the WAA argues that once athletics had become established as a competitive sport for women it 'took a firm hold on the popular imagination' and was 'increasing daily in popularity':

> [In 1922] we had then 1 club and about 20 girls; we now (in 1925) have over 500 clubs and over 25,000 girls. Our clubs embrace all classes from university clubs to Factory Girls' Clubs.
>
> (Eliott-Lynn 1925: xi)

Athletics had a greater working-class following than many other female sports. It was seldom taught in elite girls' schools because it was considered to be 'unladylike', 'not a sport for nice girls', so it was slow to get established in the college and university sectors. The Inter-University Athletics Board opposed women's athletics in 1919, yet undergraduates from Manchester University established a team in 1921 and the Women's Inter-Varsity Athletics Board was formed two years later. The first schoolgirls' athletics championships were held in 1925. Like other female sports, athletics attracted spectators. The WAA organized its first championship meeting in 1923, which had good support, but was outclassed the following year by a meeting organized by the *News of the World* and sponsored also by the *Sporting Life*, and the *Daily Mirror* (Crump 1989). The event, held on 4 August, Bank Holiday Monday, at Stamford Bridge, was called 'The Women's International and British Games'. During the preceding weeks it was promoted as a uniquely exciting entertainment, with the promise of heroics and spectacle: 'We shall offer a most remarkable programme, such as has never been seen in this country in the history of athletics. . . . In reality it will be the Olympic Games for Women' (*News of the World*, 29 June 1924). As well as a full range of athletic events for women (100 yards; 250 metres; 120 yards hurdles; relay races of 220 and 110 yards; long jump; high jump; javelin throw; short-put; discus throw) between athletes representing Belgium, Canada, Czecho-slovakia, France, Great Britain, Italy, Switzerland and the United States, 'some special scratch races and record attempts for men' were planned (ibid.). It was reported that 'No such meeting has been held before in England and it is anticipated that some thrilling sport will be witnessed. . . . We can be sure that our girls' will do their utmost to maintain their world supremacy in athletics' (*News of the World*, 6 July 1924). The public were informed of the names of British world-record holders and those from other countries who would be competing. Information about additional attractions was given as well: 'A grand net-ball match will be played by two picked teams' (*News of the World*, 3 August 1924), and 'Impressive displays will also be given by picked gymnastic girls of the principal Polytechnic Schools, and the British Physical Training Association is assisting to make this a great feature of a wonderful programme' (*News of the World*, 27 July 1924). 'The massed drums and fyfes of the Brigade of Guards' were to provide the final touch to what was envisaged as a 'magnificent spectacle' (*News of the World*, 29 June 1924).

The manifestly public nature of women's athletics and the celebration of women's sporting feats were reflected on the front page of the *Daily Mirror* the following day. It was devoted entirely to seven action pictures of female athletes at Stamford Bridge with the caption 'SEVEN WORLD RECORDS FOR WOMEN'S SPORT!' (*Daily Mirror*, 5 August 1924). Writing in the *News of the World* (10 August 1924), Joe Binks – the ex-mile record holder – described the 'Women's Olympiad' as 'an historic event' and 'a brilliant and unqualified success'. The technique of personalization and assessments of femininity were mixed in with acounts of athletic feats: 'The heroine of the meeting . . . was Miss Mary Lines, a London clerk. . . . A strongly-built woman of 5' 5" and 30 years of age, who trains very seriously on the Battersea Park track.' (She went on to win the 120 yards hurdles – breaking the world record in her heat – and then on the same afternoon she won the 250 metres and beat the world record.) Mlle Morris – the French woman who won the shot-put and the discus – was applauded as 'a remarkable woman' not only for her athletic prowess, but also for her motor-racing achievements when she was fre-quently the only woman competing, 'yet not only held her own, but in many instances either won outright or secured a place'. The article concludes, 'Her nerves, like her muscles, must be like iron, and those who saw her at Stamford Bridge will agree that she is one of the finest-built women on the face of the earth' (ibid.).

But there were mixed reactions to this event. The apparent public approval of women's athletics, not only as an entertaining spectacle, but also as a focus of praise for a new, more vigorous and athletic image of womanhood, was paralleled by reactionary, backward-looking attitudes. And opposition could not be ignored because it came not only from some authority figures from the public worlds of politics, medicine and education, but also from members of the athletic establishment who had the power to control the future of the sport for women. There was consistent hostility to female athletics throughout the inter-war years, when opposition to other female sports was dying down. Individual athletes had to deal with personal frustrations and disappointments – for example, during the 1930s Muriel Gunn (British long jump record holder) was forbidden by her mother to take part in bare legs and so she had to compromise by running in flesh-coloured lisle stockings, and Vera Searle (OBE for her service to athletics) retired from athletics when she got married at the peak of her career – it was, as she said, 'the done thing' (Channel 4 1990). Antagonists ignored and reinterpreted the successes of female athletes who were publicly exposing conventional 'scientific' arguments as nothing more than ideology. For example, there was heightened opposition to long-distance events when Violet Piercy ran unofficially in a marathon, completing the distance in 3 hours 40 minutes 22 seconds without ill-effects (Coates 1989: 20). Athletics were said to be unsuited to women's physique, destructive of the prospects of motherhood, and, by implication, injurious to the human race. It was argued that athletics would turn women into an 'unnatural race of Amazons', and it was treated as synonymous with indecency – a corrupting influence for a 'properly brought-up girl' (Winter 1979 Pt 111: 12). Although from the first decade of this century an increasing number of doctors were reassessing the dominant, hostile medical accounts of the effects of athletics on the female body, and, in co-operation with physical training colleges and associations of women teachers, producing arguments to support women's participation in exercise, their position did not represent a particularly radical shift, but rather a compromise. They incorporated the assumptions of their adversaries about Social Darwinism and eugenics, sharing the view that women were 'primarily designed as mothers' and should, therefore, be aware of the long-term effects of over-vigorous exercise. The focus of their reports was still the relative frailty of the female body and the belief that intense activity would harm a woman's reproductive capacity. This was the position adopted by those women who were the administrators of the WAA. They were cautious rather than radical about the development of female athletics and in 1925 sponsored Leonard Hill to provide a medical appraisal of their sport, which they accepted without reservation. He argued that:

> even if one does not see any ill results at the time from too strenuous devotion to athletics, the final result may be very deleterious to the girls' health and natural functions. As one great authority has it, 'it is only when children begin to come or ought to begin to come, that many women find

they are having to pay a pretty heavy price for a very temporary period of athletic enjoyment and glory'.

(Eliott-Lynn 1925: ix)

Because from its inception the modern Olympics was the premier international sports event and athletics was the principal Olympic sport, controversy about female participation in athletic events intensified, and has been a major site of conflict over the female sporting body ever since. But it was not just the Olympics that was a focus of conflict during the inter-war years; for example, there was also controversy about the inclusion of female athletics at the first British Empire Games in 1930. Even with the precedent of female athletics in the Olympics in 1928, the all-male organizers of this event made the decision that only swimming and diving events for women would be included. (The struggles over Olympic athletics for women during the inter-war years is discussed in Chapter 9.)

The theory of constitutional overstrain, discussed in Chapter 3, which had provided the dominant account of female physiology from the middle of the nineteenth century, was still being applied to female athletes at the end of the first quarter of the twentieth century. It was a strangely hostile reaction to the emerging image of the athletic woman; and out of character with changing images of femininity invoked by the previously traditional male work-roles that women had taken on during the First World War, or by the energetic Charleston dancer. By this time many women had overcome earlier stigmas associated with their involvement in activities outside the home. The public face of the 'new woman' was increasingly apparent in, for example, education, the medical profession, journalism, commerce and even local government. Hers was increasingly an image of confident independence, action and energy – in contrast to the lethargy and uselessness of the idealized, conventional feminine role of the previous century. But although changing images of femininity made athletics more plausible for women, ironically, the more popular the sport became, the more vehement were the reactions against it (ibid.).

The power invested in the female sporting body symbolically challenges the traditional idea that muscularity is a sign of male power. Foucault (1980) asserts that the power that resides in the physical body has a material existence in action which is transmitted through its own specific discourse, but can be undermined, and rendered fragile, by contradictory discourses.

The discourse of female sports during the inter-war years accommodated to reactionary accounts of female biology as well as challenging them: the new athletic image of womanhood both embodied power *and* was vulnerable.

THE 'NATURAL' BODY

Less vulnerable were the image and discourse of the 'natural' female body, exemplified by the physical culture movements of the inter-war years. They provided alternative forms of physical recreation to mainstream sports. By celebrating a 'free' use of the body, essentially 'at one' with nature, they were ideologically opposed to harsh exercise regimes. The concept of physical culture became firmly established during the 1930s throughout Europe and in North America; its popularity is exemplified by the Women's League of Health and Beauty – founded in England in 1930 by Mary Bagot Stack with just sixteen members. She trained the pioneers of the movement at the Bagot Stack Health School and her protégées opened up centres in London and throughout the provinces. The movement spread dramatically, and by 1939 the league had its largest-ever membership in England of 166,000. With her ideal of 'Universal Love and Service', Mary Stack initiated a world-wide expansion. In 1935 two of her teachers opened the first overseas centre in Canada and then the movement spread to Australia, Denmark, Hong Kong, New Zealand and the United States.

From the start, the league gave demonstrations in central London venues – the first was in Hyde Park in June 1930, with 100 participants, and the first national display was in the Royal Albert Hall in 1931. In subsequent years, in order to accommodate the increasing numbers of performers, displays were held at Olympia and then at the Empire Stadium, Wembley. Mary Stack was influenced by the Sokol movement in Czechoslovakia which stimulated the idea that when masses of people perform in perfect formation it creates an intoxicating symbol of unity and harmony (Bagot Stack 1979). Demonstrations were supported by well-known dignitaries and members of the ruling class and, in the founder's words, 'the newspapers published fine articles about us'. In the same way that the gymnastic displays were a cause for national pride (discussed in Chapter 5), celebrating the work of the league was a way of demonstrating to the public that British women were healthy and beautiful.

The league's motto, 'Movement is Life', was the first line of a verse written by the founder Mary Bagot Stack:

Movement is Life.
Stillness is the attribute of death.
The stagnant pond collects the weeds
which will finally choke it.
But the moving river clears itself.

(Barter 1979)

The symbolism is clear. 'Naturalness' is synonymous with purity, beauty with goodness, movement with life. The wholesome 'back-to-nature' cult had spread from Germany where it challenged the 'decadence' of the Weimar Republic; it represented a 'whole way of life' which embodied the 'essence' of womanhood and simplicity, in direct contrast to the emergence of contrived images of the female body influenced by the cosmetic, fashion and advertising industries. The imperative of 'naturalness' made even nakedness permissible in a society where in other contexts uncovering the body was still associated with shame – a legacy to a large extent of Protestantism. Although the spread of nudism did not share the league's image of respectability, it was fostered by the British Gymnastic Association and was part of the fitness movement.

The work of the league made bodily form pre-eminent, revealed in thin, loose and flowing clothes. Greek-style costumes were designed to allow complete freedom of movement, producing a sense of the fluid, mobile, plastic female body. Characterized as anatomical realism, this trend presented an image of the female body which incorporated a sense of joyfulness, physical freedom and healthy living, less suggestive of overt sexuality than of chastity, sexual innocence and purity.

But this image embodies contradictions and is linked to more general attitudes to female physicality and sexuality. Anne Hollander argues that the ideal of female slenderness asserted itself in the 1920s and that the 'look' of possible movement became a necessary element in female beauty and an important feature of modernization:

> The strong appeal of female slimness in the twentieth century is usually accounted for by social and economic changes rather than through a purely aesthetic development of style. Feminine emancipation from many physical and moral restraints, the increasing popularity of sport for women, together with new possibilities for gainful employment and political power, all eventually contributed to the new physical ideal. Good sense and good health, mental and physical, were seen to be properly served by freedom and activity and feminine clothing evolved so as to allow for these and (more importantly) for the look of these. What is meant by 'modern' looks developed after the First World War with the aid of clothing that expressed (though it did not always provide) an ideal of comfort and the possibility of action.
>
> (Hollander 1980: 152)

Sports were also expressions of a restless spirit and eroticism. 'This was naturally best offered', Anne Hollander suggests, 'in a self-contained, sleekly composed format: a thin body, with few layers of covering' (ibid.). For example, the 'Annette Kellerman' one-piece bathing costume which freed the arms and legs and clung provocatively to the contours of the body symbolized immanent sexuality. As in the Victorian period, there were varied discourses of sporting sexuality, some of which obviously sexualized the body and some of which attempted to control sexuality. Nevertheless, as Foucault argues (1981, 1987), they were all connected to the desire of one's own body and although the discourses were different they were not discrete, and together consolidated the existence and significance of sexuality.

WOMEN'S BODIES AND THE STATE

In the 1930s the 'freeing' of the female body in sports was gaining momentum dramatically – there were more resources, and the numbers of women involved were increasing. As we have seen, much of the impetus for this growth was to do with the educational and commercialized sectors, but there was an important political dimension as well. The development of strong, healthy women was part of the British government's concern to improve the fitness of the nation, to a large extent as a reaction to the spread of fascism in Europe. The 1937 Physical Training and Recreation Act reflected this fear and was a new political incentive to deploy the beneficial effects of sports and recreation in order to improve the health and well-being of the nation. The National Fitness Council (NFC) which engineered a National Fitness Campaign resulted from this legislation. An energetic publicity exercise ensued, including the production of posters with slogans 'Fitness Wins' and 'Get Fit – Keep Fit'. Government-sponsored propaganda films, such as *Pennies for Health* and *Road to Records* were shown before the Second World War at local cinemas throughout the country. They urged people of all classes, all ages and both sexes to participate in some form of sport or exercise. Traditional ideologies about female exercise were finally shifting and girls and women had moved from a marginal position to a more equal place on policy agendas. Women were now being encouraged, through different channels, to take part in physical exercise. In 1935 the United Women's Team Games Board had been founded and in 1937 the NFC funded an office for a national organizer to promote team games for women in England and Wales. The campaign was successful. Local government schemes including evening classes, coaching courses, residential courses and holiday provision were popular. In a Board of Education publication entitled *Recreation and Physical Fitness for Girls and Women* (1937: 3), the Chief Medical Officer of Health wrote: '"Keep Fit" classes are multiplying, and girls and women are showing themselves to be as enthusiastic as their brothers and husbands for open-air games and pastimes, where the oppor-tunity is given them to take part.' The years 1919–39 saw local authorities embark upon schemes funded from rates and grants from such bodies as the National Playing Fields Association, and women benefited from a marked increase in the municipal provision of park facilities, playing fields and swim-ming pools. As a result they were able to participate in greater numbers in such activities as boating, bowling, golf, swimming and tennis.

But state-sponsored schemes could be successful only because other agencies – mostly voluntary – were working at the same time, and in a similar way, to promote female participation. Increasing numbers of women were involved in a more public way in administrative and promotional roles. For example, it was the initiative of Phyllis Coulson that led to the establishment of the Central Council of Recreative Physical Training (CCRPT) in 1935, later known as the Central Council of Physical Recreation (CCPR). The general rubric of this body was to encourage and co-ordinate physical recreation in the population, but the influence of Phyllis Coulson and other female members ensured that the 'needs of women' were given a high profile. The CCRPT produced several publications aimed at female participants – *Daily Dozen for Girls and Women, Twelve Simple Dances, The Use of Music in Recreative Gymnastic Classes*, and the report of an investigation into *Recreative Gymnastics for Older Women*' (Evans 1974: 40). In 1939, just before the onset of war, teams of British girls and women were funded by the NFC to go to the Lingiad in Stockholm – a celebration in memory of Per Henrik Ling – the founder of Swedish gymnastics.

INCREASED DEMOCRATIZATION

Throughout the inter-war years middle-class women still constituted the majority of those who actively participated in sports and recreation, but gradually during this period more and more working-class women became involved. For example, the Sunday School Union Women's Hockey League contained six divisions with eleven teams (on average) in each, which suggests that hockey was more popular among working-class girls than its middle-class, private-school image might suggest (Jones 1990).

Numerous clubs and associations which included women's sports and recreative activities on their programmes were run vigorously at this time. Many of them, however, were set up by the middle classes and working-class girls and women who joined them were generally incorporated into middle-class standards of respectability. Some associations had religious or philanthropic connections, with antecedents in the rational recreation movement of the beginning of the century – for example, the YMCA, the YWCA, the Girl Guides and the factory girls' clubs. The National Council of Girls' Clubs co-ordinated the activities of all the organizations providing recreational and social facilities for young women. There were also some associations with political affiliations which provided sports and recreational opportunities for working women. Many of these were formed and grew rapidly during the inter-war years – for example, the Co-operative Holidays Association, the Youth Hostel Association, the Ramblers Association and the British Workers' Sports Federation. Particular youth associations used outdoor recreation and sports specifically to disseminate socialist ideas among their members (Jones 1986). Although youth associations in general tended to focus on young men, part of the socialist strategy was to have mixed groups or girls' sections – for example, the Independent Labour Party (ILP) Guild of Youth, the Labour Party League of Youth and the Woodcraft Folk. In addition, there were numerous voluntary associations and commercialized organizations which catered for women's sports and leisure, as well as the thousands of British firms that provided sports facilities and sports clubs for their employees.

The majority of sports and physical culture groups continued to be all-female. In some cases women were explicitly in favour of single-sex organizations (for example, those who formed the women's Pinnacle Climbing Club), and some men's associations were resistant to mixed participation (for example, the National Association of Boys' Clubs refused invitations to be affiliated to the London Union of Girls' Clubs in 1923 or to join forces with the National Association of Girls' Clubs in 1925). But between the wars mixed participation became increasingly popular, and sports venues became social meeting places. For example, the open-air movement which was part of the 'back to Nature' cult and symptomatic of attempts to escape from industrial environments, provided popular opportunities for women to participate in mixed activities. Whilst there had been rambling and hiking clubs in existence since the last half of the nineteenth century, during the 1920s they increased in numbers, and by the 1930s hiking and rambling had become fashionable crazes (Holt 1987). The railway companies offered cheap day-return tickets for such excursions as the 'Hikers' Mystery Express' and the 'Ramblers' Harvest Moon Special'. Huge numbers of people, of both sexes and from varied class backgrounds, turned out on these special occasions for a day's walk in the country and the numbers were swelled by young people in their late teens and early twenties who used the walks as unchaperoned opportunities for meeting the opposite sex (Walker 1985). For the same reasons cycling became a craze as well – in the early 1930s there were thought to be at least ten million bikers, and it has been claimed that 'on all the main roads throughout the summer could be seen great groups of young cyclists, the girls often dressed in a similar fashion to their boyfriends in shirts, shorts and jackets finished with the newly invented zip fastener' (ibid.: 146). Bicycles could be bought for under £5 and paid for on the instalment system, or hired for twopence a day – prices that were affordable for young, waged, working-class women.

Although there was a notable increase in the participation of working-class women during the 1920s and 1930s, it was mostly a result of the involvement of younger women who were in full-time employment between leaving school and getting married. Stephen Jones (1990) tells us that in Manchester between the wars, 62 per cent of members of those clubs affiliated to the National Council of Girls Clubs were under 18 years of age. But patriarchal relations in the home restricted women's access to leisure – most of all after marriage. During the inter-war years the majority of working-class women seldom participated in recreational and sports activities outside the home. Working-class people in general had less surplus time and money for leisure than the middle classes, and men always had a monopoly of what there was. It was particularly after marriage that problems of gender combined with problems of class to severely limit the freedom of working-class women to control their own leisure.

WORKERS' SPORTS FOR WOMEN

Women's sports at this time were not to any extent part of the struggle between mass and elite culture. But there were some instances where, in common with male sports, women's participation had political importance. In the 1920s, trade unions and local labour organizations encouraged workers' sports and this resulted in a proliferation of clubs and teams. The British Workers' Sports Federation (BWSF) was inaugurated in 1923 and survived until 1935. It was linked to the communist movement and it aimed to align the British movement to the international one. Then the National Workers' Sports Association (NWSA) was founded in 1930, becoming the official labour and trade union sports organization. Although there were serious ideological differences between the two associations, they both campaigned for working men and women to have better facilities and opportunities for sports, to have access to the countryside, and to be able to play sports on Sundays (Jones 1985, 1986a, 1986b). However, most of the organized sports activities were for young men – in part the effects of working-class cultural traditions and ideologies. As Margaret Phillips pointed out in a study of working-class hobbies in 1922, young men were interested 'in sport, or in engineering and mechanical inventions connected with their work', whereas girls were interested in 'housecraft or clothes' (quoted in McKibbin 1983: 129). Nevertheless, women's sports sections became active during the 1930s – particularly in major urban areas like London – and it is likely that women participated in quite large numbers in rambling and cycling, and in smaller numbers in other activities such as gymnastics, netball, swimming and tennis (Jones 1985). There were also women's football teams – a unique example of women breaking into the most popular male working-class sport. It is probable that because the participation of working-class women is under-researched, it is also underestimated. Newspaper reports provide evidence that local Labour parties selected women to participate in the International Workers' Olympiads (*Kentish Independent* 1931), and that women were involved in politically inspired meetings, such as the Tolpuddle Celebration Sports (*Kentish Independent* 1934). Guttmann (1991: 162) suggests that in 1930 'some 18 per cent of the BSWF's 6,000 members were women'.

In other European countries workers' sports were more developed than in Britain – Germany was the European country with the highest percentage of working-class women involved in organized sports (Guttmann 1991: 160). Part of their rhetoric was similar to that of the Women's League of Health and Beauty – a quest for 'naturalness' and a free use of the body, symbolized in like fashion by the drawing of a naked girl (ibid.: 162). But for working-class women the notion of empowerment through exercise was linked not only to a desire for physical invigoration, but with the instrumental need for physical strength to deal with the harshness of their working lives:

We want to bathe our bodies in light, air, and sun, to do our sports while as lightly clothed as possible . . . and . . . take to the swimming pools and the sports grounds to refresh our bodies and make them elastic enough for us to return on the morrow, with renewed strength, to the struggle for existence.

(Borg 1929, cited in Guttmann 1991 from Pfister 1980)

By 1930 workers' sports associations were flourishing in many areas of North and South America and Asia, as well as in Europe. Of a total membership of over 4 million, more than one sixth were women. The international workers' sports movement was explicitly opposed to all forms of racism and sexism and to the elitism of traditional bourgeois sport. Workers' teams from Britain competed against communist teams from western Europe and the Soviet Union, and working women entered big international workers' competitions, like the 1925 Workers' Olympics and the 1930 Workers' Wimbledon Tennis Championship. The third Workers' Olympics – organized in direct opposition to the Nazi Olympics – were scheduled to take place in Barcelona in 1936, but they never materialized: the fascists took aggressive action on the morning of the opening ceremony: the Spanish Civil War had begun.

The inter-war years had provided a brief period during which working-class women were able to forge 'alternative' sporting opportunities for themselves which were distinctly different from female sports modelled on conventional, bourgeois lines. But although organized workers' sports during this period probably held the greatest potential for the development of sports for working-class women on a wide scale because they were linked directly to the context of work, it was a potential that was never realized because of the intervention of war and the subsequent demise or weakening of workers' sports organizations.

PLAYING MEN'S SPORTS

The small amount of evidence available suggests that the links between women and football go back to at least the late Victorian period. Although few women played the game, substantial numbers became regular spectators and enthusiastic fans (Williams and Woodhouse 1991; Williamson 1991). But it was the new experiences of women during the First World War that acted as an impetus for the development of the women's game afterwards. Women working in wartime munitions factories formed football teams and, according to Williams and Woodhouse, following the war 'the establishment of the new factory and charity women's football teams . . . boasted women from both working-class and middle-class backgrounds' (ibid.: 13). But most women football players were working-class and in 'respectable sporting circles' football was considered to be an unsuitably rough sport for middle-class girls. The popularity of women's football was greatest in the North of England and the Midlands where the game was quickly rationalized to provide regular league and charity matches. From humble beginnings, women's football captured the public imagination and grew rapidly. Dick Kerr's Ladies was the best-known team, formed in 1917 by women munitions workers at Kerr's engineering works at Preston, in the North of England. During 1920 Dick Kerr's Ladies played thirty matches, by which time they had become the unofficial English national team, playing against both Scotland and France in that year, and later in America. Their success was dependent on male entrepreneurs who secured for them the use of pitches owned by clubs that were in the men's Football League, including those in the First Division. They were therefore able to play in front of large crowds – for example, on Boxing Day in 1920 they played at Everton to an audience of 53,000 (10,000 were turned away), taking over £3,000 in gate receipts for local charities (ibid.). They also played matches against men's teams. Williamson (1991: 15) describes the extraordinary public interest in women's football:

> By early 1921 it was as if the country had been gripped by ladies' football fever. Teams now covered the country with every major town having its own side and the major cities having several, especially in the North. Whether at the weekend or in the middle of the week there was a ladies' match being played somewhere.

By the end of 1921 there were probably around 150 women's football clubs in England and at that time the first national English Ladies' Football Association was formed. But as soon as the women's game was consolidated and reached a peak of success, so the seeds of its downfall were being sown. Williams and Woodhouse (1991: 18) suggest that one cause was a shift in social conditions:

> the charitable causes and the social context of wartime Britain upon which the female game was built, and which remained the raison d'être, were by 1921, beginning to fade from the collective memory.

But it was the Football Association (FA) that had the power to damage the women's game irreversibly. Whilst it had originally provided the support needed for the game to flourish – most importantly, in the provision of pitches – by the end of 1921 this help was withdrawn. The FA claimed to be responding to complaints about the appropriation of charity money, but supported its position with a conventionally male-chauvinist statement that 'the game of football is quite unsuitable for females and should not be encouraged' (ibid.: 17). The players had to contend with contradictory attitudes – support from the liberal-minded, but opposition from public sources and indeed sometimes from their friends and families, too. Alice Stanley, for example, one of the original members of Dick Kerr's team, played football without the knowledge of her mother, who was angry when she found out and who reprimanded her daughter for having her hair cut to shoulder-length because it was 'too mannish' (Channel 4: 1990).

The case of women's football provides another example of the unusual spread of untypical female sports during this period and the incursion of greater numbers of working-class women into sports. Like other female sports which had grown rapidly at this time, football illustrates how in some cases women needed the support of men and men's organizations to develop their game. The case of football also illustrates the power that men had to impede the smooth progress of women's sports and the way in which they did so when the success of the women's game seemed to be threatening the enactment of traditional masculinity. The women's sports that survived without a break in continuity were in general those which formed their own separate national organizations and international federations, and which were not dependent on male support and control of resources and events.

'LOW-LIFE' SPORTS

There were also some sports that women participated in which were quite marginal to the orthodox ones. Whereas mainstream women's sports had a mark of respectability, whether or not the participants had middle-class or working-class backgrounds, some other activities – not usually looked at in books about 'women's sports' – were associated with the 'unrespectable' worlds of the circuses, travelling booths, pubs and working-class gyms. Trapeze artistry, acrobatics, boxing, weight-lifting and wrestling are examples. Female performers were on the margins of society – in general members of the lower classes who were poorly paid professionals. For example, there is evidence of female wrestling contests during the nineteenth century, and from the early years of the twentieth century promoters were exploiting the 'drawing power of women'. During the 1920s and 1930s women wrestlers were popular, and gimmick matches drew large crowds. For example, although conventional wrestling was best known, in 1938 at the Winter Gardens in the South London suburb of Clapham, a mud-wrestling match between an English woman and a French woman was the key feature of an evening's programme (Kent 1969: 184). Female wrestling became popular all over the world and, in spite of its 'low-life' ambience, it became a serious competitive sport with European and World championships (ibid.: 188). Female wrestlers trained hard and were often weight-lifters as well, celebrating muscularity, physical power and aggression – normally considered to be essentially male sporting attributes. However, because these women were outside conventional female sporting circles, they were ignored by the ideologues of female sports, including members of the medical profession. Women's boxing was also a form of entertainment about which there are few records because it was an 'underground' sport, characterized as disreputable and dangerous, and self-contained in working-class venues. Little is known, either, about forms of professional sport for women – pedestrian and swimming competitors, for example, who gave demonstrations or raced for money. Their manifest abilities to perform activities involving speed, strength and endurance, without suffering any harmful effects, were ignored in the arguments about female sports.

CONCLUSION

The development of women's sports is often presented as if it has been an evolutionary, progressive process. But the evidence of the period between 1919 and 1939 suggests it was both uneven and complex. There were similarities between different sports and different contexts, but also differences and contradictions. It is clear that some female sports during these years showed a continuity of past practices. But there were also changes – various sports for women emerged and new arrangements were secured. Even in the same sport old traditions were reproduced and defended at the same time as new ideas and practices were occurring. Many female sports between the wars reflected new consumer patterns and were more secular than in Victorian times. Usually women had to struggle hard to gain anything at all, but sometimes change was relatively easy and they broke new barriers and used their bodies freely and powerfully. In general, organized sports for women in institutional settings like schools, colleges and clubs remained conservative in orientation, but coexisted with sports where individual women flouted convention and presented new, provocative physical images. Although there was a relaxation of conventional attitudes about women's supposed physical limitations, however, women's sports careers usually ended when they got married, and almost always when they had children. Although working-class women participated in increasing numbers, they came mostly from 'respectable' working-class backgrounds and were single, waged women. In general, sports for females retained a middle-class character and it is misleading to imply that they had become thoroughly democratized.

The inter-war years show clearly that there were continued gender struggles over the consumption of sports and that many unexpected changes occurred. Women's sports were very different in 1939 from what they had been in 1919.

Chapter 7

Femininity or 'musculinity'?
Changing images of female sports

INTRODUCTION

This chapter is about the feminine character. More specifically, it is concerned with images of the female in western sports, and how, in conscious and unconscious ways, they are constructed, reproduced and changed. These processes are overlaid with ideologies, some of which go back a long way in history and are so much a part of everyday life that for the vast majority of people they seem eminently sensible. But ideologies are not fixed – they are the result of struggles over meaning and of constant reassessments. In sports, as in other areas of life, conventional and stereotyped representations of femaleness coexist alongside progressive and oppositional ones: there are those which are part of a broad ideological structure of power which severely limits female autonomy, and those which are expressions of an active redefinition of the female sporting body. This is why Michael Messner (1988) describes the female athlete – and her body – as 'a contested ideological terrain'.

But we can understand images of the female in sport only in relation to those of the male. Competitive sports are celebrations of physical differences – between people of the same sex, but also, and in a most profound way, between males and females. Throughout their histories, modern sports have been powerful sources of male imagery. The idealized male sporting body – strong, aggressive and muscular – has been a popular symbol of masculinity against which women, characterized as relatively powerless and inferior, have been measured. Masculinity and femininity are relative concepts which are socially and historically constructed, and as Connell (1987: 85) observes, 'The meanings in the bodily sense of masculinity concern, above all else, the superiority of men to women, and the exaltation of hegemonic masculinity over other groups of men which is essential to the domination of women.'

We have seen in the previous chapters how during the nineteenth and early twentieth centuries power relations between men and women in sports, predicated on representations of physical difference between the sexes, were starkly uneven. And although during the inter-war years sportswomen were more adventurous and athletic, there were still influ-ential ideological assumptions about the harmful and masculinizing effects of exercise on the female body. The acquisition of strength, muscularity and athletic skill has always been empowering for men, whereas for women it is valued far less and in some cases is denigrated. For huge numbers of men the image and experience of the body are intimately linked to sporting experiences: for the majority of women, the image and experience of the body have very little or nothing to do with sports. These differences are the result of generally held images of men and women, and although some women are creating radical ideas about female physicality, the assumption that it is 'unwomanly' to have a muscular physique is still widespread. Even at the end of the twentieth century, sportswomen are pressured to present popular images of femininity to avoid such labelling. The question posed in this chapter – 'FEMININITY OR "MUSCULINITY"?' – is concerned with the acceptance or overcoming of conventional images of and ideas about the female body and femininity in a range of agencies including the family, the school and the media. This is a question about gender.

GENDER – AN ORGANIZING PRINCIPLE

. . . *sex* should properly refer to the biological aspects of male and female existence. Sex differences should therefore only be used to refer to physiology, anatomy, genetics, hormones and so forth. *Gender* should properly be used to refer to all the non-biological aspects of differences between males and females – clothes, interests, attitudes, behaviours and aptitudes, for example – which separate 'masculine' from 'feminine' life styles.

(Delamont 1980: 5)

The distinction between sex and gender in this quotation is clear, but in everyday life these categories are used as if they are the same. Although 'masculine' and 'feminine' are *social* realities, there is a mystique about their being predetermined by biology. Biologism is an ideology which explains social and cultural differences between males and females according to scientific criteria. For example, the commonplace claim that men are *naturally* more aggressive, more competitive and, therefore, better at sports than women suggests that these are inherent conditions and hence un-changeable. But it is illogical and inaccurate to argue that because relatively more men than women display aggressive and competitive behaviour, these characteristics are exclusive to the male sex. This is not to deny that there are essential differences between the sexes, but to resist the strong tendency to treat as natural everything that is customary. To regard gender as a biological category works to sustain relationships that we think we know about; biologism condones sexual stereotyping and ignores the power dimension of differences in male and female behaviour; it also underestimates the common capacities of men and women and the ways in which scientific explanations have changed historically. Differences between the sexes in displays of aggression and competitiveness can be explained as a result of social and cultural experiences – part of a process which starts at birth.

Infants have a biological sex when they are born, but no 'masculine' or 'feminine' identity. However, because they emerge into a social world where gender differences are intrinsic to everyday life, they rapidly acquire one. Gender is to do with expected behaviour based on unitary conceptions of sexual character. There is a widespread assumption that all girls and women have a set of characteristics which is constant and common to them as females, and which is distinctly different from the set of characteristics common to boys and men. In social analyses of sports the most popular way of explaining how individuals acquire gender identities has been to use the concept of socialization. It is argued that the family is the primary agency of socialization – a place where, from infancy, boys and girls internalize particular ways of behaving which correspond to social expectations for their sex and influence their future involvement in and attitudes to sports (Coakley 1990: 192–7).

GIRLS AND BOYS COME OUT TO PLAY

Research has shown that the behaviour of parents and other adults towards children (even when they are newly born) differs according to the sex of the child (Belotti 1975; Deem 1978; Delamont 1980; Grabrucker 1988; Whyld 1983). From the earliest hours of life the physical body is the focus for the construction of gender, and because gender is experienced through the body, 'masculinity' and 'femininity' seem absolutely intimate and fundamental. We understand our gender because we are given names, colour coded, dressed, talked to and treated in particular ways which accord with our sex. Girls tend to be handled more gently; boys are tossed around and wrestled with more frequently and vigorously; girls are more closely supervised and allowed less physical freedom; boys are encouraged to be adventurous and to play vigorous out-of-door games; girls are given domestic toys, skipping ropes and Barbie dolls; boys are given fighting toys, footballs and Action Men; girls are restricted in methods used and distances covered when travelling; boys are allowed more freedom when travelling away from home for sports meetings.

Not surprisingly, from an early age there are observable differences between the motor characteristics of many boys and girls (Ryan 1985): the former tend to be physically more active and adventurous; the latter tend to favour quieter activities and smaller-scale movements. Iris Young (1990: 145) discusses the differences that Strauss observes between boys and girls: 'Not only is there a typical style of throwing like a girl, but there is a more or less typical style of running like a girl, climbing like a girl, swinging like a girl, hitting like a girl.' It seems sensible to believe that such differences reflect 'natural' abilities, and Iris Young (141–59) compares the explanations of Erwin Strauss with those of Simone de Beauvoir. The former claims that because differences between the sexes are manifest at an early age, they must be biological, whereas Simone de Beauvoir argues that expressions of masculinity and femininity are fundamentally historical, cultural, social and economic. This typifies the way in which the opposition between biological and social explanations for human behaviour is exaggerated and marginalizes the complex interrelationships between them. The concern to point out ways in which sexual differences are socially constructed has arisen because biological explanations, still prevalent and popular, are used to legitimate the different treatment of males and females, and to justify male domination.

In most families gender stereotyping is part of everyday life and so there is a qualitative difference in the psychological experiences of being male or female. Even when parents set out to undermine gender-based child-rearing practices, they cannot prevent their own subliminal responses. Children quickly understand set ideas about what it is to be a girl or a boy by their daily experiences in the world around them – in relationships with other members of their families, with neighbours, and with other children – in the home, in the park, in the supermarket – and in response to representations in books and magazines, in advertisements and on television. Iris Young (1990: 158) discusses a survey of textbooks for young children which reveals that 'children are thirteen times more likely to see a vigorously active man than a vigorously active woman'. Constant exposure to a social world that is full of cultural signs of sexual difference makes it very difficult for children to behave so that their biological sex is not convergent with their gender. It is impossible to prevent the influences of contemporary child culture which still labels girls for being 'tomboys' and takes notice when they 'play with the boys', and is always cruel to 'cissy' boys who prefer the company of girls, or are frightened of taking part in rough games. Boys seem to suffer greater anxiety over sex identity than girls, and particularly in their younger years have fewer opportunities, without suffering stigma, to express themelves in ways which are different from conventional norms of masculinity:

A girl may refuse the constraints of femininity during the period of childhood which the psychoanalysts have called 'latency' – that is, between the ages of about 7 and 11. She may climb trees, play football, get into scrapes and generally emulate acceptable masculine behaviour, *but only on the condition that she grows out of it*. No such tolerance is extended to the male. He can never, even temporarily, abdicate from his role. The boy who goes around with girls, plays girls' games and rejects his male peers would probably be referred to Child Guidance.

(Comer 1974: 261, quoted in Talbot 1990)

Differences are magnified as children get older, and their experiences of sports become firmly based on principles of gender. Margaret MacNeill (1988: 198) argues that 'without ever being taught or told, children learn that certain activities are more appropriate for girls and others are more suitable for boys'. She talks about the common practice in Canada of sending girls to figure-skating classes while boys play ice-hockey. In England a similar situation arises when masses of young boys play Little League (a term borrowed from America) soccer, whilst in gymnastic clubs and dancing classes there is a predominance of girls. Throughout the western world huge numbers of young boys (and at increasingly young ages) are inducted into highly competitive sports. And they are encouraged to be aggressive, tough and even violent. Although aspiring parents also encourage young girls into competitive sports, they take part in smaller numbers and usually participate in those sports characterized as aesthetic and expressive. Children's ideas about sports are consolidated through their relationships at home with siblings and parents. Through sports discourse and the sexual division of labour in the family, they learn about the intense physicality and hypermasculinity of male sports and about the special importance of sports in men's lives.

GENDER DIFFERENCES IN CHILDREN'S WEEKLIES

Images of gender differences in sports are also reproduced in children's comics and magazines. The hidden ideology is very powerful. In Britain, most popular weeklies are produced for 'all-boy' or 'all-girl' readerships, and there is far less attention given to female sports than to male ones.[1] The process starts early: in comics for young boys (under 12), sports, and in particular football, have a very high profile. Football is treated as an adventure, a way of being 'macho' and 'one of the boys' in a 'separate' world of masculinity. Girls are never portrayed *playing* football, and are only occasionally seen looking on. The most common features in these comics are action-packed adventures, often with military or fighting themes. Sports and other physical pursuits are portrayed as central in the lives of young boys and as contexts for early male-bonding. In marked contrast, in girls' comics sports have a low profile: some attention is given to 'feminine-appropriate sports', but they are seldom treated as a focus. It is more usual in girls' comics for sports to be used as background activities for the main story-line which is often to do with relationships between individual girls or cliques of girls. A popular setting is the all-girl boarding school (with which working-class girls have no organic connection), and the theme of the story is often a moral one – for example, when the school swimming champion breaks a leg, a sad and misunderstood newcomer is persuaded to compete in the match against the rival team, and by doing so brings glory to her new school and makes friends who help her to come to terms with being recently orphaned. Stories in girls' magazines are often home-based, concerned with relationships, and usually have moral overtones. They seldom portray girls' athleticism and love of sports. A serial about synchronized swimming in the girls' comic *Bunty* (1991–2) is unusual. In magazines produced for an older, mixed readership (12–16), male sports are given a lot of space and are always presented as popular and appropriate activities for young males, with the hidden message that if boys are good players (again, usually at football), the 'girls will come running'. In comparison, there are only sometimes articles about sports for girls, including occasional features about non-conventional female sports, such as football, and minority sports for girls. But although making girls' sports visible in this way seems to be a radical shift and an attempt to reduce gender differences and to treat sports as appropriate for both sexes, it is clear in these publications that girls' sports are an afterthought. Because they are not treated in the same way as boys' sports – as 'everyday' activities – they remain marginalized, not integrated. Gender differences are further emphasized by the production of 'specialist' boys magazines, such as *Shoot*, which are devoted entirely to football. There is one sports magazine for girls which focuses on pony-riding and gym-kanas. There are no magazines which treat sports as everyday 'mixed' activities.

The display and emphasis of gender differences in comics and magazines for young readers may seem unimportant when considered in isolation, but because they are visible and public symbols of differences between males and females which are constructed and reproduced in other spheres as well, the ideological message is a very powerful one indeed. Together with other experiences, the comics and magazines which are consumed by young girls shape their understanding about the female body and about sports. It is impossible for anyone to develop gender-free images of everyday experience and conversation, or to be unaffected by those institutions that shape our existence. Gender is an organizing principle, reproduced and disseminated – publicly and privately – in all social contexts; it pervades the cultural sphere. Nevertheless, the process of gender assimilation is exceptionally complex. Femininity is not a static condition (which the socialization and sex-role models, as well as the biological one tend to suggest), but an experience that changes historically, and according to specific economic, ideological, political and social structures. Furthermore, it is the result of an *active* engagement in a world of gender images which are put into practice on a day-to-day basis and hence become part of everyday life – a 'lived condition'. The older children get, the more complicated the process becomes. Although we come across conventional images of gender most frequently and understand them most easily, they are not the only ones. The transmission of gender incorporates contradictions, struggles and changes – a process that can be recognized in the school.

GENDER DIVISIONS IN PRIMARY SCHOOLS

Schools do not exist in a social vacuum – girls and boys start their education with definite ideas about what is appropriate for their respective gender, ideas which are reinforced by orthodox sexual divisions in the classroom, in the playground and on the games field. But schools also have the potential to modify children's perceptions of gender roles and to challenge sexist behaviour. The complexities of the issue of gender in schools are further compounded by the relative autonomy that teachers in British schools have enjoyed and also by the tremendous differences between schools (for example, private/state/single-sex/mixed), and within schools.

In spite of increasing attention to equal rights issues in education, gender divisions are still apparent at all levels of schooling throughout Britain and, in many ways and in most cases, the organization, classroom management and teaching methods of schools polarize girls and boys and reinforce their ideas about and previous experiences of gender divisions:

> Schools segregate the sexes in many ways. For example, lavatories, changing rooms, cloakrooms and even playgrounds may be segregated. Pupils are commonly listed separately on the register, lined up in separate groups, and offered different subjects.
>
> (Delamont 1980: 24)

Physical sex segregation is often engineered by children themselves. In a number of studies it has been observed that in mixed playgrounds, and in other areas of the school environment, boys monopolize the physical space and play more vigorous games than girls who tend to become marginalized watching the boys from the side (Leaman 1984; Mahony 1985; Wolpe 1977). In mixed physical education (PE) classes in Australia it was observed that 'boys tended to dominate the setting and determine the pace and direction of the game being played' (Evans 1989: 84).

Although for years the philosophy of primary education (5–11 years) in general, and of primary physical education specifically, has been full integration, this has not always been put into practice and the hidden curriculum has continued subtly to engender children's schooling. However, the process of gender reproduction in PE is not without contradictions and struggles. In many schools it has been intended that the teaching of PE should undermine and reshape traditional practices, attitudes and images of gender in sports. This has happened in a number of ways: some primary schools have encouraged total integration of the sexes in all aspects of the subject and for children of all ages; the teaching of dance to girls and boys in mixed classes has provided a creative and aesthetic movement experience for both sexes, usually associated with 'femininity'; the teaching of a range of small-side games to both sexes has moved the focus away from gender-appropriate competitive games; and the organization of mixed school teams (in particular, football) reassesses the link between traditional male sports and 'masculinity'. Increasing numbers of primary-aged girls want to play football and compete in junior leagues. (The early efforts of primary girls to play football are discussed in the following chapter.) But such programmes coexist with traditional incentives. In many primary schools, the older girls and boys are separated for competitive team games, on the grounds that mixed PE is 'only appropriate for younger children', and throughout the country there are local junior leagues for football and netball where the tradition of single-sex competition and the associated images of gender remain intact. Anne Williams's research (1989) shows how primary-aged girls and boys have sex-linked attitudes and abilities in sports and PE, linked to their experiences outside school. Separate programmes of games are what many children expect and accept.

PHYSICAL EDUCATION IN SECONDARY SCHOOLS

The history of PE in secondary schools (11–18 years) has been characterized by images of difference. A blueprint for separate development was set in the nineteenth century: while boys were being pushed into worlds of toughness and aggression playing organized games in public schools and performing military drill in elementary schools, girls were enjoying 'feminine-appropriate' sports and games and doing Swedish gymnastics. Then, throughout the inter-war years assumptions about gender provided the basis for subsequent, though more varied, programmes of PE in schools for both middle-class and working-class girls (see Chapter 4). After the Second World War economic factors forced women back into the home to release jobs for men, and the ideologies of the family and of sexual difference were re-asserted in secondary education. The Crowther Report (1945) was explicit: 'The incentive for girls to equip themselves for marriage and home-making is genetic' (cited in Beddoe 1983: 61). And nearly two decades later, the Newsome Report (1963) urged that 'our girls should be educated in terms of their main social function – which is to make for themselves, their children and their husbands a secure and suitable home and to be mothers' (cited in Beddoe 1983: 61). At a time when the ideology of gender difference and education for motherhood was integral to educational theories and practice – for example, while boys were taught metalwork and woodwork, girls were taught needlework and cooking – not surprisingly, PE continued to be sex-specific. The two distinctly different systems of physical education for boys and girls were consolidated after the establishment of men's specialist colleges of physical education (Carnegie was the first in 1933). Student teachers were trained in a specifically 'military' style of gymnastics and aggressively masculinized and highly competitive team games. Rigid sexual divisions continued from the time when the tripartite system of schooling was established in the state sector of education in 1944. In spite of fundamental changes in educational philosophies with the inception of comprehensive education from the 1950s onwards, with few exceptions, girls and boys in secondary schools had distinctly different PE curricula (in content, teaching methods and attitudes). Further developments have done little to change conventional ideas which normalize gender differences in PE (Delamont 1980; Fletcher 1984; Flintoff 1990; Hendry 1978; Scraton 1986, 1992). In the 1950s and 1960s, modern educational dance and modern educational gymnastics were introduced into the PE curriculum for girls, whilst most boys' schools continued with a traditional programme. The philosophy underpinning these two new elements of girls' PE derived from the ideas of Rudolph Laban, who had been working with female physical education specialists since the 1930s on a more creative and expressive method of teaching (Foster 1977). The resultant new discourse of girls' PE was incorporated into the concept of 'movement education'. It fitted in well with the developing 'child-centred' theme of 'progressivism' and the emphasis on creativity and discovery methods of learning. Movement education, based on Laban's analysis of movement, was diffused throughout the women's colleges of physical education, girls' secondary schools and the primary sector. Swedish gymnastics had been completely displaced. However, men's physical education teacher-training continued to adhere to the disciplined, fitness and competitive games tradition, underpinned by the natural sciences and behavioural psychology, thus cementing the images of and divisions between 'feminine-appropriate' and 'masculine-appropriate' activities. Although for the first three years of secondary schooling (11–14 years) it has been usual to introduce both sexes to compulsory 'core' activities (including athletics, dance, games, gymnastics and swimming), in many schools boys and girls continue to be taught separately and differently. Even when some aspects of the curriculum are taught to mixed classes, ideologies of sexual difference continue (see Chapter 8), and traditional divisions along lines of gender are almost always retained in games. The shared experience of mixed PE in primary schools seems to do little to diminish the power of traditional ideas about gender in secondary PE or to change the expectations and experiences of pupils. It is therefore the case that most secondary-aged boys are systematically shut off from an expressive movement experience and are schooled into physical robustness and aggressive competition, whilst girls are schooled into creativity and co-operation.

In common with the formative years of PE from the nineteenth century, in recent times much of the impetus for the development of the subject for older girls has come from teacher-training establishments, but new incentives and the discourse of change have centred on the state schools and not the private sector. Sheila Scraton (1986, 1992) claims that the notion of 'separate' and 'different' physical opportunities and experiences for boys and girls remains a central concept in the planning of PE programmes. She argues that teachers have stereotyped ideas about the different abilities of girls and boys based on the ideologies of motherhood and sexuality, and she found consistent examples of sexist behaviour and language in the schools she observed. It is immaterial whether teachers believe that differences between girls and boys are rooted in biology or culture if PE departments continue to operate programmes on the basis of gender difference and when teachers themselves articulate sexist sentiments. Physical education in secondary schools plays a vital part in shaping attitudes to the body. Whenever differences between the sexes are institutionalized, and left unchallenged, they are very hard to change.

BREAKING TRADITIONS

However, it is mistaken to imagine that mainstream gender images in PE are constructed and reproduced with no resistance. By urging girls to be physically active and to participate regularly in sports or physical recreation, teachers are encouraging a redefinition of femininity. And, although in small numbers, certain mixed schools have made a positive effort to establish new educational principles and to break with the stereotyped images of 'male-appropriate' and 'female-appropriate' PE. They have instigated mixed classes in the core curriculum for younger pupils – notably in the teaching of gymnastics and dance. Mixed sessions for older pupils are nothing new. Since the 1960s PE programmes for fourth years upwards (15–18 years) have been based on the concept of 'education for leisure', and optional courses for both sexes have been offered in recreative and leisure pursuits. Barbara Humberstone (1986) argues that outdoor activities in mixed-sex groups can present a challenge to traditional notions of gender differences. Her research shows that when girls and boys are exposed to risk together, gender boundaries are weakened, and an unusually co-operative atmosphere develops between pupils of different sexes. However, there are also indications that older girls choose options, not so much out of interest in a particular sport or activity, but rather for social reasons. The timetabling of mixed PE for older pupils provides a setting where adolescent girls and boys can meet and where dating can occur.

The issue of mixed PE is a controversial one and has been highlighted in discussions about the Educational Reform Act and the National Curriculum for PE (discussed in Chapter 8). What is clear is that gender-stereotyping in PE can be limiting and damaging to those children who do not conform, and, it can be argued, also for those who do. There are boys who hate the images and conventions of masculine-style sports and find compulsory games a brutalizing experience, and, together with those who relish the aggressivity and macho connotations of compulsory games, they are denied opportunities to move creatively and to develop a wide vocabulary of motor ability: and there are girls who are labelled as 'masculine' and 'unfeminine' for expressing a preference for playing traditional male sports, and whose opportunities to participate in activities which require explosive and powerful movements are limited. However, the trend for girls to participate in those sports that have traditionally been all-male ones is established and expanding. This is happening slowly in Britain and more quickly in other parts of Europe – for example, during the last two decades in Norway and Sweden football has become, respectively, the fourth and second most popular sporting activity for girls (Flintoff 1990). There is no equivalent initiative or research to show that 'feminine-appropriate' sports are becoming more popular with boys. The idea that both girls and boys should have a positive experience of PE tends to assume that girls should be doing the same thing as boys – not the other way round. The result is that images of femininity in sport and PE are diversifying more quickly than masculine images.

DROPPING OUT

It is still the case, however, that sports are not generally popular amongst adolescent girls. Cockerill and Hardy (1987) asked fourth-year secondary schoolgirls (14–15 years) about their attitudes to PE and their ideas about femininity. They revealed the pressure they felt to conform to mainstream images of femininity, and their feelings that participating in vigorous sports was unfeminine. Because being good at sports is inextricably linked to popular perceptions of masculinity, for secondary schoolboys success brings prestige and boosts self-image. But sports are far less important in the lives of adolescent girls, who, encouraged by peer group pressure, seek other activities linked closely to their preferred perceptions of femininity (Hendry 1978).

The act of dropping out of PE is linked in complex ways to physical and emotional experiences during puberty, as well as to commercial influences and practical and ideological constraints. Although there are no biological or medical reasons why the onset of menstruation and the accompanying and often dramatic changes in body shape should inhibit girls from participating in physical activities – in practice, they do. Sheila Scraton (1992: 105) discusses the social construction of young women's biology – what she calls the 'ideology of biology' (i.e. the expectations placed on young women as to how they *should* be reacting to these changes):

It is reasonable to assume that for some young women the changes of puberty produce such distinct changes in body shape that it becomes difficult to retain the levels of mobility and movement which they had developed as children. . . . However, it is important to emphasize that social and ideological pressures, linked to sexuality and body physique . . . together produce inhibitions on mobility and movement rather than a biologically determined restriction.

Because girls go through puberty at different ages and rates, pre-pubertal and post-pubertal pupils find themselves in the same PE classes together. 'Early developers' can become inhibited about changing and showering in front of their peers when their breasts and pubic hair are growing and their hips are spreading, and the lack of privacy in communal changing rooms increases the difficulty of coping with menstruation. Paradoxically, 'late-developers' can be made to feel awkward and unnatural in a room of girls talking about periods and bras when they are still flat-chested and physically childlike. Hendry's research in schools uncovered the inhibitions felt by adolescent girls (particularly those who were overweight) about changing into sports clothes which did not enhance their appearance (1978: 50). He collected evidence from different research projects to show that adolescent girls do not value PE or join in extra-curricular activities as much as boys. Those who do tend to be mesomorphs with stereotypically 'beautiful' bodies – quite lean and muscular, not overweight and flabby, or underweight and skinny.

The cultural emphasis on images of sexuality and femininity heightens the self-consciousness of adolescent girls about their developing bodies and expected ways of behaving. The construction of adolescent femininity is now so firmly linked to consumer culture that girls are bombarded with idealized images of the female shape that are impossible to ignore and difficult to oppose. The effects are insidious – adolescent girls and young women rarely feel at ease with or proud of their bodies unless they conform to some notional ideal. Not surprisingly, they tend to show interest in those forms of physical activity which are designed to 'improve' the body and enhance 'attractiveness'. There appears to be limited interest among adolescent girls in physical activity for its own sake. Ironically, the introduction in some secondary schools of 'feminine-appropriate' PE options for the older pupils, such as aerobics, disco-dancing, keep-fit and pop-mobility, whilst catering for the interests of the pupils, does nothing to change the dominant ideologies surrounding adolescent gender.

THE CULT OF ADOLESCENT FEMININITY

There is tremendous peer group pressure on adolescent girls to immerse themselves in an 'anti-school' culture of femininity, which, amongst certain groups, resembles a cult within which there is no place for sports. Both working-class and middle-class adolescent girls are influenced by a personal culture of femininity passed on to them by female relatives and by the public culture of femininity, heavily influenced by commercialization. But their experiences are different (McRobbie 1991). Working-class girls tend to visualize their futures as being limited by marriage, housekeeping and child-rearing, and their attitudes to leisure and sports are influenced by these ideas. Middle-class girls are not unaffected by the ideologies of romanticism and domesticity, but, in comparison, they tend to accept more readily the value-system of schooling and its promise of interesting work in the labour market and access to leisure. While at school they participate in greater numbers in varied extra-curricular activities, including sports. This class-based trend continues after girls leave school, when fewer working-class young women participate in sports than their middle-class counterparts. It is clear that during adolescence class and gender are articulated together in the construction of female sports.

Angela McRobbie's research (1978, 1991) shows how the leisure culture of working-class girls is determined by their material position, but also embodies sets of meanings and practices which they creatively work out for themselves. Much of female adolescent culture is home-centred (Deem 1978; McRobbie and Garber 1976; McRobbie 1991; Sharpe 1976). Girls spend a lot of time in their bedrooms – trying on make-up and clothes, reading fashion, romance and music magazines, listening to pop music, and talking with friends. They go out to meet friends for coffee, to dance and to date. The focus of the culture is the presentation of a 'trendy' and 'sexy' image in order to be accepted by girlfriends and attractive to boys. The relationships of adolescent girls to other young people of both sexes are mediated through their bodies – their stances, clothes, make-up and hairstyles, etc. Theirs is a culture that accentuates images of femininity and sexuality which, although circumscribed in many ways by practical and ideological influences, is also a way of grasping power. Young working-class women create their own preferred values and ways of presenting themselves to the world.

In contrast, most working-class boys immerse themselves in a culture of physical activity and conquest. Talking about motor-bike boys, Paul Willis (1978) points out that although they are not interested in *organized* sports, nevertheless, they display a particular masculine style that is physical and aggressive. Playing and watching sports, reading football and motor-cycle magazines, meeting mates for a drink, and messing about with cars and motor-bikes – all accompanied by sexist behaviour (Willis 1977, 1978) – are the activities that for working-class boys are ways of creating particular images of masculinity and virility. Bedroom culture and the cultivation of the female sexualized body, socializing and going out with boys are the equivalent activities for girls in their creation of feminine identities. Most working-class girls get their exercise at the disco rather than on the sports field or in the gym or swimming pool. Sports for them have no connection with their idealized images of femininity.

THE POWER OF GIRLS' WEEKLIES

The attitudes that adolescent girls have about sports and physical activity correspond to the particular images of femininity made accessible to them through the personal worlds of such weeklies as *Jackie* (average readership age 10–14) and *Just Seventeen* (readership – over 15 years – which has replaced *Jackie* as the most popular weekly magazine). *Jackie* has a heavy commitment to romance, whereas *Just Seventeen* focuses more on 'fashion, pop, problems and personal realization'. Angela McRobbie (1991: xiv) notes a change in the portrayal of femininity in the last two decades: she describes *Jackie's* 1970s world of adolescent femininity as oppressive because, she says, it urges working-class girls to find 'a steady boyfriend and potential husband at all cost and preferably as soon as possible' (xvii), and she points out how 1980s magazines present a more independent, less passive version of femininity – embodying self-image and self-satisfaction – concentrating on 'the potentially sophisticated and discerning young consumer' (146). In the 1990s fashion and beauty features which feed the ideology of self-realization continue to take up more space in girls' magazines than the idealization of romanticism and 'getting a man'. In *Just Seventeen*, in particular, adolescent girls are urged to pay attention to the maintenance of their bodies through attention to healthy living, diet and exercise, together with the aid of numerous beauty and fashion products. The idealized image of the adolescent female body is of one that is, through regular attention, and costly procedures, beautified and sexualized. Sports that are associated with adventure, sweat and muscularity are not part of the feminine culture of *Jackie* and *Just Seventeen*: in these weeklies exercise is synonymous with keep-fit and aerobics, presented as part of a 'caring-for-the-body' package aimed to make girls attractive to boys. Images of clean, sleek, young and gleaming bodies are popularized in advertisements for 'trendy' sportswear, such as trainers, tracksuits, sweatshirts, ski-suits, high-cut leotards, and lycra-skin shorts and tights. Female models pose in 'casual' stances, displaying the sportswear for fashion rather than for practical use, with captions such as 'The sports-look goes smart in flowing silk'. Although the evidence suggests that very few adolescent girls actually take the idea of regular exercise of any kind seriously, it is clear that they treat fashion and other forms of body care as priorities. Teenage femininity is thus coded in the language of consumerism and profit.

IMAGE-MAKING AND THE SEXUALIZED FEMALE BODY

In common with adolescent culture, the gradual growth of female sports and other types of physical recreation in recent years have become inextricably linked to the commercialization of the female body and the commercialization of sexuality. Image-making is the cult of modern capitalism; it reflects the obsession about the body which affects modes of everyday life and personal responses. The proliferation of images of sports with sexuality reflects the prevalence of images of women's bodies in western culture – a process that is coded in the language of consumerism and profit (Sparkes 1988).

Body presentation which makes more visible the form and sexuality of the female body has become increasingly noticeable in particular female sports. Those which emphasize balance, co-ordination, flexibility and grace (such as gymnastics, ice-skating and sychronized swimming) are characterized as 'feminine-appropriate' because they affirm a popular image of femininity and demonstrate their essential difference from popular images of sporting masculinity. Not surprisingly, these are the sports which have been most visibly and systematically sexualized: the performers conform to the female norm of heterosexuality; the routines contain 'ultra-feminine' postures and gestures, sensuous symbolism, sexually suggestive movements, and even sometimes provocative poses bordering on the erotic.

Modern sportswear (for these sports and other leisure activities) is manufactured specifically to promote a sexy image. This is one way in which sports have become inextricably linked to the commercialization of the female body and the commercialization of sexuality. Fashion seems increasingly to be taking its energy from sports, and sportswear and leisure-wear are not just practical, but sexy and modish. Sportswear makes statements about femaleness and enhances sexuality; it both reveals the body *and* conceals the body, promoting an awareness of the relationship between being dressed and being undressed. For example, elasticated body-stockings and lycra leggings provide a dynamic image with an explicit focus on body definition and no clear distinction between body and material. Clinging clothing highlights sexuality and eroticism, as do particular designs – leotards cut high above the thigh, and skin-coloured inserts between the breasts, for example. Young models with firm and nubile bodies which look good in tight-fitting materials are used to promote sales. Sportswear contributes to the making of a self-conscious, narcissistic individual image, and it is worn by women who are active participants as well as those wno wear it just for effect. And sportswear is combined with other beauty aids to construct a total image: in addition to wearing sportswear-based fashion, women seek to enhance their appearance by their styles of walking, postures and gestures, by shaving axillary, pubic and body hair, by dieting, by wearing particular underwear, by having fashionable hairstyles, by adding adornments to hair and body and by wearing make-up. These public and commercialized body presentations are perceived as unequivocally heterosexual: they are everyday 'lived practices' which subtly aid in the reproduction of a system of 'dominant heterosexuality' which permeates sports.

Although some sportswomen seek actively to reject trendy and provocatively heterosexual images, and choose to present themselves in alternative, less contrived and non-objectified ways (by wearing loose-fitting, comfortable and 'unmemorable' sportswear without accoutrements), there are huge varieties of tracksuits, shorts and running shoes, for example, which have been marketed as designer-wear in ways which exaggerate sexuality.

All sports styles incorporate insignia of femininity and sexuality, and, as Anne Hollander (1980) argues, even modest dress can have an erotic pull by making the inferred body seem more, not less desirable:

> For six centuries fashion has perpetually re-created an integrated vision of clothes and body together. There is a strong eroticism in this method, since it plays on the dialectic of dress and body while constantly changing the rules. Fashion is in itself erotically expressive whether or not it emphasizes sex.
>
> (Hollander 1980: 85)

BODY MAINTENANCE AND 'THE LOOK'

Women also try to restructure their bodies and enhance their appearance by exercising, as well as through fashion. Mike Featherstone argues that body maintenance and its surface representation or the 'look' of the body have become obsessions of consumer culture: 'Images of the body beautiful, openly sexual and associated with hedonism, leisure and display, emphasize the importance of appearance and the "look"' (1982: 18). The power of consumer culture derives from its ability to harness for profit people's desires about their bodies – a form of 'control through stimulation'. It is a process that has become marked in the exercise industries: body maintenance requires hard work and discipline, but the perceived end-product of a well-toned and sexy body induces women to participate in one or another of the numerous exercise programmes available. Although there are aerobics classes, for example, that take place in community facilities rather than commercial venues, and cater for women who are more interested in the enjoyment of exercise and the social interaction with other women than with the ideal of a beautiful body, they are in the minority. Aerobics has been successfully packaged to persuade women, specifically, to participate in order to lose weight and improve their sex-appeal, rather than for reasons of fitness and enjoyment or for competition. (Although aerobics has become a fiercely competitive sporting activity – see Chapter 10 – the vast majority of participants are not interested in participating for competition.) The focus of publicity is on appearance (the athletic-looking body), fashion (the trendy-looking image) and physique (the sexy-looking shape); rather than on movement (the active-looking woman). The idea of exercise is blurred with sexuality through neologisms such as 'sexercise' and 'exersex' and 'slimsexy' (Featherstone 1982: 182). The body is the visible sign of sexuality, and since in sports and other exercise regimes the focus is on the physical body, they provide obvious channels for its sexualized display. Not surprisingly, this potential is exploited in advertising and the visual media,[2] where, as Roland Barthes (1977: 229) argues, 'pictures . . . are more imperative than writing [because] they impose meaning at one stroke, without analysing or diluting it'.

Even in magazines which promote the values of sports and fitness, the ideology of health with sexiness is made explicit. Female subjects are frequently idealized and presented as if reducible to a set of bodily attributes – fit, with beautifully proportioned and conditioned bodies, erotic, and posing as if sexually available. Horne and Bentley (1989: 4) argue that since the end of the 1970s 'the "worked on" female body has become not only permissible, but presented as desirable'. They write about women's 'Fitness Chic' magazines that give the promise of fit and shapely bodies through exercise, whereas the real issue is less to do with fitness than 'the look'. According to Featherstone (1987), the message is only relevant to a small percentage of women, in particular the new petite bourgeoisie who are motivated through anxiety to participate in body maintenance techniques; it has no relevance to the majority of working-class women, or to black women or those from other ethnic minorities. Although 42 per cent of British women are size 16 or more, nevertheless, representations of the slim female body as sexually desirable in heterosexual terms are profitable and abundant. The idea of 'keeping in shape' in order to be attractive to the opposite sex is a way of controlling women's bodies: it is a powerful idea which has induced some women to have surgical operations, go on liquid diets, take laxatives and exercise compulsively. It has also caused clinical depression and such conditions as anorexia nervosa and bulimia.

Susan Bordo (1990: 85) argues that the preoccupation with fat, diet and slenderness is 'one of the most powerful "normalizing" strategies of our century, ensuring the production of self-monitoring and self-disciplining "docile bodies"'. Because women more than men are the objects of these controls, it follows that they function in the reproduction of gender. The idealized contemporary female body is slender and has to some extent become homogenized – across class, ethnic and age divisions. However, Susan Bordo points out that the athletic and muscular image of femininity, although more solid and bulky-looking, has become highly desirable. This, she argues, is because tautness and containment have become more highly valued than thinness, and any form of excess, sagginess or wrinkling – even on a thin body – spoils its line and firm appearance. Whereas in the past, muscularity has been associated with masculinity, it has now become a glamorized and sexualized condition. Muscularity through work-outs is a symbol of both control and desirability, and for both men and women. In the same way that muscularity has always symbolized the empowerment of men, representations of the female athletic body can also be understood as a symbol of empowerment and escape from traditional images of femininity and domesticity. However, in common with popular women's magazines, in journals expressly concerned with sports and fitness, female muscularity is overlaid by techniques of sexualization, falsifying the notion of fitness, and trivializing female sports.

OBJECTIFYING THE FEMALE BODY

The sexualization of the body is also a favoured image in magazine and press photographs of well-known female athletes (Duncan 1990). Glamour poses which ignore the skills of performance and those which highlight sexuality transform athletes into objects of desire and envy, providing an unambiguous message that sportswomen are sexual women. Annette Kuhn (1985:12) argues that a glamorous image is one that is manipulated and 'is peculiarly powerful in that it plays on the desire of the spectator in a particularly pristine way: beauty or sexuality is desirable exactly to the extent that it is idealized and unattainable'. Although glamorous representations of sportswomen occur most frequently in the tabloids, they are found in quality newspapers as well[3] – for example, at the time of the Seoul Summer Olympics in 1988, newspapers of all persuasions had photographs of Florence Griffith Joyner (Flo Jo) in poses focusing on her carefully nurtured, long fingernails, as well as highlighting her physicality and sexuality; they also all had photographs of Katarina Witt at the Winter Olympics the same year which captured the allure of the event and Witt's obviously provocative 'look' and sexy poses, emphasizing shots which focused on particular parts of her body and clothing – a convention of sports photography. Photographs are accompanied by blatantly sexist comments which confirm the message of the image – for example, in the *Wimbledon Television Viewer's Guide 1987*, Gabriela Sabatini is referred to as a 'pin-up' and 'an eye-catcher both on and off the court. . . . As graceful as a jungle cat, with flashing Latin eyes'; Flo Jo is regularly characterized as 'leggy', 'lithe', 'gorgeous' and 'pouting'; Monica Seles is noted for being a 'fashion plate . . . constantly adding the latest designer-wear to her sizeable wardrobe. . . . Right down to her varnished fingernails, she looks the perfect product' (*Daily Mail*, 26 June 1989); in the *Daily Express* (24 August 1988) Fatima Whitbread is observed to be 'tall, elegant, and at close quarters astonishingly pretty' and to have 'finely-tuned feminine shoulders'; and in several newspapers, accounts of the Commonwealth Games (1991) showed a photograph of Sharron Davies in a sexy pose and with a glass of champagne, modelling a new swimsuit that she had designed herself with captions such as 'Suits you, Sharron'. Although female athletes who are glamorous in a commercialized way, or who are sexually 'different' or 'deviant', are those who are photographed or written about most frequently, the sexualized image is a favoured one for *all* female athletes. But female sports stars are not simply passive subjects in this process – although they are caught up in the imperatives of modern consumer culture in ways which provide gratification for other people, they also exploit their own sexuality to get media attention, public interest and money (Heaven and Rowe 1991).

STEREOTYPED FEMININITY

Although there are national and regional differences in the representation of gender in the media between and within different countries in the West, there is an accelerating process of homogenization of images of femininity and sexuality (Boutilier and San Giovanni 1983, Cary 1990, Duncan 1990, Heaven and Rowe 1991, Klein 1988, McKay and Rowe 1987). Throughout western Europe, North America and the Antipodes, the construction of images of males and females is stereotyped as if the differences between them are real and 'natural'. Men tend to be portrayed as physical and aggressive, and their actions and accomplishments are highlighted, whereas women's femininity is symbolized as we have seen through glamorous and sexualized shots, or through implied masculinization, by the use of informal and intimate names, and by references to athletes' roles as girls, wives and mothers. For example, it was claimed that Fatima Whitbread was 'sacrificing any thoughts of children by being the world's best javelin thrower' (*Today*, 24 September 1988); and references to Liz McColgan's role as wife and mother were more numerous than references to her athletic successes. In the *Guardian* (31 August 1991) there were two photographs of Liz McColgan who had just won Britain's first gold medal at the World Athletic Championships in Tokyo – neither of them was an action shot. The first was on the front page and showed her draped in a large Union Jack flag – this was a cause for nationalist celebration – the second was a tiny photograph tucked at the bottom corner of one of the sports pages, showing her wrapped in the arms of her husband Peter – and in the text we are told that they will shortly be 'winging their way home to their baby daughter Eilish'. Taking up the rest of that page and the adjacent one was a huge action photograph of Mike Powell executing the new world long-jump record, with a caption 'Powell leaps into the 21st century. . . . A giant step forward for mankind . . . Mike Powell flies across the sandpit to shatter Bob Beamon's record.'

The body is a signifier of sexual difference and the ideology of gender difference is a trademark of the sports media. In newspapers and magazines images of sportsmen in action proliferate, but we constantly see symbols of women's femininity, rather than pictures of female athleticism. Popular versions of masculinity and femininity which suggest sexual difference are repeated and become commonplace, universalized, so that they feel 'natural' and acceptable, whereas in reality they are preferred, constructed images. Women's implied vulnerability and dependence on men are often the focus of sports pictures and reporting. For example, men tend to be presented as the advisers, monitors and facilitators of female sportswomen: Steffi Graff's father is described as 'the driving force behind her success' (*Daily Mail*, 3 July 1989) and John Lloyd as Caterina Lindqvist's mentor' (*Daily Mail*, 6 July 1989; Cary 1990). During the 1988 Seoul Olympics victorious female athletes were invariably photographed in the arms of a male associate – husband, fiancé, father or coach (Seton 1989), and their emotions were a major focus of attention. In contrast to action shots of male athletes, we see female athletes supported or embraced by husbands or boyfriends; crying with elation or disappointment; in situations and poses that have no apparent connection with sports; in domestic contexts; pregnant or with children; and with special hairdos, make-up, and clothing . . .

Sportswomen are treated ambivalently – on the one hand they are news-worthy for their athletic efforts and successes, but because sport still poses a threat to popular ideas about femininity, readers are assured in various ways that they remain 'real' women. Similar procedures occur on the television:

> The audience is reassured that *despite* their involvement in sport, they are still real women, an assertion backed up by reference to family, husbands and children (the implication being that sport is a mere diversion). Where they are too serious, too self-evidently fit, and especially if they're not British, they may be implicitly admonished for being not real women, either physically (hence the notorious imposition of sex-tests on some athletes) or sexually.
>
> (Whannel 1992: 127)

In the case of Wang Junxia, the 20-year-old Chinese athlete who slashed the women's 10,000 metre world record by an astonishing 42 seconds, the *Guardian* (9 September 1993) detracted from her athlethicism in a number of ways. At first glance, the account is brief and apparently inauspicious, with a small accompanying photograph depicting only her upper body, in direct contrast to the celebration of Mike Powell's long-jump record, dis-cussed on p. 163. The headline – 'Wang almost too good to be true' – was positioned next to a 'Drugs in Sport' report and, together with the claim in the text that her achievement will 'add to the pressure on China to show they are achieving these results by fair means', strongly implies, without evi-dence, that it was a drug-induced victory and not a 'real' record.

TECHNIQUES OF SEXUALIZATION

A recently popularized model of sports photography is the shot of the sportswoman which has an erotic quality. In her research in the USA Duncan (1990) shows how female athletes are sometimes photographed in poses similar to those of women in soft-core pornography, where the camera lingers on the signifiers of sexuality – for example, parts of the body such as buttocks, breasts, thighs and genital region; a facial expression which is sexually inviting such as parted lips or a pout; an intimate shot of the athlete suggestive of sexuality – as she adjusts her bathing suit or leotard. She argues that such presentations appeal to the young male heterosexual voyeur. One example is a photograph of the Soviet rhythmic gymnast Marina Lobatch (*Sports Illustrated*, 10 October 1988) – the focus is on her crotch as she does a standing split, one leg positioned near her ear (Duncan 1990: 30).

The sexualization of the female body occurs on television as well. Helen Lenskyj (1986) writes about the 'obscene' portrayal of women in American television exercise shows and Margaret MacNeill (1988: 203) goes into detail about a Canadian television programme, *20 Minute Workout*. She shows how 'the predominance of aerial and upwardly tilting camera shots helps create sexual images rather than images of physical activity', and describes the tendency to focus on the mid-section of the body (hips, thighs, buttocks) which 'objectifies an image of the "sexually active" female body'. She analyses camera angles and techniques, the choreography and directions of the production crew, and the use of music and commentary, which, she argues, combine together to 'sell sex appeal rather than fitness development'. Margaret MacNeill (208) argues that 'the television viewer is situated in the role of voyeur capable of exerting domination over the image of active women'. On keep-fit programmes for women on British television, the sexualization of the female body is less crude and less frequent, and there have been attempts to break down such stereotyping and to encourage women with different abilities, backgrounds and physiques (the elderly and those who have recently had babies, for example) into regular exercise regimes. There have also been a number of initiatives to produce serious and informative programmes about women's sports on British television, but the time devoted to them is minimal and the tendency is to overshadow the athletic image by the sexualization of the athlete. For example, the language of the male commentators is regularly and often quite explicitly riddled with observations about the appearances of female performers and with sexual innuendo. In a 40 minute programme about football,[4] less than three minutes was devoted to the first-ever Women's World Cup. Having praised the standard of play in general, the commentator, noting the comparative weakness of the goal-keeping, looked at the camera in the sure knowledge that he would raise a laugh with the cameramen and said, 'You'd think they'd have got it right – being good at netball and "handling the balls"!' Another example is provided by the commentator during the 1989 World Ice-Skating Championships who made a blatantly sexist remark on BBC television when he was observing Claudia Leizint's performance: 'There are a lot of men here who think she should be at the top of the rostrum – but I don't think it's because of her skating!' Individual comments of this sort tend to be treated as unimportant and 'just a good laugh', but their effectiveness in objectifying sportswomen and belittling women's sports is because they are one tiny element of a huge structure of gender relations of power. Because sexualized images of female athletes are just one example of the general bombardment of sexualized images of women, the message that female sexuality is more important than sporting ability is very powerful. Because sexism is part of the everyday discourse of sports – a taken-for-granted way of thinking and behaving – it forms the basis of institutionalized discrimination.

The media do not treat women's sports in an exclusively sexist fashion. Recent American research about the coverage of basketball and tennis on television reveals that 'commentators today are less likely than their pre-decessors to sexualize or trivialize women athletes overtly' but that the language used 'tends to mark women's sports and women athletes as other, infantalize women athletes, and frame their accomplishments negatively or ambivalently' (Messner, Duncan and Jensen 1993: 133). The quality press in Britain occasionally publish informative and analytical articles and there are some programmes on television which portray women's sports in a sensitive and interesting way. However, non-sexist treatment provides a clever decoy which suggests that women's sports *are* being treated reasonably. The reality is that the coverage of women's sports in the press and on television is minimal in comparison with men's sports (Sports Council 1992; Messner, Duncan and Jensen 1993; see Chapter 8), and only a tiny percentage of time and space overall is given to 'serious' reporting and programming. The overall message, therefore, is that men's sports are the 'real' thing, and women's sports, by comparison, are unimportant. So the variety of messages put out by the sports media gives the idea of objectivity some legitimacy which makes effective the way the media as a whole continue to reproduce popular and specially constructed ideas about what constitutes 'masculinity' and 'femininity' in sports.

SPORTS AND EROTICIZATION

Sporting images are particularly popular in advertisements that use erotic sexuality to promote the sales of women's health, fashion and beauty prod-ucts (whether or not the product has anything to do with sports). We are presented with images of contrived, alluring bodies, rather than 'real', everyday ones: the sporting connection is incidental; the sexual one is of paramount importance. This manoeuvre is apparent every year at the Recman confer-ence (the GB Sports Council's annual 'flagship' conference), where exhibitors use women's bodies as commodities to sell equipment (in contradiction to the Sports Council's rhetoric of gender equity and positive action towards that end). The meanings we apply to representations of this sort are based on ideas we already have about femininity and sports from our everyday lives. Janice Winship (1980: 218) argues that these ideas are 'anchored by the patriarchal relations in which we as individuals have a history and which we already know about'. Such signification of the female body depends on sexual imagery and, more specifically, on the female as a sexual person: these images eroticize the female body and present it as an intimate object made accessible to the voyeur. Again, they trivialize female sports, using them simply as channels for the commodification of the female body. In these instances female sporting images derive their meanings from the link with commercial representations of the female body: the marketing of the female body through sports is extremely profitable.

Not surprisingly, sports photography has become a significant part of the mass market in pornography. Models in immodest, suggestive or erotic poses, holding and wearing sporting accoutrements, make popular pornographic images. Snooker cues, cricket bats, boxing gloves and footballs are such obvious symbols of manliness that for bare-breasted women to be holding them suggests a provocative sexual message: that 'real' sports are for men, and women are there to provide excitement and arousal. It is as if women's bodies are part of the equipment – apparatuses of male 'sporting' pleasure – 'playthings' for men. Sportified images of female sexuality are metaphors for male desire. As in advertising, this is a case of stereotyping females according to their sex and using their sexuality as an apparent vehicle for male pleasure. Whether female images are used in advertisements for selling products, or explicitly to titillate male voyeurs in order to increase sales, is immaterial – they are both representations similar to soft-porn, and examples of eroticized subordination. Because sports are popular culture – usually understood as male culture – to combine them with images which exaggerate the insignia of female sexuality produces a provocative illusion. This is why sporting pornography has become a surprisingly popular feature of the commodification and exploitation of female sexuality that permeates modern life.

REDEFINING SPORTING IMAGES

But the link between sports and female sexuality is not without contradictions. In sports there is a strange intersection between the notion of the 'natural' and artificial. Sportswear has shaped and reshaped the female body – hidden the body, revealed the body, flattened the chest, and lengthened the legs. But sportswomen are not simply passive dupes yielding to the dictates of fashion and commercialization. The issue that is seldom addressed is that women are just as interested in sexuality as men – the important question is whether they are treated as active subjects or as objects (Williams 1990). It is clear that female athletes are making positive choices and creating images which are radically different from previously stereotyped ones of women in sports. Not only are sportswomen making new displays of physical power, but also new displays of sexual power. Flo Jo, for example, presents herself in a manner which is an unequivocal display of her own femaleness as well as her supreme physicality and athleticism – she weight-trains to promote muscle development, puts on tight-clinging and modish athletic gear, nurtures long and painted fingernails, and wears make-up and jewellery. The 'look' of the female body in sports has changed not only with changes in sportswear, but also with changes in the dimensions and musculature of the body resulting from training, dieting and drug-taking. Both clothed *and* naked female bodies in sports are socially constructed. In some contexts, the recent combination in sports of fashionableness with sexiness, self-consciousness, youthfulness and fighting fitness produces a radical and powerful image of aggressive femininity which is influencing the production of feminine identities in sports. Because sports are media for the justification for the female body being scantily clad, they are some of the few public contexts where men see women in this state and so can be used as vehicles for fantasy. But new images of female athleticism seem to contradict the popular sexual idea that women are passive and compliant – commodities for voyeurism and possession. Physical power has come to be understood as synonymous with sexual power, and exercise is recommended for women who want to be confident and *active* lovers. Although the marriage of female sports with the sexualization of the female body has never been stronger, the relationship is complex: sportswomen can be understood to be actively sexual *and* sexually exploited.

The idea of power being invested in the female sporting body is understood most clearly in those modes of sport seen as being suited to males which have been taken up by women as new forms of identity. Female body-building represents a form of female power which can be interpreted as a positive act by women to take control of their own bodies. The focus is the physique – the body itself. The body is the raw material and the sport is intended to transform weak and undefined flesh into strong and well-defined muscle. Body-building is described as an art form – the aim is to work on the body, to perfect it, and to display it. It is both ascetic and aesthetic, treating hard work and muscularity as beneficial to women. Female body-building makes an unashamed display of the female physique, and creates radical notions of the female body, beauty and sexuality. But the creation of muscular women puts the 'natural' order of gender under threat, so that female body-building is also characterized as a sport which produces a distorted masculinized body upon which stereotyped symbols of femininity are imposed. Female body-builders are in a position of contradiction – to become muscular they adhere to strict diets in order radically to reduce body fat and enhance muscle definition, but because this process eliminates breast definition, 'in order to balance muscle and sex appeal, some contenders are undergoing silicone breast implants to artificially meet the criteria' (MacNeill 1988: 209). If a woman is physically strong and muscular (a traditional symbol of male power), then power is actually and symbolically invested in her body, but if she is also adorned with the accoutrements of mainstream femininity (wearing a bikini, with ribbons in her hair and wearing make-up and nail varnish), she is making a statement which overrides the athletic image. These are the contradictory techniques of female body-building – those that enhance fitness and muscularity and symbolize the empowerment of women, and those for the display of contrived femininity which symbolize manipulation. In the case of female body-building idealized femininity and sexuality are *prior to* and become *more significant* than muscularity and athleticism. Furthermore, the tremendous growth of the sport over the last decade has been mediated by male-defined standards of femininity, illustrated by the International Federation's guideline for 'assessing the female physique':

> the judge must bear in mind that he or she is judging a woman's body-building competition and is looking for the ideal *feminine* physique. Therefore, the most important aspect is shape, a feminine shape. The other aspects are similar to those described for assessing men, but in regard to muscular development, it must not be carried out to excess where it resembles the massive musculature of the male physique.

The notion of a 'feminine shape' implies narrow definitions of femininity and sexuality and marginalizes or masks alternatives. The diversities of images of female sexualization in sports and their apparent liberative tendencies are limited by the privileging of a powerful heterosexual code. The only publicly acceptable sexual orientation for female body-builders is heterosexuality and, in common with other sportswomen, many of them have a deep fear of being labelled lesbian, hence their concern to construct images which are not sexually ambivalent. It is not, therefore, at all clear in what ways the potentially radical form of sporting femininity in female body-building is connected to the broader structures of gender relations of power in society (to what extent it may be supporting them or challenging them).

HETEROSEXUAL FEMININITY AND THE FEAR OF MASCULINIZATION

We have seen in this chapter how sports produce a visual language of the physical body, obsessed with gender, and embodying images of femaleness and sexuality. And it is also apparent that these images have symbolic and ideological significance because they are based on conventional heterosexual assumptions. In mainstream sports heterosexuality is viewed as the only rational, 'natural' and acceptable orientation; the reason why sportswomen, like body-builders, feel the necessity to conform to dominant images of heterosexual femininity, is because female muscularity is treated as a sign of masculinization. The anxiety about effeminization among males is paralleled by the fear that female athletes will acquire masculine characteristics. In sports, as in other areas of public life, the construction of heterosexual femininity is a powerful form of control.

Although there has been a broadening of definitions of sporting femininity, and well-honed athletic female bodies are now openly embraced as sexually attractive according to heterosexual criteria, nevertheless, athletes who are heavily muscled, small-breasted, and do not display on their bodies the usual insignia of conventional femininity, face insinuations about defeminization. There was a classic example in a report in the *Sunday Times* at the time of the 1984 Summer Olympics: the Czechoslovak runner, Jarmila Kratochvilova, was castigated for her implied 'deviant' sexuality and contrasted with Mary Decker, who was celebrated for fulfilling the stereotype of idealized heterosexual femininity:

> [Mary] Decker is the all-American female retort to the heavy artillery of Eastern Europe . . . pretty, sexy Mary Decker who, in this Amazonian world, wears make-up on the track and shaves her legs. . . . In the 3000 and then the 1500 metres, Decker simply whipped those hard-faced East Europeans with the ambiguous biceps.
>
> (Freedman 1984)

The sexual ambiguity of female athletes is pounced upon in the media with greater frequency and is given more pernicious treatment than the homosexuality of sportsmen. Martina Navratilova (1985: 207) argues that

> Women and men are treated differently even in something as private as sexuality. Sports-writers have no problem asking a woman, 'Is it true you're sleeping with other women?', but they'd never ask a man whether he was sleeping with other men!

Navratilova's lesbian sexuality has been exposed to the glare of the media, but she has also argued that, regardless of sexual preference, women are treated less sympathetically than men by the media. When referring to Magic Johnson, the American basketball player who after admitting he was HIV positive was given public sympathy, she said:

> If I had the Aids virus, would people be understanding? No, because they would say I'm gay – I had it coming . . . they're accepting it with him, because supposedly he'd got it through heterosexual contact. If it had happened to a heterosexual woman who had been with a hundred or two hundred men, they would call her a whore and a slut, the corporations would drop her like a lead balloon and she would never get another job in her life. . . . It's a very big double standard. I had a very good endorsement possibility about seven years ago and it came up to the president of the company and he said no, because she's gay.
>
> (*Guardian*, 21 November 1991)

Although in recent years cultural and artistic investigations and portrayals of lesbian relationships have been treated more sensitively and seriously than in the past (for example, the 1982 film *Personal Best*, which tells of a love affair between two penthaletes), nevertheless, as Lenskyj (1986: 107) points out, greater lesbian visibility has not solved the problems of homophobia in sports. Tracey Edwards, who led an all-female yachting crew, makes explicit the usually unarticulated views of many sportswomen in her response to the rumours that her boat could be renamed 'Lesbos':

All-male crews have been yacht-racing for centuries and no-one has ever suggested they're a bunch of raging queers. But the moment an all-women crew gets together it's assumed we're all lesbians.

(Daily Mail, 18 October 1990, quoted in Cary 1990: 33)

Sports have been classified as 'masculine-' and 'feminine-appropriate' because of fiercely defended heterosexist traditions. Conventional femininity does not incorporate images of physical power and muscularity and female athletes who have such physiques have always stood the risk of being treated in a derogatory way. Women who play traditional male sports, such as cricket, football and rugby, face the greatest criticism and exposure to ridicule. The implications that athletes may be 'pseudo-men', 'unfeminine', 'gay', 'masculine', 'mannish', 'butch', 'dykes', or 'lesbians' put pressure on heterosexual sportswomen to play the 'femininity game' and stigmatize homosexuality. It is a device which separates from one another women with different sexual preferences. Sports construct differences between different femininities (and masculinities) as well as between males and females. Because lesbians are made to feel uncomfortable in the fiercely heterosexual world of mainstream sports, they tend to hide their sexuality, or, not surprisingly, form their own sports clubs and associations where they can 'be themselves' and feel 'free' (see Chapter 10). Images of sexual deviancy produce the conflict that many women feel between sports and their preferred concept of femininity.

If compulsory heterosexuality were no longer a legitimizing force in women's sports they would, as Lenskyj (1986: 57) suggests, 'be feminine simply by virtue of female involvement, not by reason of [their] alleged compatibility with the ideals of femininity or heterosexual appeal'. But it is tremendously hard to change ideas about 'normal' sexuality and to tackle discrimination against homosexuality in women's sports when organizations that are supporting their expansion continue to work with an implicitly heterosexual model. It is also a problem that is rooted in men's sports and in society. Changes in women's sports cannot happen unilaterally when boys continue to be schooled through sports to accept an aggressive model of masculinity that embodies compulsory heterosexuality, the subordination of women, and the marginalization of gay men (Pronger 1990; Messner and Sabo 1990), or when gender divisions and heterosexuality are organizing principles that permeate society.

Messner and Sabo (1990: 7) point out how role theory simplifies the complexities of gender. They argue that the tendency in role theory to 'insist on the existence of "a male sex role" and "a female sex role" inadvertently legitimizes and normalizes dominant forms of masculinity and femininity while marginalizing others'. When 'masculinity' and 'femininity' are defined and talked about, the automatic assumption is that we all know what the terms are referring to – heterosexual ideals of what it means to be a man and to be a woman. The 'silences' are powerful – these terms do not imply a man who is small and gentle, for example, or a woman who is muscular and aggressive. Furthermore, they imply gender relations based on difference and separateness – ideas which we have seen are systematically reproduced and naturalized in family situations, in schools, in the media, and in sports and leisure. In most settings, these are relations of male dominance and female subordination – part of a comprehensive structure of power and a 'whole way of life'. This is why Connell (1987: 183) argues that while 'hegemonic masculinity' usefully describes the global dominance of hetero-sexual men (constructed in relation to various subordinated masculinities as well as in relation to women), there is no parallel hegemonic femininity. He prefers the idea of 'emphasized femininity': heterosexual femininity is the 'emphasized' image of femininity in sports which, as in other areas of life, though less vulnerable than marginalized lesbian femininity, can be under-stood only in the context of the overall subordination of women to men.

CONCLUSION

The power of images is essentially ideological – they reflect a common system of values and meanings. And ideologies about female sports are not just abstract ideas; they constitute a material force which permeates experi-ence and is difficult to change. However, although there is a tendency towards the standardization of images of female sports – a preference for 'emphasized' femininity – images of gender are changing and sportswomen are making different and personalized statements about themselves. We have seen in this chapter, how, through imagery, sports link the worlds of sexuality, fantasy and consumerism which severely limits women's choices. But ideology is deeply contradictory, and in some contexts, girls and women are constructing alternative sporting identities. There are important incen-tives amongst sports feminists in Britain to build new images of women in sports which could transform traditional attitudes and stereotypes. One such incentive has resulted in collaboration between the Sports Council, the Women's Sports Foundation and Hobson's (publishers) to produce a new magazine entitled *Women and Sport*. Still in the pilot stage, it is intended to promote the idea of 'Sport for All' and to provide positive images of women in sports.

Although women are treated as objects in sports much more than men, John Berger's idea that 'men act and women appear' (1972: 47) treats women as passive dupes rather than active agents. It ignores the ways in which power can be invested in the female sporting body. This chapter has focused on dominant ideas about female sports and, in particular, images of sexuality because, in their contemporary forms, sports appear to celebrate and make public female sexuality. However, there are different and emerging images of female sports which are questioning past conventions and new forms of dominance, which will be examined in the last two chapters. Current representations of the female sporting body show some collapse of conventional points of reference, some acceptance of values which have previously been marginalized, and the emergence of new, radicalized images of female physicality. These representations are part of a process of continuing conflicts and contradictions. In the 1990s there are no universal conventions of female sports and no universal representations of the female sporting body. But although cultural value is much less clear, this is not a result of random events, but a result of our experience, history and culture.

The question 'FEMININITY OR "MUSCULINITY"?' points to the connection between female sports and sexual politics which has been seriously neglected in feminist sports literature. Since bodily skill, strength and muscularity have symbolically been the source of the empowerment of men, feminists should look to sports in their struggle for greater autonomy.

Chapter 8

Gender relations of power
Institutionalized discrimination

INTRODUCTION

One of the continuities of the post-war period has been the persistence of inequalities in cultural power between men and women. Although in sports there has been some narrowing of the gender gap, male domination continues to be a foundational principle of their social organization. The power structures of most sports are heavily weighted in favour of men and, in general, female sports have an inferior status both socially and financially. The ideas dealt with in Chapter 7 (about symbolic representations of difference between males and females) provide a basis for looking here at structural inequalities of gender. More specifically, this chapter is to do with different ways and contexts in which men wield power over women in sports – i.e. with partriarchal relations of power.

The power relations of gender in sports are complex, contradictory and controversial. The situation is not static and women are becoming increasingly aware of the nature of discrimination and are struggling to change it. Optimism about change is linked to the sure knowledge that no set of cultural arrangements can be totally monolithic; the ideologies of the powerful in sports are not the only ideologies. Henley (1977: 205) explains that 'Neither the history, nor the pervasiveness, nor the intricate workings, nor the seeming inexorableness of power make it immutable . . . power is constantly being broken down and overturned'.

GENDER RELATIONS AND THE STATE

State intervention in leisure and sports has increased in recent years, resulting in more opportunities in the public sector which, together with the expanding scope of commercialized enterprise, has arguably produced a greater choice for women than ever before. However, large numbers of women in British society, in common with those from other countries in the West, are unable to take advantage of existing opportunities, and lack the power to formulate choices for themselves. Although liberalism embodies the idea that the state is a neutral, benevolent institution and that sex inequality can be put right by legal processes and public spending, the government in the United Kingdom has failed to deal with the particular problems that women face in sports and leisure. Furthermore, even though governments have provided openings for equality between the sexes, no such legislation can be properly effective as long as the power of men over women subtly permeates society.

In 1975 the UK Sex Discrimination Act (SDA) was passed. It makes discrimination on the basis of sex illegal in the general contexts of employment and education; in the provision of goods, facilities and services; and in the disposal of premises. The Equal Opportunities Commission (EOC) is a quasi-governmental organization set up to implement the legislation and help individuals to challenge discrimination based on sex. However, although the purpose of the Act is to eliminate public forms of discrimination, it is constructed in such a way as to make it difficult to do so whenever people resist change, and whenever there are different opinions about what constitutes sex discrimination. This has been the case in sports and physical education. For example, because the terms of the Act do not apply to single-sex educational establishments, it was only in 1986, in reaction to the arguments of the European Commission and the European Communities that the SDA contravened the EEC Equal Treatment Directive of 1976, that mixed physical education teacher-training courses became obligatory (Talbot 1987: 13). However, the British government failed to play a pro-active role – the Department of Education and Science (responsible for PE) did not positively comply with the European Directive, but rather decided not to challenge it. Not surprisingly, the resultant changes in teacher-training have had a limited influence on the traditions of single-sex PE programmes in secondary schools. They are justified on the grounds that they are 'equal but different' (ILEA 1984: 22; Scraton 1992; see previous chapter). It is tremendously hard to alter the entrenched attitudes of those in positions of power when they underpin the lived practices of institutions. The Act does not compel local authorities to provide additional resources in order to facilitate equal opportunities in PE, nor does it require positive action in favour of a disadvantaged sex. Therefore changes to radicalize gender relations in PE have been minimal.

Outside education the problems of shifting uneven gender relations are greater. According to sections 29 and 34, private and single-sex clubs and voluntary associations are exempt from the Sex Discrimination Act, and since most sports clubs and associations in the UK fall into these categories, they can legitimately continue to function in ways that subordinate women. As the Sports Council (1992: 3) points out, private clubs can operate 'overtly sexist policies and discriminatory practices without legal penalty'. ERICCA (Equal Rights in Clubs Campaign for Action) was a women's action group which set out to change the gender traditions of working men's clubs by challenging the power wielded by men in the Clubs and Institutes Union.

The group campaigned for a change in the SDA legislation so that voluntary clubs with a mixed clientele would be obliged to give women full membership rights. The specific stimulus for this incentive was the frustration experienced by female snooker players who could not get equal access with men to snooker facilities. It is because men in such sports as cricket, crown green bowling, golf and snooker have a hugely unequal monopoly of resources that women who are keen to participate are seriously disadvantaged. It is common practice in male-controlled clubs and associations for women to have only associate membership – this means that they are prevented from having equal access to facilities, they have minimal playing time, and they are denied voting rights so that they can do nothing to change the rules of the club within its constitutional framework. In numerous contexts, women are absolutely dependent upon the goodwill of men to be able to play at all. Therefore, in 1988, in an effort to improve the position for those women who wanted access to male-controlled resources, the EOC proposed to parliament that amendments to the SDA be made to 'require clubs and organizations who have allowed women members in the previous three years to give women full, rather than associate, membership and voting rights' (Sports Council 1992: 3). These proposals have never been given parliamentary time (which suggests that no member of parliament considers the issue important) and, anyway, even if they were adopted, all-male institutions which have privileged resourcing would not be required to admit female members. If there were new legislation to embrace all clubs and associations, it would, ironically, threaten the autonomy that women enjoy in all-female groups. The idea that it is simple to use legislation to equalize relationships of power between different groups is misleading. Because of tradition, the problems of change are complex and shifts towards more equal sharing of power between men and women in sports have been more the result of unrelenting pressure from women, and from men campaigning on their behalf, than from government legislation.

Section 44 of the Act is another exemption clause which has disadvantaged women. Because it refers to activities where 'strength, speed and physique' are important so that the 'average' man or woman would be at a disadvantage, it sanctions the banning of mixed competitions. This clause has always been used to argue that females, because of their physiques, should not be allowed to play against males. It has been applied not only to adult competitors, but also to pre-pubertal youngsters, at which age girls are on average bigger and stronger than boys. The best-known example occurred in 1978, when a 12-year-old girl, Theresa Bennett, was banned by the Football Association (FA) from playing football with boys in a local league. In a court case, 'Theresa Bennett versus the Football Association', the FA's decision was initially overturned on the grounds that it had failed to provide her with recreation facilities, but then the FA won an appeal under section 44. Although Theresa's defence argued that since she was pre-pubertal she was not disadvantaged physically by the greater strength of her male peers, nevertheless the judgment hinged on outmoded biological beliefs that 'Women have many other qualities superior to those of men but they have not got the strength and stamina to run, kick, to tackle and so forth' (ILEA 1984: 23). This result became case law and for another decade was used to prevent other young girls from playing in mixed football teams. Nevertheless, it generated growing interest in the particular problems of schoolgirl football, sensitized primary schools to the contradiction between their equal opportunity policies and actual practices, and resulted in active opposition to FA policy. By the end of the 1980s, more primary schools were including football for girls in their curriculums, and finally in 1990, after years of resistance, the FA capitulated to the constant pressure demanding a change in its rule disallowing mixed football for children under 11 years of age. At the same time the English Schools' Football Association was made responsible for girls' as well as boys' football and it is now the FA's policy to promote the women's game (see Chapter 10). The example of the FA's original intransigence over schoolgirl football and its subsequent ungenerous policy change demonstrates again the failure of legislation to influence change directly. It is also the case that poorly formulated legislation can lead to confusion – for example, the EOC Schools Unit has particular problems about taking action because school *sport* is subject to section 44 of the SDA (because of the role of governing bodies), whereas *curriculum PE* is not subject to section 44 (because it is an educational service). Not surprisingly, the action of individuals outside the legal framework can result in more immediate and effective changes in institutionalized gender relations than legislation.

But in spite of its drawbacks the SDA has been used in some court cases to challenge discrimination. It has been used successfully in changing policies about female referees in judo and rugby league and in facilitating the promotion of women physical education teachers. But progress is slow – very few cases of discrimination are ever taken to court because individuals have fewer resources than the institutions they are opposing – and because discrimination against women in sports occurs every day in unconscious as well as conscious ways. Nevertheless, although the SDA has had limited direct influence on the implementation of non-discrimination in sports, together with pressure from action groups, it has been a catalyst for change. Sex-equality legislation in Britain has provided legitimacy for people's opposition to traditional structures of power.

State intervention is not necessarily progressive in its effects on gender relations. An example is the Local Government and Finance Act of 1988, which incorporated a framework for compulsory competitive tendering (CCT – putting out to private tender the running of local authority facilities). In 1989 CCT legislation was extended to the management of leisure and sports facilities, and its implementation was required during 1992. CCT focuses on money: it came at a time of recession, when the government was monitoring local authority spending, and when leisure services were already vulnerable. Public leisure centres, playing fields and swimming pools, for example, are still owned by local authorities, but run commercially. Contracts can be won by local authorities themselves, private individuals, or companies. The popular understanding of the Act is, therefore, that public facilities have been privatized. CCT legislation *allows* local authorities to make certain stipulations about how their facilities are run (for example, by regulating prices, by insisting on positive discrimination in favour of those social groups which cannot afford competitive prices, or by requiring that crèche facilities be provided), but does not *require* them to do so. The reaction to CCT is therefore mixed – in some areas local authorities have ensured as much as possible the continuity of existing services; in other areas there is a blatant attempt to cut costs and make profits. It is inevitable, however, that throughout the country contractors given the tender will promote services that make money and cut back on services that do not. The work of local authorities has been drastically reduced in recent years anyway (Houlihan 1991), by government legislation and by the recession. Throughout the 1980s the British government systematically cut revenue to local authorities and the grant was further reduced for overspending. All local authorities have therefore been forced to cut back on spending on sports and recreation; all local authorities have reduced, and some have even halted, capital investment in sports; and some have been unable to continue maintenance work (ibid.). The local authorities which have been worst hit are those with radical welfare policies, almost all in working-class areas. Although it is impossible so soon after the implementation of CCT to assess how it will affect the position of women, it is likely that middle-class women who can afford competitive prices will in general be little affected by this legislation, whereas the participation interests of vulnerable groups (for example, women with young children, those who are single parents and those with low-waged partners) will diminish because they are less profitable than those of other user groups. There is also increasing concern that, with broadening competitive tendering, the management structures of 'public' sports and leisure facilities will become even more fiercely masculine.

The Education Reform Act (ERA), passed in 1988 and implemented in 1990, is another example of government legislation which has indirectly disenfranchised some women. The Act allows for the Local Management of Schools (LMS – the delegation of financial control to individual schools), which has had consequences for some local communities where there has been dual use of school sports facilities in the past. A number of schools with some of the best capital sports resources have sold them (especially playing fields) in order to survive educational cut-backs, so that what used to be a public resource has become private property. And where sports facilities have not been sold, they are increasingly being opened in the evenings and during vacations in order to bring in revenue for the school. In such cases, it is inevitable that unprofitable, disadvantaged groups will not be catered for, and the raised costs of sports participation will militate in particular against such groups as low-waged women and single mothers. It is not that some groups of women are the only ones who are affected in this way, but they suffer from the 'double discrimination' of symbolic constraints and those of economic disadvantage. The political abandonment of welfarism illustrates clearly the combined effect of gender and class on sports participation.

EQUAL OPPORTUNITIES IN THE USA

In the United States legislation has been used more directly in the fight for equal rights in sport; nevertheless, it has also failed to eliminate discrimination against women. The 1972 Title IX of the Education Amendments (to the Civil Rights Act of 1964) was intended to remove preferential treatment on the basis of sex in any education programme or activity receiving federal funds. As soon as it was passed, Title IX was used by sportswomen to push for equality with males, resulting in an immediate increase in resources and participation rates (Gaccione 1991). Before Title IX there were enormous inequities between spending on male and female sport, sometimes on the scale of 50:1, and there were huge differences in participation figures for boys and girls. Figures for school-age girls, for example, increased dramatically: 'In 1971, only 294,015 girls participated in high school sports, compared with 3,666,917 boys. By the 1989–90 academic year, there were 1,858,659 girls participating in high school sports, compared with 3,398,192 boys' (Messner, Duncan and Jensen 1993: 122). However, during the following years, after men's and women's programmes and departments were merged in response to the legislation, men reaffirmed their dominance in collegiate sport by taking the most powerful positions in the new mixed departments, effectively disadvantaging women more than had been the case when they ran their own programmes. Since Title IX, collegiate sport in the USA has experienced a decline in the numbers of women coaching women's sports, and a devastating drop in the percentage of women's programmes headed by women – from 79 per cent in 1974 to 15 per cent in 1986 (White 1991a: 12). Hult argues that Title IX has led to male control of amateur sports in high schools, colleges, non-school agencies, and the Olympic movement. She claims that 'Title IX has left untouched pervasive fundamental inequities in leadership, decision-making authority, coaching systems and the role models for girls in all athletic situations' (Hult 1989: 259).

The demise of the Association for Intercollegiate Athletics for Women (AIAW) also illustrates the contradictory effects of legislation specifically intended to improve the position of women. The AIAW was formed in 1971 with a membership of 278 institutions, growing rapidly to a peak of 970 in 1979. It assumed the leadership role for women's athletics in the United

States, embodying a student-centred, education-oriented approach, and resisting the professionalized model of men's college athletics. However, Title IX's mandate for parity between men and women pushed the AIAW towards a more competitive model of sports and provided the incentive for a merger with the men's association. In 1984 the AIAW was disbanded after losing its struggle with the predominantly male National Collegiate Athletic Association (NCAA) to control female athletics (Hult 1989; Wilson 1988). Ironically, the demise of the AIAW has also resulted in fewer championship opportunities for women – 'in the last years of the AIAW, 34 championships were held for women in 21 sports. This past year (1990-1991) 41 championships in 19 sports were offered for both men and women in the NCAA' (Gaccione 1991: 11).

TARGETING WOMEN IN SPORTS

The development of women's sports has been affected not only by legislation that is indirectly concerned with sports, but also by legislation and programmes directed specifically at sports and women's participation. Throughout the West, sports have become increasingly politicized and are part of the agenda of liberal welfarism. During the last two decades, most western governments have made explicit their shared philosophy that sports are not luxuries for the rich, but should be available for every citizen. But the rhetoric about the particular needs of women varies – for example, in Britain there is a marked difference in the policy statements about sports of the two major political parties: whereas the Conservative Party's broad concern for a 'Sport for All' programme makes no reference to gender (Department of Education and Science 1991b), the Labour Party, in its *Charter for Sport* (1991: 14), identifies women as a needy group:

> We will make special efforts to involve those sections of the community that are, at present, under-represented in sport, particularly women, the disabled and the retired. . . . Sport Centres will be encouraged to make participation by women easier, for example by the introduction of women-only sessions and the provision of crèches. . . . We will use, and where necessary strengthen, existing equal opportunities legislation to prevent discrimination in sport.

Sports programmes are initiated not only by central governments, but also by local governments, and autonomous, voluntary and commercialized agencies, or a combination of these. For example, in the UK, local authorities have been mainly responsible for sports development and, although varying in their approach to gender inequalities, many local authorities have appointed sports development officers with special responsibility for women's sports, and have organized women-only sessions and provided crèche facilities. In addition, the central and regional Sports Councils (government-funded, but autonomously run) have made it clear that resources should be used to increase women's involvement. In 1982, for example, the Sports Council aimed to increase women's participation in indoor sports by 70 per cent and their participation in outdoor sports by 35 per cent by 1993 (Sports Council 1982: 34).

In contradiction to its own policy, the Sports Council was encouraging gender discrimination by funding organizations that chose to spend more on men's than on women's activities. Therefore, in 1987 it made it obligatory for mixed organizations that received Sports Council grants to provide equal opportunities for men and women. The following year, the Sports Council (1988) assessed changes:

> Nearly one million extra women have been attracted into indoor sport in the past five years – marginally short of the target, but nevertheless a major social phenomenon. . . . Conversely, the number of women taking part in outdoor sport has fallen by about 100,000 during the past five years.
>
> (Sports Council 1988: 1 and 25)

Reaffirming its strategy to work towards equality between men's and women's participation, the Sports Council (1988: 2) planned to encourage an extra 1.25 million women to take part in sports over the next 5-year period (1988–93). Part of its strategy was to work in liaison with local authorities, sports-governing bodies and other agencies, such as the National Coaching Foundation, supporting programmes to encourage participation at all levels – in community sports, elite sports, coaching and leadership, for example. But the Sports Council's 1982 and 1988 strategies were concerned with quantitative changes within the existing structures of sports and they failed to address fundamental issues of discrimination to do with the culture and traditions of sports. To some extent this is changing, and policy-makers are more sensitive to the problems and complexities surrounding the issue of women's sports. For example, it is generally recognized that the category of 'women' is unwieldy and often 'too diverse to use as a basis for realistic planning of strategies and programmes' (White 1991b: 4). This is why local authorities and regional Sports Councils have tended to focus on specific subgroups, such as young mothers, the over-sixties, and Asian women. And in the Sports Council's (1992) consultation document, *Women and Sport*, there is a much greater sensitivity to the complexities of change. The new radicalized philosophy is a reaction to the failure of most sport-specific organizations, including the Sports Council itself, 'to develop effective equal opportunity policies and practices', and a recognition that 'achievement of equality of opportunity requires unequal distribution of effort and resources' (p. 29).

However, at the same time that the Sports Council is encouraging other sports organizations to follow its lead in taking affirmative action in favour of women, it also has a plan for 'larger grants' and 'fewer schemes' which is likely to militate against 'outsider' interests, including female participation. Lelliott (1991) explains that in future the Sports Council will expect local authorities and other local sources to cater for community needs because its policy is 'shifting away from supporting a large number of small, local schemes in order to invest in larger, strategic facilities where Sports Council resources can have a unique influence'. The Sports Council's policies clearly contain contradictions, and it is unlikely that its apparently radical philosophy about women will be comprehensively implemented. Unless account is taken of the effects on local provision of recent legislation discussed earlier, and of the difficulties of disseminating new values and forms of action throughout a sports world which continues to be riddled with sexist practices and where men wield most of the power, change is likely to be minimal. The Sports Council itself is still a male-dominated institution; its official policy on gender is the result of constant pressure from a feminist minority and is not necessarily the precursor of equally radical practice. The relationship between theory and practice has always been problematic.

INTERNATIONALIZATION OF WOMEN AND SPORTS

Sports policies about women in Britain are not insular. With the opening up of Europe and the increasing globalization of sports, no individual country can remain unaffected by international influences. The positions of sports feminists in individual nation-states have assumed greater credibility by the internationalization of the 'women and sport' question. The International Association of Physical Education and Sport for Girls and Women (IAPESGW – an association aimed to build links and provide knowledge and support to individuals) and the Women's International Sports Coalition (WISC – an association with a mission to achieve equity for women in and through sports by facilitating communication and the collecting and sharing of information, and by building a network of support amongst national and international women's sports organizations) provide international forums for women from different parts of the world. Although gender issues and problems for women in sports are infinitely variable across the world, and although women from the West are taking the lead in international organizations, nevertheless, there is a sense of solidarity about tackling gender inequities in sports which transcends traditional boundaries. Networking is spreading out from countries in the West to those in other parts of the world, including some developing countries.

Statements made by various European organizations which have an interest in sports have given credibility to feminist ideals and put pressure on the constituent countries to implement change. In the case of the European Sports Conference (a consultative group constituted from leading representatives of national sports organizations and government sports agencies from eastern and western Europe), its *Charter* states that sports in Europe must be 'kept free of any kind of discrimination on the grounds of religion, race, sex, politics or social status' (1989: 185). The more specific concerns about gender inequalities were laid out in the recommendations of the *Women and Sport* working party, accepted by the conference in 1991. The report articulated the intention 'To increase the involvement of women in sport at all levels and in all functions and roles'. It emphasized the need to take into account the knowledge, experience and values of women as well as men; to increase the scientific knowledge about women and sports; and to increase the numbers of women at all levels of coaching, advisory, decision-making and administrative work. The work of this group continued in 1992 and 1993. The Council of Europe also promotes the general principles of equality of opportunity, and applied them to sports originally in the 1976 *European Sport for All Charter*, and in the revised 1992 *European Sports Charter* which was produced to take account of recent developments in the countries of central and eastern Europe. It states clearly that 'No discrimination on the grounds of sex, race, colour, language, religion, political or other opinion, national or social origin, association with a national minority, property, birth or other status, shall be permitted in the access to sports facilities or to sports activities' (p. 26). The Council of Europe Committee for the Development of Sport has been sympathetic to the cause of women (Council of Europe 1989). Equal opportunities is also an issue which has high priority in the European Economic Community (EEC), and although the European Parliament has as yet no worked-out sports policy, there are individual members who are lobbying for one to be drawn up; some of them are involved in the issue of women's participation and sex discrimination.

In all western countries, philosophies about equalizing gender relations in sports are becoming legitimized through the legislative procedures of governments and sports organizations. And whenever positive action has been used, there has been a quicker and more far-reaching shift in the traditional patterns of male domination. For example, in 1984 the government-funded Norwegian Confederation of Sports sponsored a women's committee whose first project was to work for equal male and female representation on all boards and committees, and then to seek quotas for women in senior administrative positions. In order to facilitate these changes and enable women to take on powerful roles in sports, a leadership development course, entitled 'Can, Will, Dare', has been successfully implemented. In Canada also, federal as well as provincial legislation has been extremely successful in improving women's rights in sports. Federal sports policy in Canada is well articulated and includes a 'Women in Sport' programme and, as in Norway, projects to encourage women to advance to high levels in administration and coaching (Lenskyj 1986; White, Maygothling and Carr 1989: 20). The philosophy of inclusiveness is embodied in a recent report, 'Sport: The Way Ahead', which makes clear the intention to integrate women at all levels of the sports system (Government of Canada 1992a). The strategy includes working with provincial governments and sports associations to develop policies and programmes for equity, as well as channelling funds for this purpose. But an unprecedentedly radical development for gender relations in Canadian sports, and probably in the world, has been connected with the foundation in 1992 of the Canadian Sport Coalition – 'a truly national sport umbrella group'. From the start, gender equity was built into every level of its structure in the following ways:

> Each delegation to the Coalition's general assembly must consist of one person from each gender.
> The overall goal of the general assembly is 50/50 gender representation; member groups have made the commitment to work towards achieving this goal within the next few years.
> *Effective immediately*, all governing and working committees struck by the coalition will have a gender balance of not less than 40% of one gender.
>
> (Government of Canada 1992b)

To a great extent these reforms in Canada have been the result of continual lobbying by the Canadian Association for the Advancement of Women and Sport and Physical Activity (CAAWS). The parallel association in the USA, the Women's Sports Foundation, has received federal government funding for its development work, and state-funded projects have been set up to encourage women to take high-status administrative and coaching positions. In Australia, the government's Sports Commission (ASC) set up the Women's Sports Promotion Unit (WSPU) – to target women as part of the broader 'Sport for All' campaign, and the 'Active Girls Campaign' is aimed at counteracting some of the effects of socialization by creating an attractive picture of sports for girls (Heaven and Rowe 1991). The situation now is that programmes promoting women's sports are operating in every state and territory in Australia.

These are just a few examples which illustrate some of the practical implications of central government policies and equity programmes. But although official support provides legitimacy for change, it is articulated within the framework of existing sports structures. Government intervention does little to alter the structural and cultural patterns of discrimination that many people take for granted in their ordinary lives, and which have been the major causes of discrimination in sports in the first place. Male hegemony in sports is a daily process – a subjective feeling produced by uneven gender relations. It occurs automatically and is an unquestioned, lived experience. Hegemony is not a simple matter of domination, it occurs through direction – a product of habits and customs. It is not, however, established in one place only, it is rooted in the lives of different communities and through different institutions. The institutionalization of unequal gender relations in the home, the school, the media and sports organizations, presents a powerful barrier even to the most radical legislation.

GENDER RELATIONS AND THE HOME

Gender relations in the home are relations of power which, as we have seen in the previous chapter, are established at an early age and fundamentally affect attitudes to sports. Women's sports, however, are shaped by class as well as gender relations. Research done in the UK shows how important the family is in influencing the sports participation of young women (White 1989). It is more usual for girls from middle-class homes to be encouraged to participate in extra-curricular activities such as sports, and to receive practical help from their families – in terms of cost, ease of travel, etc. – than for girls from working-class backgrounds. The general pattern of the leisure of working-class girls, in particular, is home-based, and linked to romantic ideas about their future roles as wives and mothers. Women derive much of their meaning of life and their understanding of leisure and sports from their husbands, lovers, fathers and brothers. Even when young women leave school, their leisure is frequently structured more by their relationships with men than by their move to waged work (Wilson 1988: 50). Although earning power usually enhances opportunities, it is the unpaid work which they do in the home that most limits women's autonomy. Yet because higher numbers of working-class girls leave school early and marry much younger than their middle-class counterparts (and than working-class males), their leisure opportunities are curtailed the most (Delamont 1980: 67). And many working-class girls have already been trained in the family to service others: they often have to look after younger siblings and help with the domestic chores – tasks seldom demanded of older boys in the family. Boys and girls at home are thus 'encultured' in ways that shape their future leisure patterns. The uneven sexual division of labour in the home is responsible, in large part, for an uneven sexual division of leisure – both are components of a broad structure of male dominance inherent in modern capitalism. Popular, culturally rooted ideologies about female sports (see Chapter 7) constitute an additional obstacle to women's involvement in this specific form of leisure:

> Gender and class . . . (as opposed to employment status) are overarching constraints operating on all women, but mostly with differential effects; however, gender constraints are such that few women, of whatever social class or employment status, would find themselves at ease on the rugby field, in a pub otherwise full of men, or jogging late at night on dark streets; nor are many likely to return from Sunday morning sport to find their lunch waiting on the table, and an offer from their partner to wash their sports gear.
>
> (Deem 1984:13)

Although in some families there has been a transformation of gender relations, in many others traditional gender divisions based on male physical
and economic power continue. It remains commonplace for women to
service men's leisure. Some of the most enduring forms of patriarchal power
over women's labour in the family are manifest in sports. The following
account of women's servicing role in the context of men's rugby in New
Zealand is replicated in numerous sports and countries throughout the
western world:

> the domestic labour of New Zealand women has always serviced rugby.
> One is able to cite an almost endless list of chores traditionally done by
> women for the benefit of the men and boys who play rugby. It would
> include providing meals, catering for visiting teams, shopping for,
> laundering, mending and ironing team uniforms, transporting sons to
> practices and games, waiting on the sideline, attending to injured bodies
> and egos.
>
> (Thompson 1988: 206)

It is women's domestic and child-care roles that to a large extent dictate
gender differences in the meaning of leisure (Deem 1984; Green, Hebron
and Woodward 1987; Hargreaves 1989; Talbot 1989). The leisure of women
– particularly working-class women and those living with male partners – is
inextricably interwoven with their responsibilities as wives and mothers.
Most women have fewer, different and less convenient opportunities for
leisure and sports than most men, and it is difficult to separate work from
leisure for women who watch television as they iron or feed their babies;
read a book while supervising their young children in the park; or chat with
friends while shopping in the supermarket. That is not to say that men, in
common with women, do not experience obligated, domiciled and
family-based leisure – repairing the car, digging the garden or playing
football with the kids – but in general their choices are reduced less than
those of women. Talking about Australia, Brown (1984: 64) relates the
popularity of sports in male culture to the problem of women's leisure:

> it is not true that a majority of men are beginning to share the domestic
> role of housework and child-care; and it is taken for granted by most men
> that 'family time' used as a spectator with the boys or as a participant of a
> sport is their sole right.
>
> (Cited in Talbot 1989: 9)

Although increasing numbers of women are in paid work, including those
who are married and those with young children, the *idea* that women's
proper place is in the home remains influential. Because money determines
value in capitalist societies, and women's position in the labour market is still
marginal to men's, men's labour outside the home is highly valued. In contrast,
labour done at home, including child-care, though physically demanding,

time-consuming and socially essential, is valued less (Beechey 1982; Benston 1982). This is a distinctly male definition of work which is linked to the belief that men have the right to engage freely in leisure activities so that they can return fresh to their jobs. There is a strong tendency in this popular idea to ignore the oppressive characteristics of the private sphere of the home, especially for women. Women's leisure away from home is rarely taken as a right, and even when some women (usually middle-class) do get some 'away-from-home leisure', it often takes the form of 'family leisure'. Although family leisure is not necessarily a constraining experience (Talbot 1989), women usually assume the role of carer and provider, in addition to participating, or instead of doing so. In general, men have infinitely more disposable time and income for leisure and sports than women, and they find it easier to take part in activities *of their own free will.* Women's leisure is frequently highly constrained, rather than free from constraints.

The literature relating to the richer countries of the western world reveals similarities between comparable groups of women. Those who are middle-class are more likely to have help in the home and with child-care, and in general they have more money for leisure and easier access to private transport. Because sports activities take place outside the home and frequently require regular blocks of time, as well as money for participation and travel, working-class women participate in smaller numbers. The difficulties increase for women with young children, and are greatest for those who are single parents. Most single parents are women. Streather makes the following point which, although written at the end of the 1970s, is still valid: 'leisure centres and palaces of fun will offer one-parent families little if the pressure of poverty, low status, social isolation, and unrelieved parenting go for nothing' (1979: 185). The financial and social problems associated with single parents and other women with responsibility for young children who are low-waged or unemployed transcend the problems of access to leisure, and to sports in particular. The politics of women's leisure and sports moves from the personal to the public sphere when the health of women who are malnourished or simply exhausted from domestic labour and childcare would be put more at risk through exercise (Wimbush 1986).

Even for women who are not so seriously constrained and who are keen to take part in sports, there are cultural factors and traditional practices which militate against their doing so. Women have limited access to many sports facilities which are located in private clubs dominated by men, or in mixed settings when males tend to monopolize the space and equipment. Women often feel intimidated by the fierce masculinization of public sports venues. There is no equivalent female culture to that of the male-bonding, back-slapping scenes in the pub after the match; or to the rowdy and bawdy joke-telling, chauvinist changing-room scenes; or to the sports hospitality meetings where male business executives meet to do deals. Such places and events wield symbolic power – they confirm in popular consciousness the idea that the male worlds of sports and work are powerful ones from which women are excluded. And male control of female leisure also occurs in ways that are connected with the wielding of power in a very personal sense. It is commonplace for working-class men to control the amount of leisure time and the type of activity which their wives, daughters and girlfriends enjoy (Green, Hebron and Woodward 1987). Working-class women in general lack private transport and are therefore afraid to go out after dark for fear of physical abuse and sexual harassment. This is a limitation that is imposed on women and mediated by male and female attitudes to sexuality.

The problems of women's leisure become more complex if other variables are taken into account. Because women have diverse cultural and economic resources, they experience the general patterns of gender-based inequalities differently, according to such factors as age, disability, ethnicity. But sports have never been important aspects of female culture for any particular social group; to break this tradition, day-to-day practices have to be changed and affirmative action taken. Much of the impetus for change has come from schemes which have attempted to address the ways women have been constrained in the past. For example, the Sports Council has funded a number of 'National Demonstration Projects' based on 'the principle of marketing and providing sport in a way that fit(s) with women's lifestyles rather than expecting women to adjust to a male model of sport' (1991: 12). Classes have been organized for women with specific needs and interests (e.g. ante- and post-natal sessions, sessions with crèches, mother and toddler classes, mother and teenage classes); at suitable times and locations; and marketed to be attractive to women and to avoid stereotypical assumptions about what constitutes 'women's sport'.

RELATIONS OF POWER AND EDUCATION

The school as well as the home is implicated in the reproduction of gender inequalities in sports, and this section will examine the issue of equal opportunities for boys and girls in physical education (PE). The British 1988 Education Reform Act (ERA) included in its rubric the intention to promote equal opportunity programmes in schools through the establishment of a national curriculum for all children in maintained schools. But although the ERA provides a legal framework for challenging and changing unequal gender relations and sexism in schools, it has not made the implementation of equal opportunities obligatory, and in the case of PE has failed to produce radical changes. The national curriculum is made up of core and foundation subjects (PE is one of the latter), to be taught to pupils in four consecutive key stages during compulsory schooling from 5 to 16 years. The government appointed a Physical Education Working Group to make recommendations (Department of Education and Science 1991a) before it published *Physical Education in the National Curriculum* (Department of Education and Science

1992), which specifies attainment targets and programmes of study for PE, implemented at the start of the new academic year in 1992.

The *Final Report of the Physical Education Working Group* is a radical document. It proposes that in PE there should be 'no barriers to access or opportunity based on race, sex, culture or ability' (Department of Education and Science 1991a: 5), and it recommends that six areas of activity – athletic activities, dance, games, gymnastics, outdoor activities and swimming – should be included on the PE programme at some time during key stages 1 to 3 (ages 5–14). The aim is to provide all children, regardless of sex, with a broad movement experience. The most radical proposal is that dance should be compulsory for both sexes until the age of 14 years. But the report goes further; it recognizes that to equate access with opportunity is mistaken and clearly places responsibility on teachers to 'question the sterotypes which limit children's behaviour and achievements; and to challenge, whenever necessary, instances of racism and sexism'. It states that working for equal opportunities in PE requires 'an understanding and appreciation of the range of pupils' responses to femininity, masculinity, and sexuality', and will require 'both in initial and in-service training, a critical review of prevailing practice, rigorous and continuous appraisal and often a willingness to question long-held beliefs and prejudices' (ibid.: 15). The report's recommendations are unequivocal – that children of both sexes, regardless of their different rates of development and experience, should be offered the same PE curriculum to avoid 'future undesirable sex stereotyping activities' (ibid.: 57). 'In particular,' it argues, 'a broad and balanced programme of physical education, sensitively delivered, can help to extend boys' restricted perceptions of masculinity and masculine behaviour' (ibid.: 58).

But the government-appointed National Curriculum Council, who advised the Minister for Education, chose not to incorporate the radical guidelines of the working group. Dance will be compulsory for younger children (5–11 years), but at key stage 3 (12–14 years), only games is obligatory (together with a choice of three out of four other activities). The result is that at a very impressionable age, when boys are consolidating a sense of the masculine, it is likely that their curriculum will exclude dance and that traditional gender identities in PE will be reproduced (see Chapter 7). A copy of the first-ever Physical Education National Curriculum was sent out to every school in the country, together with a pack containing non-statutory guidance for teaching and assessing the programme. At no point in either of these official documents are there observations or recommendations about the problems of equalizing gender or dealing with sexism.

The relationship between masculinity and dance is at the root of the more general 'problem of gender equality' in PE. Margaret Talbot (1990: 2) argues that activities such as dance, which are normally associated with women and girls, are treated as low-status activities and that dance has the potential to play 'a central role in questioning ideologies and practices which many of us regard as anti-educational and abhorrent'. This is an implied criticism of the macho, aggressive and fiercely competitive orientation of many boys' PE programmes. She points to research showing the antagonistic attitudes of some male PE teachers who argue that dance should not be included in the curriculum at all and who want the term 'physical education' to be abandoned in favour of 'sports education' (ibid.: 3). An additional problem is that since single-sex departments have become amalgamated, approximately 75 per cent of the heads of mixed PE departments are men (Sports Council 1991: 26), and as the number of mixed schools increases it is likely that the number of female heads of department will decrease. Any implementation of equal opportunity programmes is therefore certain to be premised on a deficit model for girls, rather than on one which acknowledges that if boys lack the experience of creative and artistic movement, *they* are fundamentally deprived. The tendency is for new programmes to be constructed according to male values and male experiences which fails to question the underlying assumptions about 'masculinity' incorporated in traditional programmes of boys' PE.

Another controversy surrounds the comparison of single-sex and mixed-group teaching. The debate has been going on for years – for example, a 1975 government report entitled *Curricular Differences for Boys and Girls* was critical about the separatist policy of PE in secondary schools, and in 1984 an Inner London Education Authority publication, *Providing Equal Opportunities for Girls and Boys in Physical Education*, made the following opening statement:

> During the current debate on equal opportunities, accusations are increasingly being made that physical education is one of the most sexist school subjects. It has traditionally started to separate the sexes as they approach puberty and allowed different programmes to develop thereafter. Many teachers are now saying that they cannot continue to justify such separatism but that they need evidence with which first to challenge stereotypic assumptions regarding pupil potential and then suggestions to help them reorganise their programmes.

During the last decade there has been a marked shift, in line with the ideology of this report, in the attitudes of increasing numbers of PE teachers who believe that, as a first step towards changing patterns of discrimination based on sex, wherever possible, children should be taught in mixed groups throughout the whole of their education. They believe that single-sex teaching is underpinned by ideological constructions of 'femininity' and 'masculinity' that symbolically articulate *differences* and mask similarities between boys and girls.

But through the years, other PE professionals have argued that programmes should be *equal, but different.* Such a position coincides with the belief that equal rights in education, laid down in the United Nations Resolution of 1967, should mean 'of equal value', but not necessarily 'the same'. The Sex Discrimination Act also allows sex differentiation as long as neither sex is disadvantaged. Studies of classroom interaction have shown that in mixed groups boys tend to be given more attention by the teachers than girls, and there is concern that if mixed PE replaces single-sex teaching, the same might happen. There is evidence that in mixed schools both boys and girls are expected to conform to dominant stereotypes more than they are in single-sex schools. Mahony (1985) shows how girls in mixed groups tend to be dominated by boys in a number of ways. For example, in order to prove their 'manliness', boys are pressurized to demonstrate muscular strength to their peers and are not infrequently provocatively sexist. Their behaviour may include verbal and even physical forms of sexual harassment. Further-more, as Mahony's research shows:

> boys who do not display sufficient evidence of masculinity, or more rarely those who actively challenge the sexist behaviour of other boys, are prime targets for a good deal of what is called in their case 'bullying'.
>
> (Mahony 1985: 52)

Such examples have prompted some educationalists (see Evans 1988) to argue that because assumptions about gender-appropriate ability and be-haviour may be more difficult to break down in mixed classes, and because girls in single-sex schools are more interested in physical activities than girls in mixed schools, then to begin with positive action may be a more effective way to implement the principles of equal value and equal opportunity. Single-sex PE is argued for in specific cases which relate to ways in which girls' experiences of gender mediate with other aspects of their lives. For example, as Carrington and Leaman point out:

> In schools with a significant proportion of Muslim pupils, mixed PE will not be an option available to staff. . . . Muslim parents frequently raise objections to it on both religious and moral grounds, arguing that mixed PE may bring their daughters into direct contact with males in what is regarded as a shameful and potentially compromising position.
>
> (Carrington and Leaman 1986: 222)

Anne Flintoff (1990a: 88) argues that many PE teachers fail to address seriously the ways in which 'their practices reinforce, and reproduce, social inequalities'. Even if specifically anti-sexist PE programmes could be made obligatory, on their own they would not change the broader patterns of gender inequities in schools, or the sexist practices throughout society. Children themselves reproduce attitudes about gender divisions that they come to school with, and, in turn, gender divisions in schools consolidate those in other social spheres. Although some schools and some PE depart-ments are trying to overcome the most obvious aspects of sexism and sex-role stereotyping, nevertheless, the power of sexism in schools is such that it operates unconsciously in the hidden curriculum (see Chapter 7) – in the classroom, in the playground, and on the sports field; and between pupils and in relationships between pupils and teachers.

The future of PE is already threatened by factors which are not directly linked to equal opportunities. It looks likely that in most schools PE will lose some of its timetable allocation to 'the demands of the core subjects', and in numerous local authorities PE has already suffered cut-backs as a direct result of the Conservative government's punitive financial policies discussed earlier. It is likely that the position in many schools in the future will be that, for both boys and girls, there will be less time and fewer resources for PE. Anne Flintoff predicts a possible route that schools might take to save money:

> it is the case that most girls would be relieved to see PE disappear from school programmes, the few boys interested in playing sport would find the sports development officers the Ministers are currently encouraging to come into school, very willing to take them on, and headteachers will be rubbing their hands with glee having saved large amounts of money previously spent on PE equipment and staff.
>
> (Flintoff 1990a: 95)

The national physical education curriculum is fiercely contested. There are those who are clinging to tradition and privilege, and those who seek change. The divisions are about gender in the PE curriculum, but are not along strictly gender lines – men and women agree and differ – but in the foreseeable future it is likely that those in the greatest positions of power will ensure that 'undesirable sex stereotyping' will continue unabated in the PE curricula of British schools. The effects of the ERA illustrate the conservatism of state intervention.

Although one would expect the situation in higher education to be different, there are marked gender differences in sports participation in colleges and universities which reflect the school experience. In general, facilities are good, and male and female students can claim equal funds from student unions for sports activities. Nevertheless, students often have fixed ideas about sports when they come to college and male students, in general, come with a wider vocabulary of experience leading them to take greater advantage of the opportunities to play college and university sports than their female counterparts. Rosemary Deem (1978: 95) suggests that this may be because there is a tendency for women students to retreat into a 'home-based domestically oriented culture' while at college. The problem of gender reproduction is exemplified on many degree courses in dance and sports studies. Whereas during the 1960s and 1970s dance and sports were together incorporated into movement studies or physical education degree pro-grammes, in many institutions they are now partitioned off into separate departments and separate disciplines. Students must then select *either* sport *or* dance. So the symbolic representations of the 'physically competitive body' and the 'aesthetically creative body' are institutionalized 'in degree programmes. Although there are increasing numbers of male dance students, most courses have a predominance of female applicants and female staff. It is also the case that outside the colleges themselves male dance students still get labelled as 'unusual' or castigated as homosexuals. Evidence from an investigation carried out by Anne Flintoff (1990b) shows that since college courses in physical education and sports studies have become mixed, they have also become more male-defined and women's positions have become increasingly threatened. Although there are approximately equal numbers of male and female sports studies students in colleges and universities throughout the country, most courses focus on male models of competitive sports and, increasingly, on top level sport. Furthermore, sports scientists and psychologists tend to concentrate on differences between male and female performance and to be blind to the distinction between sex and gender (Talbot 1989). Not surprisingly, research in the sports sciences (biomechanics, exercise physiology, psychology, etc.), is biased in favour of the male subject (White 1991a: 11), and it is customary for generalizations to be made on the basis of male examples and an essentially male sports culture. Historical and sociological analyses of sports, which include examining gender relations of power, tend to be allocated less time, and many male students, whose hidden agendas are heterosexist and homophobic, are antagonistic to feminist analyses.

Many sports studies and dance students will seek careers in teaching, recreation management and commercialized leisure and fitness venues. They will hold key positions in the future and the fear is that they will reproduce traditional gender relations of power in their fields, rather than encouraging change.

THE IMBALANCES OF GENDER AND THE MEDIA

The previous chapter examined ways in which ideologies of sporting femininity and images of sexuality are reproduced in the media and act as a material force on women's participation in sports. The focus here is on the under-representation of women's sports in the press and on television and radio. We receive a very limited and partial view because attention is given almost exclusively to top-level, competitive and 'feminine-appropriate' events, or to the sporting feats or aspects of the lives of sportswomen that are deemed to be unusual, spectacular, controversial or newsworthy. On very few occasions, and only in some newspapers and on certain television programmes, women's sports receive more serious and comprehensive treatment. And although cultural meanings attached to sports are different in various nation-states, nevertheless, in all countries in the West men's competitive sports and idealized images of masculinity are promoted systematically in the sports media; in comparison, women's sports are marginalized and trivialized (Blinde, Greendorfer and Shanker 1992; Fasting and Tangen 1983; Gaccione 1991; Heaven and Rowe 1991; Klein 1988, 1989; Lee 1992; Robinson 1993; Sports Council 1991; White 1991a).

THE PRINTED MEDIA

All British national newspapers concentrate on men's sports. There are, however, differences between the quality press and the tabloids. (See Chapter 7, note 3, for a list of these newspapers.) In general, the former cover more women's sports than the latter, and they present them in a more objective and less sensationalized way. However, the overall percentages of sports items devoted to women are woefully low. In both categories of newspapers there are times when there are no references whatsoever to women's sports, although this happens more frequently in the tabloids, and sometimes for days on end. Research reported by the Sports Council (1992: 28) estimates that 'only 0.5%–5% of total sports space in [British] national newspapers is devoted to women's sport'; and during different 4-week periods in 1988, 1989 and 1990, research showed the percentage of the total sports coverage devoted to women's sports to range between 0.5 per cent and 11 per cent in the quality newspapers; and between 0 per cent and 4.8 per cent in the tabloids.[1] In addition, women's events tend to be given less prominence than men's events: for example, coverage of the finals of the 1989 Women's World Snooker Championships was placed at the end of a report of the Rothman's Grand Prix men's snooker competition (*Daily Telegraph*, 21 October 1989); and during the Seoul Olympics *The Times* newspaper placed accounts of all female swimming competitions after those of the men, and all the photographs depicted male swimmers (Seton 1989). Also in *The Times*, the 1989 Women's Oxford vs Cambridge boat-race received 5 per cent of the written space allocated to the men's race one week later, and there were no photographs. In the *Sunday Express*, the same event was treated as marginal to the men's race, and most other newspapers made no reference to it at all. Even during Wimbledon (1990), the overall coverage of women's tennis matches was given far less prominence and space than the coverage of men's events (Cary 1990).

It is also the case that the numbers and sizes of photographs devoted to women's sports are far fewer and smaller than for men, and there are much lower numbers of action photographs of sportswomen (see Chapter 7). For example, in the British press during the Seoul Olympics, there was a marked difference between the numbers of photographs of male and female competitors, as shown in Table 8.1. The relatively few photographs of female athletes tend also to be individualized and sexualized images – especially in the tabloids – and accompanied by references to marital status, femininity, private lives and personal problems. Even in some specialist sports magazines (for a list of these see Chapter 7, note 2; see also Leath and Lumpkin 1992; Robinson 1993) aimed at mixed readerships of keen participants and followers of specific sports, coverage is disproportionately oriented towards males, most of the articles are written by men, most of the photographs are of male participants, and advertisements of sports clothing and equipment present sexualized images of women. Similar obervations have been made about specialist sports magazines in North America (Blinde, Greendorfer and Shanker 1992).

TELEVISION SPORTS

The forms of discrimination in the printed media's coverage of women's sports are paralleled by discrimination on television.[2] Men's boxing, cricket, football, horse-racing, motor-racing, rugby, snooker and 'imported' men's sports such as American wrestling, American football, baseball, rally cross and sumo wrestling fill most viewing hours. Magazine programmes such as *Grandstand, Match of the Day, Saint and Greavesy, Sportsnight* and *World of Sport* concentrate on men's sport, and at times when such events as the men's Cricket, Football, Rugby or Snooker World Cups are on, television is saturated with these events. Sometimes, for days at a time, no women's sports are televised. The reverse is never the case. It is also men's sports that are usually shown at peak viewing times. It is only on the occasions of popular mixed competitions, such as the Commonwealth Games, European Championships, the London Marathon and the Olympics, that there are more female sports on television than at other times. Popular 'feminine-appropriate' sports such as gymnastics and figure-skating are highlighted and given approximately equal viewing time when compared to men's events. Because equestrianism is an open event, unusually, women are treated on a par with men, but in sports such as professional golf, and rowing, men's competitions receive comprehensive coverage, whereas

Table 8.1 Press photographs of male and female Olympic competitors, 17 September – 1 October 1988

Newspaper	Percentage of pictures of females		Percentage of pictures of males
The Times	35.8	:	64.2
The Independent	25.4	:	74.6
Daily Express	24.5	:	75.5
Today	23.4	:	76.6
The Sun	20.2	:	79.8

Source: Seton 1989

the women's equivalents are given relatively little attention. Even traditional women's team sports – netball and hockey – receive minimal coverage, and women playing traditional male sports, such as cricket, football, rugby and snooker, are seldom seen on television.

There are further discrepancies between the sexes in television sports. For example, in sports quiz shows such as the BBC's *A Question of Sport*, it is not unusual for the quiz master and panellists to be all men, and for most of the visual material and the vast majority of questions to be about male sports and male subjects. Although the new topical sports programmes produced by commercial companies, such as *Transworld Sport*, have widened their range to include minority sports and those indigenous to countries all over the world, the overall focus is still on male events. Even taking into account documentaries and feature programmes about female sports, and educational programmes for young people, overall, the viewing time for female sports is probably less than 12 per cent of that for male sports.

The following argument about the media in general can aptly be applied to the sports media more specifically:

> It matters profoundly what and who gets represented, what and who regularly and routinely gets left out; and how things, people, events, relationships are represented.

> (Hall 1986: 9)

The relative neglect of women's sports and the ways in which they are represented (discussed here and in Chapter 7), confirm for many people ideas that they have already internalized from other experiences. Because we are bombarded in the sports media with action-filled stereotypes of male athletes, in comparison to a relative dearth of highly 'feminized' pictures and accounts of sportswomen, young females fail, on a regular basis, to see varied and vigorously athletic images of women. The construction and marginalization of female sports provide a hidden, but very powerful, message that they are less important than men's sports and that men are keener to participate and naturally better suited to do so.

SPORTS MEDIA PROFESSIONALS

The hidden agenda of the sports media has an important impact on the lives and minds of young people, linked here to the power to signify events in particular ways. The sports media shape public consciousness about gender. But although women's sports tend to get recurrently signified in ways that are associated with dominant ideas about gender, these ways are not the only ones. The processes of signification and embodied ideologies are not fixed and unchanging, but rather sites of struggle and negotiation over gender values and understandings. A good example is the case of women's football. For years the British media have been saturated with men's football and its ethos of 'masculinity' and have resisted covering the women's game. However, after growing public interest in women's football and pressure from players and supporters, during the 1980s the media slowly and reluctantly began to take notice. Their reluctance was clear when England reached the final of the first UEFA Cup in 1984 – whereas their Swedish opposition arrived with 'a TV crew and 36 press personnel', the game was 'barely mentioned in the British press' (Williams and Woodhouse 1991: 32). It was not until 1987 that a BBC2 documentary gave the game national exposure on British television for the first time. Since then, the 1989 Channel 4's screening of a series of 1-hour programmes has boosted the game's popularity at home, and the England team's successes in an expanding field of international competition have resulted in slightly more media exposure. But the increased coverage of women's football has been extremely slow and in no way comprehensive throughout the different media outlets. It has not been based on a consensus, but is indicative of conflicts of interests and values. The situation is one of contradiction – in the British sports media anti-female football sentiments and pro-female football sentiments coexist: on the one hand there has been some breaking down of conventional barriers, but sexist treatment still prevails. In the USA a similar observation can be made about the NCAA Women's Basketball championships – a great breakthrough occurred when the championships were televised at prime weekend time with female commentators (Gaccione 1991), but at the same time the television networks continue to 'convey and transmit gender stereo-typic ideology' (Blinde, Greendorfer and Shanker 1992: 111).

The media are supposed to be impartial, but it is clear from this account that the sports media, specifically, present a gendered view. The struggle for change goes on at two levels – first, lobbying for more space and time, and second, tackling the *ways* in which women's sports are constructed by the media. There have been some incentives to publish articles and illustrations of women's sports which promote a radical image, but these have been outside the mainstream media outlets. Not surprisingly, there is opposition to change from members of the sports media profession, which, with very few exceptions, remains a bastion of male privilege and domination. Sports media professionals justify the status quo by arguing that programmes are chosen and survive only if they are profitable and if they are what the public wants. This position was articulated by John Bromley, Head of BBC Sport, when he was tackled about the poor coverage of women's sports. He said, 'We do cover women's sports. For example, we give just as much time to the women's final at Wimbledon, to female athletics, and to gymnastics. There is no audience for women's hockey' (Channel 4's *Open Air* programme, 14 April 1989). Such an argument is a justification for holding on to power and privilege and reproducing stereotypes. And it is flawed, because sports such as gymnastics, snooker and sumo wrestling only became popular audience events after being shown on television. It is also the case that the audience does not necessarily know 'what it wants' until it has all the choices. Nevertheless, it is men's sports that in general are those that are added to the viewing repertoire.

The Sports Council has published the following figures concerning sports journalism:

> Of the 120 British print and photographic journalists who received accreditation for the 1988 Olympic Games in Seoul, Korea, only two were women. Of the 513 members of the Sports Writers Association of Great Britain, only 24 are women. There are no women sports editors of national daily or Sunday newspapers. Of the 90 British print and photographic journalists accredited at the 1990 Commonwealth Games, only two were women.

> (Sports Council 1992: 27)

The uneven balance between the sexes occurs in other areas of the sports media as well – for example, although there are slowly increasing numbers of female radio and television sports presenters and commentators, the vast majority are still men and those in high-status positions are all men. With few exceptions, sports media professionals reinforce rather than undermine gender inequalities. As we have seen, they do so by marginalizing women's sports and by treating female athletes differently from male athletes. This is a systematic process and a symbolic expression of a power relationship between the sexes. In general, media sports professionals reproduce prejudices upon which patriarchal structures and sexist ideologies are based. They construct for the readers and viewers a sense of the reality of sports which is culturally encoded.

SPORTS ORGANIZATIONS AND GENDER

Unequal power relations between men and women are also prevalent in the staffing patterns of commercial, public and voluntary sports agencies. With some exceptions, the marked trend is for men to hold posts of authority and for women to occupy lower-status positions. White and Brackenridge found this to be true when (between 1960 and 1985) they studied the gender composition of the personnel of a selected number of British sports associations and some of the 'newer professional fields of sports coaching, management and administration'. 'It is clear', they said, 'that the proportion of women with power and influence in British sports organisations is very small, far smaller than the number of women participants would warrant on the basis of proportional representation' (1985: 104). White and Brackenridge suggest that with increased professionalization, bureaucratization and state influence of sports, women are losing some of the power they used to have. This is confirmed by the Sports Council (1992: 19) which acknowledges 'a decline in the proportion of women in influential and decision-making positions'. The Sports Council itself has a marked gender imbalance in its staffing: out of the 650 people employed by the Central Council in 1991, there were no women directors, and all regional directors and National Centre directors were male. However, in line with the Sports Council's recommendation for gender equity, 'the National Coaching Foundation (NCF) has a woman director and there has recently been an increase in the number of women appointed to middle and senior management positions' (Sports Council 1992: 21). Furthermore, the Sports Council has recommended that it should set targets for equitable representation of women at all levels through-out its organization because it lacks credibility as 'a major promoter of sport for women when it is so visibly male-dominated' (Sports Council 1992: 31).

GENDER BIAS IN SPORTS LEADERSHIP

There is no doubt that the implementation of equal opportunity policies has resulted in the emergence of some women into areas of control that were previously exclusively male, but it is misleading to assume that even with the rapid expansion of the leisure and sports industries, this trend is in any way comprehensive, or that it necessarily augurs well for a comprehensive re-distribution of power and ideas. For example, although a woman holds the important post of director of the NCF, coaching remains one of the most prestigious areas of sports which embodies grossly unequal gender relations and the NCF publicity and information material is not as radicalized on gender as it could be (some of the distance-learning resources are obviously male-centric). In 1993 the NCF launched a project to provide a lead on gender equity issues in order to fulfil its aims to ensure 'equal represention of women and men in the coaching profession' and 'that the coaching of female athletes [be] given equal status to that of male athletes' (*Coach* 1993, Vol. 5, No. 1). Although a few women hold prestigious positions, they are in a tiny minority and there is little leadership on gender issues 'from the top'. For example, although recreation management is a growth profession and women are taking up careers in the field (reflected in the rising female membership of the professional association, the Institute of Leisure and Amenity Management), a traditional, and distinctly male, orientation prevails. Few women display the competitiveness and ambition required for promotion to senior management positions. The Sports Council observes that women usually have lower-paid secretarial and administrative positions: in 1990, 'out of the 33 London boroughs only two Directors of Leisure were women' (Sports Council 1992: 20; Lucas 1990). Similarly, a study of staffing at sports centres in the north-west exposes 'traditional hierarchies, with men dominating the management levels and women clustered at the lower levels' (Sports Council 1992: 16).

In other countries, similar research also shows that with increasing profes-sionalization women are failing to fill the important posts. For example, in a study of almost seventy Canadian national sports organizations, it is revealed that 'nearly half of the entry-level positions (programme coordinators) are held by women, whereas they comprise only 28% of the executive directors, 23% of the technical directors, and less than 10% of the national coaches'. In contrast, 90 per cent of the support staff are female (Hall, Cullen and Slack 1990: 1–2). The gender-bias in the leadership positions of Canadian sports has remained fundamentally unchanged, in spite of the government's well-organized programmes to encourage the entry of women into sports administration and their advancement to the top levels of management.

It is ironical that new patterns of discrimination against women are emerging as a result of measures that have been implemented to equalize gender relations. For example, the identification of women as a target group has led to the creation of positions of responsibility for 'women's affairs'. These posts have usually been filled by women who are considered to best understand the needs of other women. This in itself is generally viewed as an advance towards gender equality – it has allowed women to infiltrate sports management, and to work for the benefit of women as a whole. But in most contexts the overall power has remained with men – a sexual division of labour based on traditional assumptions about male and female abilities. It is also the case that the merging of men's and women's associations has tended to increase rather than decrease discrimination. When women had control of their own sports organizations, they had considerable power, but, as has happened in schools and colleges, with the creation of mixed organizations, women have tended to lose power. For example, women are almost invisible in the top echelons of the British Athletics Federation (BAF) (which resulted from the recent amalgamation of the separate governing bodies of men's and women's athletics):

> None have been elected to the top five offices, only one has a vote on the management board, and only one is an officer on the six new commissions – for track and field, road running, cross country, race walking and tug of war – which will coordinate the sports' disparate divisions.
>
> (*Independent*, 10 October 1991, quoted by White 1991a: 14)

POWER IN COACHING

The common assumption that men are better at managerial skills (taking the lead, making decisions, being forthright and instrumental), and women are better at doing support work because they are 'naturally' expressive, co-operative and caring (White 1988, 1990), is used as a justification for the appointment of men to powerful positions and women to lower-status ones – a situation which can be understood as part of a wider structure of power that permeates society and works to the advantage of men and to the disadvantage of women (Whitson and MacIntosh 1989). If women are underrepresented in powerful roles, their positions can easily be marginal-ized. This is the case in the coaching milieu. Most women who work as professional coaches have exclusive responsibility for women's sports; very few women indeed coach men; and a tiny minority have national coaching responsibilities. Table 8.2 shows the disproportionately low percentages of female coaches of elite Olympic athletes during four Summer Olympic Games. It also shows that their numbers do not increase in parallel with the increase in numbers of female participants.

The same study shows that in 1986 the inequalities in athletics (arguably the most popular Olympic sport) were extreme, particularly at the top levels, 'with 100% of National coaches and 98% of Event coaches being male' (ibid.: 9). Even in those individual sports which are popular with women – tennis (approximate ratio of male to female players 50:50); badminton (66:44); and gymnastics (more female than male participants) – the proportion of female coaches, particularly in senior positions, is smaller than that of men and is lower than in previous years. In badminton, for example, there are no women coaches at national level and only one to every five male coaches at county level. In gymnastics, which has a history of women coaching women's disciplines and men coaching men's disciplines, by 1980 there were more men coaching women's disciplines, but no equivalent involvement of women in the men's events – only 13 per cent (Sports Council 1992: 23–4). The marginalization of female coaches was symbolized in a 6-week promotion of children's sport in the *Sunday Observer* (1991): the six experts chosen to offer 'specialist knowledge in teaching their sports' were all men. These trends are apparent in other western countries where it is also the case that experienced male coaches see new financial and championship oppor-tunities in women's sports which were previously closed to them. In the USA, for example, it has been estimated that in 1988 more men than women were coaching women's sports (Gaccione 1991: 11).

Because male coaches greatly outnumber female coaches (particularly in senior positions), and men are increasingly involved in coaching women's

Table 8.2 Numbers of male and female Olympic athletes and coaches, 1976–88

| | Athletes | | Coaches | |
	M	F	M	F
1976	73%	27%	96%	4%
1980	68%	32%	91%	9%
1984	68%	32%	98%	2%
1988	66%	34%	92%	8%

Source: Constructed by White, Maygothling and Carr 1989: 3, from the official reports of the Olympic Games and the British Olympic Association Handbook

sports, there are very few role models to encourage young women to take up coaching. In Canada, for example, Borys has shown that it is commonplace for girls who attend rural high schools always to be taught PE by a man who is the only teacher of the subject in the school, hired because of the ideology that women can't coach men's teams. The institutionalization of unequal gender relations in coaching, as in other realms of sport, is ideologically powerful and extremely difficult to change. The increase in the numbers of male coach/female athlete relationships also augments the potential for exploitation by male coaches of female athletes. Regardless of the sex of each person, the coach/athlete relationship is an inherently unequal power relationship – 'coaches have power of knowledge, power to enforce training regimes, power over athletes' private lives . . . and in some cases, power of decision as to whether the athlete steps on the court or stays on the bench' (White 1991a: 13). In addition, male coaches can wield *sexual* power over female athletes. Because of the relatively low numbers of female coaches, young athletes frequently have no choice but to have a male coach and can become trapped with one who abuses his authority. Until recently there has been a silence about this dimension of power in sports, but recent research suggests that sexual abuse and sexual harassment of young female athletes by older male coaches, though generally hidden, are widespread (Brackenridge 1990, 1992; Crosset 1986; Lenskyj 1986; Yorganci 1992). Brackenridge (1992) points out that the likely extent of child abuse by sports coaches is alarming. The disproportionate number of male coaches means that their influence becomes exaggerated: the potential for abusive relationships and sexual harassment could in large part be avoided with a larger percentage of women coaches.

In some men's associations and among some male controllers there has been a gradual shift in recent years to a position that is less oppositional to women's sports, and less resistant to women coaches. Surprisingly, it is becoming increasingly typical now for the governing bodies of traditional male sports, which in the past have been fiercely chauvinist and opposed to women's participation, to support the expansion of the women's game. For example, the Amateur Rowing Association actively promotes women's rowing and has employed two national coaches specifically to develop the sport for women and, exceptionally, for several years during the late 1980s and early 1990s, a woman held the most prestigious coaching position – the Director of International Rowing. The British Amateur Rugby League Association encourages women to enrol on coaching courses that are part of its national coaching scheme; and the FA is promoting women's football in a number of ways. But in spite of these incentives, the world of rowing remains largely controlled and directed by men (White, Maygothling and Carr 1989: 55); only two out of sixteen teams playing women's rugby league are coached by women; and it has been argued that 'women's football is now controlled by men', in the sense that female teams depend on men for access to pitches and for coaching and sponsorship. Although women continue to have power and control of some specifically female sports such as netball and synchronized swimming, there are other examples of sports with a strong female tradition that have become increasingly infiltrated by men – gymnastics has already been mentioned; another example is the All-England Women's Hockey Association which has appointed a male development officer and a male coaching director. Although there are initiatives to reverse this trend – for example, the National Coaching Foundation is planning women-only courses and other women-friendly approaches – it is impossible as yet to assess their success.

The infiltration of women into the 'corridors of power' in sports is not inevitably beneficial. Men tend to be authoritarian and aggressive in their styles of management and coaching (White 1987), and when women are appointed to leadership positions it is usually because they have demonstrated those values and ways of behaving that are essentially masculinist and confrontational. There are very few incentives to change the structures of sports and the attitudes of those in power, to adopt more sensitive and democratic forms of control, or to appreciate that the special skills and experiences of women could be used in the most prestigious positions in sports.

PERFORMANCE AND PROFESSIONALS

Many of the problems which affect women's participation as recreative performers are exacerbated if they want to take their sport more seriously. There are relatively few courses for more advanced players, fewer facilities and competitive opportunities than for men, and there is a general lack of coaching and finance. The Sport Aid Foundation, in common with other resource agencies, tends to support established sports, thus reinforcing gender inequalities and also those between majority and minority sports. The Sports Council is addressing some of these inequities by prioritizing facilities that will benefit top-level sportswomen: founding a national centre for field hockey, a national competition centre for women's bowls and a national arena for movement and dance (Sports Council 1991: 19). Because of the blurring in many sports of the traditional amateur/professional divisions, there are vast differences in the opportunities for top performers in various sports. Nevertheless, in almost all sports, men are in a beneficial position in relation to women.

In general, the governing bodies of women's sports have fewer capital assets than men's governing bodies and most women's sports are struggling to stay solvent. They are dependent on personal and club subscriptions, small donations from patrons, sometimes grants from the Sports Council and local authorities and, in unusual cases, support from sponsors. Because women's events attract less attention from the media, corporate sponsors in particular are discouraged from supporting them. Apart from a handful of women's sports (athletics, golf, gymnastics, horse-riding, skiing and tennis, for example), sponsorship deals are unusual and far less lucrative than those for men. 'Feminine-appropriate' sports have the greatest chance of securing support; women playing traditional male sports have fewer opportunities and for those playing minority sports funding is rare. Although in a very small number of sports (athletics and tennis, for example), the top female performers earn huge amounts of money on a par with some of the men, for the majority, the differential between the financial rewards for males and females is tremendous. Women's performance sports tend to survive as a result of an essentially amateur approach supported by unpaid labour and dedication. For example, there was a failure to attract sponsors to the inaugural Women's Rugby World Cup which took place in Wales in 1991 (with Canada, England, France, Italy, Japan, the Netherlands, New Zealand, Spain, USSR, Sweden, USA and Wales competing). Hundreds of applications were made to a range of sponsors, including corporations which support the men's game: refusals were based on traditional ideas about masculine and feminine appropriateness – 'But it's a men's game' and 'They don't drink lager'! The twelve competing countries as far as possible paid their own expenses, but the event ran into a deficit for which those who organized it were legally responsible. (The Sports Council and the men's Rugby Football Union between them were persuaded to pay it off.) It has been claimed that lack of sponsorship for women's professional snooker has nearly killed the game – even though there are sixty or more women snooker players who are as good as men players, they fail to secure adequate sponsorship. Sponsors say that they do not want to take risks with sports that have no proven record of audience interest, particularly during a recession. Poor media coverage and financial support tend to mask the rapid increase in the numbers of women participating in sports (see Chapter 11) and reproduce the present system of privilege.

The top women players in professional golf and tennis have considerable advantages over those in other sports, yet there are marked differences between the positions of men and women in these sports. The creation and subsequent high profile of organizations which represent the interests of female professionals have given them improved bargaining power and have assisted in securing better conditions and rewards. The Women's Profes- sional Golf Association (WPGA) was set up as a reaction to the reduced powers that women had under the (men's) PGA (it has existed in its present form since 1988), and the Women Professional Golfers' European Tour (WPGET) was subsequently formed to represent women golfers in Europe. But even so, there is a massive discrepancy in prize money for men and women, and in 1989 there was a failed attempt to narrow the gap. For example, approximately £19 million was paid out in total for the 1991 men's European Tour in comparison with £1.4 million for the WPGET; the 1991

'Volvo' Order of Merit winner (Ballesteros) earned £545,353, in comparison with the 'Woolmark' Order of Merit winner (Dibnah), who won £89,058; players in fortieth place earn £106,191 and £10,696 respectively. The average purse in men's European tournaments in 1991 was around £500,000; for the women's tour it was £93,000. On the American professional tour discrepancies are less (Schofield 1992). Although top women golfers are wealthy, for those who are ranked lower – especially if they are black – sponsorship is difficult to secure, which, together with the high cost of travel and accommodation and the limited prize money, makes it difficult for them to make ends meet. It is also desperately difficult for women professional players to become professional coaches. Vivien Saunders, a founder member of the WPGA, was forced to purchase her own club after she had unsuccessfully applied twenty-six times for positions as a coach (Barraclough 1991). This catalogue of difference is rooted in the history of golf. Gender has been an organizing force which has been established, institutionalized and reproduced in the everyday affairs of golf, as well as in the professional arrangements for over a century (see Chapter 11).

Because women's tennis is a high-profile media sport, prize money for top players has always been relatively high. In 1971, Billie Jean King became the first sportswoman ever to win 100,000 US dollars in a year; soon after, Chris Evert became the first sportswoman ever to win $1 million; and that record was quickly broken when Martina Navratilova won over $4 million. By 1992 Martina Navratilova's total career earnings from tennis purses had exceeded $18 million, but she had been overtaken as the athlete who had earned more from sport than any other woman by Monica Seles whose winnings were in excess of $24 million. At 17 years of age Monica was the youngest woman tennis player ever to hold the number-one ranking position; by 1992 she had become the highest paid female athlete in the world. At that time she was also the twelfth highest paid athlete (male or female) in the world, but not so much as a result of the prize money she had won from playing tennis, as from multi-million-dollar endorsement deals with Perrier (mineral water), Yonex (rackets), Canon (photography equipment), Fila (tennis shoes) and Matrix (hair products). The globalization of the television coverage of women's tennis has made it possible for all the stars to earn vast amounts from endorsements. In large part, the success of women's professional tennis has been the result of the influence of the Women's Tennis Assocation (WTA – founded in 1973, with 25 members; it now has over 500). The WTA has been a powerful voice for women's tennis, effectively representing the interests of its members and operating its own Grand Prix circuit. However, the WTA has so far failed in its struggle to obtain equal treatment for women players at Wimbledon and the French Open. (It was successful in achieving equal pay at the other two Grand Slam tournaments – the Ford Australian Open and the US Open.) Unequal prize money was established at Wimbledon when it was first introduced in 1968: Rod Laver received £1,000 and Billie Jean King £750. In 1991 and 1992 the men's Wimbledon champions received £240,000 and £265,000 respectively. The comparative figures for the women's champions were £216,000 and £240,000. In 1992 women received only 70 per cent of the men's money in the early rounds and 90 per cent in later rounds. Incorporating 'per diem' payments and qualifying expenses, as well as the share of mixed doubles winnings (but excluding the masters' events), the total compensation paid to the men in 1992 was £2,345,960, and the total for women was £1,896,860 (ITF 1992). By 1993 prize money for the men's and women's champions was increased but not equalized – Pete Sampras won £305,000 and Steffi Graf £275,000.

The WTA made a stand in 1991 that it would not sanction the new Grand Slam Cup (even though it was planned to be the richest prize in women's tennis – approximately £2 million), unless women players were guaranteed equal prize money and an equal draw size at all the Grand Slam events and at the Grand Slam Cup itself. In its struggle over women's tennis, the WTA touches on the essential cause of discrimination – the idea that men's sports are better and more entertaining than women's sports. The WTA is questioning the relative values of the repetitive, low-rally, power-game of the men, when compared with the longer rallies and more varied game of the women. The argument is that the entertainment value provided by women tennis professionals is at least equal to that provided by the men. Although this is a matter of important principle and a challenge to male power, and if the WTA wins its battle it will be a symbol of equality for all sports, the irony is that the struggle is a financial one, engaged in the interests of an already highly privileged group of sportswomen who earn obscene amounts of money. The struggle for equal pay for male and female professional tennis players is more about the commodification of sports than about essential gender equality.

The careers of female athletes are influenced not only by the sports they play, but also by the images they portray. Some exceptional sportswomen can demand huge fees primarily because of their skill and success (for example, in 1989 Fatima Whitbread was the highest-paid athlete in Europe, male or female), but whereas for men athletic ability is the main determinant of earning ability, for most female performers the additional dimension of sexual attractiveness is what secures sponsorship and media coverage. For example, during a remarkably brief span of time the East German athlete Katerina Krabbe earned huge sums of money from sexualized images of herself in advertising, far in excess of what she earned from athletics. Sportswomen who play 'male' sports and are powerfully muscled are far less likely to get financed than those who are sexy and glamorous, and sponsorship opportunities are reduced for lesbian sportswomen who make public their sexual orientation. The exploitation of female sexuality – a major demand of capitalism – has permeated sports at all levels (see Chapter 7), and compulsory heterosexuality plays an important part in determining the careers of female athletes.

It has been argued that sportswomen are forced to market their bodies because this is what the sponsors demand (Blue 1987; Boutilier and San Giovanni 1983). Women's golf provides a good example. Popular images of femininity have become a vehicle for selling the sport, and players such as Jan Stevenson accept the glamorous portrayal of themselves in the press and magazines because they are sponsored by commercial companies like Avon Cosmetics whose raison d'être is to sell heterosexual glamour (Lenskyj 1986: 102–3). Players who are openly friendly with one another on the circuits are particularly vulnerable to allegations of lesbianism, and they are impelled to mask any hint of masculinity or suggested sexual 'deviance'. Talented players who do not fulfil the sponsors' criteria can be ignored or marginalized, whereas for other players golf is a 'vehicle for what is essentially a career in modelling'. Such players are paid for their appearance, not their skills:

> This was certainly the case in the 1991 'Henessey Ladies Cup' played at St Germain in Paris. The two LPGA Tour players, Tammie Green and Deborah McHaffie, were each paid £7,000 plus expenses to play the event. . . . The promoter, Lionel Provost, admitted the pair had not been invited to take part because of their golfing ability, but more '. . . because they are exceptionally attractive'.
>
> (Schofield 1992: 43)

Women's golf is trivialized by these procedures, but the WPGA lacks the power and support of its members to tackle the ideological imperatives of commercialism. Some of the players are in a contradictory position – they are highly critical of the demands made of them, but are controlled by a system that they feel unable to do anything about.

SEPARATISM

The question of how to overcome uneven gender structures and practices is linked to the issue of separatism. Women in women-only sports groups play important decision-making roles and are able to control funds and other resources which would otherwise have to be negotiated with men. In these ways all-female institutions provide greater autonomy and, as Anita White (1991a) argues, strong women's organizations can lobby effectively on behalf of their members. They can also be an effective form of positive discrimination when there is an overall gender bias in favour of males in the distribution of scarce sports resources. It is also the case that for many women single-sex sports provide the only acceptable way to enjoy physical activity because they feel protected from the fierce male chauvinism of other settings. Viewed in this way, separatism confers power.

But it can be argued that in the ways it has been applied to sports, separatism is narrow in vision because it tends to confirm ideas of difference and lower status. Separatism may be an important form of positive discrimination that is a first step towards equality, but long-term separatism institutionalizes gender divisions. Pronger (1990: 18) describes it as a 'technique for maintaining a socially constructed difference between men and women, symbolically preserving through sports the power of men over women'. Because men monopolize sports, women in separate organizations are easily defined as outsiders and cut off from the struggle to share from the common pool of resources. Rather than strengthening women's position, it can be argued that separatism excludes women from power, status, money and interaction with others in the 'real' world of sports. The feminist slogan 'The personal is political' is recognition that the personal must be understood as part of a broader political struggle, not as separate from it. Unless separate development for women can threaten the male ethos of sports, it can be said to personalize rather than politicize women in sports.

The major alternative solution to inequalities between men and women has been to assimilate women into male-constructed sports organizations. But there are problems with this process as well. We have seen that in mixed sports organizations women seldom hold key positions and are marginalized if they do. As an American woman who was a member of the NCAA Council for five years has put it, 'Women are outsiders on the inside. Women rarely lead; at best, they influence' (Gaccione 1991: 11).

The problem of inequality cannot be solved by a few exceptional women who hold powerful positions; women are needed in approximately equal numbers with men. In mixed organizations it is essential for them to be at all levels of management in order to make a distinctive contribution to sports policy and practice as a whole, as well as having special responsibility for women's affairs. But some sports feminists argue that quantitative change is not enough, and it is essential that women are fully integrated and accepted as equals in decision-making procedures. In other words, sports must be 'feminized' – influenced by those values and ways of behaving which are shared by most women. As Kari Fasting (1989: 15) argues, 'If there exists a feminist sport culture it is probably partly suppressed and invisible. Making it visible must be given a priority.'

CONCLUSION

Sports feminists who want to change the position of and ideas about women in sports do not have an easy task. Gender relations in sports are relations of power which are hard to shift because they have strong connections with a whole range of other social practices – in particular, those in the family, the school, the media and the state – and they permeate the structure and culture of sports organizations themselves. But they are not inviolable. Gender relations in sports are part of a constant process of negotiation, struggle and change.

Chapter 9

Olympic women
A struggle for recognition

INTRODUCTION

This chapter looks at the history of the modern Olympic Games, characterized as the most prestigious of all international sports competitions. There is a popular tendency to idealize the Olympics and to ignore that they have always been imbued with extreme expressions of male chauvinism and enduring examples of female subordination. The particular difficulties of Olympic sports for women have tended to be exaggerated examples of problems and complexities intrinsic to women's sports in general.

The International Olympic Committee (IOC) is the central administrative authority for the Games. Since its foundation in 1894, it has been an undemocratic, self-regulating and male-dominated institution. At the start, all members were upper-class Anglo-Saxon men, many of whom had strong aristocratic connections, and for almost a century the IOC remained elite and exclusively male. The founder of the modern Olympics, Baron Pierre de Coubertin, was its major ideologue; he wielded power because he was the sole benefactor of the IOC, as well as its president (Mitchell 1977). Until his death in 1937, de Coubertin was intransigent in his opposition to women's participation in Olympic competition, and made his views known through IOC publications. He claimed that 'women's sport' was against the 'laws of nature' and 'the most unaesthetic sight human eyes could contemplate' (cited in Simri 1979: 12–13). 'The Olympic Games', he declared, 'must be reserved for men', for the 'solemn and periodic exaltation of male athleticism' with 'female applause as reward' (quoted in Gerber 1974: 137–8). Under de Coubertin's tutelage the IOC resisted the participation of women in Olympic sports. From the start, the modern Olympics was a context for institutionalized sexism, severely hindering women's participation. They were a powerful conservatizing force, making an indelible mark not only on the development of Olympic sports for women, but also on the development of international competitive sports in general. However, the original model of Olympic sports encapsulated demands for change as well as resistance to them. The history of the Games starkly demonstrates women's struggles, failures and successes.

THE EARLY YEARS

The first modern Olympics, which took place in Greece in 1896, exemplifies sport as a bastion of bourgeois male privilege. Women were excluded from these Games, but there is a story about one *unofficial* female participant – a Greek woman called Melpomene – who 'crashed' the marathon in protest. Her action symbolizes the efforts of those who have struggled over the years to overcome male domination of Olympic sports. Although at the first Olympics the members of the IOC unanimously opposed women's participation, there were other men in the Olympic movement, and in the newly formed International Federations of sport, who supported women in their struggle for Olympic recognition. These men were involved in the development of women's sports in their respective countries. The period covering the first few Olympic Games coincides with the formative years of organized sports for women in the West (see Chapters 3, 4 and 5). It was during this time that national and international organizations for women's sports were formed, and there was a steady growth of competitions, giving sportswomen increasing visibility and legitimacy.

Ironically, the entry of women into the Olympics occurred as a result of laissez-faire arrangements in the early years. In 1900, and again in 1904, the IOC (which had the ultimate power to control the Olympics) rather casually handed over the responsibility for arrangements to the organizing committees of the host cities, Paris and St Louis. Under these conditions women were admitted to the Olympics without the official consent of the IOC (Mitchell 1977). Then, in a more formalized way, the British Olympic Association took charge of the 1908 Games in London and allowed women's archery, lawn tennis and figure-skating competitions. But advances were slow and contested. In 1912, at a time when the International Federations were growing in number and importance, and there was increasing popular support for women's sports, the IOC made the decision to reassert its authority over the Olympic programme. With a characteristically sexist and reactionary stance, it systematically blocked women's progress and could only be persuaded to allow a few 'feminine-appropriate' events to take place outside the official programme. But even when women's events were made official, they were not given equal status with men's competitions until 1924. During the first few Olympic Games only very few women were involved. They came from privileged backgrounds, with adequate time and financial resources to make participation possible. But the 1920s marked a watershed for women's participation when controversy over athletics (which had a more popular base of support and were the major Olympic sports) reached a peak.

CONTINUED RESISTANCE TO ATHLETICS

In spite of consistent opposition to women's athletics on the grounds that they were particularly unsuited to the female physique, they were growing in popularity and showing early signs of democratization throughout Europe and in the British Commonwealth and North America. Women were therefore in a position to take militant action. It was in 1917 that a Frenchwoman, Alice Milliatt, representing all female athletes, challenged the IOC's rule which prevented women from competing in the Games. She founded a French women's sports organization through which the demand that women's athletics be put on the Olympic programme of 1920 was made. Although de Coubertin's response was to reiterate his demand that all women's events should be terminated, the majority of members of the IOC voted to allow tennis and swimming competitions. The opposition of the IOC to all female participation was no longer total – some of its members now saw women's sports as part of a more general emancipatory trend, which included the entry of women into spheres of work, education and leisure, previously monopolized by men. However, they were unanimously intransigent about women's athletics. In defiance of IOC policy, a group of women from Europe and America arranged an athletics meeting in Monte Carlo in 1921. The programme included a range of events (60 metres; 250 metres; 800 metres; 300 metres and 800 metres relays; 74 metres hurdles; long jump; high jump; shot put; and javelin) which established the composition of future internationals. For campaigns to be successful, groups must be organized and have leaders and supporters; and strategies must be well thought out to win support and change opinion. The female athletes at Monte Carlo fulfilled these criteria: they consolidated a women's international athletic movement with the creation of the Fédération Sportive Féminine Internationale (FSFI), which became an important pressure group for women's international athletic competition and helped to accelerate development world-wide. The FSFI organized its own alternative *Women's* Olympics in Paris in 1922. The name was changed to the Women's World Games (because the IOC claimed the exclusive right to use the term 'Olympic'), and continued as a popular festival of women's athletics – in 1926 in Gothenburg in Sweden (when ten countries took part); then in 1930 in Prague in Czechoslovakia (seventeen countries); and a fourth and last time in 1934, in London, England (nineteen countries) (Mitchell 1977; Simri 1979). These competitions were unexpectedly successful, attracting large numbers of competitors and spectators from western Europe, the Commonwealth and North America, clearly establishing athletic events as growth sports for women on a widespread scale. In the face of hostility from the world's major sporting organization, women had occupied for them- selves an autonomous realm of sport which they could control and develop.

The IOC could no longer ignore the evidence that throughout the West women were participating in athletics in greater numbers every year, and attracting crowds of spectators. By this time it was a prerequisite that there be an already established International Federation, and an organized programme of international competitions, for a new sport to be considered for the Olympic programme. Although the FSFI was firmly established, and the Women's World Games were expanding, it was only when the all-male International Amateur Athletic Federation (IAAF) agreed to take control of women's events that their status as sports for Olympic competition was acknowledged. Although female athletes were again refused permission to compete in the Olympics of 1924, it was no longer a unanimous decision, and the IOC could not ignore the growing controversy. The problem of the legitimation of female athletics was, therefore, the subject of their Pedagogic Conference in 1925. Medical evidence, considered to be 'authoritative' and 'scientific', was the key presentation, later published in a paper entitled 'Women's Participation in Athletics'. The arguments laid out in this publication provided the justification for slowing the advance of women's athletics during the following years.

The first part of the report seemed to reflect a positive attitude to the female body and a radical understanding of gender:

> There are two main features which have to be examined in facing this most difficult problem, which is daily becoming more difficult. The first is that the male and female are derived from the same parent stock. They have been evolved together, and their methods of life are similar. . . . They have somewhat similar organic systems, the differences in skeleton and muscular formation being minor. The differences in the nervous and the blood systems being still less noticeable. . . . The present adaptation of Womanhood itself to the demands created by the labour market, bring her still closer to Manhood in her habits of life. . . . This feature of the question seems to indicate that the recreations and physical exercises taken by men might be found advantageous for women.
>
> (Cited in Eliott-Lynn 1925: 111)

But then the orientation of the report changed, focusing on the differences between male and female athletes, the limitations of female biology and, in particular, the potentially harmful effects of athletics on women's reproductive potential:

> The second feature is that the basic function of men and women is totally different. Women's function is highly specialized, and when it is brought into play those minor differences which I mentioned a moment ago become strongly pronounced, and the woman becomes a totally different creature from that which she was before her role of motherhood was entered upon. . . . The differences which appear in the nervous, skeletal and muscular systems are all necessary adjuncts of the great work of

parturition and anything that might tend to hinder or make this more difficult must be very heavily deprecated. . . . We have therefore before us the problem of finding a suitable mean between those sports which tax the muscular frame and put a strain on it, and which are, of course, wholly unsuitable for the feminine organism, which is more delicate and should conserve its energy for the great work before it, and those recreations which are not sufficiently physically energetic to assist the woman towards the most healthy development she may attain. . . . It seems to me, therefore, that if those sports and games which are suitable for men be modified and reduced so that they cannot in any way injure the woman, and if we can create organizations which will enforce these modified regulations stringently, we will have gone a long way towards achieving our objects.

(Eliott-Lynn 1925: 111)

This medical report was a reaffirmation of the popular nineteenth-century theory of constitutional overstrain (see Chapter 2). By compounding the social with the biological, the discourse of the report shared the ruling class's moral concern for social progress and national welfare, arguing that female athletics should contribute to a 'workable system of eugenics', comparable to that practised in ancient Sparta. The report supported the idea of 'feminine-appropriate' exercise, urging caution about the type and amount of exercise, particularly for young girls between the ages of 13 and 18 years, claiming that 'it is then that their bodies need a tremendous amount of care and attention' (ibid.: ix, x, 27, 114). Importantly, the report provided the national sports associations, the IAAF and the IOC with a 'scientific' justification for limiting women's participation in track and field athletics during the following years.

ASSIMILATION OR SEPARATION?

Ironically, the lure of the Olympics, which had been the major stimulus for the organization of women's athletics, was now the bait for women to surrender control to the IAAF, in exchange for a recommendation that female athletic events be put on the next Olympic programme. In 1926, after extended and difficult negotiations, the IAAF recommended a women's athletics programme which was accepted for the 1928 Games – 100 metres; 800 metres; high jump; discus; and 400 metres hurdles. It was no coincidence that women athletes were finally admitted into Olympic competition during the year following de Coubertin's retirement from the presidency of the IOC; nor was it surprising that there were only five events on the women's Olympic programme, instead of the eleven in the Women's World Games. In accepting this offer, the FSFI made a fundamental compromise. It was a decision surrounded by controversy, and in protest at the limited number of events, British women athletes, strongly supported by their male colleagues, boycotted the new track and field programme for women at the 1928 Amsterdam Olympic Games.

The example of athletics illustrates the problems women face when they are assimilated into an association where men have the power to make decisions about female sports. Some of the British female athletes had previously argued for separate development in order to retain control of their own sport:

> We strongly object to the mixing up of men and women in the Olympic Games or at any other meeting. If this actually happened it would kill our movement, and we should be absorbed by men as in other countries.
>
> (Vera Searle, quoted in Lovesey 1980: 66)

Women could more easily insulate themselves from opposition in the separate sphere of their own association; in a mixed association they were rendered weak and vulnerable. The nineteenth-century stereotype of woman as a physically limited creature still provided the focus of controversy. When several of the female athletes collapsed in the 800 metres final at the 1928 Games, the event was immediately removed from the women's athletics programme, and provided the IOC with a 'biological' justification for opposing women's participation. Nevertheless, some members of the FSFI believed they were in a position of strength. Following their Olympic debut, female athletes were admitted to the second Empire Games in London in 1934, which gave their events further legitimation; and by this time the FSFI was a vibrant organization with thirty member countries. Female athletics had become popular spectator events in Europe and North America, and so the FSFI was, ironically, now able to use the threat of withdrawal from the Olympics as a lever in the continuing struggle with the IOC. It also planned to continue its own World Games. But the 1938 Women's World Games never materialized because Austria (the intended host country) was annexed by Nazi Germany and war was threatening. Furthermore, much of the impetus was removed when the FSFI was assured in meetings with the IOC that it would have a full athletics programme in future Olympics – a promise that was never fulfilled. The momentum of the FSFI was suddenly halted and women athletes lost their bargaining power. Although there was a new world record set in every women's event in the 1932 Games, even so there were still only 328 women competing in 1936 in just 4 Olympic sports (athletics, fencing, gymnastics and swimming), whereas 3,738 men competed in 11 Olympic sports and in a far greater number of events than women.

The Olympic debate over women's athletics (and by implication competitive sports in general) was complicated further because the women involved in it were not a homogeneous group. In the USA, a lobby against the 'improper' nature of Olympic sports was gaining momentum, spearheaded by the Women's Division of the American Amateur Athletic Federation. This group was composed of physical educators who held powerful positions in education and female sports. They were knowledgeable about prevailing arguments concerning exercise for women and about progressive educational philosophies – ideas which influenced their hostility to high-level competition. They were vehemently opposed to the exploitation of the athlete and to the increasingly commercialized features of male sports, arguing that such trends should be resisted in women's sports. They therefore wanted control to be in the hands of women, and opposed the decision of the Amateur Athletic Union (AAU) to send a women's track and field team to the Women's World Games, and to the Olympics in 1928, 1932 and 1936. In 1932 they sent a formal protest to the IOC in an attempt to suspend athletic events for women from the Los Angeles Olympic Games, and they planned an alternative festival, including singing, dancing, music, mass sports and games: the focus was to be on 'play for play's sake', in direct contrast to the stress and over-specialization associated with individual sporting accomplishment. They also joined forces with members of the medical profession and representatives of other sports organizations to express their fears that competitive sports would render women incapable of bearing children and would have a masculinizing effect on the female physique (Gerber 1974, 1975; Hult 1989; Kennard 1977).

On the one hand, the leaders of women's physical education in the USA appeared to be ahead of their time; they had a critical appreciation of the potentially harmful affects of top-level sports, and a belief in the philosophy of 'activity for all'. They were actively promoting the idea of 'a sport for every girl and every girl in a sport' (Segrave and Chu 1981). But it has also been argued that because they considered athletic events to be low-status, associated with black and working-class women, their position embodied mainstream ideas, implicitly supportive of class and ethnic divisions in American society (Leigh 1974). Furthermore, by adopting a separatist stance and reproducing the establishment's version of female biology, these women had minimal influence on the accelerating impetus of international competitive sports and the commercialized and exploitative characteristics of which they were so critical. Nor did their policy reduce in any way the seductive appeal that the Olympics had for most sportswomen; it rather strengthened gender differences and helped to make it easy for the IOC to slow the expansion of women's Olympic sports during subsequent years.

The issue of female participation in the Olympic Games shows clearly the complexities of analysis. The early history of women's Olympic sports is a history of struggle and diversity – power and control were fought over, not just between men and women, but between different groups of women. It illustrates the importance of drawing attention to contradictions and conflicts within the broad history of women's oppression in sports.

GENDER STEREOTYPING

By the 1940s, organized sports for women in Europe, the British Commonwealth and North America were spreading in scale and popularity, and the
machinery of national and international competition was in place with the
establishment of governing bodies of sport and International Federations.
The feats of outstanding female athletes, such as Mildred 'Babe' Didrikson
from America and Fanny Blankers-Koen from the Netherlands, had captured
the public imagination and done much to dispel the myth of the physically
limited female. 'Babe' Didrikson was hailed as the 'greatest female athlete of
the twentieth century' for her record-breaking ability in track and field events
in the 1930s, and Fanny Blankers-Koen demonstrated that supreme athletic
ability is not incompatible with popular images of femininity and motherhood. Between 1938 and 1948, she set seven world records in five different
athletic events; won four gold medals at the 1948 London Olympics; and
then achieved two additional world records in two different events. She
produced these outstanding achievements while having and raising a family
– at the 1948 Olympics she was 30 years old and three months pregnant.

Contradiction, however, has been a feature of all phases of the Olympic
story for women. At the same time as sporting heroines were providing
conspicuous exceptions to traditional images of womanhood, conservative
efforts to limit participation to 'feminine-appropriate' sports and events were
strengthening. Avery Brundage, who was a powerful member of the IOC and
became its president in 1952, articulated this view. For example, after the
Berlin Olympics in 1936 he said, 'I am fed up to the ears with women as track
and field competitors . . . [their] charms sink to less than zero. As swimmers
and divers, girls are beautiful and adroit, as they are ineffective and un-
pleasing on the track.' And in 1949, he expressed disgust at the vision of
'muscular' women in the new shot-put event, arguing that it should be
removed from the Olympic programme: 'I think women's events should be
confined to those appropriate for women – swimming, tennis, figure-skating
and fencing, but not shot-putting' (cited in Simri 1979). Opposition to women's
field events came also from women themselves, and gained momentum in
1966 when members of the IOC, who tried to get the shot-put and discus
events removed from the Olympic programme, were supported by the
Women's Board of the US Olympic Development Committee, which
vehemently claimed that 'Often the feminine self-image is badly mutilated
when women perform in these two sports'.

Gender stereotyping has been an integral feature of the development of
Olympic sports; it has always been easier for women to gain access to those
events that it has been argued are more suited to female biology and less
threatening to dominant images of femininity. Arguments based on traditional notions of female ability have been used repeatedly to limit the
number of Olympic events for women. For example, the banning of the 800

metres after the 1928 Olympics slowed the development of women's distance running tremendously: it was not reinstated as an Olympic event until 1960, and other longer-distance events came much later. Despite repeated appeals to have the 3,000 metres put on the programme, the IOC refused to include it in the Moscow Olympics because the committee said it was 'a little too strenuous for women' and would adversely affect their metabolism. Yet in view of the growing scientific evidence that women may be better suited than men at endurance events (Dyer 1982), and because women were achieving exceptional results in long-distance running outside the Olympics, the IOC's position was visibly weak. Finally, the IOC capitulated, and included the 3,000 metres, together with the marathon, for the first time in the 1984 Olympics. Women have also been systematically blocked from Olympic competition in the longer-distance events of other sports, and in those that emphasize strength, require physical contact and are potentially dangerous (Boutilier and San Giovanni 1983). Arguments are still made to justify women's exclusion from the triple jump, the pole vault, boxing and weight-lifting, on the grounds that women's reproductive systems are vulnerable to injury in these sports. The evidence that there are no medical reasons intrinsic to women that should prevent them, *any more than men*, from participation, is disregarded (Dyer 1982). The female reproductive organs are firmly positioned and thoroughly protected inside the body cavity and are probably less susceptible to injury than those of men. And women, like men, can wear protective apparatus to cover vulnerable parts – their potential for injury is similar to, not greater than, men's. The ethics of arguments to ban dangerous sports such as boxing are as appropriate to men as they are to women; the reason they are applied only to women is cultural, not biological. The inclusion, for the first time in the 1984 Olympics, of two exclusively female Olympic sports – rhythmic gymnastics and synchronized swimming – may have been greeted as a victory, but it only confirmed gender-based associations.

CONTINUING INEQUALITIES

It is more difficult than ever before to justify continuing inequalities between men and women in the Olympic programme. By their improved performances in high-level competition, women have themselves done a great deal to dispel myths about female biology and sporting potential, and have put pressure on the decision-making bodies of Olympic sports to enlarge the women's programme. Even so, the increase in the number of sports has been minimal over the years, although there has been a steady increase in the number of events. For example, in athletics the 400 metres was introduced in 1964, the 1500 metres in 1972; then, as we have seen, it was more than a decade before the 3,000 metres and the marathon became Olympic events for women in 1984. The decisions to include these events were, without exception, the result of conflict and negotiation. For example, preceding the 1984 Summer Olympics in Los Angeles, eighty-two female athletes from twenty-one different countries, with the assistance of the American Civil Liberties Union, failed in a court case to force the IOC and the IAAF to put the 5,000 metres and the 10,000 metres on the women's Olympic programme. Although the case was lost, it was an aggressive demonstration that sportswomen across the world were prepared to fight, and that the issue of female sports had entered the public agenda. Conflict of this sort acts as a lever for change, and the following year the IOC and the IAAF agreed that the 10,000 metres should be put on the women's programme. The struggle continues over the 5,000 metres, the 3,000 metres steeplechase, the pole vault, the triple jump, the hammer throw, the 20,000 kilometres walk and the 50,000 metres walk.

In spite of advances, there is still a large discrepancy when the numbers of male sports, events and competitors are compared with female ones. For example, at the 1984 Los Angeles Olympics, there were 168 all-male Olympic events, 73 all-female events and 15 'mixed' events, and

> Men competed in twice as many events as women . . . and comprised seventy-nine percent of all competitors. Attempts appear to have been made to broaden women's participation – of the fourteen new events at Los Angeles, three were for men, ten for women and one was open to both sexes – yet many events continue to exclude women. These include several running events, soccer, hammer, judo, rings, pole vault, weight-lifting, boxing, wrestling and water polo.
>
> (Williams, Lawrence and Rowe 1986: 82)

At the 1988 Summer Olympics the imbalance between men's and women's events was reduced somewhat – there were 26 sports and 165 events for men; compared with 22 sports and 83 events for women, but there were still twice as many male as female competitors. At the Winter Olympics in that year, there were 11 sports and 30 events for men, but only 6 sports and 17 events for women. At the Summer Olympics in Barcelona in 1992 women were only 40 per cent of the total number of competitors. New sports for women were judo, canoe slalom and windsurfing, but men's events still outnumbered those for women – there were 28 sports and 171 events for men, in comparison with only 24 sports and 98 events for women. There were 3 sports and 12 events for mixed competition. At the Winter Games in Albertville 29 events were for men, 22 for women, plus 4 mixed demonstration events.

Table 9.1 provides participation figures for each of the Summer Games since 1896. It shows the numbers of male and female competitors; the number of females as a percentage of the total number of competitors; the numbers of countries sending male and female competitors; and women's events.

Table 9.1 Summer Olympic Games 1896–1992

Year	Host city		a) No. of competitors			Women's events
			Male	Female	% Females	
			b) No. of countries with competitors			
			Male	Female		
1896	Athens	a)	311	0	0%	None
		b)	13	0		
1900	Paris	a)	1,319	12	0.9%	Tennis (unofficial)
		b)	13	5		Golf (unofficial)
1904	St Louis	a)	617	8	1.28%	+ Archery
		b)	12	1		
1908	London	a)	2,034	43	2.07%	Tennis
		b)	28	3		Archery
	(One woman took part in an open sailing event.)					Skating
1912	Stockholm	a)	2,491	55	2.16%	Swimming
		b)	28	10		Tennis
1920	Antwerp	a)	2,628	76	2.89%	Skating
						Tennis
		b)	29	12		Swimming
1924	Paris	a)	2,956	136	4.4%	+ Fencing – foil
		b)	44	20		
	(Women's events were finally given full status.)					
	(Figure-skating was transferred to the programme of the first Winter Games in Chamonix.)					
1928	Amsterdam	a)	2,724	290	9.62%	+ Gymnastics (team events)
		b)	46	24		+ Athletics
	(No tennis – dropped until 1960)					
1932	Los Angeles	a)	1,281	127	9.02%	+ Javelin
		b)	34	17		+ 80 metres hurdles (No gymnastics)
1936	Berlin	a)	3,738	328	8.07%	+ Gymnastics
		b)	49	26		
	(Women were still competing only in athletics, fencing, gymnastics and swimming. An appeal to open equestrian events and hockey to women was refused by the IOC.)					
1948	London	a)	4,062	385	8.66%	+ Long jump
		b)	58	33		+ Shot-put
						+ Canoeing
1952	Helsinki	a)	4,407	518	10.51%	First individual gymnastic events
		b)	69	41		
	(For the first time women took part in open equestrian events.)					

(continued)

Table 9.1 Continued

Year	Host city		a) No. of competitors			Women's events
			Male	Female	% Females	
		b) No. of countries with competitors				
			Male	Female		
1956	Melbourne	a)	2,813	384	12%	
		b)	67	32		
1960	Rome	a)	4,736	610	11.41%	Reintroduction of
		b)	84	47		800 metres
1964	Tokyo	a)	4,457	683	13.29%	+ Volleyball
		b)	93	53		+ 400 metres
1968	Mexico City	a)	4,749	781	14.12%	+ Pentathlon
		b)	112	53		

(First female shooters took part in mixed event.)

Year	Host city		a)			Women's events
1972	Munich	a)	6,086	1,299	17.59%	+ 1500 metres
		b)	122	61		Archery reintroduced
1976	Montreal	a)	4,834	1,251	20.56%	
		b)	92	65		

Events open to women

100 metres, 200 metres, 400 metres, 800 metres, 1500 metres, 100 metres hurdles, 4 × 400 metres relay, high jump, long jump, shot, discus, javelin, pentathlon, archery, basketball,* canoeing, kayaks, fencing (foil and team foil), equestrian, gymnastics, handball,* swimming, volleyball, rowing* (* new sports)

(In the Winter Games women took part in 14 out of 37 events.)

Year	Host city		a)			Women's events
1980	Moscow	a)	4,238	1,088	20.43%	+ Field hockey
		b)	81	57		
1984	Los Angeles	a)	5,458	1,620	22.89%	+ 3,000 metres
		b)	140	95		+ Marathon
						+ Shooting
						+ Rhythmic gym
						+ Synchronized swimming
1988	Seoul	a)	7,105	2,476	25.84%	+ 10,000 metres
		b)	158	119		+ Tennis
						+ Table tennis
1992	Barcelona	a)	6,658	2,708	28.91%	+ Canoe slalom
		b)	169	135		+ Windsurfing
						+ Judo

Source: Information was gathered from a number of different sources including publications of *Olympic Review* and official figures from the British Olympic Association. Also Mitchell (1977) and Simri (1979).

MALE CONTROL OF FEMALE SPORTS

The main problem for women now, in their quest for equal opportunities in Olympic participation, is that they lack direct power to make changes because they have minimal representation on decision-making bodies. The National Olympic Committees (NOCs), which are in control of Olympic sports in individual nation-states; the International Federations of Sport (IFs), which have the monopoly of power to propose the introduction of Olympic events; and the IOC itself, which makes the final decision about which sports and events are included in the Olympic programme, are all heavily male-dominated organizations. During the 1980s a handful of women infiltrated the top management levels of international sports organizations, but they are exceptional, and have made very little impression on the overall power of men. Only seven women hold the position of president and four women that of secretary-general out of the 167 national Olympic committees. A woman is president of the Equestrian Sports Federation – the only female president from forty-eight International Federations of Olympic sports. There are two women who hold the position of secretary-general. Between 1884 and 1981 there were no women members of the IOC: the only way a woman could be appointed was for men to campaign on her behalf. But although Lord Killanin did so from the time of his election as president of the IOC in 1972, most of the other members remained fiercely opposed to female membership (Simri 1979). In 1977, for example, when the IOC elected twelve new members at the same time, they were *all* men; and in that year the IOC also resisted the setting up of a tripartite committee (IOC, NOCs and IFs) for women's sports. It was not until 1980, when Juan Samaranch was president, that two women were finally co-opted as members. (Monique Berlioux did hold office as director of the IOC from 1973 until 1985, but this is an administrative position with no voting power.) Samaranch has actively incorporated women into the IOC: he has invited them to serve on various IOC commissions and has appointed them to responsible positions on the secretariat. In 1993, out of a total of ninety-three, the IOC still had only seven female members; the president was male, there were four male vice-presidents, and of the rest of the executive board, who numbered six, only one was a woman. The male-weighting tends to be self-perpetuating because nominations for the IOC come from the National Olympic Committees, where women have low status, and because the IOC is a self-electing body whose members need not resign until they are 70 years of age (this rule does not apply to those who are already over 70 – they can remain in office until they die!). The IOC therefore still retains an essentially upper-class character, with royal and aristocratic fractions; its members are influential in their own societies with access to those who are politically and economically powerful. It is unlikely, therefore, that the IOC as a whole would be responsive to grass-roots opinion, or, in particular, to suggestions about eradicating gender divisions.

The Olympic movement is not simply to do with attitudes: it is a *system* of power based on gender. The femininity control test, which is obligatory for all female Olympic competitors (IOC 1991: 46), is the most potent symbol of the concern to prove that there is an absolute distinction between the sexes. 'Sex testing' (Dyer 1982; Ferris 1991; Lenskyj 1986) was introduced in order to prevent males from competing in women's events, and so it also symbolizes the idea of male athletic superiority. The IOC's interest in biological definitions of femininity was made public with the first large-scale testing carried out at the 1968 Olympics in Mexico. It was at a time when sportswomen, particularly from the eastern bloc, were producing outstanding performances and regularly breaking records. Not surprisingly, the western media were quick to castigate them as ambiguous women. The first official tests, which required all female Olympic competitors to undergo a physical inspection, were particularly demeaning, but even the more modern chromosomal tests present female athletes with a psychological hurdle which men do not have to surmount. In addition, the procedures have been insensitive and, for some, the results have been horribly destructive. By stereotyping femininity according to heterosexual standards, the tests force women to 'prove' themselves and can be particularly threatening to those women who are naturally flat-chested and heavily muscled. But some sportswomen, who have lived their lives believing themselves to be unambiguously female, and who have been found to have chromosomal irregularities (which have rendered them ineligible for competition even when they do not confer any sporting advantage), have had their lives shattered. Although the sex chromatin test is less of an obvious invasion of privacy than the original physical examination, Elizabeth Ferris (1991: 19) argues that it 'is more likely to exclude athletes unfairly than to detect those who cheat'. During the two and a half decades that femininity tests for female Olympic athletes have been in operation, although no male has been found to be masquerading as a female, women have improved their Olympic performances remarkably, and in many sports continue to narrow the performance gap with men.

In reality, as Dyer makes clear, sex differences are not straightforward, absolute and unchanging:

> In every phase of sex differentiation – chromosomal, hormonal, anatomical, psychological and social – there are overlaps, ambiguities, uncertainties and changes of sexual identity. Changing medical and social practices will increase their frequency and raise their visibility rather than lower them and hide them. Any definition of sex is an arbitrary one subject to change as social pressures change.
>
> (Dyer 1982: 65)

In response to vigorous petitioning over a number of years for new testing methods for female eligibility, which would eliminate the destructive effects on those athletes found to have anomalous chromosomal arrangements, the IAAF agreed that the femininity test should be discontinued for the 1991 World Athletic Championships in Tokyo. It was replaced with a health test for all athletes, regardless of their sex. Elizabeth Ferris (1991) argues that if a person has lived as a woman and has always believed herself to be so, then she should be allowed to compete as a woman. And if a woman has a sporting advantage for any anatomical or physiological reason, it should not bar her from competition. For example, those who are very tall are not barred from participating in basketball or volleyball. A proper health check, carried out thoroughly and ethically, would stop anyone from calculated cheating, in the same way that drug tests are carried out in order to stop athletes from gaining an unfair advantage. The IOC, however, refused to instigate new testing procedures for the 1992 Barcelona Olympics and so some competitors in those Games had eligibility certificates from the IAAF, based on a health test, and others still had to undergo a sex chromatin test. The different treatment of individual sportswomen at the Barcelona Olympics should put pressure on the IOC to follow the lead of the IAAF.

Male supremacy in the IOC has ensured that, throughout the history of the modern Olympics, men have made decisions about women's participation, and male standards have become generalized standards. However, public awareness of gender issues has inevitably influenced the IOC to make changes, and the female membership of the IOC, however small, should help. An example of the IOC's response to external pressure can be found in the *Olympic Charter*. Whereas the category 'sex' used to be omitted from the clause on discrimination (Hargreaves 1984a), it is now included: 'Any form of discrimination with regard to a country or a person on grounds of race, religion, politics, sex, or otherwise is incompatible with belonging to the Olympic Movement' (IOC 1991: 9).

The necessity to redress the imbalance between male and female participation in different member countries is acknowledged in the IOC rule which states that 'only sports widely practised by men in at least seventy-five countries and on four continents, and by women in at least forty countries and on three continents, may be included in the programme of the Games of the Olympiad' (IOC 1991: 52). However, the IOC is considering changing the rule which allows one athlete from each country to compete in an event without having reached the qualifying time or distance. Only if more than one athlete is entered are they required to meet qualifying standards. If the rule is changed so that everyone has to reach the Olympic standard, it would inevitably militate against women from developing countries where the infrastructures and standards of women's sports are often basic, but where women need international contacts and competition to enhance growth.

The IOC, in common with other powerful, male-dominated institutions, has created patterns of participation and control that are difficult to change. Also in common with other institutions, however, the IOC has not been able to insulate itself entirely from changing attitudes to gender outside its immediate influence.

POLITICAL INTERVENTION

The concern for equivalence with men at the Olympics coheres with a liberal feminist perspective. Liberal sports feminists have been campaigning for the same opportunities as men in training, competition, media coverage and sponsorship in order to have the same chances to reach the highest levels in sports. But the issue has been treated as an insular one, and in the early years of the modern Olympics, because the IOC was an all-male body and wielded exceptional power, the struggle for equivalence with men was understandably, although incorrectly, conceptualized as exclusively male vs female. Although the IOC is still powerful, it has less autonomy and authority than in previous years, and other factors influence the character of Olympic sports for women to a greater extent than has ever been the case before. However, although political and economic imperatives have influenced IOC decisions and made the balance of power more complex than ever before, there have been remarkably few organized initiatives which, in common with the lobby of the American physical educators in the 1930s, have questioned the essential value of the Olympics and the relationship to wider social, economic and political issues.

The interweaving of sports with politics, and the efforts of individual countries to accumulate Olympic medals, have provided a major incentive to improve the standards of elite sports for women and make women's events integral to national sports policies. The debut of the USSR into the Olympics in 1952 spearheaded the fierce competition between eastern- and western-bloc countries that accelerated the creation of Olympic sportswomen as medal collectors. Because international sports, in general, and Olympic sports, in particular, were predominantly male, it was possible for a country without an established sporting history to make an impact on the international stage by concentrating on the medal potential of its women. The eastern-bloc countries did this incredibly successfully by making elite female sports a central component of their sports systems (Riordan 1985, 1986). In 1968, when East Germany entered the modern Olympics for the first time as a separate nation-state, the dramatic way in which its women dominated international athletics and swimming further strengthened the political dynamics of female sports. A decade later, eastern European women were pre-eminent in athletics, swimming, gymnastics and rowing, and held 86 per cent of world records in track and field athletics. In 1976 women from communist countries won 73 per cent of all the Olympic medals. The incredible successes of sportswomen from the eastern bloc, and the production of sports heroines, such as Soviet gymnast Olga Korbut, who captivated the imagination of people across the world at the 1972 Olympics, increased the visibility and popularity of sports for women, and stimulated the expansion of women's international sports.

The explicit sports ideologies and systems of the USSR and the GDR provided models for all communist countries, and also infuenced western countries and developing nations. Under communism relatively equal resources were devoted to male and female sports; and during the 1970s the Soviet and East German Olympic teams were composed of a higher proportion of female athletes than western teams, and the women in their teams won a higher percentage of medals than the men. (All countries that have done well in the medal tables have a relatively high percentage of female competitors.) Female champions were used as national assets to promote patriotism at home and political prestige abroad.

Since the demise of the USSR and the unification of the two Germanies in 1990, criticism of the social construction of sports under communism has intensified. The past has been narrowly and exclusively defined in terms of alternatives and opposites – East versus West; communism versus capitalism – and the apparent absolute victory of liberalism has exposed the problems of the sports systems of the old communist states. These countries made instrumental use of their women by concentrating on the individuals, sports, events and methods that would produce medals: from a very young age female champions were systematically engineered by identification, isolation, testing and coaching procedures. Most highly criticized was the officially sanctioned use of drugs and other performance-enhancing agents. Commentators from the West claim that sports under communism were hugely expensive, profoundly authoritarian and riddled with deceit and corruption (Hargreaves 1990). But the implication that sports in the West are uncorrupted is misleading: early specialization, intense training, fierce competition, cheating and high wastage have become common components of elite female sports in all industrialized countries. The concern to do well in international competition is one of the reasons why state intervention in the West has increased in recent years, and why elite sports for women are being encouraged. Olympism also has its own specific imperative which is inextricably linked to capitalist market forces, and young girls get sucked into a competitive system in which they are encouraged to perform like machines in order to become famous and wealthy. The emphasis on success, the exaltation of records, and the cult of sports heroes and heroines have been characteristics of elite sports under capitalism as well as communism; together with the marketing of champions, the system produces a very powerful influence on aspiring Olympic performers. It is not unusual for children to be pushed into the system at 3 or 4 years of age, and in the USA the term 'battered child athletes' is used to describe children who are physically and psychologically damaged as a result. Since girls peak earlier than boys, the problem is more acute for them. Very young girls are regularly subjected to stress and danger in order to increase the level of technical skill and spectacle; 'over-use injuries' are commonplace, and there is a lack of preventative screening (Wilkinson 1984). Although East Germany has been rightly criticized for its official programme of drug-taking, the systematic drug-taking that has always gone on in the West (ibid.) exposes the hypocrisy of western analyses of communist sports and the inherent corruption of Olympic sports. The commercial and media manipulation of top-level sportswomen under capitalism (see the previous chapter) has been highlighted since ex-East German athletes, like Katerina Krabbe, instantly became million-dollar performers in the West.

The de-colonization of the old totalitarian regimes has ended some forms of repression and hardship, but has brought new problems. Sports, in general, and women's sports, specifically, have undoubtedly been affected. In the new eastern European nations elite sports are less privileged, and it is unlikely that their women will continue to dominate Olympic sports. (It has been argued that the dove-tailing of East Germany's expertise with West Germany's financial power provides great potential for the sportswomen of the united Germany to predominate in future Olympics – although this did not seem to be the case at the Barcelona Olympics.) There are effects as well for 'ordinary' women in the new units of the old USSR and the newly democratized nations of eastern Europe: whereas sports were previously virtually free of charge for all citizens, and the encouragement of female sports did much to eliminate sexism, these patterns are changing radically. In the new Czech republic, in common with other newly established states, serious economic problems and privatization have resulted in a lack of funding for the maintenance of sporting infrastructures (Mikan 1993). In addition, people are working harder and for longer hours and participation rates are dropping radically (ibid.). Communism held down traditional differences and rivalries that are now emerging as new expressions of religious, cultural and racial exclusiveness; the breakdown of integrative trends will inevitably mean that in the future women from the old communist states will be excluded from access to sports resources in the same way that those who live in other countries with cultural, ethnic and economic divisions are. Capitalist market forces have always discriminated against women in sports – there are no signs that the new systems of demo-cratization in the old communist states will be different. Because socialism has been devalued in the West as well, there has been a resistance in democracies like Britain to the discourse of caring and community. The resultant fear that welfare-based sports may be dismantled, and commercial-ized and elite sports encouraged, is an ironic twist. It is certain that in future the commodified characteristics of international sports, and specifically Olympic ones, will predominate in the East and the West. It is also likely that this trend will be present as organized sports spread through the developing world, and more women from developing countries enter Olympic com-petition. For example, the recent shift in various African states away from

socialist strategies of development towards a market economy and democratic pluralism (Tordoff 1992) will facilitate the universalization of Olympic
sports for women.

GLOBALIZATION OF WOMEN'S OLYMPIC SPORTS

The entry of the USSR into the Olympics in 1952, together with Israel, New
Zealand and Uruguay, signalled the spread of Olympism to countries with
less well-established sporting histories. Since 1952, most of the countries that
have joined the Olympic movement have been developing countries from
Africa, Asia and Latin America, where sports have been state-controlled for
utilitarian purposes and used as agents of social change (Riordan 1986).
Although the participation of these countries has increased the scale of the
Olympic movement, it has been the result of an increase in male rather than
female competitors. In general, the greater the economic and social resources of a country, particularly in terms of education, health care and
nutrition, the more likely it is that women will be part of a general national
sports scheme. But developing societies are relatively poor with limited
resources. In addition, other variables, such as religion, tend to militate
against the development of women's sports. In general, the status of women
in the developing world is far behind that of women in the developed world,
and although in some cases sports have undoubtedly contributed to the
social emancipation of women, most developing countries have only a small
number of female Olympic competitors, or none at all. Between 1952 and
1972, the number of countries in the Olympics rose from 69 to 121 – an
increase of 75 per cent; the number of countries that entered women rose
from 41 to 61 per cent – an increase of only 49 per cent. In 1976, when the
African nations boycotted the Montreal Games, the effect on women's
competitions was minimal; if the boycott had not occurred, the percentage
of countries with no female competitors would have risen to 64 per cent.

By 1988, although the percentage of countries with female competitors
had increased, there was still a marked imbalance. At the Summer Olympics
in Seoul there were contenders from 160 countries; 42 countries sent only
male athletes and 1 country sent only female athletes. Of those that had
mixed contingents, the great majority had more males than females in their
teams. The figures in Table 9.2 show, first the number of male competitors
from each country, followed by the number of females, and then the percentage (to the nearest whole figure) of females in each team, starting with
the five countries that had more female than male competitors. These figures
can be misleading because when the overall numbers are very small, one or
two sportswomen can produce a high percentage. In the case of Burma, for
example, two athletes constitute the whole contingent, or 100 per cent. And
the percentages of women do not reflect a spread across different sports. The
case of Peru illustrates how a team sport can exaggerate the figures – twelve

Table 9.2 Numbers of male and female competitors in Olympic teams, 1988: countries sending more females

	Males	Females	% Females in team
Burma	0	2	100%
Ivory Coast	16	18	53%
Malaysia	5	8	62%
Peru	7	14	67%
Romania	34	39	53%

of the fourteen female representatives were members of the volleyball team. The case of Romania reflects more accurately the involvement of women from eastern European countries in a range of sports, and the generally high percentage of women in their teams.

Table 9.3 shows capitalist and socialist countries with established sports traditions. They all had much bigger teams, and the figures indicate more realistically a general pattern of participation. Although they all had more

Table 9.3 Numbers of male and female competitors in Olympic teams, 1988: countries with established sports traditions

	Males	Females	% Females in team
China	158	135	46%
GDR	173	115	40%
Belgium	39	26	40%
Bulgaria	122	74	38%
USA	388	224	37%
GB	238	132	36%
USSR	351	173	33%
Denmark	62	26	30%
Canada	265	117	31%
FRG	288	119	29%
Australia	216	79	27%
France	225	82	27%
Finland	76	27	26%
Japan	213	75	26%
Brazil	138	35	20%
Italy	243	53	18%
Spain	231	42	15%

men in their contingents than women, China, the German Democratic Republic and Bulgaria had the highest percentages of women and the Soviet Union had a 'respectable' one third of its team who were women. In the capitalist countries the percentages of women were higher in those with a tradition of women's sports and lowest in Spain, Italy, Brazil and Japan, where gender inequalities in sports and throughout society are greater.

All countries that sent no female athletes were from the developing world. In all developing countries gender differences are magnified by comparison with gender divisions in the developed world. There are numerous other factors that militate against women's participation in sports – for example, poverty, weak economies, political instability, race and religion – and various combinations of such factors are relevant to different countries. Of those selected in Table 9.4, Bangladesh, Iran, Iraq, Pakistan and Saudi Arabia are all Muslim countries where religion is a powerful deterrent to the development of public sports for women, but where other factors vary in their effects. Zambia represents African countries where culture and the economy are the major material constraints on female participation.

The majority of developing countries have very small teams and they either send no women at all, or have a tiny number in one or two sports only. The overall participation of women from developing countries and repressive regimes is minimal. There are very few organized sports for women who are more likely to take part in indigenous games which do not fulfil the criteria to be Olympic sports. There are some developing countries with reasonably sized teams and a substantial percentage of female competitors. These are representative of countries where there is an established sports infrastructure, particularly as part of education. This is the case in the Bahamas, Jamaica and India, for example. Even so, most mixed teams from developing countries contain much lower percentages of female athletes than teams from developed nations. The focus on male athletes from some African countries, such as Kenya and Nigeria, has spearheaded a growing interest in female athletes as national resources although, overall, the per-

Table 9:4 Numbers of male and female competitors in Olympic teams, 1988: countries sending no females

	Males	Females	% Females in team
Bangladesh	6	0	0%
Iran	27	0	0%
Iraq	35	0	0%
Pakistan	32	0	0%
Saudi Arabia	14	0	0%
Zambia	31	0	0%

centages of female athletes from most African countries remain very small or nonexistent. The growth of regional competitions (African Games, Asian Games, Commonwealth Games, for example) is a prerequisite for the development of Olympic sports in these countries.

Although the figures in Table 9.5 give us a general idea about the distribution of women in various national Olympic teams, like all 'evidence' of this sort, it is incomplete and can be interpreted in different ways. Only a selection of Olympic countries is presented here, because otherwise the figures and variables would be too unwieldy. In developed countries where women have been participating in international sports since the end of the nineteenth century, the percentages of female Olympic participants are understandably higher, and are representative of grass-roots participation in a spread of sports throughout those societies. Olympic participation of women from developing nations tends to be in a much narrower range of sports and is much more variable between countries. The figures do not show the size of populations, however, and in some cases, the relatively small numbers of female participants represent surprisingly substantial percentages. In Canada, Finland, the GDR, Jamaica, and Trinidad and Tobago, for example, the numbers of women participating represent much higher percentages of the total female populations of those societies than the figures for the USA and the USSR – the two countries that have sent more athletes than any others.

It is difficult to generalize about factors affecting women's participation in the Olympics on a global scale. They are culturally specific and relate to the economic and political systems of different nation-states. Religious ideologies, for example, tend to be backward-looking, but the attitudes to

Table 9.5 Numbers of male and female competitors in Olympic teams, 1988: developing countries

	Males	Females	% Females in team
Ghana	11	7	39%
Jamaica	24	11	31%
Angola	22	7	24%
Bahamas	13	4	24%
Zimbabwe	23	7	23%
India	43	8	16%
Bolivia	6	1	14%
Nigeria	66	9	12%
Algeria	41	4	9%
Kenya	71	5	7%
Barbados	17	1	6%

women's sports of, for example, the Protestant, Catholic, Greek Orthodox and Muslim faiths vary, and the same religion has different effects in different countries. In general, however, assessed in a framework of western ideology, the influence of Islamic ideologies has slowed the liberative potential of sports for women (see Chapter 10). At the 1988 Summer Olympics in Seoul, 21 Muslim countries sent only male competitors, although Riordan (1986) gives the examples of Albania, Afghanistan and the former USSR, with sizeable Muslim populations, where state strategies have been used to break down traditional barriers to women's participation in sports. In the case of Nigeria, women have made considerable inroads into a previously exclusively male preserve, although most Nigerian sportswomen originate from the predominantly Christian south of the country and not from the Muslim north. In most Islamic states where sports are accessible to Muslim females, it is usually in single-sex schools, but many schools provide no opportunities; when girls leave school, participation is closed to them unless there are facilities where exclusive use by women can be guaranteed (because of the cultural and religious traditions of Islam which disallow women from participating in public). Women are forced to participate during unsocial hours and to wear unsuitable clothing in order to keep their bodies covered and away from the eyes of men. But, anyway, most sports resources in Islamic countries are for men and many men will not allow their wives or daughters to take part. In some Islamic states, however, there has been a planned drive to develop women's sports in recent years – for example, in Bahrain (a modern Islamic state with a population of only half a million people, a comprehensive education system and free health care), a head of women's sport has been appointed and in just over one year (1992–3) the number of sports centres for the exclusive use of women (mostly in girls' schools) rose from five to nineteen (with 2,5000 participants) (Hijris 1993). However, the laws and traditions in some Islamic countries make the development of sports for post school-age females painfully slow. In Jordan, for example, the government passed a law in 1993, proposed by the Muslim Brotherhood (the single largest political bloc), to ban mixed sports centres throughout the country. It is inevitable that this will delay the development of sports for women. In Algeria female athletes are being used as political pawns. The recent increased power of the Front Islamique du Salut (FIS) – the Muslim fundamentalist movement – is likely to reverse the liberating tendencies of women's sports. Hassiba Boulmerka, who is only the second Arab woman to win major sporting titles (1500 metres champion at the 1991 World Athletics Championships and Olympic Champion in 1992), was denounced by the FIS and her safety was threatened for running in public in running shorts and vest. She now lives in exile in Italy. When Muslim women participate in public they become symbols of struggle; therefore the FIS is targeting female athletes in its attempt to halt the progressive political and religious trends of recent years.

Female sports are resisted in Muslim countries because they represent and reinforce radical and westernized ideas about women and women's bodies which threaten established gender values and relations. There are increasing numbers of Muslim sports feminists, however, who are struggling for the growth of women's sports in their own countries and throughout the Muslim world. Some of these women want Islamic attitudes to change so that Muslim women can participate freely in international sport. Their efforts have been strengthened and co-ordinated by the formation of the Islamic Countries Sports Solidarity Congress for Women. The struggle involves demands for more sports resources for women, including facilities, equipment and trained coaches. In most cases the struggle remains confined to the Muslim world – for example, the first World Women's Islamic Games (which have been dubbed the Muslim Women's Olympics), held in Tehran in 1993, was an all-women affair involving competitors from thirteen Asian and African Islamic nations in eight Olympic sports. All events were held behind closed doors and audiences were all-female; none of the events could be shown on television and winners were required to wear chadors (traditional face-masking robes) for photographs. But the shift required to enable Muslim sportswomen to participate in events that are not controlled by Islamic traditions and to allow them to see outstanding female athletes such as Hassiba Boulmerka competing in the Olympics is massive.

Race as well as gender is a variable affecting the Olympic potential of women in countries such as Zimbabwe and South Africa. Although independence was achieved in Zimbabwe in 1979, there are still fewer black than white female athletes because sports have been part of the tradition of white culture and have been better resourced in white communities. Stark gender inequalities in the black communities diminish the likelihood that the numbers of black sportswomen will increase dramatically. Modern sports have never been a part of the culture and traditions of black women in Zimbabwe – there is still tremendous pressure for them to stay at home and have the total responsibility for domestic work and child-care. And there are no women in the top levels of the governing bodies of sports in Zimbabwe to act as a pressure group – black women are involved more in the development of dance and other cultural activities. Cultural pressures will inevitably present a powerful constraint to black South African women as well. Although South Africa re-entered Olympic competition during the early stages of the dismantling of apartheid, black women face a tremendous struggle to be represented in their country's elite sports squads. The only South African sportswoman who was successful at the Barcelona Olympics was a white woman, Elana Meyer – the sporting potential of the black female South African population is untapped and unknown. Their sports resources have always been impoverished and they have no sports tradition to build on. Although the new multiracial sports associations are obligated to open up sports in the black townships, most of the development so far has built on the existing traditions of sports for black males. A huge investment in sports resources is required if black women in South Africa are to achieve equity in sports either with white women, or with black men. However, equity issues in South African sports are already topical and women are involved in the debates. In the same way that South African feminists are working through the Women's National Coalition to ensure that women's rights are embodied in the new constitution, black and white sports feminists are actively campaigning for their rights in South African sports. They were represented at the first Olympic Academy of the non-racial National Olympic Committee of South Africa (NOCSA), held in 1993, when the issue of gender equity was debated (Berck 1993).

It would be wrong to underestimate the positive benefits that sports have brought to the lives of increasing numbers of women from developing countries and the importance of sports as symbols of women's liberation in those countries. However, the ethical dimension of Olympic sports for women in the developing world is masked by quantifying and describing participatory trends. More than two-thirds of the world's women come from developing countries, and for huge numbers of them survival is a way of life; they live daily with poverty and sickness. Spending money on a sporting elite can be a critical drain on the resources of a nation with famine, malnutrition, poor housing and limited education, health and medical services. In many African and Asian countries, the social position of women remains one of extreme subordination, and they bear the brunt of poverty and famine. When women are struggling to survive multiple pregnancies, when infant mortality is excessively high, and when few women are educated, it is inappropriate to consider sports participation as a serious issue. In such countries as sub-Saharan Ethiopia and Somalia, where people are dying of starvation and disease, it seems obscene to debate the likelihood of Olympic participation for those few women who have escaped the deprivations of the majority. Nevertheless, the unprecedented success of Ethiopian Derartu Tulu, who won the 10,000 metres in the Barcelona Olympics, was a symbol of hope for women in third world Africa. She was the first black African woman to win an Olympic gold medal. From a family of ten children, she used to run 5 kilometres to school each day and to take part in competitions while at high school. Although the communist government collapsed in mid-1991, and the new regime is practically bankrupt, she is still revered and allowed to be a full-time athlete – on her return from Barcelona to Addis Ababa she was cheered, showered with gifts, presented with a lump sum (£6,700) by the government, and promoted to the rank of major. Derartu Tulu has been described as the most famous woman in Ethiopia and 'more success will make her a wealthy woman in a land of immense poverty' (Nichols 1993). Her success demonstrates a poignant contradiction: on the one hand she has broken the pattern that Olympic sports benefit only the elites in developing countries who are predominantly male; on the other hand, like western foods, popular literature and music, Olympic sports have been imported by transnational corporations to the developing world, regardless of the political, economic and social climate – in spite of Derartu Tulu's success, it is still the case that for the majority of women in the world, the modern Olympics are an irrelevance.

CONCLUSION

For increasing numbers of more fortunate women from the developing world the desire to escape from a life of labour and hardship can be the incentive to win an Olympic gold medal. The global popularity of the Olympics demonstrates the cultural power of sports which pulls more and more women from across the world into their ambit. Yet with remarkably few exceptions, women are moving to fit into the existing patterns of participation and structures of control, rather than arguing for qualitative changes. It is even more difficult for underprivileged women from the developing world to understand the elitism and commodified form of the Olympics, and the associations with political nationalism and a whole number of corrupt practices, than for women who live in the West. Because women's experiences are culturally specific, there is no generalized notion of consciousness which can be applied to 'women in the Olympics'. The IOC and its affiliated organizations continue to be a 'world of men', infiltrated by a tiny number of women. But women need *direct* power in the Olympics, equally with men, not indirect or 'irresponsible' power as surrogate males. Power in the Olympics should not only be to do with having a choice from a number of alternatives, but rather to be involved in the formulation of those alternatives.

Chapter 10

Sports for all women
Problems and progress

INTRODUCTION

The following brief account of some of the main events in women's sports in Britain since the Second World War sets the scene for recent changes and debates.[1] Although during the war many events stopped altogether (for example, roller- and ice-skating rinks, swimming pools and sports grounds were closed), there was a surprising continuity in some female sports. Ironically, the evacuation of schools and factories from London, where women's sports were well established, facilitated growth in other parts of the country. In the case of netball, for example, club tournaments and county trials continued so that when the war was over all levels of national competition could be resumed quickly. Netball had become the most widely played game in girls' schools and colleges (in comparison with hockey, which required large grassed pitches and was more difficult to play in wintry conditions). In other countries, where the war had a less direct influence on people's lives, the development of women's sports at national level was also fully established. This was a necessary prerequisite for the growth of international organizations and competitions. For example, in 1960 the International Netball Federation was instituted and international rules were drawn up, and in 1963 the first World Tournament was hosted by England.

But women's competitive sports at this time were run on a shoe-string, militating against the full growth of competition, coaching and umpiring programmes. In contrast with men's sports, grant-aid and sponsorship were negligible (for example, although the British Ministry of Education subsidized a national netball coaching scheme, most other women's sports lacked funding, and although the Central Council of Physical Recreation (CCPR) gave grants to individual sports, the governing bodies of mixed sports, such as swimming, allocated more to the men's activities). Inequities between men's and women's sports, sustained by the philosophies of amateurism and voluntarism, were apparent in all western countries. They worked to the disadvantage of working-class women to a greater extent than their middle-class counterparts; those who could not afford travelling expenses at home and abroad were prevented from participating.

Physical education in Britain continued to be sex-segregated, and under the tripartite system of education most grammar schools had better facilities than technical and secondary modern schools. The ideologies of familism and domesticity re-emerged after the war, which, together with the constraints of waged labour and lack of spending power, structured the sports participation of working-class women in particular. Nevertheless, there were some predominantly working-class school- and club-teams which flourished, although female sports overall continued to have a very strong middle-class character, and were controlled by women with traditional ideas. In addition, women's sports were features of an essentially 'white' culture – first generation immigrants, predominantly from the Indian subcontinent, the Caribbean and Africa, were not integrated into mainstream sports. Class and ethnic differences, as well as gender differences, were thus effectively institutionalized in sports. However, the establishment of comprehensive education nudged school sports in the direction of greater democratization, although class, gender and ethnic inequalities changed only partially. In addition, the provision of sports for women, viewed as an aspect of welfarism, resulted in community programmes which have been some of the most radical examples of grass-roots development. The various state apparatuses – those of central government, local governments and quasi-government organizations – have been centrally involved in sports provision for women. Although the focus here is on the British context, and each nation-state has specific cultural, economic and political differences which mediate women's sports, there are many parallels between the British context and other countries in the West. The interface between sports and one or more of such factors as class, education, ethnicity, ideology, gender and politics is significant to them all.

There were influences also from outside the West. The year 1952 – when the Soviet Union made its debut in the Summer Olympics – marked a watershed. From that time women became an important part of international sports strategies. Countries in the West looked to the apparently anti-sexist sports systems of eastern European countries as symbolic of success. A reappraisal of western sports policies and state provision followed. It has generally been acknowledged in the West that efficient systems of mass sport have to be established in order to maximize talent, and that tapping the potential of girls and women is an important aspect of such a philosophy. Although it was not until 1972 that the government-funded British Sports Council was founded, and only during the next decade that women were targeted as a needy group, there had already been a gradual expansion of the organizing mechanisms of women's sports and a more professional and businesslike approach to development.

Women's sports have also been greatly influenced by burgeoning commercialization. The rapid globalization of sports (with the development of sophisticated communications and technology and cheap travel) has strengthened the link between sports and commerce. As we have seen in Chapter 7, producing female sports as glamorous and spectacular, systematically sexualizing and personalizing sporting females, and promoting physical activity as an aid to female health and beauty, have become profitable features of leisure and 'showbiz'. Commercialized forms of female exercise have been central to the increase in sports consumer expenditure and the sporting female has been successfully commodified for pleasure and profit.

To imply that women have been simply manipulated by the imperatives of governments and capitalists, however, is misleading. The present situation in women's sports is highly complex and has varied and contradictory features. Some women have little choice in their lives and are seriously constrained by cultural, economic and political structures; other women have achieved relative autonomy in their sporting lives; there are women who still cling to past traditions and ideas; and there are those who are forging radical policies. The idealized image of the 'ladylike' sportswoman, dominant in the first two decades of the twentieth century, has been challenged, and to a large extent replaced, by a more dynamic, self-confident and truly athletic image. Women are constantly breaking fetters with which they have historically been bound; they are beating men's past records; out-performing men in direct sporting competitions; and their skills, speed and endurance are continually improving. The dominant trend has been 'to catch up with the men' and to model female sports on the values and traditions of male sports to which aggressive competition, sexism, commercialization and political nationalism are endemic. Although this tendency makes change difficult, nevertheless women who dislike the dominant characteristics of sports have forged for themselves radical alternatives. This chapter is concerned with questions of freedom and constraint and the conditions under which, and the extent to which, women have been able to control their own activities.

'SPORT FOR ALL': GENDERED FACTS AND FIGURES

The ideal of 'Sport for All' emanates from the principles of social democracy and human rights; it implies non-discrimination, non-elitism and popular alternatives to mainstream sports. 'Sport for All' is an ideal concerning equality of opportunity – for those of different ages, classes, ethnicities, genders and sexualities; those who are disabled as well as the able-bodied; and those with varying levels of talent and aspiration.

During the 1960s the philosophy of equality of opportunity filtered into sports discourse in response to public debates focusing on inequalities in education and work. Although the feminist movement of the 1960s had failed to look at sports seriously, it raised awareness about the subordinate position of women in all areas of life, and stimulated the growth of sports feminism. By the 1980s, attention had become focused on the huge gap that still existed between the sports participation rates of men and those of women, and policy-makers targeted women as a group for special treatment in order to redress inequalities. Public bodies openly acknowledged that women are a category of special need and the GB Sports Council has played a leading role in the development of policies and practices for women's sports. As the leading government agency for sports, the council reflects the 'establishment position'; it has an influential public voice, and the financial means to shift the gender relations of power in sports by deciding on whom, for which sports and in support of what schemes its annual grant from the central government shall be spent. In the financial year 1988/9 the grant was £38,412,000; in 1989/90 it was £41,877,000; in 1990/1 £44,747,000; in 1991/2 £46,008,850 and in 1992/3 £48,762,000. Although the amount of money available to the council each year is very small in comparison with the total amount of public spending on sports (most is spent by local authorities), the Sports Council is in a uniquely powerful position. Because it works in partnership with numerous other agencies (for example, local authorities, health and education authorities, youth services, commercial firms, govern-ing bodies and sports clubs, and other voluntary associations), its influence is pervasive.

The Sports Council's aim in 1982 was to increase women's participation in indoor sports from 3.1 million to 4.1 million and in outdoor sports from 4.8 million to 5.7 million (over a 5-year period up to 1987). For indoor sports the increase was marginally short of the target (from 19.5 per cent to 24.2 per cent – almost 1 million), but the number of women participating in outdoor sports actually fell during that time (from 25 per cent to 24.3 per cent – about 100,000). Over the next five years (1988–93) the aim was to increase women's indoor participation by 70 per cent and outdoor participation by 35 per cent (an extra 1.25 million). Although the figures are for 'women' as a unitary group, the emphasis has changed to take account of the different needs of various groups of women – particular priority being given to the 13–24 and 45–59 age groups (Sports Council 1988a). Throughout the 1980s and into the 1990s 'partnership projects' have been organized to increase women's par-ticipation in sports in innovative ways, some of which have been hugely successful. Through its regional offices, the Sports Council liaises with people from other agencies in local communities throughout the country. Some of the most notable developments have been local authority ones where the sporting franchise has been extended to groups which have traditionally found it difficult to participate. In this respect, local authorities have a far better record than private and voluntary providers. Courses are organized that focus on specific activities, specific groups of women, and/or their specific needs and problems. All types of arrangements have been made to encourage wider involvement – day courses, weekend courses, evening courses, residential courses, courses in the locality and courses at more distant venues. Increased participation has been the major aim of these activities and outreach work has been particularly successful. More recently, courses have been organized to promote women into leadership and coaching roles in order to increase the scope of involvement of women in sports, the range of activities that can be offered by women, and the power that women wield in sports. In addition, sports-governing bodies, associations and clubs are involved in sports-specific development work: numerous schemes have been devised to attract girls and women of all ages and abilities to particular sports, although the focus in most cases is on programmes for youth and the potential for success in international sports.

Much of this work has been done by sports development officers who have special responsibility for women. They are employed by local authorities and sports-governing bodies, often partly funded by the Sports Council; their work in the main is auxiliary to the work of leisure centre departments. The specific brief for most development officers is to provide a service for those women in the community who do not go to leisure centres or belong to a sports club. Most of these women are in low-user categories – for example, single parents, the low-waged, overweight and elderly, those from ethnic minority groups, those who have no access to private transport, or who have played no sports since leaving school. Because many women find sports venues difficult to get to, expensive and intimidating, cheap 'women-only' sessions at venues which are within easy reach of residential areas, and where the environment is welcoming, have been the most successful. The Sports Council (1992a) confirms that for provision to be appropriate for girls and women there should be ease of accessibility by public transport; proximity to residential areas; good safety measures such as plentiful lighting, especially around the access routes and car parks; changing areas which provide for flexible use (family changing/private cubicles); child-care provision; pleasant social spaces and a friendly atmosphere; women-only classes and spaces; classes arranged at times when women are most likely to have free time; and cheap rates.

In most cases these criteria are lacking, and there are other problems as well which militate against female participation. A major one is the problem of funding – there is quite simply too little money to provide a service which deals adequately with the specific needs of all groups; there are too few development officers responsible for huge numbers and areas; the range of possible options is severely restricted; and in many cases money is only provided to instigate a course, and then if continued the course is expected to be self-financing. Activities such as keep-fit and aerobics are relatively cheap and therefore tend to attract women from different social backgrounds, whereas a course for 'Women in the Outdoors', which incorporates activities such as rock-climbing and hang-gliding, is expensive and attracts more or less exclusively middle-class women. Not surprisingly, much of the expansion of women's sports has been linked to stereotyped ideas about what women want – aerobics, keep-fit, swimming and yoga are highly favoured. Because in many contexts they are the only activities available, the idea that they are all that women want is confirmed. However, when women are offered subsidized 'tasters' of a less predictable kind, the evidence shows that a surprising number choose to take part. The likely interest of women in a variety of sports has probably been greatly underestimated (Women's Sports Foundation 1990).

Local authority adult education programmes for women's sports have been some of the most radical because they tend to reflect 'what women want rather than what someone else thinks they want' (Women's Sports Foundation 1990: 9). Many women avoid the machismo and aggressive competitiveness found in a lot of sports contexts and mixed courses, and prefer programmes that cohere with their own values and life-styles. For example, combinations of short courses and drop-in courses, women-only groups, female coaching, a wide range of activities to choose from at a minimal cost or without charge, crèche facilities, a friendly, supportive environment, and links with other women's issues (including health and alternative medicine) have been high recruiters. Those projects that make sports attractive and accessible to women, with staff and organizations that value a 'woman-friendly' philosophy, have consistently been the most successful in attracting new participants.

Nevertheless, in spite of the great amount of time, energy and resources deployed to increase the numbers of women taking part in regular exercise, figures are still far below those for men. In 1986 there was a big discrepancy between male and female participation overall: 56.9 per cent men/37.2 per cent women – about 10 million men and 7 million women (Sports Council 1991: 10), and in the 1990s there are still big gender differences. A survey entitled *Sports Market*, published in 1991 by Mintel, shows that:

39 per cent of active sportsmen take their sport seriously or quite seriously, compared to only 17 per cent of sportswomen. And 33 per cent of the women questioned never take part in any sport, compared with 17 per cent of the men. And in the traditional male sports such as football and rugby, men still massively outnumber women. In golf, male players outnumber female players by seven to one, though in athletics and jogging the ratio drops to three to one. Squash has seen a fall-off in female players over recent years and tennis, traditionally enjoyed by both sexes, has more male players. Only keep-fit and aerobics appeal almost exclusively to women, and, interestingly, weight training has gained popularity with women (6 per cent of women compared to 14 per cent of men). Marginally more women are still taking a dip, and swimming is by far the most popular sport enjoyed by both sexes.

(*Sport and Leisure*, Vol. 32, No. 2: 4)

A regional study carried out in the north-west (NWCSR 1991: 6) confirms the findings of previous surveys showing that the gap between men's and women's participation is greatest in that part of the country. Women are the largest group (around 3 million) who are under-represented in sports in the region, and the figures for the participation of women aged between 25 and 60 is lower than the national average. The gap between men's and women's participation in indoor activities in the north-west has closed slightly from 20.3 per cent to 16.3 per cent, but for outdoor activities it has increased from 12.67 per cent to 18 per cent. In common with other depressed areas of the country where there is a high level of unemployment and the lack of a tradition of women's sports, even with a highly creative approach, it is difficult to persuade women to participate.

Research shows that the improvements in women's participation rates have been uneven, and the Sports Council has acknowledged the problem:

> One million more women have been attracted to sport in the past five years BUT the benefits of increased participation are not being shared by all women. Particularly under-represented are: black and ethnic women, girls and young women, housewives, single mothers, unemployed women, those on low incomes, and women with disabilities.
>
> ('Sport for all Women' pamphlets)

The facts and figures above illustrate the problems of treating women as unitary subjects. They also make assumptions about the value of encouraging women to take part in sports and the types of programmes that should be offered. The projects of the Sports Council and other public bodies are examples of piecemeal reforms which fit into principles of liberalism. The emphasis has been to make token provision in terms of equal access and choice and to quantify the results; there have seldom been strategies to understand and overcome the obstacles that cause disadvantage. Margaret Talbot (1981: 1) argues that both the concept of 'Sport for All' and the means to its fulfilment have not been understood in countries in Europe where policies are based on 'more of the same' rather than on radical ideas which get to the root of the reasons for non-participation. She points out that if 'Sport for All' is to become a reality, the willingness of providers to 'rethink strategy and policy is absolutely essential' (1981: 14).

To a very small extent, this appears to be happening, although changes in rhetoric can be interpreted in different ways. In official sports discourse the term 'equality' has recently been replaced by the term 'equity' – a change which reflects the idea that identifying a group as a target may in itself be discriminatory. Sports-targeting policies marginalize low-users as separate and different, with discrete problems and needs. The alternative is to *assume* that all groups of women will be given comparable time, access to facilities, representation in planning and provision, and resources and funding. This represents a shift away from the idea that it is *women* who are the problem, and firmly establishes, at a subtle level, that it is the *system* that should be flexible and change radically in order to be able to cater for everybody. The idea is that all women, in common with the disabled and ethnic minorities, for example, should be equally represented in all plans and practices.

The term equity is used throughout the Sports Council's consultation document *Women in Sport* (Sports Council 1992a). This document is the most radical establishment statement on the subject, arguing that there should be a move away from treating women as a target group towards a more comprehensive strategy which takes account of the needs of all the various groups of women and a commitment to equity principles throughout the structure and culture of sports organizations themselves (White 1991; see also Chapter 8). However, the very low response (13 per cent) to the Sports Council's request for comments (sent to all public agencies which work with women in sports) suggests a lack of interest or a resistance to change. The Sports Council is seen as 'separate' and 'elite' by many people actively involved in community work, and the massive 'silent majority' reflects a cynicism about the council's real intention to put policies into practice. The Sports Council has been criticized for treating its own role uncritically and for misunderstanding or underestimating the very real difficulties of those work- ing in the community. It is argued that the document fails to recognize the ideological and cultural problems associated with non-participation and the ways in which present practices institutionalize discrimination. The major criticism of the Sports Council is its failure to make a concrete and financial commitment to tackle the problems it recognizes. In summary, the document is argued to be another liberal strategy which effectively de-politicizes women in sports.

WOMEN-ONLY PHILOSOPHIES

Most sportswomen participate in conventional or mainstream activities. But there are increasing numbers of women who are actively seeking something different – for example, those who reject organized sports that emphasize physical performance and competition; those who are opposed to aerobics and exercise classes which idealize youthfulness and physical perfection (Rail 1990); and those who are keen to compete, yet who feel alienated from the dominant images, personalities, values and practices associated with their sports (see next section). Much of the increase in women's sports is the result of groups of such women who are constructing and controlling their own authentic female sports cultures. The historical focus of women's struggles in sports has been over inequalities with men; and the attempts of women to wrest power away from men and to have more equal access to resources suggests that all women share a common philosophy. But women are not a homogeneous group and do not have identical needs and desires. Different women see the social world of sports in different ways and struggle amongst themselves, as well as with men, over definitions of women's sports.

All-women sports groups are being set up for a variety of reasons. In some cases, the impetus, quite explicitly, is to escape from the domination of men and from experiences of sexism and discrimination; and for Asian women, for example, separate sports development is desired for religious and cultural reasons. But for many women, the desire to participate in women-only groups is because they positively value female company and benefit from a collective, social experience. Shared pleasure in sports bonds women together, as it does for men. In many mainstream contexts, the constant comparisons made between men and women, the intimidating atmosphere and 'sports-talk', and the narcissistic reminders of the notional ideal female body have deterred women from participating, whereas all-female environments can provide a setting where girls and women can take part without feeling threatened or inadequate. This is reflected clearly in the 56 per cent female usage of the Newham Leisure Centre – a purpose-built facility in a predominantly working-class area of the East End of London – where the design brief ensured that the building is cosmetically pleasing with pastel colours and contains comfortable social areas; where the whole centre, including the men's changing rooms, is turned over to women three times a week to ensure privacy; where varied activities are timetabled for women; and where there are regular crèche facilities. The following statements are typical of the reasons why many women prefer all-female settings:

> I feel more comfortable with other women . . . we all have our saggy bits and plump parts to contend with, but we all encourage one another. . . . Men put pressure on other men to be macho . . . women quite frankly are a lot more sensitive and caring of one another . . . you come away feeling good, and after a few sessions, you feel the benefits of regular exercise as well. (Age 41)

> I hated PE at school. It made me shy and awkward about my own body . . . I used to skive off whenever I could . . . a girlfriend persuaded me to join this group and everyone was so welcoming and somehow I've developed confidence in my body . . . I feel physically stronger and more co-ordinated . . . but most important are the friends I've made. (Age 26)

> I'd never go near the leisure centre unless it were all-women . . . everyone's good mates . . . you can have a good laugh . . . and sit and chat if you don't want to join in. . . . And it's good with the crèche . . . it's like it's for *me* . . . I feel good about myself . . . funny thing is, I feel more energetic. (Age 33)

> Companionship and fun come first and the spin-offs are increasing self-awareness, confidence and fitness. (Age 46)

The most successful community sports programmes for women are those which make no artificial separation of the sporting and the social. This idea underpinned an experimental project called 'Friends for Fitness' (launched jointly in 1991 by Online Leisure, the Sports Council and Thames Television). The aim was to encourage women from London and the south-east of England keen to participate in some form of exercise to make telephone contact with other women interested in the same activity. During the first six months the scheme was remarkably successful: out of a sample group of 500, 51 per cent took up a new fitness activity. The majority were between 25 and 55 years old, 74 per cent per cent were over 30 years of age, and many had done no form of sport for a long time (Sports Council 1992a). Being with another woman or other women gave them confidence to try an activity for the first time and then the incentive to participate regularly.

During the last decade, 'women-friendly' projects have been remarkably successful, which suggests that there are huge numbers of potential participants for whom the right opportunity needs to be made available. This is reflected in the history of the 'Reebok Running Sisters' which grew in a decade from a simple idea to become what is probably the largest non-facility-based sporting activity in the country. In 1983, when a small advertisement was placed in the back of *Running* magazine asking experienced runners (Big Sisters) to volunteer to help beginners (Little Sisters) train for a 10-mile race, over 700 women responded. After just five months of training 150 novice runners finished the Avon Cosmetics National 10-mile road-race championships, within eighteen months the network had 4,000 women members, and after just two years the Running Sisters were able to secure sponsorship from Reebok UK. Pairing up women of similar ability (Twin Sisters) was then included, and membership has increased to approximately 5,000. Although there is now a national co-ordinator, a number of regional organizers, nation-wide advertising, and plans to liaise with local sports development officers, the initial philosophy remains – the Sisters are essentially a self-help group that 'works a bit like computer-dating' putting women in touch with each other for 'fitness, fun, friendship and safety in numbers'. They have created a network of runners *for themselves*, running at times and in ways with which they feel comfortable. Women of all ages, standards, shapes and sizes are encouraged to join, and Alison Turnbull, the founder, says the organization provides a stepping-stone into the athletic system for those women who love the sport but are intimidated by experienced and competent runners who speed off and 'leave them for dead'. Those who have joined the scheme claim that they have benefited in numerous ways – physically, psychologically and socially, and that the single most significant gain has been the acquisition of new friendships (Turnbull 1985; interview 3 September 1992).

There is a plethora of schemes which make 'sports connections' for women and provide attractive publicity through leafleting, posters and local radio, etc. Networking is a favoured method of attracting women to take part. Because it is personalized, women can very quickly be made to feel welcome, regardless of experience or physical type. Although throughout the country there have been numerous highly innovative schemes which have successfully attracted women to sports, nevertheless the increased numbers do not reflect a representative balance of women from different class and ethnic backgrounds. For example, although a variety of women have joined the Sisters network – 'committed feminists and leisured house-wives in carpet slippers' – it is an essentially white middle-class organization. The problem of mixed-class and mixed-ethnic recruitment, greatest in inner-city areas where there are larger numbers of working-class and ethnic minority women, is graphically explained in the following statement:

> If you don't know anybody, if you can't speak English, if you are afraid for your personal safety, the chances of your finding out about anything that is going on in your area are likely to be limited. Many Southwark women are in this situation.
>
> (Southwark Women's Equality Unit 1984)

Southwark is an inner-city area in the south-east of London with a long history of deprivation and a high percentage of working-class women and women from ethnic minorities. In spite of enthusiastic sports initiatives, large numbers of Southwark women are in the same situation ten years after this statement was made. This is not to ignore the successes of projects in inner-urban areas and the increasing numbers of working-class, Asian and Afro-Caribbean women, for example, who participate in sports, but even particularly sensitive and creative approaches, combined with generous funding, cannot compensate for the economic and social deprivations which act as powerful constraints on the lives of large percentages of women living in such areas.

THE COMPLEXITIES OF SEPARATE DEVELOPMENT

The problems of democratic participation in community sports programmes for women is widespread. This is a problem for the innumerable voluntary agencies that provide sports opportunities for women, as well as the Sports Council, local authorities, governing bodies and private organizations. A number of voluntary associations have their historical roots in the nineteenth century or early in this century, and their concern for the general welfare of women has continued over the years. Their work in community sports today is integral to the national drive for health and fitness, contributes to the ideology of 'Sport for All' and is influenced by the commercialized focus on women's bodies and positive life-styles. Some of these associations actively promote women's sports as a way of popularizing their image. For example, the Young Women's Christian Assocation (YWCA) is the world's oldest and largest women's organization with branches in more than eighty countries; throughout its history it has provided sports opportunities for women and girls as part of its social work programme. But the Young Men's Christian Association (YMCA) has a more comprehensive and well-organized timetable of sports and exercise classes for women. In 1967 it was agreed that female membership should be on an equal basis with men, and the Central YMCA (in central London) was rebuilt to include suitable facilities for women. The YMCA provides more leisure and fitness facilities than any other voluntary association in Britain; about 40 per cent of those who use them are women, and the numbers are increasing all the time. The YMCA employs a national sports health and fitness innovator and PE directors who run a range of courses for women. Daytime courses at the Central YMCA are predominantly health-related, described as 'not just cosmetic'. They attract mostly professional working women, between the ages of 20 and 40, who travel to central London each day for their work; but a special seniors' programme, which recruits women between the ages of 50 and over 90, is popular as well. The women's programme at the YMCA is built on the ideology of exercise for health which attracts mostly those who are quite young, single or childless, and relatively affluent. The association has responded to market forces and recent trends in the demand for exercise classes from this group of women – for example, they have instigated 'step training' sessions and put on teacher-training courses for 'Exercise to Music' and 'Fitness Training'.

Interest has also been shown in sports by the Women's Institute (WI – an educational/social association for women which spread from Canada to Britain where the first group was formed in 1915). This occurred as recently as the mid-1980s, as part of a general expansion into the field of leisure. The WI aims to replace the stereotype of 'cardiganed ladies' with a more positive, active image and a healthy life-style philosophy. In common with other associations, the WI's strategy for sports has become 'professionalized': the association gets grant aid from the Sports Council, it has appointed national and regional co-ordinators who work with sports development officers, there are regular teams and nation-wide competitions, and popular 'taster days' for unusual activities such as hot-air ballooning, gliding, various watersports, orienteering and trampolining, as well as traditional activities. However, in common with other associations such as the Keep Fit Association, the Margaret Morris Association, the Medau Association, the Women's League of Health and Beauty, and the new professional bodies for aerobics, body conditioning and exercise teachers, the WI has made only small inroads into attracting other than middle-class women to its sports and exercise programmes.

Women-only community groups have a very different history from the separate development of PE and sports in schools, colleges and clubs. (See Chapters 2, 4 and 5.) However, in both cases the exclusionary nature of participation appears to give women power to control their own sports development. In mixed associations power-sharing has always worked in favour of men. The Pinnacle Club provides an interesting example. Formed during the inter-war years (see Chapter 6), it remains the only all-women's rock-climbing club in Europe, with the same philosophy as it had then: to foster 'the independent development of rock-climbing and mountaineering amongst women'. Although there are a growing number of women climbers in Britain, in most mixed clubs there is a competitive edge, many women feel intimidated, and most of them 'trail behind' their boyfriends, husbands and partners. In comparison, the Pinnacle Club encourages female independence in climbing, and trains its members to lead climbs so that they can get the sort of experience denied to them in mixed, male-dominated clubs. Whatever the grade of climbing, the emphasis is on enjoyment of the sport and commitment to the club. The club also supplies a unique opportunity for members to meet other women climbers, provides for them a communication network and stimulates long-term friendships.

Some all-female activities have developed complex and contradictory characteristics. For example, Chapter 7 has argued that the *public* image of aerobics perpetuates patriarchal notions of femininity and limits personal perceptions of the female body. But for those women who participate in church halls rather than commercialized studios, who enjoy the movement experience in non-competitive and non-threatening environments, who value the social interaction and support of other women, and who are critical of the dominant obsession with the idealized female body, there is a clear contradiction between the personal and the popular. The popular image of aerobics, however, is very powerful and puts a lot of women off. There are huge numbers of aerobics classes which skilfully market the ideology of individualism – politically powerful in Britain for the past two decades. They are settings for female narcissism and competition rather than for companionship and co-operation. Fashionableness, sexiness, self-consciousness, youthfulness and fighting fitness have combined to produce a distinct image of commercialized and aggressive femininity (Lenskyj 1986: 129) which influences the production of self-identities. Increasing numbers of young women take seriously the public message that they must be personally responsible for their own health and fitness, and they exercise obsessively to keep a well-toned youthful appearance. The added influence of mixed aerobics has produced a hardness and seriousness about training which is typical of masculine sports. There are national and international aerobics organizations and championships; and competitions including individual, pairs, mixed pairs and group events which are fiercely contested. Reebok sponsor the British National Aerobic Championship, the winners of which represent Britain in the World Aerobic Championships. The national organization is campaigning with other countries to have aerobics acknowledged as an Olympic sport – its latest slogan is 'Aerobic Gold for Britain'.

It is clear that groups that are run *by* women *for* women vary tremendously from one context to another and do not necessarily prioritize giving support and encouragement to their members ahead of improving standards of performance and competition. To do so is described by some feminists as a humane philosophy and one that has 'feminized' sport, but others suggest that by highlighting differences between male and female participation, gender divisions in sports are consolidated. Those who believe that separate development is backward-looking and who want reciprocal relations between the sexes are involved in constructing ideological alternatives that are for both sexes rather than for women only.

IDEOLOGICAL ALTERNATIVES

Korfball is an unusual example of a mixed sport because it was invented specifically to enable males and females to play together. The idea of the game is to blend the positive aspects of both male and female sports cultures, rather than accepting the norms of men's sport as standard norms for female participation. 'Biculturalism' is the term used to describe korfball's relinquishment of the 'traditional bipolar conceptualization of masculinity and femininity' and 'release of the dominant ethic of competitive sport' (Crum 1988: 234). Each player marks another player of the same sex, otherwise there are no special rules for either sex; co-operation between players of the opposite sex is encouraged, and physical aggression discouraged. Korfball is therefore said to be an egalitarian sport which promotes sex equality and breaks down traditional sex barriers. It is argued that the rules are devised so that the varying abilities, heights and skills of the players are utilized, and as a result there is a very different attitude to women from the popular chauvinist one associated with male players in other sports. The ethos of korfball is to undermine sexist stereotypes not only philosophically, but also in the practice of the game. It is promoted as the 'co-ed sport', based on the belief that 'sex equality will always remain an illusion as long as the macho character of modern competitive sport dominates' (Crum 1988: 233).

New Games go even further in breaking with traditional ideas about the meanings of sports. In addition to the transformation of gender barriers, those between old and young players, between the able-bodied and the disabled, and between people with different cultural and ethnic backgrounds are changed. The New Games Movement arose in opposition to the high levels of specialization, the aggressively competitive ethos, and the impersonality which regulate many sports today; it rejects the ways in which the body is appropriated by political and economic systems, especially in high performance sports. Fluegelman (1976: 9) argues that 'because our own sports are so highly competitive, we may tend to believe that all human beings, especially males, are born competitors, driven by their genetic nature to the proposition that "winning is the only thing"'. The games of many cultures, however, have no competitive element whatever. With this in mind, the idea of New Games is that everyone can play a game together, regardless of sex, age and ability, and that rules are formulated as the game progresses to suit the specific participants. Multicultural games and co-operative games share a similar philosophy, 'challenge without competition'. Orlick (1978: v) describes his initiative to 'humanize contemporary games' as a dedication 'to the women of the world for maintaining some sanity and tenderness in our children, our games, our existence, and for giving me some legitimate hope for the future'.

Both korfball and New Games are rejections of the masculine traditions of mainstream sports and opposed to discrimination of any kind. They have both become popular in some countries and contexts. Korfball was established in the Netherlands at the beginning of the century and spread quickly to other countries in the developed world. The International Korfball Federation (IKF) was established about sixty years ago and there are now thirty-two affiliated countries from all continents. In the Netherlands the sport is very popular, with 10,000 players and 700 clubs; in Britain it is less well known, with between 3,000 and 4,000 players and 87 clubs, but growing rapidly as a result of Sports Council and local authority support for development work in schools and youth clubs. New Games originated in California in the 1970s and spread to other parts of North America and to western Europe and Australasia. From the start they have been viewed as a means of enhancing community links – the movement has a strong following in Australia with state funding for New Games' programmes and sponsoring of 'Life Games'. In Britain local authorities have developed pockets of New Games and these have been incorporated into youth sector programmes. In the 1970s sports in youth clubs were viewed as macho and aggressively competitive, and non-competitive games were favoured; and the Woodcraft Folk (the mixed 'socialist' alternative to the Boy Scouts and Girl Guides) play co-operative games, many of which are based on Innuit culture which embodies the idea that people work together to achieve the outcome.

Although korfball and New Games are promoted as ideological alternatives, as in the case of aerobics they stand the risk of developing characteristics in common with mainstream sports. In spite of its fiercely anti-sexist philosophy, close observation of korfball shows that men tend to play more controlling roles in the actual game and hold more high-level administrative and coaching positions than women (Crum 1988; Summerfield and White 1989). Furthermore, korfball has become a very 'serious' and competitive game; it is played at the world games for non-Olympic sports and the IKF is applying for Olympic status. New Games have also become institutionalized, competitive and commodified, and in the youth services the profile of sports has been raised and as a result more competitive sports and fewer co-operative games are played. The processes of organization, codification and institutionalization – even for mixed sports or 'open' events – tend to embody conventional forms of gender divisions which women have to struggle to overcome. The statement made in 1988 by the first woman to contest a lawn bowls superbowl final, playing, she said, 'for every woman in the UK', symbolizes male/female inequalities to which korfball and New Games' players are becoming vulnerable. Activities that are able to retain a high level of spontaneity and autonomy and usually take place outside an institutionalized setting, such as hiking, hill-walking, rambling, orienteering and swimming (the most popular holiday recreations in the UK), retain greater equality between the sexes.

POLITICIZING WOMEN'S SPORTS

Historically, women have enjoyed the greatest autonomy in those sports characterized as 'feminine-appropriate', and they have suffered the worst forms of discrimination and faced the greatest struggles in traditional 'masculine' sports. But the problems of autonomy are more complex than this generalization implies – no single female sport has ever had a unified position, and those women who are organizers and players struggle among themselves for the way forward. Recent developments in netball and football illustrate this point.

As a non-contact game, played and controlled by women throughout its history, and linked to the school and college contexts, netball has all the attributes of a 'feminine-appropriate' sport. It is the most widely played female sport in the country, with over 3,600 adult clubs and 6,000 members registered with the All England Netball Association (AENA), an unknown number who do not affiliate, and approximately 3,000 schools who belong to the England Schools Netball Association, and over a million schoolgirl players (AENA 1993). Playing figures are estimated to be increasing by about 7 per cent each year, but there is a fear that netball will get squeezed out of the PE curriculum. The AENA is therefore working to make the game more visible and popular in the community through its youth development pro- gramme and play-day schemes. Although the association receives some funding and sponsorship, the amounts are limited, arguably because the game gets poor publicity. In Australia and New Zealand, for example, netball obtains good television exposure which is the key to winning good sponsorship.

There are some netball players, however, who feel alienated from the dominant images, personalities, values and practices associated with the game. A netball club called 'Queens of the Castle' comes into this category. The club is situated in an inner-urban area of south-east London, and the members all have working-class roots and are predominantly black. Although they are committed to the game, with high standards of attendance and performance, the Queens believe that mainstream netball is 'strait-laced and socially restricting' with a St Trinians' schoolgirl image. So they have created their own netball culture which combines a radical appearance with a radical philosophy: their playing kit is non-conformist and flamboyant, in contrast to the uniformed character of conventional netball clothing, and they have a democratic and 'politicized' approach. The Queens of the Castle run their club in a way that is 'in touch' with young working-class London women. It is in contrast to traditional netball philosophy which their founder sees as a way of submerging individual identities into the concept of a team through the inculcation of highly disciplined, unquestioning and 'girl-like' responses. All the members of the Queens' club are involved in the construction of its values and practices, which are openly discussed and negotiated. The club has a truly caring ethos providing a support network for those with personal and financial problems and showing opposition to all forms of discrimination – for example, the white players will not countenance racial harassment aimed at their black team-mates. The success of this approach is clear – after only two years the Queens of the Castle were running four regular teams with an enthusiasm for netball which is uncharacteristic of other young women with similar working-class roots and allegiances. However, the cultural values and behaviour that these young women bring to the game are not favoured by the official ideologues of netball – a difference which 'has a lot to do with race, and class, and money, and how you live and what language you use' (Angela Farley, interview 5 May 1992). The Queens of the Castle believe that playing netball their way stands a good chance of becoming the 'trendy thing to do' among city women; their long-term aim is to get the game recognized as an exciting, forward-looking sport that will be given television coverage and sponsorship, rather than a sport which is played out of the public's eye and in a schoolgirl atmosphere. At the moment, although netball is the major female sport in the country, and most young women play at school, there are no popular role models. The contrast with boys' football is stark. The struggle over meaning in netball is between young women who might have been characterized as 'drop-outs and problems', and those who are in positions of power to make decisions about the future of the game. It suggests that netball policy-makers have failed to understand the specific needs of young, urban, working-class women.

In comparison with netball, women's football has had a more recent history and one that has incorporated constant opposition. But in the last few decades, women's struggles to participate and gain recognition have gained momentum. Although England has lagged behind other countries in Europe and in North and South America, there are now more players and more people interested in women's football than ever before – 'with TV audiences of up to 2.8 million' (Williams and Woodhouse 1991: 5). The Women's Football Association (WFA – the original governing body) was founded in 1969. At the end of the 1992/3 season (shortly after which time the WFA was taken over by the [men's] FA), there were 450 clubs and over 10,000 members affiliated to the WFA. Since the inauguration during the 1991/2 season of the first national league with three divisions, women's football has had a nation-wide structure (ibid.; WFA 1992). These developments illustrate women's infiltration into the most popular men's sport in the world – one that has historically unified men and marginal-ized and trivialized women. Huge numbers of boys are inducted into sports by men and come to identify themselves as male through sports – and the world of football plays a key role in this process. It is for this reason that football so strongly symbolizes male power. The idea of sports being dominant patriarchal institutions through which, Messner (1990: 99) claims, 'men's separation from and power over women is embodied and naturalized', is most easily understood when applied to traditional male sports such as football. So when women play it, popular definitions of masculinity are threatened; on the surface the partici-pation of women in sports which have hitherto been reserved more or less exclusively for men is seen as an important swing of power and a radical act.

But men wield a great deal of power over the development of the women's game: in 1993 the WFA was taken over by the (men's) FA, men play key roles in the running and control of women's clubs, and most women's teams have male coaches. There are now over forty men's English Football League clubs with a women's section, many of which are given financial and practical support – for example, free use of the club's pitch, physiotherapist and minibus, free coaching, and full kit supplied free of charge. Because women's football lacks resources, such arrangements have clearly assisted the development of the game. However, it is inevitable that if men have so much influence, they will impose on the women's game their own values and practices, and women footballers are being effectively schooled to copy what men do. It is not surprising that the women's game is viewed as a pale copy and a weaker version of what men do best.

But female footballers do not all agree about the way in which their game should progress. For example, written into the constitution of Newham Women's Football Club is that women should run the club and have absolute control of all its affairs. The publicity leaflet claims that it is 'the only [football] club run entirely by women where any girl can rise to achieve full potential'. They have negotiated for the lease of the first-ever women's football ground in the country, in order to have a site specifically for their game, and to generate income from hire charges. A central pillar of the club's philosophy is to provide role models for the next generation of female footballers by 'putting women in control' – members are therefore supported to go on refereeing and coaching courses, to do assertiveness training and to learn computing skills and counselling techniques. The women who run Newham Football Club are also working for a radical and creative way to play the game – what they call 'a women's philosophy of football'. They have piloted a task-book about tactics and attitudes, concentrating on positive ways of playing, in contrast to the way they see the men's game progressing. Other clubs, they argue, have been influenced negatively by the men's game and play defensively, protecting the goal. Newham women want to win imaginatively, rather than 'trying not to lose'; their style of play is therefore attacking and forward-looking. They want women to spearhead new ideas and to be inspirational about a way forward that is authentically female, rather than producing a female replica of the men's game. Their position is part of the debate about whether the (men's) FA should have taken over the running of the women's game (discussed in Chapter 11). Although the Newham Women's Football Club is critical of many values and practices in women's football, it would not argue for the destruction of the legacy of past struggles and achievements. What its members believe, however, is that things could be better and that the struggle for greater autonomy must go on. They operate to this end from within the dominant system, trying to persuade those in power to reflect better the needs of women. As the club's founder puts it, 'Change should be creative, not destructive'.

The scope of the club's ideology extends beyond the game of football – as with the Queens of the Castle, it is an explicitly caring one, based on an empathy with the needs and problems of young urban women. Newham is a predominantly working-class area of London and, with very few exceptions, all the players have working-class roots and links with the local community. The club has taken an overtly political stance on women's issues and on issues of discrimination. The term political here is used not simply to describe the exercise of power related to the activity of the state, but to describe the exercise of power to define and control culture, meanings, values and practices. One Newham player articulates the philosophy: 'Politics is part of everyday life. Politics *is* life – the things that we do and the way that we do them.' Newham WFC actively seeks women from all groups in the community – for example, those with different social backgrounds, ethnic identities, sexual preferences and religious beliefs. The explicit aim of the club is to work, through football, to encourage the empowerment of women as a gender. This is a starting point, because as the club develops it intends to consider in more detail the links between gender, class, ethnicity and sexuality, and the particular problems of marginalized groups. The club claims to have a *radical* equal opportunities philosophy – it does not intend only to open its doors to different women, or only to challenge discriminatory values and practices, but also actively to create practices that will implement in a positive way the values it holds. For example, it is the club's intention to challenge all forms of sexism. As in all sports, there are women of different sexual preferences who play football; and Birgit Palzkill (1990) suggests that lesbians are attracted to sports like football because the characteristics required are in opposition to those associated with popular images of femininity. But because football is characterized as a 'masculine' sport, sexuality becomes a particular issue; players are frequently labelled in a derogatory way as hard and butch and lesbianism is implied. Heterosexual players have blamed lesbians for bringing women's football into disrepute. These are surface manifestions of conflicts which reflect the deep problem of homophobia in sports. This problem has not been tackled by any official sports organizations or ideologues whose collective non-action allows the institutionalization of sexual difference to continue. The Newham club will not ignore this issue; the leaders make it clear that in their club sexual preference is unimportant (players are not forced to deny their sexuality or to make it explicit) and only women who will tolerate sexual difference are welcome and respected. The Newham Women's Football Club makes its position about sexism clear – that *to do nothing* is irresponsible.

Racism is not tolerated either, and positive steps are being taken to increase the ethnic mix in the club. For example, because the number of Asian players is minimal and unrepresentative of those in the community, training times have been arranged to fit in with religious and cultural commitments; in order to build links with the Asian community meetings are being set up in local schools to enable Newham players to welcome Asian girls to their club and assure their parents that it is a safe, all-female environment. There is a positive intention to try to understand and confront the forms of discrimination that Asian women experience, and to work with them towards ethnic integration in the club. This initiative shows some practical understanding of the 'importance of treating race as a relationship of power, rather than continuing to treat it as a variable' (Birrell 1989: 186).

The politicization of women's sports is unusual. For the most part, sportswomen see sports in an insular way and claim that there is no connection between participation and politics. As a result discrimination goes unchallenged: a deaf ear is turned towards people who make sexist and racist remarks, and nothing is done to change the practices of clubs that (often unintentionally) discriminate against certain groups so that they remain marginalized, alienated and powerless. Dominant structures and discourses are exclusionary; they are the basis of institutionalized discrimination which is very hard to shift. There have been few organized initiatives in women's sports which look beyond the struggle for greater equality with men, and which relate the gender dimension to wider social and political issues as a part of the everyday experience of participation. The Newham WFC philosophy is the result of democratic processes and non-hierarchical relations; values are not imposed but negotiated, and all members are encouraged to join in the decision-making procedures. Since the club's inception, an atmosphere of openness and friendliness has been nurtured, and discussions have become franker and freer.

The examples of the Queens of the Castle and Newham Women's Football Club suggest that a new generation of young working-class women is seeking actively to redefine the mainstream values and practices of women's sports. The proponents confirm that struggles over women's sports occur not just between men and women but between different groups of women with contrasting views of the social world of sports – those who belong to the 'establishment' and those who are relatively powerless. Both these clubs believe in power-sharing and the elimination of discrimination, and they both have an awareness of the relationship between sports and the wider social context. By pushing back boundaries and setting alternative standards for running women's sports, they demonstrate an unusual sensitivity to the relationship between values, practices and consciousness. These examples also point to the ways in which we should understand how gender, class, ethnicity and sexuality are constructed together in sports. Their success in putting radical ideas into practice also has a political character – both these clubs are funded by local authorities controlled by the Labour Party where there are powerful feminist lobbies. Across the country, Labour authorities have the best record of funding women's sports in working-class areas, but government restrictions on local authority spending are likely to make this more difficult in the future (see Chapter 8).

UNDERSTANDING RACISM AND ETHNICITY

Black and Asian feminists argue that feminist literature in general has marginalized issues of ethnicity and racism – the same criticism can be made about feminist literature on sports. There is a tendency for generalizations to be made about all women in sports from examples of white women. More specifically, stereotypes of sporting femininity are almost always stereotypes of bourgeois, heterosexual, western, white women; sometimes replaced by black or Asian women who have become thoroughly westernized. Otherwise, black women are referred to as 'black' and Asian women as 'Asian'. The white stereotype means that black and Asian women are marginalized – treated as 'different' from the 'norm' in certain ways. There has been a tendency, therefore, to look at 'problems of blackness' or the 'problems of being Asian', rather than 'problems of gender and relations between gender and ethnicity'. In recent years, a small amount of investigative work has stimulated more serious treatment of the issue (Birrell 1989; Carrington, Chivers and Williams 1987; Carrington and Williams 1988; Lovell 1991; Lyons 1988). Some research has been done in the UK into black women whose roots are in the Afro-Caribbean and in Africa, but the bulk of work has been about Asian women whose origins are in India, Pakistan, Bangladesh, Sri Lanka and East Africa (Lovell 1991; Lyons 1988). There has been a tendency to stereotype black women as 'naturally' good at sports and Asian women as those who need to be targeted because of low participation rates and negative attitudes. But the focus on these ethnic groups in Britain (and, for example, on Afro-Americans, Hispanics and North American Indians in the USA) masks the diversity of ethnicity and the complexity of the sports-ethnicity question. For example, there has evidently been no work done in Britain on the participation in sports of women from other ethnic minorities whose roots are in such countries as China, Italy, Poland, the Ukraine, or Vietnam, or work that systematically looks at the political, economic and social components of the sports/gender/ethnicity relation.

Afro-Caribbeans have been the most visible single ethnic group in women's sports. But their outstanding successes tend to present a misleading idea about the general position of black women in sports and in society. Whereas the successes of white women in sports are assumed to be the result of dedicated training and self-sacrifice (or drug-taking, particularly in the case of eastern Europeans), the visibility of elite black sportswomen is assumed to be because they are genetically predisposed to be superior athletes (Lashley 1991). It is for this reason that black girls have been encouraged to participate in school sports rather than in intellectual work. The following schoolgirl experiences are typical examples taken from interviews carried out with young Afro-Caribbean women who joined sports clubs after leaving school:

> Even when O-levels was coming up the PE teacher was always on to me to come to practices and be in the team. . . . She got really pissed off when I said I wouldn't. . . . I didn't want to. . . . I was a bit unusual . . . doing exams.

> The teachers who were nicest to us were in the PE Department. If you could run fast and jump and stuff then they wanted you for the school . . . they was always interested in us black kids . . . you know, they expected us to be good . . . no one was like that for your English . . . no one took much notice of my work . . . they didn't think you'd be any good at brainy things . . . so they didn't bother.

Tessa Lovell (1991) argues that racial stereotyping facilitates the integration of Afro-Caribbean women into British sporting cultures, but militates against the integration of southern Asian women. She points out that Afro-Caribbean women are considered to be aggressive and dominating – characteristics supposedly suited to sports – whereas Asian women are often characterized as weak and passive, so that teachers typically assume that they will not be interested in sports. Attitudes about 'natural ability' tend to mask alternative cultural explanations for differences between women from different ethnic backgrounds. For example, a survey carried out in the London borough of Newham shows that while Afro-Caribbean women and Asian women enjoy keep-fit, the former prefer team games and weight-training, whereas the latter enjoy swimming, badminton and water aerobics – differences that could be explained according to the diverse attitudes to femininity in the two communities. However, overall participation rates for both these groups are low. Although some black sportswomen have had outstanding successes and have become public figures (for example, Tessa Sanderson, Judy Simpson, Fatima Whitbread and Mollie Samuel from Britain and Florence Griffith Joyner, Jackie Joyner-Kersee and Zena Garrison in the USA), it is not across a comprehensive range of sports. Black women tend to predominate in athletics and to participate in large percentages in certain other sports, such as volleyball and basketball. By comparison, there are relatively few who take part in swimming and tennis, which are two of the most popular female sports. Nevertheless, the successes of a few black sportswomen, in a limited range of sports, misleadingly imply that sports provide equality of opportunity for all women. The reality in multiracial societies like Britain and the USA is that low percentages of women from ethnic minority groups achieve success in sports overall, reflecting their low participation rates at grass-roots level. In many situations, the interaction of ethnicity and class makes it impossible to assess which predominates in the way they militate together against women's participation. Work needs to be done on the particular ways in which class and ethnicity interact with gender. Furthermore, racism has deep cultural roots in British and American societies and is a continual and major influence on the participation of women from ethnic minorities. For most women from ethnic minorities, racism *deters* them from participating, but Tessa Lovell (1991) argues that racism often *leads* black women into sports in the first place. The increase of all-black or predominantly black female sports clubs illustrates the attempts of black women to escape from the racism that occurs in mainstream sports. It is also a mechanism for cultural control which compensates for the low numbers of ethnic minority women in positions of power in mainstream sports organizations. Founding all-black women-only sports clubs is a way of dealing with the double discrimination of racism and sexism.

There is a problem here about characterizing 'black' and 'Asian' women as if they are discrete ethnic groups with their own cultural identities, relationships and traditions. Black women have different ethnicities and different cultural resources one from another: most come from the West Indies, others from Africa, and within each group there are women with varied economic resources, educational backgrounds, interests and experiences which affect their involvement in sports. Asian women are not a homogeneous group either: they come from various parts of the Indian subcontinent, and some from Africa, and they have different religious affiliations (mostly Hindu, Muslim, Sikh, or Christian) and marked generational differences, and their interactions with other communities in Britain influence their values and experiences in sports.

It is the very low participation rates of Asian women in general, however, that has resulted in their being targeted by policy-makers as a needy group (Sports Council 1988b). A study of Muslim women in Birmingham (Lyons 1988), which suggests that their especially low participation rates is the single most important factor linked to poor health, provides a persuasive reason to organize sports programmes for Asian women. Jarvie (1991: 4) articulates the concern:

> If one Asian housewife does not seem able to find the opportunity to train or participate in sport, the problem might be nothing more than a personal trouble, but if Asian women in general cannot develop healthy,

recreational life-styles, then this personal trouble . . . transcends from the level of individuality to being a more public issue.

Of all Asian groups, Muslim women appear to be the most restricted in their public leisure and to have the very lowest participation rates; Sikh women in general are more westernized and participate in greater numbers in sports. The popular conception of Muslim women is that the rules of Islam prevent them from participating, although Muslims point out that there is nothing in the Koran to say that women should not take exercise, only that the body should not be exposed and curves should not be apparent. There is opposition not so much to the activity itself as to the rituals of participation and to the environment in which most sports take place. Modesty and chastity before marriage are essential components of Muslim femininity, and for Muslim women to go to venues where there are men, to wear sports clothing in public and to take part in mixed activities are viewed as threatening to their safety and virtue, and are therefore unacceptable. The contrast between the provocative commodification and sexualization of the female body in western culture, and the Muslim ideal of the female body conceived of as private and precious, highlights the feeling for many Muslim women of being 'between two cultures'. But the assumption that Muslim culture is oppressive is understood by Muslims themselves to be an example of westernized and racist thinking. As Sadhna Raval (1989: 239) points out, 'many Asians are proud of their tradition and cultural heritage, which they wish to preserve and pursue as it forms part of their identity'.

The research of Carrington, Chivers and Williams (1987), Carrington and Williams (1988), Lovell (1991) and Lyons (1988) shows that there are cultural similarities in the attitudes to women and their participation in sports between all the British Asian communities. In common with Muslims, there are no religious laws for Hindus or Sikhs that stop women participating in sports, but in none of these communities are sports highly valued cultural activities for women. For example, although Kabbadi (a traditional game from the Punjab) is played by girls and young women in schools and colleges in India and Pakistan and has been played in the United Kingdom by men of Asian descent for the past thirty years, it was played by Asian women in the UK for the first time only in 1990, and in a spontaneous fashion as part of an Asian festival. Although Lyons (1988) points out that Asian women are valued as homemakers, and their domestic responsibilities severely limit out-of-home activities, it is the deep feeling that modesty is the essence of femininity, together with the fear of racism and sexual harassment, that most deters women from participating. Asian men oppose female sports participation only because they wish to protect traditional gender values and they fear for the safety of their wives and daughters. Raval (1989: 239) argues that analyses of the relationship between Asians and sports in Britain tend to explain low participation rates among women without taking sufficient note of 'the crucial issues of racism (at both structural and personal levels) and white patriarchy'. The problem of non-participation is fundamentally linked to the westernized standards of sports providers, organizations and facilities. Asian women often feel out of place and intimidated in sports venues – facilities do not meet their cultural standards, they are often ignored, not made to feel welcome, have a language problem and a lack of knowledge about what to do.

In most areas of the country where there is a sizeable Asian population, development work has been aimed at increasing the numbers of Asian women who participate in sports. Initially the approach was to target the group and then provide a number of activities and classes, generally speaking in the same way as for white women. The approach now is more sensitive to the specific needs of Asian women, for example, by providing information in Urdu, Bengali and Punjabi, as well as in English; ensuring a female-only 'safe' environment; organizing crèche facilities, low-price or no-price sessions; training and employing members of the Asian community to take classes to provide role models and a feeling of solidarity; arranging classes for schoolgirls at times which fit in with religious commitments, and providing transport home; and doing a lot of outreach work so that the families and leaders of the local Asian community understand what is going on. But it can be difficult, even when there is a programme of positive action, to ensure that all the criteria are met. For example, the success of taster classes (in horse-riding, climbing, pot-holing and archery) during a residential weekend exclusively for Asian women, could not be followed by regular sessions because the special arrangements were too costly. And there are other problems which are not easy to solve in multicultural contexts. For example, pupils in a London girls' secondary school who are 75 per cent Asian, and mostly Muslim, do all aspects of the PE curriculum in tracksuit trousers. But in the summer, in particular, if they are really energetic they can get seriously over-heated and exhausted. And during Ramadan, when Muslim girls are required to fast during daylight hours, they can become ill if they are physically active.

In general, sports policy-making assumes that Asian culture, and in particular Muslim culture, oppresses women. The model is, therefore, one of cultural deficit. Asian women, when asked about their low participation rates, however, point to examples of institutionalized racism as the main problem – not only overt racist abuse, but examples of discrimination that are built into the structures of sports. As a result the points of convergence between Asian women and white women tend to get overlooked – for example, the specifically Asian ideologies of femininity and domesticity are argued to militate against sports participation, whereas women as a gender experience similar forms of patriarchal discrimination in sports that have developed within the context of western capitalism. Although at an individual level the provision of special classes for Asian women is beneficial, it

is an example of piecemeal reform which places the blame for low participation rates on the target group, rather than dealing with the deeper causes
of racial stereotyping, harassment and discrimination (David 1991). If there
is to be any major increase in the sports participation of Asian women,
creative and radical practices which combine anti-racist and anti-sexist
policies must be implemented. It is essential not only to eliminate racial
stereotyping and racial harassment and to set in place culturally sensitive
arrangements, but also to oppose explicitly the varied forms of sexism which
have traditionally deterred huge numbers of women from all social and
ethnic backgrounds from participating in sports.

The British sports system reflects traditions that can be traced back to the
nineteenth century – and many of its values and practices are inappropriate
for a modern, multiracial society. British sports policies reflect 'white' culture
and codes of thinking which celebrate individualism and promote a spurious
sense of free will. That is why the discourse of racism in women's sports has
to a large extent been repressed. Neither black nor Asian women hold
powerful decision-making positions in sports and are therefore unable directly
to influence policies in ways which might lead to a re-examination of
existing values and practices. Women as a gender lack power in sports
administration (White 1991), but those relatively few who do fill prestigious
decision-making positions in general reflect the mainstream model in female
sports which is white, middle-class, western and heterosexual – unrepresentative of women as a *whole*. Their relative lack of experience of discrimination results in the lack of a language to articulate and deal with
problems of discrimination for other people. That is one of the reasons why
the sports establishment has failed to grasp the need to empower all groups
of women to make decisions about their own sports participation, rather
than imposing values and practices on them.

PROBLEMS FOR LESBIANS

The sports establishment has also failed to create a discourse to explain and
deal with discrimination against homosexuals and, more specifically, against
lesbians in sports. Silence implicitly condones taken-for-granted ways of
thinking and behaving, which occur subtly and during informal activities,
and which are hurtful and harmful to non-heterosexuals. But the non-action
of sports agencies, organizations and ideologues is justified on the grounds
that lesbians have not articulated a problem. There is no acknowledgement
that discrimination is the reason they remain silent in the first place. Because
in recent years issues of sexuality have become more public, and gays and
lesbians have spoken out about their experiences in sports, it is no longer
legitimate to deny there is a problem.

Although sexuality is intensely personal, it is constantly mediated by
structured practices and experiences. And in sports, as in other social institu-

tions, compulsory heterosexuality is part of a system of domination that perpetuates patriarchal relations and the wielding of power over other sexualities. Young men are inducted into a fiercely heterosexual world of male toughness and competitiveness which embodies a fear of the effeminate and subordinates gay men (Messner and Sabo 1990; Pronger 1990). Pressure is put on sportswomen to display heterosexual signals and to fear the stigma of masculinization. Because male sports emphasize the link between masculinity and the physical, muscular body, muscularity and athleticism are only considered to be desirable female characteristics if they are bonded with a heterosexual orientation. Women who are flat-chested, physically powerful and well-muscled stand more risk of being labelled deviant or lesbian than women who conform to dominant ideas of femininity. The notion of 'male' and 'female' roles in sports implies narrow and biased definitions of masculinity and feminity, and marginalizes others. Lesbianism is stigmatized because it is perceived to violate popular stereotypes, and this has a powerful effect on the attitudes and behaviour of sportswomen, whatever their sexual preferences. Heterosexual sportswomen have a deep fear of being labelled lesbian, and lesbians feel driven to 'pass' as straight because of the fear of victimization. The overriding concern about sexuality in sports results in divisions between women with different sexual preferences, and in this way sports structure relations between different femininities.

Homophobia (a fear, intolerance and hatred of gay men and lesbians) has been described as 'the glue that holds sexism together' (Griffin and Genasci 1990: 213–14). The basis of homophobia is the assumption that to be heterosexual is 'normal' and to be a lesbian is 'deviant' – an attitude which becomes consolidated and reproduced every day in sports. For example, sexist and heterosexist jokes and innuendoes in the changing rooms, generally treated as innocent and humorous, are part of the everyday discourse of sports which bonds heterosexuals together. Because heterosexism is seldom challenged, it achieves a credibility based on the assumption that everyone listening is heterosexual. Dominant discourses are exclusionary; they are the basis of institutionalized discrimination which is very hard to shift. Heterosexist discourse alienates and marginalizes gay men and lesbians; it is a form of harassment that usually goes unnoticed. For example, gay men and lesbians on sports studies courses are often deeply offended by the fiercely heterosexist attitudes of their colleagues, but feel unable to speak out for fear of being ostracized and misunderstood. They therefore stay silent and 'pass' as heterosexuals. A gay man explains his reaction to the heterosexist discourse of male students and its effect on everyone in the group:

> It's a terrible pressure not to be able to be yourself . . . every day they're making dirty jokes about their exploits with women or they're making jokes about gays . . . and some are really hostile . . . they really hate

gays. . . . These students are so reactionary . . . and really intolerant. . . . They fancy themselves as studs and think all the women in the group are going to fall over them . . . they talk about the female students . . . whether they'd be any good in bed . . . and they're really shitty about some who look a bit butch. . . . They laugh at pictures of muscly [female] athletes . . . openly . . . in lectures . . . they seem even more disgusted at the idea of lesbians. . . . But no one says anything . . . sometimes some of the more outspoken girls will tell them to shut up . . . and some of the quiet ones look a bit uncomfortable . . . but no one talks about it . . . they never seem to consider that anyone in the group is gay.

Lesbian students feel the same pressures to remain silent about their own sexuality:

We've come here to study sport and you'd think students would be interested to learn about different ideas . . . some of them are . . . but most of them seem to have closed minds . . . I think they feel threatened by the idea of lesbianism . . . it's so obvious they think it's disgusting and un-natural. . . . Sometimes I want to say something . . . to come out and be myself . . . and shame them . . . but I'm really scared to face the conse-quences . . . I'm really an outsider. . . . There are a couple of us on the course so far as I know . . . and we get on quite well with some of the other female students, but hardly any of them are feminists . . . they laugh with the guys . . . you don't even have to say anything, they just laugh when you show a slide of some Eastern European woman putting the shot or something like that . . . and everyone knows why they're laughing.

Although very little research has been done on the issue of sexuality, the limited evidence available suggests that most lesbian sportswomen react to homophobia and harassment by hiding their sexuality and 'passing' as heterosexual. The case study of a young lesbian PE teacher (Sparkes 1992) suggests that PE students are exceptionally conservative and biased in their attitudes to sexuality. When she was at college she found that 'attempts to raise issues relating to gender and equal opportunities were deflected by members of the group and openly ridiculed by a few' (ibid.: 15–16); once she was a qualified teacher she found the process of condoning the homophobia of colleagues and pupils who were ignorant about her sexuality a form of self-denial which was painfully oppressive. In common with other sports professionals, out of necessity, she lives a discrete personal and professional life.

Sportswomen also hide their sexuality in order to protect their sporting careers. Martina Navratilova has become a spokesperson for lesbians, but she is unusual. Remarkably few women in top-level sports or in sports coaching or administration are prepared to risk the likely discrimination that results from 'coming out'. For example, Kidd (1983) writes about the abuse and loss of opportunities experienced by lesbian sportswomen in Canada; Lenskyj (1990) argues that lesbian sportswomen, coaches and administrators are not selected for teams or jobs because of their sexual orientation; and in a publication entitled *Unity*, there are numerous examples of anti-lesbian discrimination, including 'dyke bashing', loss of sports scholarships, loss of revenue, and exclusion from Olympic squads. In a video entitled *Running Gay* (Sheffield Film Co-op 1992), a former Canadian Olympic athlete describes how she was fired from the position of national coach, which she had held for three years, after it was discovered that she was a lesbian; one athlete talked about rumour-mongering and slander; another about the problems of not meeting the 'feminine' image; another about the impossibility for known homosexuals to secure sponsorship; and another claimed that if the sexuality of an athlete is known to be gay, his/her career will be finished and he/she will never be hired as a coach. One lesbian professional golfer expresses the reason for remaining closeted: 'I'm not willing to be a martyr and give it all up. It's painful, it makes me unhappy, but it's the way things are. Period.' The following analysis of lesbian professional golfers illustrates the contradiction faced by all lesbian athletes who 'pass' as heterosexuals:

> the silence, designed to protect reputations and purses, deprives those who are hiding of a sense of community and history, restricts their cultural and political affiliations, and engenders fear and even paranoia. In this instance it also exacerbates the homophobia of the men who own, finance and control women's sports.
>
> (Nelson 1991a: 10)

Homophobia is expressed in particularly intense and hostile ways in sports. Even some all-women clubs with non-sexist philosophies – like the Pinnacle women's climbing club – are stigmatized by outsiders because of the standard but incorrect assumption, that the club is full of lesbians. And when sportswomen are known to be lesbian, hostility intensifies. For example, lesbians have been attracted to football in Britain in quite large numbers, but it is not uncommon for confrontation to arise between the heterosexual majority and the lesbian minority. Lesbians have been accused of corrupting young girls at an impressionable age and using sports clubs for opportuning; lesbians say they feel persecuted and have been forced to leave.

Not surprisingly, lesbian (or predominantly lesbian) sports clubs and associations have been formed as a reaction to the prejudice and sense of alienation experienced in mainstream sports. The relations of sexual power are reversed in such clubs and they provide opportunities for sexual openness and lesbian bonding and, importantly, remove the fear of abuse and victimization. The sexual divisions in women's sports, and the hostility engendered by them, is symbolized by the name of a club exclusively for heterosexual women called 'WAS' (We Are Straight), and a predominantly and openly lesbian club whose logo includes a black triangle (the lesbian symbol). There are local, sport-specific lesbian clubs, and associations at regional, national and international levels. The efforts of lesbians to come together in their own teams result from their desire to be in the majority for once, to 'be themselves' and to feel 'free'. The International Gay Games exemplify the efforts of gays and lesbians to control their own sports and illustrate the use made of sports as ideological instruments of gay politics. These Games have become one of the biggest events on the gay calendar – at the 1992 Games in Vancouver, Canada, there were 7,300 athletes from 27 countries participating in 29 sports. As many as 43 per cent were women (a much larger percentage than at the Olympics), and more than 10,000 people watched the opening ceremony. The 1994 Games are planned for New York where it is expected that there will be 10,000 athletes from 35 countries. The executive director claims that 'Gay Games IV will be a tremendous opportunity for the international lesbian and gay community, and our friends, to eradicate prejudice, achieve our personal best and create a living legacy for millions of lesbian and gay youth in the years to come' (Unity '94: 2). At the Gay Games lesbians transcend the contradictions they face because of their sexuality with their love of sports and the positive focus sports give to their lives. In this respect their only difference from heterosexual women is their preference for women rather than men as sexual partners.

The prospect of a sports system where lesbians could be open about their sexuality without suffering discrimination seems a long way off, but it is unlikely that single-sex sports can be conducive to achieving anti-heterosexist goals unless individual heterosexual sportsmen and women accept some responsibility for eradicating the widespread homophobia and discrimination suffered by lesbians and gay men in sports. A good starting point would be to lobby sports-governing bodies and official agencies such as the Sports Council and the Women's Sports Foundation which at present are doing nothing to tackle the problem.

LOOKING AFTER THE ELDERLY

There has been a marked increase in the number of elderly people in British society during the last few decades (they now constitute approximately 17 per cent of the population). Although there are more males than females at birth, women are the majority sex in the older age groups. Life expectancy has risen more for women than for men and until recent legislation, women retired earlier than men. In 1985, when most women retired at 60 and men at 65, it was estimated that almost twice the number of women to men were over the age of retirement (Reid 1989). With increased longevity and earlier retirement, women can expect to spend around a quarter of their lives pensioned and 'abundantly leisured'.

Although people live longer, the traditional model of the ageing population as pathological continues to be important. It carries with it notions of a decline in health, social usefulness and independence. Part of the discourse of the elderly is to do with disease, needs and disabilities. Age is viewed as a social problem, and in recent years sports for the elderly (essentially in the form of gentle, therapeutic exercise) have been a concern of health and social welfare agencies. Keeping the ageing body moving and functioning has become one way of dealing with what has been characterized as the 'problem of ageing populations'. Neglect of the physical body can be expensive in terms of medical care and welfare support, and exercise and sports can reduce health costs.

At the same time, and influenced by the general consumer climate of body maintenance, there has been a new emphasis on exercise for bodily preservation and the postponement of ageing (Featherstone 1982; Turner 1991). The focus on the physical body is no longer appropriate only to young people with firm flesh and abounding energy; body maintenance has become an intergenerational concern and includes cosmetic, dietary, exercise and fashion components, for young and old alike. The concern for loss of physical attractiveness amongst ageing women in particular has made them a target group for business entrepreneurs. Featherstone (1982) explains the interconnections between industries with an interest in the economic benefits of influencing older people to look after their bodies:

> The wrinkles, sagging flesh, tendency towards middle-age spread, hair loss etc., which accompany ageing should be combated by energetic body maintenance on the part of the individual – with help from the cosmetic, beauty, fitness and leisure industries.
>
> (Featherstone 1982: 178)

The youth/age opposition has been rendered problematic, in part because of the quest for youth in older people and the resultant similarities in behaviour, dress, and activities between the generations. The 'modernization of ageing' is a term used to describe the blurring of physical and psychological boundaries between age groups. The use of hormone replacement therapy and other medical advances, such as screening procedures for the early detection of cancer, have given women the potential for a longer and younger-feeling life. Research has shown that, together with a balanced diet, regular exercise is beneficial to ageing women – in particular, it helps to prevent osteoporosis which affects 25 per cent of women by the age of 60 (Health Education Authority in Sports Council, cited in Sports Council 1992b). However, if there is evidence of bone deterioration, weight-bearing activities, such as road-running, can easily lead to injury, so that other forms of exercise, such as swimming and cycling, are preferable (Turnbull 1985). Exercise has become an ideologically acceptable activity for those elderly women questing for a full life, and the wearing of fashion leotards symbolizes the modern, youthful approach. Featherstone and Hepworth argue that chronological age has therefore changed its meaning:

> As far as body maintenance is concerned, an array of evidence continues to accrue which disproves the necessary decline of mental, sexual and physiological capacities in old age. Chronological age continues to be discredited as an indicator of inevitable age norms and life-styles and a new breed of body maintenance experts optimistically prescribe health foods, vitamins, dieting, fitness techniques and other regimes to control *biological* age, which, it is argued, is the true index of how a person should feel.
>
> (Featherstone and Hepworth 1988: 374)

The reality is that the elderly are not a homogeneous group. Many old women suffer from poverty, poor health and disability (the elderly are the largest group of disabled people). Others are relatively affluent, healthy and energetic and are participating in increasing numbers in sports (although the overall percentage of participants of 60 years and over – both male and female – is lower than for any other age group). Because elderly women outnumber men in the population, one might expect that they would also outnumber men in sports participation. This is not the case. Figures for 1986 show that women's indoor and outdoor participation was only half that of the men (Sports Council 1988a). However, although there are no up-to-date national figures available, the Sports Council's programme for the targeting of elderly people, called '50 Plus – All to Play For', has successfully attracted increased numbers of women to various schemes throughout the country and the trends suggest that the gender imbalance may eventually be reversed. Many local authorities have taken up the theme and have appointed sports development officers with responsibility for establishing classes and schemes for people in this age group. Indoor bowls, swimming, aquarobics and yoga sessions have attracted predominantly female clients and the numbers of elderly women in more varied activities is on the increase as well. Evidence from across the country suggests that women over 50 are less inhibited than men about trying new activities – whereas men tend to take sports seriously, women are able to laugh at themselves and enjoy the experience. Although the ideology of sports as masculine inhibited many women in the past from participating in large numbers, all-women arrangements have provided the emotional and social support necessary to attract them to take part now they are older. These women particularly like the company and support of other women of their own age.

There are also a growing number of women who are actively redefining the conventional idea that only moderate exercise in a limited range of activities (gentle aerobics, aquarobics, swimming, bowls and yoga) is appropriate for elderly women. For example, the Duke of Edinburgh Discovery

Award, devised for the over-fifties, is modelled on the Duke of Edinburgh's Award Scheme for young people. It is intended to give older people enjoyment, a challenge, and a chance to meet other people. Recreative activities, such as fishing, hiking and orienteering, are included in the scheme. A club called the Golden Adventurers provides another example of elderly women participating in untypical activities. In this case a group of grandmothers with ages ranging from 60 to 90 (and who share the philosophy that life begins at 60!), wanted to take part in action-packed activities which they had had no chance of doing earlier in life. The formation of the club is an example of women defining their own needs and taking action to fulfil them – they have planned, organized, acquired financial backing and participated in belly-dancing, driving racing cars and army tanks, and hot-air ballooning. It is possible to find numerous examples of individuals who are challenging conventional assumptions about the physical capabilities of elderly women. For example, Madge Sharples ran her first London marathon in 1981 at the age of 64. Born in 1916, she started running in her sixties and continued to do so well into her seventies. She travelled to numerous countries, competing in over fifty marathons, as well as in shorter-distance races. Increasing numbers of older women take sports seriously, participate regularly and compete in open events and in veterans competitions. Elite sports are not always the privilege of youth – for example, some of the best sportswomen in the world who compete at certain events at the Olympics and other major international competitions are middle-aged and a few are even older. Joyce Smith ran her first marathon at the age of 41 and two years later, at 43, she was the first British woman to run the distance in less than 2½ hours. Women compete in golf and equestrian competitions into their seventies and even eighties. Most popular sports have organized competitions at national and international levels for 'mature' performers of 25 years up to 80 and over – for example, there are veterans' leagues for single-sex and mixed hockey, and veteran gymnastic and tennis competitions. Masters swimming provides a good example of the desire of older women to continue to take part in a sport that they have competed in when younger, although there is an ideological shift from the usual over-seriousness of top-level sport to a shared philosophy that competition is for 'fun, fitness, and friendship'. There are numerous local, national and international masters' swimming meetings throughout the developed world: the European and World Masters' Championships, organized for the first time in the 1980s, are two of the most prestigious. There are short- and long-distance swimming, synchronized swimming and diving events. The success of masters' swimmers exemplifies the abilities of women actively to participate in sports throughout their lives. For example, at the age of 82, Mrs Cherriman from England won six gold medals at the 1990 World Masters' Championships and set three world records; Maria Lenk Zigler, from Brazil, who was the first woman ever to swim the butterfly stroke and who competed at the 1936 Olympics, was still swimming competitively in her seventies; an English Ladies Masters' relay team swam the English Channel in 1987 – thought at that time to be the oldest European ladies' team to do so. The development of masters' events and the accomplishments of the competitors have transformed the notion that sports for the elderly are essentially therapeutic to an image of positive health and autonomy.

TRANSFORMING SPORTS FOR THE DISABLED

Disabled people (including the deaf, the blind, amputees, paraplegics, those with cerebral palsy and the mentally handicapped) form a significant proportion of the population (approximately 1 in 10 of the adult population and 3 per cent of all children under 16 – James 1990). There are more disabled women than disabled men – in part because women live longer and the likelihood of disability increases with age. Almost 70 per cent of disabled adults are over the age of 70 (Sports Council 1992b). It has been argued that in capitalist societies, disability is individualized and medicalized (Oliver 1990), and in common with the conventional image of the aged, the popular image of disability embodies physical inability and is associated with the idea of sports for therapy. In a way which is similar to that in which elderly women are challenging the conventional concept of the ageing body, disabled sportswomen are rejecting the conventional concept of the handicapped participant and are keen to be recognized for their sporting abilities and successes and not their problems (Minister of Sport 1989; Moucha 1991).

The British Sports Association for the Disabled (BSAD) is an umbrella organization which promotes and co-ordinates all types of sporting activities for people with different disabilities. Its influence is country-wide and it has a comprehensive grass-roots network. The BSAD works in liaison with the numerous associations for different disabilities, the Sports Council, local authorities, governing bodies and voluntary sports clubs. The London Sports Forum for Disabled People, set up in 1993, has a similar function for people with disabilities in the capital. In recent years there has been a marked increase in participation, and 1989 (the date the British Paralympic Association was founded) marked the start of an accelerated period of development. Since that date the emphasis has changed from sports for therapy and for people with specific disabilities, to organized activities for those with abilities in specific sports. The national governing bodies of sports for the able-bodied are systematically incorporating disabled people into their development plans, so that sports-specific competition is rapidly replacing disability-specific competition. After the Barcelona Paralympics in 1992, the newly formed International Paralympic Committee has worked through national affiliations and sports-specific federations. The idea is to build on people's abilities, not their disabilities (Marshall 1991). Although the usual pattern is for disabled athletes to compete against other disabled athletes, in some sports it is possible for disabled athletes to compete on equal terms with the able-bodied. For example, in 1982, a wheelchair archer from New Zealand – Neroli Fairhall – won a gold medal at the Commonwealth Games. It is only in recent years that disabled sportspeople have begun to be integrated into the community and have used facilities otherwise available only for able-bodied players.

In spite of being a majority, and in spite of an increase in the overall number of disabled people who participate in sports at various levels, disabled women are far outnumbered by disabled men in organized sports. In 1987 in the USA, figures for female membership of sports associations ranged from 10 per cent to 40 per cent of male membership (Grimes and French 1987: 24). It seems that the Education for All Handicapped Children Act in 1975, intended to remove the barriers to participation of all disabled children in mainstream activities, failed to shift the gender discrepancies between male and female participation (ibid.). Figures for the Paralympics and for wheelchair tennis show a considerable gender imbalance: 15 British athletes went to the Winter Paralympics in 1991, but only 1 was a woman; out of 206 athletes selected to go to the Summer Games in Barcelona, only 46 were women – 5 with cerebral palsy, 13 amputees and spinally injured, 8 who were blind, and 20 wheelchair athletes who were mostly paraplegics. There was no single female squad, whereas the men sent football, basketball and volleyball teams. The world-wide figures for the Barcelona Paralympics are as follows: 2,366 male athletes, 716 women; 686 male officials, 230 women; others 169 men, 54 women – a total of more than three times as many men as women. Eighty-four countries sent no female athletes at all, and although there was one country (Namibia) that sent no men and five others which sent more women than men, they were all small numbers. A higher number of men than women was associated with each of the disability federations – IBSA (blind) 450 men, 173 women; ISOD (amputees and les autres [the others]) 737 men, 153 women; ISMWSF (spinal injuries) 849 men, 305 women; and CPISRA (cerebral palsy) 333 men, 85 women. The numbers of male officials at Barcelona were also much higher than female officials: for example, chefs de mission (96 men, 6 women); administrators (27 men, 16 women); doctors (44 men, 12 women); coaches (469 men, 120 women); officials (82 men, 21 women). The exceptions were those who were in traditional female roles such as physiotherapists (43 men, 45 women) and nurses (4 men, 14 women). The International Wheelchair Tennis Federation estimates that there are approximately 12,000 wheelchair tennis players in the world – 11,000 of whom are men, and 1,000 of whom are women. In international competition, approximately 130 men and 47 women have an open ranking.

The reasons for the gender discrepancy are complex. More disabled people in younger age groups participate in sports than older people, and accident rates resulting in spinal injuries and amputations, most common in

younger age groups, are higher for men than for women, whereas more
women are chronically disabled. But this does not account for the general
size of the difference. A top international athlete suggests a combination of
factors:

> It's true, disabled women seem reluctant to participate and much the same
> factors militate against them participating as those that affect able-bodied
> women. Family responsibilities are important for some women . . . and
> there's nearly always a lack of money . . . and transport is often a special
> problem. . . . And so too are the influences of images of what women
> should be like.

American research shows that

> Disabled women and girls often face enormous emotional and psycho-
> logical problems. Issues of low self-esteem, inexperience with sports, fear
> of success and failure, which are already documented for able-bodied
> women are even greater problems for disabled females . . . [and that]
> disabled women view themselves more negatively and are likely to be
> viewed by others more negatively than disabled men.
>
> (Grimes and French 1987: 26)

The general environmental and financial problems 'emanating from a society
that is unwilling to adapt to the needs of the disabled' (James 1990: 14) seem
to militate against the participation of women to a greater extent than against
the participation of men. Particularly for those women who are married or
live with a partner, greater financial restrictions exist and it is usually impossible for them to do anything spontaneously – 'it's very much a matter of
juggling one's life-style'. But the media's constant portrayal of the idealized
able-bodied, slim, fit and beautiful female (see Chapter 7) is probably the
greatest deterrent against sports participation for disabled women. They are
made to feel even more distanced from the ideal body image than women in
the non-disabled community (James 1990: 25). The link between sports and
modern consumer culture clearly has a powerful influence on the physical
and psychological identities of disabled women – the commodification of
the female body beautiful implicitly undervalues and even stigmatizes the
disabled female body. Disabled women are made to feel unattractive if they
are unable to come close to the non-disabled definition of beauty. Tanni
Gray is gold medallist at the Barcelona Paralympics for the 100 metres, 200
metres, 400 metres and 800 metres wheelchair trackraces, silver medallist for
the 4 × 100 metres relay, world record holder and Paralympic record holder
for the 100, 200, 400 and 800 metres, and British record holder for all those
events and for the wheelchair marathon; she explains, 'Certainly road racing
and training are not very glamorous and you have to be thick-skinned and
determined, because people look at you as if you're a freak sometimes.'

Because sports are central to male culture, disabled men tend to be influenced to participate in greater numbers. To be able to flex their muscles and demonstrate physical power symbolizes masculinity and status among disabled men, as it does for the able-bodied. The equivalent quest for identity as a disabled women is to be able to assume the symbols of mainstream femininity in the able-bodied world. There are other similarities with gender divisions in sports for the able-bodied: disabled sportswomen find it harder to get sponsorship than disabled sportsmen, and very few women exist in sports administration for the disabled – for example, only one elected woman is on the International Paralympic Committee. Because disabled women have few role models in sports, the status quo is more easily reproduced than changed. Britain compares unfavourably with other advanced capitalist countries, notably the United States and Canada, to a large extent because sports are better integrated into rehabilitation programmes, they are better sponsored – in many cases by rehabilitation clinics, there are better facilities and training opportunities, and there is better publicity and media coverage.

Nevertheless, sports have made a substantial difference to the lives of the relatively small number of disabled women who take part. In some cases it is the only activity that gives a disabled woman confidence and a sense of achievement. As Deanna Coates (1988 Paralympic air-rifle shooting gold medallist) puts it, 'Sport has changed my life. Before I joined a sports club I didn't really do anything. Now I'm living instead of just existing.'

Disability in sports has traditionally been understood as a negative phenomenon, but with the development of vibrant national and international sports organizations for the disabled and with the increased visibility of disabled sportsmen and women in the media, public consciousness about sports for the disabled and the consciousness of disabled women themselves will inevitably change to something more positive.

CONCLUSION

This chapter has dealt with different categories of sports and sportswomen. The analysis has pointed to the relationship between sports, the structures of capitalism, and ideology. We have seen how, for women from certain social groups, gender inequalities are exacerbated by other factors so that they suffer from double or multiple forms of discrimination. But we have seen, too, ways in which women are creating for themselves participatory trends which reflect personal desires and abilities. Sports touch the lives of women with diverse cultural and personal biographies in ways which are linked to the issues of power, autonomy and control. The tendency in British society – in common with other capitalist nation-states – is to individualize the 'problem' of low participation rates and to characterize minority groups as 'outsiders' who are difficult to assimilate into mainstream sports. The ideology of 'difference' coexists with a strong concept of the 'norm' – a concept that is defended and reproduced on a daily basis so that existing inequalities are continued. Individualism rests comfortably with the ideology of equality of opportunity, but both attract attention away from deep-seated and widespread forms of discrimination. They make it seem sensible that individuals should adapt to existing sports systems, rather than focusing on the idea that sports environments should be changed. These ideologies make it hard for those with minority interests to be in decision-making positions about changing the structures of power, dealing with institutionalized discrimination and distributing limited resources. However, the relationships between the individual and society, women and sport, autonomy and control, agency and structure are constantly shifting and this chapter points to the diversity and complexity of the politics of sports and to the need for individuals to form organizations to work for radical reforms.

Chapter 11

Into the twenty-first century
Diversity and empowerment

GETTING INTO MEN'S SPORTS

It is clear that the development of women's sports is not a coherent, unified process, but riddled with complexities and contradictions. Nevertheless, women's historical struggle for increased opportunities has resulted in changes that only a few years ago were unimaginable: women are now participating in a vast range of sports with varied characteristics.[1] Their radicalism is most powerfully symbolized by the inroads made into traditional male sports. Some of the fastest-growing female sports are aggressive, team sports, such as football and rugby; combat sports, such as boxing and judo; those where power and musculature are important, for example, body-building, weight-lifting and throwing events; and those that have been traditionally male for cultural reasons, such as snooker, bowls and darts. For example, the UK Women's Rugby Football Union (WRFU) was formed in 1983, with 12 founder members, yet just ten years later 2,000 women were playing each week, and 22 new clubs were registered with the WRFU during the 1992 season, making a total of 142, some of which run two or three squads on a regular basis. Scotland has recently organized its first national team and Ireland is setting up clubs for female players. Another example is rugby league – a staunchly male game – which has powerful roots in working-class communities in the north of the country. It is mostly in those regions that women are playing. The north/south, working-class/middle-class orientations of men's rugby league and union respectively, are reflected in the women's games. In 1985 the Women's Amateur Rugby League Association (WARLA) was formed, and from that time there was a gradual expansion of the game so that by 1993 there were two divisions with 16 teams and 250 registered women players. A recently founded Girls' Rugby League Association, which already has 11 member teams, also exists (Thompson 1992: 23).

Women who play rough, physical sports requiring strength and speed express the sense of satisfaction and exhilaration they get from participating. The following two extracts are from transcriptions of interviews with a rugby union player and a football player:

I don't care how tough it gets, or how filthy I get . . . I love to pit my strength against other women and outwit my opponents . . . I really don't care if people smirk when they know I play rugby . . . for me, it's the best game in the world. . . . It's very physical . . . the physical contact . . . that's what gives me a buzz . . . I don't like 'girly' sports – they do nothing for me.

Football's fantastic . . . think of it . . . why do you think so many men play it? . . . Why shouldn't women play it? . . . What business is it of theirs if they think I'm gay? It's the sport I'm interested in. . . . It's difficult to say why I like it best . . . maybe because I used to kick a ball around when I was a kid . . . with my brothers . . . even my Dad would mess around with me . . . I like the skills of the game . . . and I like to play really hard . . . [to] get really tired . . . you know . . . so exhausted you could drop . . . but afterwards it feels so good.

These women are actively redefining concepts of women's sports. Their accounts show a blurring of traditional ideas of masculinity and femininity in sports and an enthusiasm and positivity which transcend opposition based on mainstream heterosexual assumptions. They appear to be confident with their sporting identities, and with the radical images of femininity which they project. Their definitions may indicate a growing trend among young sportswomen to reject traditional attitudes about sports which they find personally limiting.

However, although women are stamping their own character on sports which used to be absolute bastions of male identity and privilege, the process has not been straightforward and without struggle. Many sportswomen playing 'men's sports' still face harsh criticism and ridicule which reflect a particularly British, class-based form of sexism. At the same time, as well, a new form of gender relations has emerged. In many cases, the historical opposition of men's governing bodies to women's entry into their sports has changed to a controlling role, so that women lack autonomy in these situations. For example, part of the work of the (men's) Rugby League National Development Scheme is to promote women's rugby league and, in the case of weight-lifting, men's opposition to women's participation continued until less than a decade ago, when the all-male governing body agreed to female membership and competitions. Women's weight-lifting in Britain remains under the authority of the British Amateur Weight-lifters Association (the original men's association). The inaugural British Women's Weight-lifting Championships were held in 1986, and since that time the sport has burgeoned, both nationally and internationally. Its popularity has spread rapidly in the West, and in other parts of the world as well – for example, the Bulgarians are pre-eminent in Europe; it is estimated that China has over 3 million female weight-lifters; and women are weight-lifting in increasing numbers in India and in Japan. The infiltration of women into traditional male sports has come first from the West and has then spread to some industrialized countries in the East. Little development of this sort exists outside the industrialized world.

The rapid growth of female body-building during the last decade has also been mediated by the male-controlled International Federation. The federation provided guidelines for 'assessing the female physique' in its 1984 rule book:

> the judge must bear in mind that he or she is judging a woman's body-building competition and is looking for the ideal *feminine* physique. Therefore, the most important aspect is shape, a feminine shape. The other aspects are similar to those described for assessing men, but in regard to muscular development, it must not be carried to excess where it resembles the massive musculature of the male physique.
>
> (*IFBB Constitution and Rule Book for Judges, Athletes and Officials*)

It was according to these criteria that Australian Bev Francis, described as having muscle definition 'equivalent to a man', failed to win women's body-building contests until she changed her shape. The film *Pumping Iron II – The Women*[2] (concerning a body-building competition held in Las Vegas in 1984) exposes the inability of male judges to provide more than a subjective and socially constructed definition of the 'feminine physique' and the 'aesthetic body'. Although there was controversy among the judges about the ideal shape for a female body-builder, the majority rejected Bev Francis's exceptionally heavy and well-defined musculature in favour of the less bulky and 'softer' frame of Carla Dunlop. Bev Francis came to body-building from power-lifting (she was the world professional champion) and in order to achieve success in her new sport, she 'worked' on different parts of her body until she had transformed her appearance. With a 'slimmer, more "feminine" waist', more 'flare in the thighs and legs' and a 'more balanced and aesthetic physique' she became the runner-up in the Miss Olympia competition (the Women's World Professional Body-Building Championships – inaugurated in 1980) in 1990 and 1991. Although the Federation has recently changed its guidelines for assessing the female physique (laid out in the 1993 edition of the Professional Rules for IFBB athletes), it protects the rights of judges to make subjective assessments according to their preferred definitions of femininity. The guidelines state that 'Women should be encouraged to develop as much muscle mass as possible as long as this development conforms to the accepted standards of bodybuilding aesthetics – symmetry, shape, proportion, definition etc'. As in 1984, the focus of assessment is the extent of muscularity that is acceptable for the female frame. '"Too big"', it is pointed out, 'is a term that applies only to whether or not a competitor has developed too much muscle mass for her skeletal structure and proportions.' The construction of sexual difference in body-building is made official in the texts of the specifically male and female rules, and the bodies of female competitors are signifiers of this difference.

Women's body-building incorporates contradictory body techniques (those that enhance fitness and muscularity and symbolize physical power, and those for the display of contrived femininity which symbolize manipulation – see Chapter 7). This opposition can be seen, and is often exaggerated, on all occasions when women infiltrate traditional male sports. Although the term 'androgeny' – the state of being neither male nor female – has been used to describe the capacity of women to combine stereotypical masculine and feminine characteristics, it is a term that has been applied to sports as if they are insulated from the demands and constraints of the rest of society. Women who play 'men's sports' have continually to negotiate their positions in traditional cultural contexts of male power and privilege, and in a general ideological framework of patriarchy and compulsory heterosexuality.

Without exception, the advances made by women in 'men's sports' have been the result of struggle and negotiation. In the case of horse-racing, Florence Nagle campaigned for twenty years to be allowed to train race-horses in her own name (Ramsden 1973). Finally, in 1966, she secured a legal victory over the exclusive male Jockey Club, compelling it to grant her a trainer's licence and therefore breaking its all-male monopoly. Florence Nagle paved the way for the future successes of female trainers. She was clear about her position: 'This was a matter of principle. I am a feminist. I believe in equal rights for women. Things should be decided by ability, not sex' (Martin 1979: 199). It was not until 1972, when the Ladies' Jockey Association was inaugurated, that women were first allowed to race on the Flat, and then in 1976 they could ride the Jumps (Grayson 1987). Female jockeys still number only a fraction of the numbers of male jockeys, how-ever, and in National Hunt racing the problems are compounded by a dogged resistance to female riders by male owners and trainers. Because the horses are bigger and there is a greater element of danger, and because some of the few successful female jockeys have been badly injured (one was even killed), traditional ideas about 'femininity' provide an ideological barrier. Female jockeys have to contend with facilities inferior to those supplied for their male counterparts and often experience abusive behaviour. Neverthe-less, they are making an impact and, in 1988, Alex Greaves was voted the top rider, male or female, on all-weather race tracks in Britain.

THE RESULTS OF TRADITION

Cricket provides a unique example of gender inequality in a traditional male sport. The Women's Cricket Association was founded during the 1920s, and since that time women have had control of their own game in a separate sphere from men. A full range exists of club, county and territorial competitions, six-a-side junior tournaments, and national teams at senior and junior levels. In 1958 the International Women's Cricket Council was formed; the first women's cricket World Cup was played in 1973; and the first European Cup

Tournament took place in 1989. But the contrast with the men's game is marked. The Lord's Taverners (a registered charity) gives support to the junior game, but sponsorship is hard to come by. No regular schedule of international tours has existed because each host country has to underwrite the costs of the visiting team, and most players have to take extended time off from work, and pay their own travel costs. In 1988, for example, members of the national squad had to find £2,000 each in order to play in the World Cup in Australia. The men's game is financially and ideologically powerful and exclusionary; women have traditionally been refused membership of major clubs and associations which wield power and control resources. The major symbol of male cricket privilege is the Marylebone Cricket Club (MCC), whose ground is at Lord's where only the all-male members have access to the famous Pavilion during matches. Over the years, proposals that women should be allowed to become members of the MCC have failed. In 1991 a letter was written to all members of the MCC explaining that

> Although the Rules of the Club do not explicitly disqualify women from membership, MCC has always been a men's club and the Rules are written upon that assumption. It would therefore require an amendment to the Rules supported by a two-thirds majority of those voting to admit women to membership.

Members were asked to vote on two resolutions: first, to decide whether or not women should be allowed to become full members of the MCC, and, second, and less radically, to decide whether or not to permit the committee to elect as honorary members 'whether for services to cricket or for any other reason', women 'the Committee considers to be especially desirable in the interests of the Club'. The latter suggestion would empower the committee to recognize outstanding services to the game of cricket by a woman such as Rachael Heyhoe Flint (ex-captain of the women's English cricket team). In both cases, there was a failure to get the two-thirds majority required to change the present exclusionary practices.

However, there have been some recent advances for women's cricket in England. Although in comparison with Australian players, who receive federal government grants, support from the Australian Sports Commission and corporate sponsorship, English players are woefully short of substantial financial support, some sponsorship was secured for the fifth World Cup held in England in 1993 – from the MCC, the Sports Aid Foundation, the Foundation for Sport and the Arts and the UK Sports Council. The final, played between England and New Zealand, took place at Lords, free of charge, and the match was televised. Media commentators praised the exceptionally high standard of play and presented the women's game as top level entertainment – a marked shift which may help to increase public interest. If women's cricket in England draws large crowds, as it does in Australia, India, New Zealand and the West Indies, it will create a stimulus for regular media coverage and increased sponsorship.

Golf is another bastion of male sporting privilege in which women have participated for many years, yet with fewer opportunities, poorer facilities, exclusion from clubs, and limited rights and powers. Only a few clubs in the country allow women to become 'full playing members' with the same rights as men; some have no women members at all, and the majority allow only men to be full members and allow only full members to have full rights. 'Lady associates' have no say in how a club is run and, since there are relatively few public facilities in relation to private ones, women have no alternative but to play at the limited times and according to the restricted conditions laid down by men. In Ireland the entrenched male opposition to golfing equality for women has become a political issue. Some have criticized the Ladies' Golf Union (LGU – the governing body for ladies' amateur golf in Britain) for failing to take a stance against discrimination; people disagree about what should be done. Some are in favour of separate clubs for women where they would have better opportunities than in mixed clubs; others argue that the only way to change male attitudes towards discrimination against women is to wage the battle in mixed clubs. Similarity exists between the symbolism of the Lord's Pavilion for cricketers and the Royal and Ancient (R and A) for golf, where, although women have access to the playing greens, they are barred from the clubhouse. Liz Khan, who was physically removed from the clubhouse during the 1990 Open, expressed her anger:

> The R and A is the home of golf and women cannot even visit the trophies, let alone become members there. How can things ever change if you've got an all-male club administering and being the establishment that every-one looks up to?
>
> (Cited in Barraclough 1991)

Although some established golf clubs have introduced changes to make membership democratic, and (recognizing the boom in women's golf) new clubs have democratized facilities for commercial reasons, nevertheless Britain still lags behind other European countries which practise gender equality in both clubs and competitions. In North America and Japan the governing bodies for golf have taken account of sex equality issues. In the case of women professionals, those outside the UK generally have a higher status and better media coverage; in America, for example, it is more typical for golf clubs to employ women professionals. Sponsorship for the women's game is much harder to acquire in the UK, and there are fewer and less lucrative tournaments than in Europe and North America.

The power wielded by men in sports is not given up lightly; it has to be fought against. As with golf, in snooker the resources are monopolized by men and the struggles for equality have been long and bitter. Although some clubs welcome women as full members now, discrimination against women players still prevails in numerous situations, especially in the north. However, the creation of the Women's Billiards and Snooker Association (WBSA) in 1976, and the World Ladies' Billiard and Snooker Association (WLBSA) in 1981, has enabled national and international competitions to grow. This has also given women some bargaining power, and done a great deal to change the face of the women's game. Nevertheless, the position of female professional snooker players is grossly unequal in relation to men. Women find difficulty obtaining sponsorship and their prize money is derisory in comparison with men's. The only lucrative prize is for the winner of the Women's World Snooker Championship, sponsored by Forte Hotels – £12,000 (approximately 8 per cent of the men's top prize). But a much greater discrepancy prevails in the ranking tournaments – the top prize for men is around £100,000, for women it is never higher than £500 (0.5 per cent). Snooker is essentially a game of touch and technique and so no physical reasons exist for separate competitions; in 1991, the world professional snooker body capitulated to pressure and changed its rules to allow any player (male or female) to turn professional. However, the huge fees demanded militate against women professionals – by 1993 only 1 female professional snooker player was in the open, but still essentially male, association; there are 700 men. All top male players are seeded and do not have to qualify – in comparison, *all* female players have to work their way through the qualifying rounds. The slow progress of women's snooker is also due to minimal and sexist media coverage. Women have struggled in a similar way to gain equality in the less widely played (in Britain) game of pool – in 1993 there was only one female professional player in comparison with twenty-nine men. She only became a member of the Professional Pool Players Organization (PPPO) because the PPPO had to accept her application in 1992 as a result of the recommendations of an industrial tribunal.

Women experience similar problems in struggling for recognition in all sports and events from which they have traditionally been excluded. In the early stages there is no history to draw upon; no role models or networking arrangements exist for interested participants; there are no female organizations or coaches; there is always resistance and a certain amount of ridicule; and it is impossible to secure financial backing. The longer men practically and ideologically appropriate an activity, the more difficult it is for women to take part. Divisions appear to be along traditional gender lines, and women tend to be dependent on male coaches and associations, the recognition of national governing bodies, and then validation by international organizations. From the start of organized athletics, for example, women have been banned from official competition in the hammer, pole vault, steeplechase and triple jump events, and there has been continual resistance to change over the years. In Britain development has been slowed by the conflict between different groups in women's athletics, in addition to opposition from powerful male ideologues. In 1986 the 'Women's Hammer, Triple Jump and Pole Vault Club' was formed in an attempt to co-ordinate interest, but it was only after a long period of resistance to pressure that in

1987 the Women's Amateur Athletic Association (WAAA), in liaison with the (men's) AAA and the English Schools Athletic Association (ESAA), agreed that the events be included in a 3-year development plan. Ironically, even when clubs and associations have been persuaded to include these events on their programmes and arrange coaching sessions, there has been a very poor response, so that further development has effectively been halted. It is always difficult to change long-standing cultural traditions; when events have been more or less always exclusively male, the ideological barriers keep out all but a tiny minority of women. This seems to be a greater problem in Britain where the development of the hammer, pole vault, steeplechase and triple jump has lagged behind that in other countries. For example, in Australia, Canada, Denmark, Ireland, the USA, the former USSR, and Germany women's struggles to gain recognition in these events have gained momentum: since the mid-1980s the national athletic organizations in these countries have officially sanctioned the events and facilitated coaching and competition procedures. However, there is as yet no international validation and a general lack of official commitment still exists on a worldwide scale, reflected in the very low response to a questionnaire sent out to eighty-two affiliated countries by the women's committee of the International Amateur Athletic Federation (IAAF – which has had control of women's international athletics since 1936). Although the committee had been considering introducing the hammer throw, pole vault, steeplechase and triple jump into the women's athletics programme, nothing more was done when a response was received from only eight countries. The IAAF has traditionally been a male-dominated body, and in the past it has only responded to demands for women's participation; it has never initiated change.

The growth of many women's sports had led to increasing dependence on mixed, but male-controlled, associations. In the case of football, for example, the women's association was assimilated into the men's association in 1993. The FA is now responsible for men's and women's football and has set up a Women's Football Committee and appointed a co-ordinator for the women's game. This development has made the debate about separatism highly topical. On the one hand, it is argued that because women now have some share of the vast resources of the FA, there is greater potential for women's football than ever before. But those who opposed the amalgamation of the two single-sex associations point out that in many instances women have had to relinquish control of their own game. Even the FA's Women's Committee has a majority of male members and, not surprisingly, in most contexts, male-defined practices and ideas dominate the women's game.

COMBATING TRADITION

Although in the sports establishment, and among sports professionals and sports academics, it is now officially acknowledged that no reasons exist why biological differences between the sexes should impose restrictions on women's participation, nevertheless it is exceptionally difficult to shift institutionalized practices and the ideas that have supported them for so many years. As increasing numbers of women become involved in traditional male sports, however, the range of behaviour considered to be appropriate for females is broadened. Since the 1960s the increased popularity of oriental martial arts among women is part of this phenomenon – for example, aikido, judo, karate and taekwon-do have been fast-growing sports among both sexes in western Europe and North America. Martial arts appeal to women as forms of self-defence, and they have become increasingly popular as competitive sports in recent years. The mystique and discipline of martial arts have rendered redundant the conventional taboo against women fighting. The advent of 'sambo' wrestling in the Pan-American Games of 1983 marked the first time that women were allowed to participate in a combat sport in an international multi-sport competition (Lenskyj 1986: 123). Judo was accepted as an Olympic sport for women in 1992 (it was a men's event in the 1964 Olympics). Judo is one of the most successful female sports in Britain, and every member of the British team receives a grant from the Sports Aid Foundation. To some extent, the traditional gender divisions that are imposed in most sports with separate male and female categories are broken down in judo. In many situations men and women train together (members of the British team, for example, train at the famous Budokai club in London) without embarrassment and without any privileging according to sex. However, US women in mixed classes have experienced harassment which, according to Lenskyj (1986: 118), is a 'purely North American brand of chauvinism'. The ability of women to use their skill, agility, timing and alertness to outclass a male opponent in direct combat threatens the concept of maleness and symbolizes female empowerment. The following quotation illustrates how images of masculinity and femininity are constantly being reassessed and reconstructed:

> In 1980, an Industrial Tribunal and the Employment Appeal Tribunal . . .
> rejected the British Judo Association's defence that it was exempt from a
> charge of unlawful discrimination against a woman referee. It claimed
> *inter alia* that women did not have the strength to separate beefy male
> fighters; and during evidence it arranged a demonstration to try to prove
> this. One demonstrator even said, 'I wouldn't feel happy on the mat with
> a woman refereeing. I think I would find the physical aspects of a woman
> controlling two hefty men on the mat a little degrading.' Neither tribunal
> shared this view, and held unlawful the ban on the woman from

refereeing the all-England men's contest while she was still allowed to referee the women's national event and all-male club and area events.

(Grayson 1987:7)

The growth of women's self-defence is a reaction to the power of sexist ideology and the fear of sexual harassment and abuse. The Women's Self-Defence Association was formed in 1980 in response to women joining martial arts classes – not because they were interested in the sport, but because they were looking for a survival technique. Although self-defence draws on the elements of martial arts such as judo and karate, it is not competitive. Its main aim is to develop self-confidence and to equip women with the skills and attitudes necessary for them to take some responsibility for personal safety. Self-defence is linked to women's fears about their vulnerability *as women*, and to their desires to be able to live safely in a society where sexual harassment and violence are commonplace. Many women who join self-defence groups have experienced harassment and violence – they have been raped, been the subjects of racist attacks and threats, been beaten up by men at home, mugged in the street, or attacked for being lesbians. Self-defence abilities enhance the link between physical and psychological power which some women find that regular sports participation gives them.

More women participate in self-defence and oriental martial arts than the western combat sports of boxing and wrestling. In some states in the USA bans against women's boxing and wrestling were lifted during the 1970s and 1980s, but, where allowed, specific regulations for female participation were applied (Lenskyj 1986: 121). Women's boxing in some European countries is also popular, but although it is legal in Britain, it is not recognized by the British Boxing Board of Control (BBBC). There are only thirty or forty women on the unofficial British circuit, fights are infrequent and take place in pubs and gyms. The best-known British female boxer, Sue Atkins, is now retired, but she was the unofficial lightweight British women's champion. But although in 1993, in an attempt to regulate and put the sport on an official footing, she launched the British Ladies' Boxing Association, it was not recognised by the men's boxing associations or by the GB Sports Council. But also in 1993, the Amateur Boxing Association of England conceded to constant pressure to allow a woman to take their coaching examination and in doing so avoided a court action. The love of boxing as a sport and the serious approach of some female competitors is to a large extent masked by the sexy and seedy connotations of women in the ring. Female boxers are parodied – treated as 'denatured', crazy, brutalized, monstrous – a difficult image to dislodge because it is reproduced by the showbiz forms of topless women's boxing and free-for-all 'tough girl' bouts. It also remains a popular conception that women's breasts will be injured when boxing, although protective equipment eradicates the risk. It may be that it is undesirable on ethical grounds for women to compete in boxing because the specific aim is to inflict injury, but such arguments should be consistently applied to boxing for women *and* men, who are equally vulnerable to brain damage or eye injuries. Conventional images of the masculine and feminine in sports have traditionally articulated women's subordination. But the increasing number of women taking part in traditional male sports is creating an emergent female sports culture which is transforming those conventional definitions. The process of reproduction is clearly complex and contradictory and results in an increasing range of sporting femininities.

CATCHING UP WITH THE MEN

In different ways, men and women are constantly being compared in sports, and differences between male and female levels of performance are used as an index of 'natural' ability. Men are on average taller, stronger and heavier than women, with broader shoulders, narrower hips and a higher centre of gravity. They have more muscle mass, a greater lung capacity, larger hearts, and therefore a more efficient delivery of oxygen to the working muscles. Sportsmen are, therefore, generally stronger, speedier and more powerful than sportswomen: they can run faster, jump higher and throw farther. Females have a comparatively lesser muscle mass, more body fat, shorter and less dense bones, a smaller lung volume and total chest capacity, and are on average more agile and flexible, though slower and less strong than men. They also have to accommodate in their sports to the physiological changes which occur during menstruation, pregnancy, childbirth and the menopause (Dyer 1982). However, although women are on average slower and less powerful than men, it does not follow that events demanding speed and strength are suited only to men. There are far greater differences within a sex than between sexes, and the fitness factor and levels of skill, agility and co-ordination can outweigh the sex factor anyway. With this in mind, in 1993 the British Athletic Federation sanctioned graded races (for athletes of comparable standards) between men and women.

Innumerable social variables exist – cultural, economic, ideological, psychological (many of which have been discussed in the earlier chapters of this book), which also affect performance. The complexities of the interplay between the biological and the social make it impossible to assess accurately the factors which are most important in any given situation. As Kenneth Dyer (1989: 97) argues:

> Physiological differences are undoubtedly responsible for some of the performance differential between the sexes but it is simply flying in the face of the evidence to label physiology the sole cause. To do that directs attention from what those other causes might be.

But differences between male and female performances in many sports are far less marked than they used to be because women's performances are improving at a faster rate than those of the men, and Dyer (1989: 86) claims that it looks as if the pattern will continue:

It is my assertion, based on the analysis of the data with all the short-comings and difficulties I have hinted at, that women's performances are improving faster than men's in virtually all events in all sports and will continue to do so for the foreseeable future.

The reasons for this trend are not clear. But Dyer (1989: 86–7) opposes the easy answer that improved performances are due only to a few outstanding or sexually dubious women, or are the result primarily of drug-taking. It is likely that the answer is linked to the increase in the number of women participating, combined with advances in sports sciences, technology and coaching, as well as changing attitudes about femininity. What is clear is that women have exploded the myths surrounding female biology and are en-gaged in a process of reinterpretation of physical ability. The trend towards equivalence with, and superiority over, men is most dramatic in endurance events such as long-distance cycling, running and swimming, and evidence shows that women may be physiologically advantaged in such activities. The theory is that trained female athletes experience more effective aerobic ventilation than trained men because they possess a high level of intra-muscular fat and have a more efficient enzyme system for utilizing it for high energy production over long periods. Coupled with a better temperature control mechanism, this means that women can avoid fatigue better than men (Dyer 1982).

Since the women's marathon was introduced as an Olympic event in 1984, women's distance running has boomed. Only 300 women out of a field of 7,500 (4 per cent) ran in the first London Marathon in 1981; in 1992, just over one decade later, the numbers had increased dramatically – out of a total of 23,783 who finished the course, well over 3,000 were women (13 per cent). Far more women are competing in all the world marathon champion-ships every year, and some are involved in unusual and little-known events as well – for example, in the third Everest Marathon held in 1991, 8 women competed out of a field of 70. 'Ultra' running (from a marathon to 1,000 miles) is a fast-growing sport among women as well as men. In 1991 the British athlete Eleanor Adams ran a distance of 83 miles 555 yards in the Interprint 12-Hour Race. She was third out of a mixed field – 4 women out of 24 started the race and 3 women out of 10 completed it. She also finished third in an open 1,000 kilometres (over 620 miles) race in a world record time of 17 days 15 minutes, and she has held just under forty world records for distances ranging from 30 miles to the Six Day Race (in 1991 this was more than any other practising athlete [Combes 1991]). In multi-day races Eleanor has run 100 miles in 14 hours 34 minutes, and 1,000 miles in 19 days 23 hours

(Hammond 1991). Women are in the top 10/20 in the extraordinarily physically demanding triathlon competitions (swimming for 2½ miles; cycling for 112 miles; and running a full marathon without a break), and are challenging men in 'short' triathlon races (swimming between 800 metres and 1 mile; cycling 25–40 miles; running 5–13 miles). The International Triathlon Union (ITU) is committed to gender equality and with this in mind set up the ITU Women's Commission in 1990. Identical prizes are awarded to both sexes. Women have also made remarkable inroads into long-distance cycling. The year 1984 marked the first Women's Tour de France (La Tour Féminine) which lasted a whole month; and in 1989 a new EEC tour was created. But there have been Women's World Cycling Championships since 1958, won by the British competitor Beryl Burton seven times between 1959 and 1967. In open competitions top women cyclists have recorded equivalent times to those of leading men and for two years Beryl Burton held the 12-hour time record in equal competition with men. Records are also held by women in long-distance swimming events – for example, British swimmer Alison Streeter holds the world record for the 20 miles across the North Channel from Scotland to Ireland; she holds the British Double Channel (England to France) record (50 miles) and the round the Isle of Wight record (60 miles); and has swum around Jersey (42 miles). Women have held records for the non-stop return swim across the English Channel; for the American equivalent two-way swim across the Catalina Channel in California; and for the 89-mile swim from the Bahamas to Florida. Finally, in long-distance walking, British Ann Sayer's 415-mile walk over the Three Peaks (Ben Nevis, Scafell Pike and Snowdon) in 7 days 3 minutes is in the Guinness Book of Records; she has also held the world record for the French 117-mile walk.

These examples give some idea of the extraordinary but generally little-known accomplishments of sportswomen. And they are paralleled in long-distance sailing, ice-skating, roller-skating and skiing events. The concern about whether or not women will ever equal the sporting achievements of men has become an obsession in sports. Because the biological gap underpinning male and female performances has been used to discriminate against women and explain their supposed inferiority, it has masked the fact that differences may be more social than biological. The very idea that women are 'catching up with the men', and the ways in which studies of differences between males and females and quantification procedures are prioritized, takes for granted the dominant masculinist framework of analysis which, as Alison Dewar (1991: 18–19) points out,

> never asks us to question why sporting practices in our culture are defined in ways that allow men to display their physical strength, speed and power. Nor does it question why the performance gap in sport is given so much attention and how this is used to bolster images of male power and dominance as natural and immutable.

Social definitions of sports place a higher value on attributes such as speed and power. If endurance, flexibility, skill, artistry, creativity and timing were accorded higher value, sports would have a very different meaning.

SPORTING DIVERSITY

Because accounts of women's sports tend to focus on conventional activities, and minority events receive poor publicity, general ignorance exists about the diversity of women's involvement. For example, little is known about the history of women's water-polo after the inter-war years (see Chapter 6), apart from evidence of some friendly international matches during the 1950s after which time the sport seemed to decline and die. It is only now being reinstated, and although Britain is behind other European and North American countries which have been playing competitively for over two decades, there are about sixty women's water-polo clubs with 260 players registered with the Amateur Swimming Association (ASA) (although it is claimed that the actual figures are higher because some players are registered as swimmers). The low profile of the game, however, discourages a rise in the number of participants and makes it difficult to secure pool time and financial support (over £100,000 was spent on the preparation of swimmers for the Barcelona Olympics and another £60,000 for accommodation and flights; women's water-polo receives a total of £12,000 per year). Although advances are slow for minority sports such as water-polo, changing attitudes about female sports and physicality have given women more incentive than ever before to take part in diverse activities. A marked increase has occurred in women's participation in other minority water sports, such as canoeing, octopush, surf-boarding, water-ski racing, and yachting.

Air sports provide examples of virtually invisible female sports cultures. Although hot-air ballooning is a costly sport (a balloon costs around £10,000 and there are heavy associated expenses), it is nevertheless an expanding female sport. About 1,000 pilots are registered with the British Balloon and Airship Club, 10 per cent of whom are women. Ballooning is reliant not on strength, but on skill and judgement, and so women take part in open competition with men. In 1988 Lindsay Muir became the first woman to win the British National Championships; since then she has won the Best British Pilot Trophy; set new British women's distance and duration records; and become the best female hot-air balloon pilot in the world when she set a new women's world distance record. Only one women's-only competition exists in the world – the Ladies' Grand Cup. Although women are able to compete on equal terms with men, clear gender inequalities exist in terms of numbers: to compete in the world championships a person has to be nominated by the organization of his or her home country and, out of 101 pilots at the 1989 and 1991 Championships, Lindsay Muir was the only woman to take part. There are other air sports, such as aerobatics, gliding, hang-gliding, paragliding and parachuting, in which women have had notable successes – for example, the World Hang-gliding Championships have been won by a woman, and the *Daily Express* has an all-woman parachute team.

Women's sports are usually defined very narrowly and so the multiple realities, languages and experiences are largely hidden. Although in smaller numbers, women participate in the full range of sports in which men participate – all those that have so far been mentioned in this book and hundreds for which there is no space. With this in mind, women's sports can be said to have a 'revolutionary' core in the sense that increasing numbers of women are taking action for themselves, participating in sports of their own choice, in their own ways, and experiencing a sense of empowerment by so doing.

EMPOWERMENT

Central to the development of women's sports is the issue of female agency and empowerment. There have always been exceptional women who have enjoyed sports, but if all women are to have real choices, the problem of the low status of women and girls must be tackled collectively, through the work of organizations with well-thought-out strategies to win support and change opinion. In most developed, western countries, a special action group for women's sports has been set up – the first one, called the Women's Sports Foundation, was founded in the USA in 1974, and the Canadian Association for the Advancement of Women and Sport was founded in 1981. The British Women's Sports Foundation (WSF) followed in 1984. It was set up by a group of women 'committed to the aim of promoting the interests of all women in and through sport'. In the early days the WSF struggled to acquire funding and recognition; it has now gained legitimation as the major association in the voluntary sector concerned exclusively with issues of women's sports and recreation, and receives support from a number of sources, including the GB Sports Council. A recent sponsorship deal with Tambrands, the makers of Tampax tampons, has resulted in the publication of a new magazine entitled *Women and Sport*, and £250,000 has been put into a Sports Award scheme for girls and young women from 11 to 19 years of age. This scheme is part of a drive to develop the potential of individual and team performance, coaching, and skill as a sports official. Special awards are given for the overall 'Young Sports Person of the Year' and 'Young Disabled Sports Person'.

Although from the start the WSF has been concerned to embrace wide social aims committed to humanistic ideals and grass-roots and 'alternative' opportunities, it is difficult to put this philosophy fully into practice. The organization has ensured that the sports establishment is constantly lobbied on the issue of women in sports, and it has worked successfully with other agencies to set up projects and provide advice, information and networking facilities. It has not, however, been able to create sufficient financial or ideological power to be the 'official' voice for women's sports in Britain. It is also difficult for those women who run the organization, who are in the main middle-class sportswomen or professionals, to represent the needs and desires of all groups of women in the community or to find ways fully to integrate different women into the work of the WSF. Nevertheless, in common with associations in other countries, the WSF in Britain has done a tremendous amount to keep the campaign for women's sports constantly alive; to stimulate interest in women's sports; to nurture talent; to educate and to inform. Together with the action of other groups and individuals throughout the nation, and with the connections and shared concerns of similar women's sports associations across the world, the WSF has provided an indispensable forum for the empowerment of women in sports. Nevertheless, it needs to go further. To date there are few incentives which are concerned with ways in which wider economic, political and social implications of sports are part of the politics of gender. Some examples have been discussed in this book – the redefining of democratic processes in women's sports and the elimination of discrimination in sports clubs based on sexuality and ethnicity. Other examples are the links which are being examined between feminism, ecological movements, sports and recreation; research being carried out to examine and eradicate sexual harassment and child sexual abuse in sports; and the activities of sports studies students who are activists on human rights issues. If sports for women are to be truly enriching then they must also be truly humane and women's sports organizations must take the lead in the transformative processes.

CONCLUSION

This book is to do with the gender relations of cultural power. Some sports have been stubbornly male-dominant, and for years biological differences have been used to obscure the uneven relations of power between men and women in sports. But the histories of women's sports show that patriarchal relations on their own do not explain women's subordination. Female sports are integral to the totality of relations of cultural power which include those between men and women; those between different groups of women; and those which are tied to economic, political and ideological relations of power. The idea that women in sports are a homogeneous group has been resisted. The hidden prototype in much writing about women's sports has been linked to the experience of white western women from Christian cultures – usually middle-class and heterosexual. This book suggests that most women in sports, even in western cultures, depart in some way from this norm. Women's relationships with men are variable and complex and such factors as age, disability, class, ethnicity and sexuality make women different from one another. We need to challenge the fabrication of a consensual 'shared experience of women'.

The issues of autonomy and control are also complex. There are no authentic, absolutely autonomous sports for women; but neither are women simply passive recipients of culture, duped by men, or impossibly constrained by circumstances. Although a strong tendency exists for sports to reproduce dominant culture, the potential also is present to transform it. Women are involved in the dialectic of cultural struggle – they are manipulated *and* resistant, determined by circumstances *and* active agents in the transformation of culture. Sports, like other forms of culture, are deeply contradictory. Some female sports are backward-looking; some are incorporated into the dominant system of values and meanings; others are radical cultures incorporating new values and meanings.

Although the active choice by some women is to 'follow in the steps of men' and to participate in traditional sports according to the conventions of those sports, other women have chosen actively to build new sporting practices sensitive to the particular problems that women as a gender face. Female sports are part of the battle for control of the physical body – an intensely personal process. In western cultures in particular there is a tendency for women to experience their bodies as sites of oppression and to harbour a vision of a different and better body. But sports have become social experiences that for increasing numbers of women are positive, pleasurable and empowering. Women's consciousness about their own physicality is changing and they are active agents in this process.

During the writing of this book I have spoken to hundreds of women who participate in sports – for recreation, to escape from the home, for social reasons, to lose weight, to get fit, to compete – and most of them talk about a sense of well-being and enrichment that comes to their lives as a result. I have spoken to other women who are also implicated in the creation of female sports – as providers, administrators, coaches and theorists. They have a sense of energy, enthusiasm and commitment, much of which is focused on humanist and progressive ideas and the elimination of discrimination. Many of them share an awareness of the inadequacies of past traditions and have a vision of new possibilities for sporting females in the twenty-first century.

Notes

7 FEMININITY OR 'MUSCULINITY'?: CHANGING IMAGES OF WOMEN'S SPORTS

Information in this chapter about sport in the media comes from my own research and from a survey carried out by Sports Studies students at the Roehampton Institute, London, during December 1988 and January 1989, and January and February 1990. During those periods two groups of approximately sixty students examined the coverage of sport on television, in the press, and in comics and magazines.

1 The comics and magazines referred to here are as follows: *Beano, Blue Jeans, Bunty, Fast Forward, Hot Shot, Jackie, Jinty, Judy, Just Seventeen, Look-In, Mandy, My Guy, Non-League Football, Roy of the Rovers, Shoot, Sindy, Twinkle.*

2 A number of magazines, including some sports magazines and sports clothing catalogues (published in the UK and USA), were analysed for their coverage of sport and exercise and for representation of the female body which had sporting connections. They included the nine most widely read women's magazines, listed here in order of popularity: *Take a Break, Bella, Woman's Weekly, Woman's Own, Woman, Me, People's Friend, My Weekly* and *Woman's Realm.* Other magazines were selected fairly randomly to give a wider representation of style and readership: *Athletics Weekly, Body Building Magazine, Chat, Cosmopolitan, Elle, The Gleaner, Looks, Mayfair, Mountain Biking UK, Muscle Digest, Nautilus Woman, New Woman, Prima, Runner's World, Surfer, Tennis, Tri-athlete Magazine, The Voice, Wimbledon Television Viewer's Guide 1987, Women's Sports and Fitness.*

3 Newspapers in Britain characterized as 'quality' ones are *Daily Telegraph, Guardian, The Independent, Independent on Sunday, Observer, Sunday Times* and *The Times.* Those characterized as 'tabloids' are *Daily Express, Daily Mail, Daily Mirror, Daily Star, Sunday Mirror, Sun, Sunday Sport, Today* and *News of the World.*

4 The programme referred to here is LWT's *Saint and Greavsie,* broadcast on 23 November 1991.

8 GENDER RELATIONS OF POWER: INSTITUTIONALIZED DISCRIMINATION

1 These figures are percentages in column inches devoted to women's sports of the total coverage of sports reporting (including text and photographs of female-only

and mixed sports). These are the results of a survey carried out at the Roehampton Institute, London (see Chapter 7, notes for details). The Commonwealth Games took place during one of the periods chosen and therefore the findings may provide a more favourable idea of the time and space given to women's sports than is usually the case.

2 Information about sport on television comes from the Roehampton survey, mentioned in note 1.

10 SPORTS FOR ALL WOMEN: PROBLEMS AND PROGRESS

1 Much of this chapter is based on extensive interviews with women from the various social, cultural and sporting backgrounds discussed.

11 INTO THE TWENTY-FIRST CENTURY: DIVERSITY AND EMPOWERMENT

1 Much of this chapter is based on interviews with women from numerous different sports contexts and backgrounds.

2 *Pumping Iron II – The Women* (USA 1985). Directed by George Butler. British distributor Blue Dolphin.

References

1 THEORIES OF SPORT: THE NEGLECT OF GENDER

Althusser, L. (1971), *Lenin and Philosophy and Other Essays*, London: New Left Books.

Anderson, P. (1976–7), 'The Antimonies of Antonio Gramsci', in *New Left Review*, No. 100.

Ashworth, C. (1971), 'Sport as Symbolic Dialogue', in E. Dunning (ed.), *The Sociology of Sport*, London: Frank Cass.

Ball, D. and Loy, J. (eds) (1975), *Sport and the Social Order*, Reading, Mass.: Addison-Wesley.

Beamish, R. (1982), 'Sport and the Logic of Capitalism', in R. Gruneau and H. Cantelon (eds), *Sport, Culture and the Modern State*, Toronto: University of Toronto Press.

Beamish, R. (1988), 'The Political Economy of Professional Sport', in J. Harvey and H. Cantelon (eds), *Not Just a Game*, Ottawa: University of Ottawa Press.

Bourdieu, P. (1978), 'Sport and Social Class', in *Social Science Information*, Vol. XVIII, No. 6.

Bourdieu, P. (1980), 'Aristocracy of Culture', in *Media, Culture and Society*, Vol. 2, No. 3: 225–60.

Bourdieu, P. (1984), *Distinction: A Social Critique of the Judgement of Taste*, London: Routledge & Kegan Paul.

Boutilier, M. and San Giovanni, L. (1983), *The Sporting Woman*, Champaign, Ill.: Human Kinetics.

Brohm, J.-M. (1978), *Sport: A Prison of Measured Time*, London: Ink Links.

Carroll, J. (1986), 'Sport, Virtue and Grace', in *Theory, Culture and Society*, Vol. 3, No. 1: 91–9.

Clarke, J. and Critcher, C. (1985), *The Devil Makes Work: Leisure in Capitalist Britain*, London: Macmillan.

Coakley, J. (1990), *Sport in Society*, 4th edn, St Louis: Times Mirror.

Department of Education and Science (1991), *Physical Education for ages 5 to 16*, London: HMSO.

Dumazedier, J. (1974), *The Sociology of Leisure* (trans. M. A. MacKenzie), Amsterdam: Elsevier.

Dunning, E. (ed.) (1971), *The Sociology of Sport*, London: Frank Cass.

Dunning, E. (1989), 'The Figurational Approach to Leisure and Sport', in C. Rojek (ed.), *Leisure for Leisure: Critical Essays*, London: Macmillan.

Dunning, E. (1992), 'Figurational Sociology and the Sociology of Sport: Some Concluding Remarks', in E. Dunning and C. Rojek (eds), *Sport and Leisure in the Civilizing Process*, London: Macmillan: 221–85.

Dunning, E. and Rojek, C. (eds) (1992), *Sport and Leisure in the Civilizing Process*, London: Macmillan.

Dunning, E., Murphy, P. and Williams, J. (1988), *The Roots of Football Hooliganism: An Historical and Sociological Study*, London: Routledge & Kegan Paul.

Dyer, I. and Murphy, P. (1992), 'Drugs, Sport and Ideologies', in E. Dunning and C. Rojek (eds), *Sport and Leisure in the Civilizing Process*, London: Macmillan.

Dyer, K. (1982), *Catching Up the Men: Women in Sport*, London: Junction Books.

Elias, N. (1978), *The Civilizing Process*, Vol. 1, *The History of Manners*, Oxford: Basil Blackwell.

Elias, N. (1982), *The Civilizing Process*, Vol. 2, *State Formation and Civilization*, Oxford: Basil Blackwell.

Elias, N. and Dunning, E. (1986), *Quest for Excitement: Sport and Leisure in the Civilizing Process*, Oxford: Basil Blackwell.

Fleming, S. (1991), 'Sport, Schooling and Asian Male Youth Culture', in G. Jarvie (ed.), *Sport, Racism and Ethnicity*, London: Falmer Press.

Garnham, N. and Williams, R. (1980), 'Pierre Bourdieu and the Sociology of Culture: an introduction', in *Media, Culture and Society*, Vol. 2, No. 3: 209–23.

Giddens, A. (1982), *Sociology: A Brief but Critical Introduction*, London: Macmillan.

Goffman, E. (1961), *Encounters*, Indianapolis: Bobbs-Merrill.

Gramsci, A. (1971), *Selections from the Prison Notebooks*, Q. Hoare and P. Nowell Smith (eds), London: Lawrence & Wishart.

Gruneau, R. (1983), *Class, Sport and Social Development*, Amherst, Mass.: University of Massachusetts Press.

Gruneau, R. (1988), *Popular Cultures and Political Practices*, Toronto: Garamond Press.

Guttman, A. (1978), *From Ritual to Record: The Nature of Modern Sports*, New York: Columbia University Press.

Hall, S. (1981), 'Cultural Studies: Two Paradigms', in T. Bennett, G. Martin, C. Mercer and J. Woollacott (eds), *Culture, Ideology and Social Process*, London: Batsford.

Hargreaves, J. A. (ed.) (1982), *Sport, Culture and Ideology*, London: Routledge & Kegan Paul.

Hargreaves, J. A. (1984), 'Action Replay: Looking at Women in Sport', in J. Holland (ed.), *Feminist Action*, Hounslow: Battle Axe Books.

Hargreaves, J. A. (1986), 'Where's the Virtue? Where's the Grace? A Discussion of the Social Production of Gender Relations in and through Sport', in *Theory, Culture and Society*, Vol. 3, No. 1: 109–23.

Hargreaves, J. A. (1989), 'The Promise and Problems of Women's Leisure and Sport', in C. Rojek (ed.), *Leisure for Leisure: Critical Essays*, London: Macmillan.

Hargreaves, J. A. (1990), 'Gender on the Sports Agenda', in *International Review for the Sociology of Sport*, Vol. 25, No. 2: 287–308.

Hargreaves, J. A. (1992a), 'Sex, Gender and the Body in Sport and Leisure: Has There Been a Civilizing Process?', in E. Dunning and C. Rojek (eds), *Sport and Leisure in the Civilizing Process*, London: Macmillan: 161–83.

Hargreaves, J. A. (1992b), 'Women and Sport: Alternative Values and Practices in Sport', keynote paper presented at the Olympic Scientific Congress, 'Sport and the Quality of Life', Malaga, Spain.

Hargreaves, J. A. (1992c), 'Bodies Matter!: Images of Sport and Female Sexualization', keynote paper presented at the Leisure Studies Association Annual Conference, 'Body Matters: Leisure Images and Life Styles', Sheffield, UK.

Hargreaves, John (1986), *Sport, Power and Culture*, Cambridge: Polity Press.

Hoch, P. (1972), *Rip Off the Big Game*, New York: Doubleday.

Ingham, A. and Donnelly, P. (1990), 'Whose Knowledge Counts? The Production of

Knowledge and Issues of Application in the Sociology of Sport', in *Sociology of Sport Journal*, No. 7.

Ingham, A. and Hardy, S. (1984), 'Sport, Structuration and Hegemony', in *Theory, Culture and Society*, Vol. 2, No. 1.

Jarvie, G. (ed.) (1991), *Sport, Racism and Ethnicity*, London: Falmer Press.

Larrain, J. (1979), *The Concept of Ideology*, London: Hutchinson.

Lenskyj, H. (1986), *Out of Bounds: Women, Sport and Sexuality*, Toronto: Women's Press.

Loy, J. and Kenyon, G. (eds) (1969), *Sport, Culture and Society*, New York: Macmillan.

Lüschen, G. (ed.) (1970), *The Cross-Cultural Analysis of Sport and Games*, Champaign, Ill.: Stipes.

Lüschen, G. (1988), 'Towards a New Structual Analysis – the Present State and the Prospects of the International Sociology of Sport', in *International Review for the Sociology of Sport*, Vol. 23, No. 4: 269–86.

MacKinnon, C. (1989), *Toward a Feminist Theory of the State*, London: Harvard University Press.

McPherson, B., Curtis, J. and Loy, J. (1989), *The Social Significance of Sport: An Introduction to the Sociology of Sport*, Champaign, Ill.: Human Kinetics.

Marsh, P., Rosser, E. and Harré, R. (1978), *The Rules of Disorder*, London: Routledge & Kegan Paul.

Morris, D. (1981), *The Soccer Tribe*, London: Cape.

Parker, S. (1976), *The Sociology of Leisure*, London: Allen & Unwin.

Parker, S. (1983), *Leisure and Work*, London: Allen & Unwin.

Rigauer, B. (1981), *Sport and Work*, New York: Columbia University Press.

Roberts, K. (1970), *Leisure*, London: Longman.

Roberts, K. (1978), *Contemporary Society and the Growth of Leisure*, London: Longman.

Sage, G. (ed.) (1974), *Sport and American Society*, Reading, Mass: Addison-Wesley.

Scott, M. (1968), *The Racing Game*, Chicago: Aldine.

Sports Council (1982), *Sport in the Community: The Next Ten Years*, London: Sports Council.

Sports Council (1988), *Sport in the Community: Into the Nineties: A Strategy for Sport 1988–1993*, London: Sports Council.

Sports Council (1992a), *Women and Sport: A Consultation Document*, London: Sports Council; reformulated (1993) as *Women and Sport: Policy and Frameworks for Action*.

Sports Council (1992b), *Sport in the Nineties – New Horizons: a Draft for Consultation*, London: Sports Council; reissued (1993) as *Sport in the Nineties – New Horizons*.

Talbot, M. (1988), 'Understanding the Relationships between Women and Sport: The Contribution of British Feminist Approaches in Leisure and Cultural Studies', in *International Review for the Sociology of Sport*, Vol. 23, No. 1.

Tiger, L. and Fox, R. (1971), *The Imperial Animal*, New York: Holt, Rinehart & Winston.

Vinnai, G. (1973), *Football Mania*, London: Ocean Books.

Whitson, D. (1986), 'Structure, Agency and the Sociology of Sport Debates', in *Theory, Culture and Society*, Vol. 3, No. 1.

Williams, J., Dunning, E. and Murphy, P. (1989), *Hooligans Abroad: The Behaviour and Control of English Fans in Continental Europe*, 2nd edn, London: Routledge.

Williams, R. (1977), *Marxism and Literature*, Oxford: Oxford University Press.

Willis, P. (1982), 'Women in Sport in Ideology', in J. A. Hargreaves (ed.), *Sport, Culture and Ideology*, London: Routledge & Kegan Paul.

Wimbush, E. and Talbot, W. (eds) (1988), *Relative Freedoms: Women and Leisure*, Milton Keynes: Open University Press.

Yiannakis, A. (1989), 'Toward an Applied Sociology of Sport: The Next Generation', in *Sociology of Sport Journal*, No. 6.

Yule, J. (1990), 'Women and Leisure Policy', unpublished paper given at the Commonwealth Games Conference, Auckland, New Zealand.

2 SPORTS FEMINISM: THE IMPORTANCE OF GENDER

Arena Review: Special Issue on Women's Sport (1984), Vol. 18, No. 2.

Banks, O. (1981), *Faces of Feminism: A Study of Feminism as a Social Movement*, Oxford: Martin Robertson.

Barrett, M. (1982), 'Feminism and the Definition of Cultural Politics', in R. Brunt (ed.), *Feminism, Culture and Politics*, London: Lawrence & Wishart.

Birrell, S. and Richter, D. (1987), 'Is a Diamond Forever?: Feminist Transformations of Sport', in *Women's International Forum*, Vol. 10, No. 4.

Boutilier, M. and San Giovanni, L. (1983), *The Sporting Woman*, Champaign, Ill.: Human Kinetics.

Clarke, J. and Critcher, C. (1985), *The Devil Makes Work: Leisure in Capitalist Britain*, London: Macmillan.

Clarke, S. (1988), 'Women and Leisure', unpublished BSc dissertation, Roehampton Institute, University of Surrey.

Connell, R. (1983), *Which Way is Up? Essays on class, sex and culture*, Sydney, Australia: Allen & Unwin.

Daly, M. (1978), *Gyn/Ecology: The metaethics of radical feminism*, Boston: Beacon Press.

Deem, R. (1986), *All Work and No Play? The Sociology of Women and Leisure*, Milton Keynes: Open University Press.

Dyer, K. (1982), *Catching Up the Men: Women in Sport*, London: Junction Books.

Eisenstein, Z. (1979), *Capitalist Patriarchy and the Case for Socialist Feminism*, New York: Monthly Review Press.

Ferris, L. (1981), 'Attitudes to Women in Sport: Prolegomena towards a Sociological Theory', in *Equal Opportunities International*, Vol. 1, No. 2, London: Equal Opportunities Commission.

Firestone, S. (1979), *The Dialectic of Sex*, London: Women's Press.

Gerber, E., Felshin, J., Berlin, P. and Wyrick, W. (1974), *The American Woman in Sport*, Reading, Mass.: Addison-Wesley.

Green, E., Hebron, S. and Woodward, D. (1987), *Leisure and Gender: A Study of Sheffield Women's Leisure Experiences*, final report to the ESRC/Sports Council Joint Panel of Leisure Research, London: Sports Council/ESRC.

Greendorfer, S. (1977), 'The Role of Socializing Agents in Female Sport Involvement', in *Research Quarterly*, No. 48: 304–10.

Griffin, C., Hobson, D., MacIntosh, S. and McCabe, T. (1982), 'Women and Leisure', in J. A. Hargreaves, *Sport, Culture and Ideology*, London: Routledge & Kegan Paul.

Griffin, P. (1989), 'Homophobia in Physical Education', in *Canadian Association for Physical Education and Recreation*, Vol. 12, No. 2.

Hall, M. (1985), 'How Should We Theorize Sport in a Capitalist Patriarchy?', in *International Review for the Sociology of Sport*, Vol. 20, Nos 1/2.

Hall, M. (1988), 'The Discourse of Gender and Sport: From Femininity to Feminism', in *Sociology of Sport Journal*, Vol. 5.

Hargreaves, J. A. (1979), '"Playing Like Gentlemen While Behaving Like Ladies": The Social Significance of Physical Activity for Females in Late Nineteenth Century and Early Twentieth Century Britain', unpublished MA dissertation, University of London.

Hargreaves, J. A. (1984), 'Women and the Olympic Phenomenon', in A. Tomlinson and G. Whannel (eds), *The Five Ring Circus: Money, Power and Politics at the Olympic Games*, London: Pluto Press.

Hargreaves, J. A. (1986), 'Where's the Virtue? Where's the Grace? A Discussion of the Social Production of Gender Relations in and through Sport', in *Theory, Culture and Society*, Vol. 3, No. 1: 109–23.

Hargreaves, J. A. (1987), 'Victorian Familism and the Formative Years of Female Sport', in J. Mangan and R. Parkes (eds), *From Fair Sex to Feminism*, London: Frank Cass.

Hargreaves, J. A. (1989), 'The Promise and Problems of Women's Leisure and Sport', in C. Rojek (ed.), *Leisure for Leisure: Critical Essays*, London: Macmillan.

Hargreaves, J. A. (1992), 'Sex, Gender and the Body in Sport and Leisure: Has There Been a Civilizing Process?', in E. Dunning and C. Rojek (eds), *Sport and Leisure in the Civilizing Process*, London: Macmillan.

Hartmann, H. (1979), 'The Unhappy Marriage of Marxism and Feminism: Towards a More Progressive Union', in *Capital and Class*, No. 8.

Hearn, J. (1984), *The Gender of Oppression: Men, Masculinity and the Critique of Marxism*, Brighton: Wheatsheaf.

Kaplan, J. (1979), *Women and Sports*, New York: Viking.

Kidd, B. (1987), 'Sports and Masculinity', in M. Kaufman (ed.), *Beyond Patriarchy: Essays by men on pleasure, power, and change*, Toronto: Oxford University Press.

Klafs, C. and Lyon, M. (1978), *The Female Athlete: conditioning, competition and culture*, St Louis: C.V. Mosby.

Lenskyj, H. (1986), *Out of Bounds: Women, Sport and Sexuality*, Toronto: Women's Press.

Messner, M. (1987), 'The Life of a Man's Seasons: Male Identity in the Life Course of the Jock', in M. Kimmel, *Changing Men: New Directions in Research on Men and Masculinity*, London: Sage Publications.

Messner, M. and Sabo, D. (eds) (1990), *Sport, Men, and the Gender Order: Critical Feminist Perspectives*, Champaign, Ill.: Human Kinetics.

Miles, S. and Middleton, C. (1989), 'Girls' Education in the Balance: The ERA and Inequality', in M. Flude and M. Hammer (eds), *The 1988 Education Reform Act: Its Origins and Implications*, Lewes: Falmer Press.

Millett, K. (1971), *Sexual Politics*, London: Sphere.

Oglesby, C. (1978), *Women and Sport: From Myth to Reality*, Philadelphia: Lea & Febiger.

Oglesby, C. (1990), 'Epilogue', in M. Messner and D. Sabo, *Sport, Men and the Gender Order: Critical Feminist Perspectives*, Champaign, Ill.: Human Kinetics.

Page, M. (1978), 'Socialist Feminism – a Political Alternative?', in *m/f*: 32–43.

Parkhouse, B. and Lapin, J. (1980), *Women Who Win*, Englewood Cliffs, NJ: Prentice Hall.

Pronger, B. (1990), *The Arena of Masculinity: Sports, Homosexuality and the Meaning of Sex*, London: GMP Publishers.

Sabo, D. (1985), 'Sport, Patriarchy, and Male Identity: New Questions about Men and Sport', in *Arena Review*, No. 9.

Sabo, D. and Runfola, R. (1980), *Jock: Sports and Male Identity*, Englewood Cliffs, NJ: Prentice Hall.

Scraton, S. (1986), 'Images of Femininity and the Teaching of Girls' Physical Education', in J. Evans (ed.), *Physical Education, Sport and Schooling*, Lewes: Falmer Press.

Segal, L. (1990), *Slow Motion: Changing Masculinities, Changing Men*, London: Virago Press.

Sports Council (1982), *Sport in the Community: The Next Ten Years*, London: Sports Council.

Sports Council (1988), *Sport in the Community: Into the Nineties: A Strategy for Sport 1988–1993*, London: Sports Council.

Sports Council (1991), *Women and Sport: A Consultation Document*, London: Sports Council; reissued (1993) as *Women and Sport: Policy and Frameworks for Action*.

Sports Council (1992), *Sport in the Nineties – New Horizons: A Draft for Consultation*, London: Sports Council; reissued (1993) as *Sport in the Nineties – New Horizons*.

Talbot, M. (1988), 'Understanding the Relationships between Women and Sport: The Contribution of British Feminist Approaches in Leisure and Cultural Studies', in *International Review for the Sociology of Sport*, Vol. 23, No. 1.

Theberge, N. (1985), 'Toward a Feminist Alternative to Sport as a Male Preserve', in *Quest*, No. 37.

Twin, S. (ed.) (1979), *Out of the Bleachers*, New York: Feminist Press.

Weir, A. and Wilson, E. (1984), 'The British Women's Movement', in *New Left Review*, No. 148.

White, A. and Brackenridge, C. (1985), 'Who Rules Sport? Gender Divisions in the Power Structure of British Sports Organizations from 1960', in *International Review for the Sociology of Sport*, Vol. 20, No. 1/2: 95–107.

Willis, P. (1982), 'Women in Sport in Ideology', in J. A. Hargreaves (ed.), *Sport, Culture and Ideology*, London: Routledge & Kegan Paul.

Wimbush, E. (1986), *Women, Leisure and Well-Being*, Edinburgh: Centre for Leisure Research, Dunfermline College.

Wimbush, E. and Talbot, M. (eds) (1988), *Relative Freedoms: Women and Leisure*, Milton Keynes: Open University Press.

3 NATURE AND CULTURE: INTRODUCING VICTORIAN AND EDWARDIAN SPORTS FOR WOMEN

Armytage, W. (1955a), 'Care of the Shape: Some Changing Views in the Nineteenth Century', in *Journal of Physical Education*, Vol. 47.

Armytage, W. (1955b), 'Thomas Arnold's Views on Physical Education', in *Physical Education*, Vol. 43, No. 140.

Armytage, W. (1964), *Four Hundred Years of English Education*, Cambridge: Cambridge University Press.

Atkinson, P. (1978), 'Fitness, Feminism and Schooling', in S. Delamont and L. Duffin (eds) *The Nineteenth-Century Woman: Her Cultural World*, London: Croom Helm.

Atkinson, P. (1987), 'The Feminist Physique: Physical Education and the Medicalization of Women's Education', in J. Mangan and R. Park (eds), *From Fair Sex to Feminism: Sport and the Socialization of Women in the Industrial and Post-Industrial Eras*, London: Frank Cass.

Bailey, P. (1978), *Leisure and Class in Victorian England: Rational Recreation and the Contest for Control, 1830–1885*, London: Routledge & Kegan Paul.

Banks, J. (1968), 'Population Change in the Victorian City', in Victorian Studies, xi.

Banks, J. and Banks, O. (1964), 'Feminism and Family Planning in Victorian England', Liverpool, unpublished paper.

Barnes, Dr Robert (1873), 'The Lumleian Lectures: The Convulsive Diseases of Women', from *The Lancet*, cited by L. Duffin (1978), in 'The Conspicuous Consumptive', in S. Delamont and L. Duffin (eds), *The Nineteenth-Century Woman: Her Cultural World*, London: Croom Helm.

Baxandall, R., Ewen, E. and Gordon, L. (1976), 'The Working Class Has Two Sexes', in *Monthly Review*, Vol. 28, No. 3.

Beale, D. (1868), evidence submitted to the Schools Inquiry Commission on the Education of Girls, Vol. VII, Appendix XII.

Beale, D., Soulsby, L. and Dove, J. (1891), *Work and Play in Girls' Schools*, London.

Best, G. (1971), *Mid-Victorian Britain*, London: Weidenfeld & Nicolson.

Borer, M. (1976), *Willingly to School: A History of Women's Education*, Guildford: Lutterworth Press.

Boyle, F. (1895), personal letter in *Madame Bergman Osterberg's Physical Training College Report*, Dartford College archives. Mrs Boyle was one of a number of old Dartford students who wrote about their experiences working in clinics and hospitals, as well as in schools and clubs. Extracts from their letters were included in Madame Bergman Osterberg's College Report each year.

Briggs, A. (1959), *The Age of Improvement*, London: Longman.

Chapman, M. (1856) *Ling's Educational and Curative Exercises*, 2nd edn, cited in I. Webb (1967), 'Women's Place in Physical Education in Great Britain 1800–1966, with special reference to Teacher-Training', unpublished MA dissertation, University of Leicester.

Cobbe, F. P. (1869), 'The Final Cause of Women', in Josephine Butler (ed.), *Women's Work and Women's Culture*, London: Macmillan.

Cole, G. and Postgate, R. (1966), *The Common People 1748–1946*, London: Methuen.

Crunden, C. (1973), 'Physical Education: The First Steps Towards Professionalization', in *Bulletin of Physical Education*, Vol. IX, No. 6.

Crunden, C. (1974), *A History of Anstey College of Physical Education 1897–1972*, Anstey College of Physical Education.

Crunden, C. (1975), 'The Care of the Body in the Late Nineteenth and Early Twentieth Century in England', in *Bulletin of Physical Education*, Vol. XI, No. 1.

Delamont, S. (1978), 'The Contradictions in Ladies' Education', in S. Delamont and L. Duffin (eds), *The Nineteenth-Century Woman: Her Cultural World*, London: Croom Helm.

Delamont, S. and Duffin, L. (eds) (1978), *The Nineteenth-Century Woman: Her Cultural World*, London: Croom Helm.

Dent, H. (1970), *1870–1970 A Century of Growth in English Education*, London: Longman.

Dobbs, B. (1973), *Edwardians at Play: Sport 1890–1914*, London: Pelham Books.

Duffin, L. (1978a), 'Prisoners of Progress: Women and Evolution', in S. Delamont and L. Duffin (eds), *The Nineteenth-Century Woman: Her Cultural World*, London: Croom Helm.

Duffin, L. (1978b), 'The Conspicuous Consumptive: Woman as an Invalid', in S. Delamont and L. Duffin (eds), *The Nineteenth-Century Woman: Her Cultural World*, London: Croom Helm.

Dunning, E. and Sheard, K. (1979), *Barbarians, Gentlemen and Players*, Oxford: Martin Robertson.

Dyhouse, C. (1976), 'Social Darwinist Ideas and the Development of Women's Education in England, 1880–1920', in *History of Education*, Vol. 5, No. 1.

Dyhouse, C. (1978), 'Towards a "Feminine" Curriculum for English Schoolgirls: The Demands of Ideology, c.1870–1963', unpublished MA dissertation, University of Sussex.

Ellis, H. (1894), 'A Study of Secondary and Tertiary Sexual Characteristics', cited in V. Klein (1971), *The Feminine Character: History of an Ideology*, 2nd edn, London: Routledge & Kegan Paul, 37–47.

Fletcher, S. (1984), *Women First: the Female Tradition in English Physical Education, 1880–1980*, London: Athlone Press.

Garrett Anderson, E. (1874), 'Sex in Mind and Education: A Reply', *Fortnightly Review*, Vol. XV.
Gathorne-Hardy, J. (1977), *The Public School Phenomenon*, London: Hodder & Stoughton.
Haley, B. (1968), 'Sports in the Victorian Era', in *Western Humanities Review*, Vol. 22.
Hamilton, R. (1978), *The Liberation of Women*, London: Allen & Unwin.
Hargreaves, J.A. (1979), '"Playing Like Gentlemen While Behaving Like Ladies": The Social Significance of Physical Activity for Females in Late Nineteenth Century and Early Twentieth Century Britain', unpublished MA dissertation, University of London.
Hobsbawm, E. (1977), *The Age of Capital*, London: Sphere.
Jewell, B. (1977), *Sports and Games: Heritage of the Past*, London: Midas Books. Brian Jewell writes about a range of commercialized indoor versions of games which were produced around the turn of the century including billiards, snooker, German billiards, bagatelle, versions of shove halfpenny, quoits, skittles, table skittles and Aunt Sally.
Kanner, B. (1973), 'The Women of England in a Century of Social Change', in M. Vicinus (ed.), *Suffer and Be Still*, Bloomington: Indiana University Press.
Kingsley, F. (ed.) (1877), 'Charles Kingsley: His Letters and Memories of His Life', cited in P. Bailey (1978), *Leisure and Class in Victorian England: Rational Recreation and the Contest for Control, 1830–1885*, London: Routledge & Kegan Paul.
Klein, V. (1971 [1946]) *The Feminine Character: History of an Ideology*, 2nd edn, London: Routledge & Kegan Paul.
McCrone, K. (1988), *Sport and the Physical Emancipation of English Women 1870–1914*, London: Routledge.
McGregor, O. (1955), 'The Social Position of Women in England, 1850–1914: A Bibliography', in *British Journal of Sociology*, Vol. VI.
McIntosh, P. (1968), *Physical Education in England Since 1800*, London: Bell.
Mangan, J. (1981), *Athleticism in the Victorian and Edwardian Public School: The Emergence and Consolidation of an Educational Ideal*, Cambridge: Cambridge University Press.
Mangan, J. and Park, R. (eds) (1987), *From 'Fair Sex' to Feminism: Sport and the Socialization of Women in the Industrial and Post-Industrial Eras*, London: Frank Cass.
Margetson, S. (1969), *Leisure and Pleasure in the Nineteenth Century*, New York: Coward-McCann.
Maudsley, Dr Henry (1874), 'Sex in Mind and Education', in *Fortnightly Review*, Vol. XV.
Mill, J. S. (1970 [1869]), *On the Subjection of Women*, 5th printing, London: Dent.
Millett, K. (1972), *Sexual Politics*, London: Sphere.
Ortner, S. (1974), 'Is Female to Male as Nature is to Culture?', in M. Rosaldo and L. Lamphere (eds), *Women, Culture and Society*, Stanford: Stanford University Press.
Partington, G. (1976), *Women Teachers in the Twentieth Century in England and Wales*, Windsor: NFER.
Pedersen, J. (1975), 'Schoolmistresses and Headmistresses: Elites and Education in 19th Century England', in *Journal of British Studies*, Vol. 15, Pt 1.
Peterson, M. (1973), 'The Victorian Governess', in M. Vicinus (ed.), *Suffer and Be Still*, Bloomington: Indiana University Press.
Pfeiffer, E. (1888), 'Women and Work', cited in C. Dyhouse (1976), 'Social Darwinist Ideas and the Development of Women's Education in England, 1880–1920', in *History of Education*, Vol. 5, No. 1.
Roberts, R. (1971), *The Classic Slum*, Manchester: Manchester University Press.

Rowbotham, S. (1973), *Hidden from History*, London: Pluto Press.

Sharpe, S. (1976), *Just Like a Girl: How Girls Learn to be Women*, Harmondsworth: Pelican.

Smith, N. (1885), 'The Physical Training of Girls', in *Work and Leisure*, Vol. X, No. 6.

Spencer, H. (1861), *Education: Intellectual, Moral and Physical*, London.

Spencer, H. (1867), *The Principles of Biology*, cited in C. Dyhouse (1976), 'Social Darwinist Ideas and the Development of Women's Education in England, 1880–1920', in *History of Education*, Vol. 5, No. 1.

Spencer, H. (1876), *The Principles of Sociology*, cited in C. Dyhouse (1976), 'Social Darwinist Ideas and the Development of Women's Education in England, 1880–1920', in *History of Education* Vol. 5, No. 1.

Spencer, H. (1892–3), *Ethics*, Vol. 1, cited in L. Duffin (1978), 'Prisoners of Progress: Women and Evolution', in S. Delamont and L. Duffin (eds), *The Nineteenth-Century Woman: Her Cultural World*, London: Croom Helm.

Thomson, D. (1950), *England in the Nineteenth Century 1815–1914*, Harmondsworth: Penguin.

Veblen, T. (1899), *The Theory of the Leisure Class*, London. The terms 'conspicuous consumption', 'conspicuous leisure' and 'conspicuous waste' were used by Veblen in this book. Although he was an American, the evidence suggests that it is accurate to apply his ideas to the British context.

Vertinsky, P. (1987), 'Body Shapes: The Role of the Medical Establishment in Informing Female Exercise and Physical Education in Nineteenth-Century North America', in J. Mangan and R. Park (eds), *From Fair Sex to Feminism: Sport and the Socialization of Women in the Industrial and Post-Industrial Eras*, London: Frank Cass.

Vertinsky, P. (1990), *The Eternally Wounded Woman: Women, exercise and doctors in the late nineteenth century*, Manchester: Manchester University Press.

Vicinus, M. (ed.) (1973), *Suffer and Be Still*, Bloomington: Indiana University Press.

Webb, I. (1967), 'Women's Place in Physical Education in Great Britain 1800–1966, with special reference to Teacher-Training', unpublished MA dissertation, University of Leicester.

Winter, A. (1979), *'They Made Today': A History of the 100 Years of the Polytechnic Sports Clubs and Societies*, Pts I, II and III, London: Polytechnic Harriers.

Wolstenholme, E. (1869), 'The Education of Girls', in J. Butler (ed.), *Women's Work and Women's Culture*, London: Macmillan.

Wymer, N. (1949), *Sport in England*, London: Harrap.

Young, G. (1937), *Victorian England: Portrait of an Age*, Oxford: Oxford University Press.

4   THE LEGITIMATION OF FEMALE EXERCISE: THE CASE OF PHYSICAL EDUCATION

AEWHA (1954), *Women's Hockey from Village Green to Wembley Stadium*, London: Macdonald & Evans.

Anderson, P. (1976–7), 'The Antinomies of Antonio Gramsci', in *New Left Review*, No. 100.

Atkinson, P. (1978), 'Fitness, Feminism and Schooling', in S. Delamont and L. Duffin (eds), *The Nineteenth-Century Woman: Her Cultural and Physical World*, London: Croom Helm.

Atkinson, P. (1987), 'The Feminist Physique: Physical Education and the Medicalization of Women's Education', in J. Mangan and R. Park (eds), *From 'Fair Sex' to Feminism: Sport and the Socialization of Women in the Industrial and Post-Industrial Eras*, London: Frank Cass.

Bailey, P. (1978), *Leisure and Class in Victorian England: Rational Recreation and the Contest for Control , 1830–1885*, London: Routledge & Kegan Paul.

Barnes, Howarth (1891), *Training Colleges for Schoolmistresses*. Over one third of the complete list of residential and day training colleges employed a tutor to teach Swedish gymnastics. At Tottenham and Whitelands Colleges, Madame Österberg was the visiting tutor (pp. 223, 261).

Bourdieu, P. (1978), 'Sport and Social Class', in *Social Science Information*, London: Sage Publications.

Bradley, S. (1892), [untitled] *The Sidcot Quarterly*, Vol. 1, No. 8.

Broman, Dr A. (1937), 'The Commemoration of Madame Bergman Österberg', in *Kingsfield Book of Remembrance*, Dartford College archives.

Burstall, S. (1907), *English High Schools for Girls: Their Aims, Organization and Management*, London.

Burstall, S. (1911), 'Medical Inspection', in S. Burstall and M. Douglas, *Public Schools for Girls*, London: Longman.

Crump, F. (undated), quoted in E. Adair Impey: *Letters of Remembrance by Some of her Family and Friends 1965*, ed. Barbara Levitt Whitelaw, Dartford College archives.

Crunden, C. (1973), 'Physical Education: The First Steps Towards Professionalization', in *Bulletin of Physical Education*, Vol. IX, No. 6.

Crunden, C. (1974), *A History of Anstey College of Physical Education 1897–1972*, Anstey College of Physical Education.

Dawes, F. (1975), *A Cry from the Streets: the Boys' Club Movement in Britain from the 1850s to the Present Day*, Hove: Wayland.

Deasey, E. (1972), 'Early Organizers in London', in *Bulletin of Physical Education*, Vol. IX, No. 1.

Dove, J. (1891), 'Cultivation of the Body', in D. Beale, L. Soulsby and J. Dove, *Work and Play in Girls' Schools*, London.

Dures, A. (1971), *Schools*, London: Batsford.

Dyhouse, C. (1976), 'Social Darwinist Ideas about the Development of Women's Education in England, 1880–1920', in *History of Education*, Vol. 5, No. 1.

The Educational Review (1892), Vol. III, No. 5 (March).

The Educational Review (1896), Vol. XIII, No. 1 (November).

Fletcher, S. (1984), *Women First: The Female Tradition in English Physical Education 1880–1980*, London: Athlone Press.

Gathorne-Hardy, J. (1977), *The Public School Phenomenon*, London: Hodder & Stoughton.

Gillis, J. (1975), 'The Evolution of Juvenile Delinquency in England 1890–1914', in *Past and Present*, No. 67.

Glenday, N. and Price, M. (1974), *Reluctant Revolutionaries: A Century of Headmistresses 1874–1974*, London: Pitman Publishers.

Greene, H. (1915–17), 'Madame Bergman Österberg – An Appreciation', *Report of the Trustees 1915–17*, Dartford College archives.

Hall, S., Lumley, B. and McLennon, G. (1977), 'Politics and Ideology: Gramsci', in *Ideology: Cultural Studies 10*, Birmingham: Centre for Contemporary Cultural Studies.

Hargreaves, J. A. (1979), '"Playing Like Gentlemen While Behaving Like Ladies": The Social Significance of Physical Activity for Females in Late Nineteenth and Early Twentieth Century Britain', unpublished MA dissertation, University of London.

Hughes, J. (1975), 'Socialization of the Body Within British Educational Institutions – An Historical View', unpublished MSc dissertation, University of London.

Huizinga, J. (1971 [1937]), *Homo Ludens*, London: Paladin.

Johnson, P. (1973), 'A Golden Era of Sport', in *Quest*, Autumn.

Johnson, R. (1970), 'Educational Policy and Social Control in Early Victorian England', in *Past and Present*, Vol. 49.

Johnson, T. (1972), *Professions and Power*, London: Macmillan.

Kenealy, A. (1920), *Feminism and Sex Extinction*, London: T. F. Unwin.

Kingsfield Book of Remembrance (n.d.), Dartford College archives.

Ling Association (1899–1909), Executive Committee Meeting Minutes.

Ling Association (1919), *The Leaflet*, Vol. 16, No. 1 (January).

McCrone, K. (1987), 'Play up! Play up! And Play the Game! Sport at the Late Victorian Girls' Public Schools', in J. Mangan and R. Park, (eds), *From 'Fair Sex' to Feminism: Sport and the Socialization of Women in the Industrial and Post-Industrial Eras*, London: Frank Cass.

McCrone, K. (1988), *Sport and the Physical Emancipation of English Women 1870–1914*, London: Routledge.

McIntosh, P. (rev. 1968), *Physical Education in England Since 1800*, London: Bell.

Mangan, J. and Park, R. (eds) (1987), *From 'Fair Sex' to Feminism: Sport and the Socialization of Women in the Industrial and Post-Industrial Eras*, London: Frank Cass.

May, J. (1967), 'The Relevance of Historical Studies in Physical Education, with special reference to Madame Österberg', in *Physical Education*, Vol. 59, No. 178.

May, J. (1969), *Madame Bergman Osterberg*, London: Harrap.

Meath, Earl of (1905), personal letter to Madame Österberg, 18 June, Dartford College archives.

Montefiore, A. (1896), comment in *The Educational Review*, Vol. XIII, No. 1 (November).

Musgrave, P. (ed.) (1970), *Sociology, History and Education*, London: Methuen.

Newman, G. (Chief Medical Officer of Health to the Board of Education) (1915), personal correspondence to Madame Bergman Österberg, 13 July, Dartford College archives.

Österberg, Madame Bergman (1887), transcript of Madame Bergman Osterberg's evidence on Physical Instruction to the Royal Commission on Education (Cross), 15 June.

Österberg, Madame Bergman (1896), 'Madame Bergman Österberg's Physical Training College', in *The Educational Review*, Vol. XIII, No. 1.

Österberg, Madame Bergman (1895–8), *Madame Bergman Österberg's Physical Training College Reports* for 1895, 1896, 1897 and 1898, Dartford College archives.

Österberg, Madame Bergman (n.d.), 'The Training of Teachers of Physical Education', unpublished manuscript, Dartford College archives.

Park, R. (1987), 'Sport, Gender and Society in a Transatlantic Perspective', in J. Mangan and R. Park (eds), *From 'Fair Sex' to Feminism: Sport and the Socialization of Women in the Industrial and Post-Industrial Eras*, London: Frank Cass.

Parry, N. and Parry, J. (1974), 'The Teachers and Professionalism: The Failure of an Occupational Strategy', in M. Flude and J. Ahier (eds), *Educability, Schools and Ideology*, London: Croom Helm.

Register of Gymnastic Teachers and Medical Gymnasts (1908, 1913), Dartford College archives.

Report of the Schools' Inquiry Commission (1868) Vol. VII, Appendix XII.

Scrimgeour, R. (ed.) (1950), *The North London Collegiate School, 1850–1950*, Oxford: Oxford University Press.

Smith, D. (1974), *Stretching Their Bodies: The History of Physical Education*, Newton Abbot: David & Charles.

Springall, J. (1970), 'Lord Meath, Youth and Empire', in *Journal of Contemporary History*, Vol. 5, No. 4.

Squire, M. (1964), 'Margaret Stansfield 1860–1951: Teaching, A Way of Life', in E. Clarke and W. Clarke, *Nine Pioneers of Physical Education*, London: Physical Education Association.

Swinerdon, L. (1895) [untitled], in *Madame Bergman Osterberg's Physical Training College Report 1895*, Dartford College archives.

Webb, I. (1967), 'Women's Place in Physical Education in Great Britain 1800–1966, with special reference to Teacher Training', unpublished MA dissertation, University of Leicester.

White, J. (1977), 'Margaret Morris: A Prophet Without Honour', unpublished MA dissertation, University of Leeds.

Wickstead, J. (1937), 'The Early Days and Development of the Ling Physical Education Association', in *Physical Education and School Hygiene*, No. 88.

Women's Herald (1891), Vol. IV, No. 138 (20 June).

Zouche, D. de (1955), *Roedean School 1885–1955*, printed for private and public circulation, cited in P. Atkinson (1978), 'Fitness, Feminism and Schooling', in S. Delamont and L. Duffin (eds), *The Nineteenth-Century Woman: Her Cultural and Physical World*, London: Croom Helm.

5 RECREATIVE AND COMPETITIVE SPORTS: EXPANSION AND CONTAINMENT

AEWHA (1954), *Women's Hockey from Village Green to Wembley Stadium*, London: Macdonald & Evans. The Men's Hockey Association refused the application of the Ladies' Hockey Association for affiliation in 1895. The reason was explicit – it had been formed entirely in the interests of men's clubs.

Bailey, P. (1978), *Leisure and Class in Victorian England: Rational Recreation and the Contest for Control 1830–1885*, London: Routledge & Kegan Paul.

Blackwell, E. M. D. (1858), 'Extracts from the Laws of Life. With Special Reference to the Physical Education of Girls', in *English Women's Journal*.

Cobbe, F. P. (1870), 'Ladies' Amusements', in *Every Saturday*, Vol. IX.

Cominus, P. (1973), 'Innocent Femina Sensualis in Unconscious Conflict', in M. Vicinus (ed.) *Suffer and Be Still*, Bloomington: Indiana University Press.

Dangerfield, G. (1970), *The Strange Death of Liberal England*, London: Paladin.

Dawes, F. (1975), *A Cry from the Streets: The Boys' Club Movement in Britain from the 1850s to the Present Day*, Hove: Wayland.

Desmond, L. (1979), personal interview (9 July).

Dobbs, B. (1973), *Edwardians at Play: Sport 1890–1914*, London: Pelham Books.

Dunning, E. and Sheard, K. (1979), *Barbarians, Gentlemen and Players*, Oxford: Martin Robertson.

Dyhouse, C. (1976), 'Social Darwinist Ideas and the Development of Women's Education in England 1880-1920', in *History of Education*, Vol. 5, No. 1.

Elleret [no initial] (1858) 'Opening of the Swimming Baths for Ladies', in *Work and Leisure*.

English Woman's Journal (1858), 'Physical Training'.

Ensor, R. (1949 [1936]), *England 1870–1914*, Oxford: Oxford University Press.

Greville, Lady (ed.) (1894), *Ladies in the Field: Sketches of Sport*, Ward & Downey.

Hall, M. (1971), 'The Role of the Safety Bicycle in the Emancipation of Women', in the *Proceedings of the Second World Symposium on the History of Sport and Physical Education*, Alberta, Canada: Banff.

Hayes, A. (1893), *The Horsewoman*, W. Thacker.

Jewell, B. (1977), *Sports and Games: Heritage of the Past*, London: Midas Books. The author claims that women have been attracted to cricket for longer than is popularly believed. There is a record of a ladies' match being played in 1745 at Gosden Common, Guildford, between 'eleven maids of Hambledon and eleven maids of Bramley'.

Johnson, P. (1973), 'A Golden Era of Sport', in *Quest* (Autumn).

Klein, V. (1971), *The Feminine Character: History of an Ideology*, reprint, London: Routledge & Kegan Paul.

Lesley, C. (1979), personal interview (2 July).

Lowerson, J. (1982), 'English Middle-Class Sport 1880–1914', in *Proceedings of the Inaugural Conference of the British Society of Sport History*, Liverpool.

Lowerson, J. (1983), 'Scottish Croquet: The English Golf Boom 1880–1914', in *History Today*, Vol. 33, No. 5.

McCrone, K. (1988), *Sport and the Physical Emancipation of English Women 1870–1914*, London: Routledge.

McIntosh, P. (1957), *Landmarks in the History of Physical Education*. London: Routledge & Kegan Paul.

Margetson, S. (1969), *Leisure and Pleasure in the Nineteenth Century*, New York: Coward-McCann.

Marshall, M. (1898) 'Tennis', in F. Slaughter (ed.), *The Sportwoman's Library*, Vols. I and II, Archibald Constable.

Meller, H. (1976), *Leisure and the Changing City 1870–1914*, London: Routledge & Kegan Paul.

Middlemass, K. (1977), *Pursuit of Leisure: High Society in the 1900s*, London: Gordon & Cremonesi.

Murray, L. (1910–11), 'Women's Progress in Relation to Eugenics', in *Eugenics Review*, Vol. II, cited in C. Dyhouse (1976), 'Social Darwinist Ideas about the Development of Women's Education in England, 1880–1920', in *History of Education*, Vol. 5, No. 1.

Österberg, Madame Bergman (1896–8), *Madame Bergman Österberg's Physical Training College Reports for 1896, 1897 and 1898*, Dartford College archives.

Pennell, E. Robins (1894), 'Cycling', in Lady Greville (ed.), *Ladies in the Field: Sketches of Sport*, Ward & Downey. The 'Cyclists Touring Club' is cited as one which had an active female membership. Before the invention of the Stanley 'Rover' bicycle – the prototype for future machines – bicycles were heavy and difficult to ride and manoeuvre and cycle clubs were all-male preserves.

Radford, P. (1993), 'Women's Foot-Races in the Eighteenth and Nineteenth Centuries: a Popular and Widespread Practice', unpublished paper presented at the ISHPEF congress on the History of Sport, Berlin, June/July.

Rawlinson, Austin (1979), personal interview (2 July). When training for the 100 yards and 200 yards backstroke event, Austin Rawlinson had to take his mother with him in order to gain entry to the swimming pool during the family bathing sessions.

Revie, A. (1972), *Wonderful Wimbledon*, London: Pelham Books.

Richardson, Dr W. (1892–3), 'Physical Exercises for Women', in *The Young Woman*, Vol. 1.

Roberts, H. (1973), 'Marriage, Redundancy or Sin', in M. Vicinus (ed.), *Suffer and Be Still*, Bloomington: Indiana University Press.

Roberts, H. (1977), 'The Exquisite Slave: The Role of Clothes in the Making of the Victorian Woman', in *Signs*, Vol. 3, No. 3.

Rowbotham, S. (1975), *Women, Resistance and Revolution*, Harmondsworth: Pelican.

Salaman, S. (1894), 'Punting', in Lady Greville (ed.), *Ladies in the Field: Sketches of Sport*, Ward & Downey.

Sheddon, Lady Diana and Apsley, Lady (n.d.), *To Whom the Goddess*, London: Hutchinson.

Sinclair, A. and Henry, W. (1893), *Life Saving*, Badminton Library, London: Longman, Green.

Slaughter, F. (ed.) (1898), *The Sportswoman's Library*, Vol. I and Vol. II, Archibald Constable.

Sports Council (1977), *Sport: A Guide to Governing Bodies*, London: Sports Council.

Thomas, R. (1904), *Swimming*, Sampson Low, Marston.

Vicinus, M. (ed.) (1973), *Suffer and Be Still*, Bloomington: Indiana University Press.

Walker, D. (1873), *Exercises for Women*, 2nd edn, London: Thomas Hurst.

Ward, M. (1896), Bicycling for Ladies, Brentano's.

Whitelaw, B. L. (1965), quoted in *E. Adair Impey: Letters of Remembrance by Some of her Family and Friends*, Barbara Levitt Whitelaw (ed.), Dartford College archives.

Winter, A. (1979a), *'They Made Today': A History of the 100 Years of the Polytechnic Sports Clubs and Societies*, Pts I, II and III, London: Polytechnic Harriers.

Winter, A. (1979b), personal interview (2 July).

Wymer, N. (1949), *Sport in England*, London: Harrap.

6 THE INTER-WAR YEARS: LIMITATIONS AND POSSIBILITIES

AENA (1976), *Golden Jubilee: 1926–1976*, London: AENA.

Arlott, J. (ed.) (1975), *The Oxford Companion to Sports and Games*, London: Oxford University Press.

Arnold, P. (1983), *The Olympic Games: Athens 1896 to Los Angeles 1984*, London: Hamlyn.

Bagot Stack, M. (1979), *The Romance of the League 1930–1980*, London: Battley Brothers.

Barter, V. (1979), *History of the League 1930–1980*, London: Martin's Press.

Beddoe, D. (1983), *Discovering Women's History*, London: Pandora Press.

Blue, A. (1987), *Grace Under Pressure: The Emergence of Women in Sport*, London: Sidgwick & Jackson.

Blue, A. (1988), *Faster, Higher, Further: Women's Triumphs and Disasters at the Olympics*, London: Virago.

Board of Education (1933), *Syllabus of Physical Training for Schools 1933*, London: HMSO.

Board of Education (1937), *Recreation and Physical Fitness for Girls and Women*, London: HMSO.

Borg, Fridl (1929), 'Die Frau im Arbeitersport', cited in G. Pfister (1980), *Frau und Sport*, Frankfurt: Fischer Verlag.

Cadogan, M. (1990), *Women With Wings: Female Flyers in Fact and Fiction*, London: Macmillan.

Clarke, J. and Chritcher, C. (1985), *The Devil Makes Work: Leisure in Capitalist Britain*, London: Macmillan.

Clarke, J., Chritcher, C. and Johnson, R. (eds) (1979), *Working Class Culture*, London: Hutchinson.

Clerici, G. (1976), *Tennis*, London: Octopus.

Coates, A. (1989), *Women and Sport*, Hove: Wayland.

Collins' Schoolgirls' Annual (1926), London and Glasgow: Collins.

Cooper, C. (1989), 'Discrimination Against Women Rowers at Cambridge University', unpublished BSc dissertation, Roehampton Institute, University of Surrey.

Cousins, G. (1975), *Golf in Britain*, London: Routledge & Kegan Paul.

Crump, J. (1989), 'Athletics', in T. Mason (ed.), *Sport in Britain: A Social History*, Cambridge: Cambridge University Press.

Dawes, F. (1975), *A Cry from the Streets: The Boys' Club Movement in Britain from the 1850s to the Present Day*, Hove: Wayland.

Desmond, L. (1973), 'Gymnastics in the Roaring Twenties . . .', in *B.A.G.A. Awards for Gymnastics*, London: Sunday Times.

Dodd, C. (1989), 'Rowing', in T. Mason (ed.), *Sport in Britain: A Social History*, Cambridge: Cambridge University Press.

Donaldson, F. (1983), *Those Were The Days: A Photographic Album of Daily Life in Britain 1919–1939*, London: J. M. Dent.

Duschek, M. (1980), 'Sixty Years as a Physical Educationist', unpublished.

Eliott-Lynn, S. (1925), *Athletics for Women and Girls: How to be an Athlete and Why*, London: Robert Scott.

Evans, J. (1974), *Service to Sport: The Story of the CCPR – 1935–1972*, London: Pelham Books.

Fletcher, S. (1984), *Women First: The Female Tradition in English Physical Education 1880–1980*, London: Athlone Press.

Fletcher, S. (1985), 'The Making and Breaking of a Female Tradition: Women's Physical Education in England 1880–1980', in *The British Journal of Sports History*, Vol. 2, No. 1 (May).

Foucault, M. (1980), *Power/Knowledge*, ed. C. Gordon, Brighton: Harvester Press.

Foucault, M. (1981), *The History of Sexuality*, Vol. 1: *An Introduction*, Harmondsworth: Penguin.

Foucault, M. (1987), *The History of Sexuality*, Vol. 2: *The Use of Pleasure*, Harmondsworth: Penguin.

Gallico, P. (1988), *Farewell to Sport*, London: Simon & Schuster.

Guttmann, A. (1991), *Women's Sports: A History*, New York: Columbia University Press.

Haddon, C. (1977), *Great Days and Jolly Days: The Story of Girls' School Songs*, London: Hodder & Stoughton.

Hargreaves, J. A. (1979), '"Playing Like Gentlemen While Behaving Like Ladies": The Social Significance of Physical Activity for Females in Late Nineteenth and Early Twentieth Century Britain', unpublished MA dissertation, University of London.

Hargreaves, J. A. (1984), 'Women and the Olympic Phenomenon', in A. Tomlinson and G. Whannel (eds), *The Five Ring Circus: Money, Power and Politics at the Olympic Games*, London: Pluto Press.

Hedges, S. (1926), 'Fancy Swimming for Girls', in *Collins' Schoolgirls' Annual*, London and Glasgow: Collins.

Heyhoe Flint, R. and Rheinberg, N. (1976), *Fair Play: The Story of Women's Cricket*, London: Angus & Robertson.

Hollander, A. (1980), *Seeing Through Clothes*, New York: Avon Books.

Holt, A. (1987), 'Hikers and Ramblers: Surviving a Thirties' Fashion', in *The International Journal of the History of Sport*, Vol. 4, No. 1: 56–68.

Holt, R. (1990a), *Sport and the British*, Oxford: Oxford University Press.

Holt, R. (ed.) (1990b), *Sport and the Working Class in Modern Britain*, Manchester: Manchester University Press.

Howkins, A. and Lowerson, J. (1979), *Trends in Leisure, 1919–1939*, London: Sports Council/Social Science Research Council.

Jones, S. (1982), 'Sport and Politics: The British Workers' Sports Federation, 1923–1935', paper presented at the International Economic History Conference, Budapest, Hungary.

Jones, S. (1985), 'Sport, Politics and the Labour Movement: the British Workers' Sports Federation, 1923–1935', in *The British Journal of Sports History*, Vol. 2, No. 2: 154–79.

Jones, S. (1986a), 'Work, Leisure and Unemployment in Western Europe Between the Wars', in *The British Journal of Sports History*, Vol. 3, No. 1: 55–82.

Jones, S. (1986b), *Workers at Play: A Social and Economic History of Leisure 1918–1939*, London: Routledge & Kegan Paul.

Jones, S. (1990), 'Working-class Sport in Manchester between the Wars', in R. Holt (ed.), *Sport and the Working Class in Modern Britain*, Manchester: Manchester University Press.

Kenealy, A. (1920), *Feminism and Sex Extinction*, London: T. F. Unwin.

Kent, G. (1969), *A Pictorial History of Wrestling*, London: Hamlyn.

Low, A. (1953), *Wonderful Wembley*, London: Stanley Hall.

Lowerson, J. (1989), 'Angling', in T. Mason (ed.), *Sport in Britain: A Social History*, Cambridge: Cambridge University Press.

Lowerson, J. (1993), 'Stoolball and the Manufacturing of "Englishness"', unpublished paper.

Lowerson, J. and Howkins, A. (1981), 'Leisure in the Thirties', in A. Tomlinson (ed.), *Leisure and Social Control*, Brighton: Chelsea School of Human Movement.

McIntosh, P. (rev. 1968), *Physical Education in England Since 1800*, London: Bell.

McIntosh, P. (rev. 1981), 'Games and Gymnastics for Two Nations in One', in P. McIntosh, J. Dixon, A. Munrow and R. Willetts, *Landmarks in the History of Physical Education*, London: Routledge & Kegan Paul.

McKibbin, R. (1983) 'Work and Hobbies in Britain, 1880–1950', in J. Winter (ed.), *The Working Class in Modern British History*, Cambridge: Cambridge University Press.

Maltby, R. (ed.) (1989), *Dreams for Sale: Popular Culture in the 20th Century*, London: Harrap.

Marston, P. (1988), 'Sportswoman Who Refused to Give up', in *Birmingham Post* (5 January).

Martin, A. (1979), *The Equestrian Woman*, London: Paddington Press.

Mason, T. (1980), *Association Football and English Society 1863–1915*, London: Harvester.

Mason, T. (ed.) (1989), *Sport in Britain: A Social History*, Cambridge: Cambridge University Press.

Modman, V. (1981), *Women Aloft*, Alexandria, Virginia: Time-Life Books.

Olwig, K. (1987), *Sport as Secular Ritual: the Case of Netball*, Copenhagen: Special-Trykkeriet Viborg a-s.

Owen, H. (1989), 'The History of Women in Golf', unpublished BSc dissertation, Roehampton Institute, University of Surrey.

Pfister, G. (1980), *Frau und Sport*, Frankfurt: Fischer Verlag.

Pilley, D. (1989), *Climbing Days*, London: Hogarth Press.

Pollard, M. (1934), *Cricket for Girls and Women*, London: Hutchinson.

Pollard, M. (1946), *Fifty Years of Women's Hockey*, All England Women's Hockey Association.

Punchard, F. (1926a), 'Badminton', in *Collins' Schoolgirls' Annual*, London and Glasgow: Collins.

Punchard, F. (1926b), 'Ball Games', in *Collins' Schoolgirls' Annual*, London and Glasgow: Collins.

Ramsden, C. (1973), *Ladies in Racing*, London: Stanley Paul.

Reed, T. (1990), 'Sunny on the Other Side', *Observer* (5 August).

Revie, A. (1972), *Wonderful Wimbledon*, London: Pelham Books.

Riordan, J. (1977), *Sport in Soviet Society: Development of Sport and Physical Education in Russia and the U.S.S.R.*, Cambridge: Cambridge University Press.

Riordan, J. (1984), 'The Workers' Olympics', in A. Tomlinson and G. Whannel (eds), *The Five Ring Circus: Money, Politics and Power at the Olympic Games*, London: Pluto Press.

Smith, W.D. (1974), *Stretching their Bodies: The History of Physical Education*, Newton Abbot: David & Charles.

Spring-Rice, M. (1939), *Working-Class Wives: their Health and Conditions*, Harmondsworth: Penguin.

Tinling, T. (1983), *Sixty Years in Tennis*, London: Sidgwick & Jackson.

Walker, H. (1985), 'The Popularization of the Outdoor Movement, 1900–1940', in *The British Journal of Sports History*, Vol. 2, No. 2.

Williams, J. (1989), 'Cricket', in T. Mason (ed.), *Sport in Britain: A Social History*, Cambridge: Cambridge University Press.

Williams, J. (1990), 'Recreational Cricket in the Bolton Area between the Wars', in R. Holt (ed.), *Sport and the Working Class in Modern Britain*, Manchester: Manchester University Press.

Williams, J. and Woodhouse, J. (1991), 'Can Play? Will Play? Women and Football in Britain', Sir Norman Chester Centre for Football Research, Department of Sociology, University of Leicester; in J. Williams and S. Wagg (eds), *Going into Europe: British Football and Social Change*, Leicester: Leicester University Press.

Williamson, D. (1991), *Belles of the Ball*, Devon: R & D Associates.

Winter, A. (1979), *'They Made Today': A History of the 100 Years of the Polytechnic Sports Clubs and Societies*, London: Polytechnic Harriers.

Woodward, A. (1926), 'Punting on the Thames', in *Collins' Schoolgirls' Annual*, London and Glasgow: Collins.

Other material

Documents from:

Chiswick Urban District Council, 1930–2

Kent County Water Polo and Amateur Swimming Association, 1930

Southern Counties Ladies' Water Polo Association 1937.

Personal letters, memorabilia and interviews with subjects including Annie Blunt, Amelia Carmichael, Alice Coppard, Audrey Court, Dorothy Creak, Lucie Hilder, Grace Jones, Connie Leslie, Gladys Lunn, Linda Nutt, Maudie Ottaway, Yvonne Price, Mary Stevenson, Margaret Tuppen, Lucretia Underwood, Pearl White, Arthur Winter and John Zimmerman.

Transcripts of *Pennies for Health* and *Road to Records*, government-sponsored films, 1935. Transcript of *Adventurous Eves*, Channel 4 transmission, 14 January 1990 which includes interviews with the Honourable Mrs Victor Bruce, Eva Gardner, Kitty Godfree, Muriel Gunn, Sunny Lowry and Vera Searle.

Some of the newspaper references cited here are incomplete because they were donated from the memorabilia of the women concerned. Newspaper cuttings consulted include: *Anglian Daily Times* 1930; *Beckenham Advertiser*, 20 and 27 July 1930, 28 May 1932, 13 September 1933; *Birmingham Post*, 14 March 1988; *Chiswick Times*, 22 July 1925, 4 August 1949; *Croydon Advertiser*, 30 June 1930; *Daily Mirror*, 4 and 5 August 1924; *Fulham Chronicle*, 1 January–30 June 1920; *Kentish Independent*, 31 July 1931 and 7 September 1934; *Kentish Times*, 23 September 1932; *News of the World*, 29 June, 6, 20 and 27 July, 3 and 10 August 1924; *Sutton Times* and *Cheam Mail*, 17 August 1937; *Teddington Gazette*, 21 May 1933; *The Times*, 22 September 1920; *West Anglian Daily Times*, 27 April 1925; *West London Observer*, 29 October 1930.

7 FEMININITY OR 'MUSCULINITY'?: CHANGING IMAGES OF WOMEN'S SPORTS

Apple, M. (1985), *Education and Power*, London: Ark Paperbacks.

Barthes, R. (1977), 'The Photographic Image', in *Image–Music–Text*, ed. S. Heath, London: Fontana.

Beauvoir, S. de (1973), *The Second Sex*, London: Vintage Books.

Beddoe, D. (1983), *Discovering Women's History*, London: Pandora Press.

Belotti, G. (1975), *Little Girls*, London: Writers & Readers Publishing Co-operative.

Berger, J. (1972), *Ways of Seeing*, Harmondsworth: Penguin.

Bordo, S. (1990), 'Reading the Slender Body', in M. Jacobus, E. Fox Keller and S. Shuttleworth (eds), *Body/Politics: Women and the Discourse of Science*, London: Routledge.

Brake, M. (1980), *The Sociology of Youth Cultures and Youth Sub-Cultures*, London: Routledge & Kegan Paul.

Browne, P., Matzen, L. and Whyld, J. (1983), 'Physical Education', in J. Whyld (ed.), *Sexism in the Secondary Curriculum*, London: Harper & Row.

Byrne, E. (1978), *Women and Education*, London: Tavistock.

Cary, L. (1990), 'The Representation of Men and Particularly Women in the Sports Sections of Daily Newspapers with special reference to Tennis', unpublished BSc dissertation, Roehampton Institute, University of Surrey.

Carrington, B. and Leaman, O. (1986), 'Equal Opportunities and Physical Education', in J. Evans (ed.) *Physical Education, Sport and Schooling*, Lewes: Falmer Press.

Coakley, J. (1990), *Sport in Society: Issues and Controversies* (4th edn), St Louis: Times Mirror/Mosby College Publishing.

Cockerill, S. and Hardy, C. (1987), 'The Concept of Femininity and Its Implications for Physical Education', in *The British Journal of Physical Education*, Vol. 8, No. 4.

Comer, L. (1974), *Wedlocked Women*, Leeds: Feminist Books.

Connell, R. (1987), *Gender and Power*, Cambridge: Polity Press.

Coward, R. (1984), *Female Desire*, London: Paladin.

Deem, R. (1978), *Women and School*, London: Routledge & Kegan Paul.

Delamont, S. (1980), *Sex Roles and the School*, London: Methuen.

Department of Education and Science (1975), *Curriculum Differences for Boys and Girls*, Education Survey 21, London: HMSO.

Department of Education and Science (1991), *Physical Education for ages 5 to 16*, London: HMSO.

Duncan, M. (1990), 'Sports Photographs and Sexual Difference: Images of Women and Men in the 1984 and 1988 Olympic Games', in *Sociology of Sport Journal*, No. 7: 22–43.

Evans, J. (ed.) (1986), *Physical Education, Sport and Schooling*, Lewes: Falmer Press.

Evans, J. (1989), 'Swinging from the Crossbar. Equality and Opportunity in the Physical Education Curriculum', in *The British Journal of Physical Education*, Vol. 20, No. 2: 84–7.

Evans, J., Lopez, S., Duncan, M. and Evans, M. (1987), 'Some Thoughts on the Political and Pedagogical Implications of Mixed Sex Grouping in Physical Education', in *British Educational Research Journal*, Vol. 13, No. 1: 59–71.

Fasting, K. and Tangen, J. (1983), 'Gender and Sport in Norwegian Mass Media', in *International Review of Sport Sociology*, Vol. 1, No. 18: 61–71.

Featherstone, M. (1982), 'The Body in Consumer Culture', in M. Featherstone, M. Hepworth and B. Turner (eds) (1991), *The Body: Social Process and Cultural Theory*, London: Sage Publications.

Featherstone, M. (1983), 'Consumer Culture: an Introduction', in *Theory, Culture and Society*, Vol. 1, No. 3: 4–9.

Featherstone, M. (1987), 'Lifestyle and Consumer Culture', in *Theory, Culture and Society*, Vol. 4, No. 1: 55–70.

Featherstone, M., Hepworth, M. and Turner, B. (eds) (1991), *The Body: Social Process and Cultural Theory*, London: Sage Publications.

Fletcher, S. (1984), *Women First: The Female Tradition in English Physical Education 1880-1980*, London: Athlone Press.

Flintoff, A. (1990), 'Physical Education, Equal Opportunities and the National Curriculum: Crisis or Challenge', in *Physical Education Review*, Vol. 13, No. 2: 85-100.

Foster, J. (1977), *The Influence of Rudolph Laban*, London: Lepus Books.

Frank, A. (1990), 'Bringing Bodies Back in: A Decade Review', in *Theory, Culture and Society*, Vol. 7, No. 1: 131-62.

Freedman, P. (1984), 'The Fastest Painted Lady in the World', in *Sunday Times* (27 May).

Gaccione, L. (1991), 'Where is the "progression" for women athletic's?', in *CSSS Digest* (Centre for the Study of Sport in Society, Northeastern University), Vol. 3, No. 2 (Summer): 11.

Gilroy, S. (1989), 'The EmBody-ment of Power: Gender and Physical Activity', in *Leisure Studies*, Vol. 8, No. 2: 163-73.

Grabrucker, M. (1988), *There's a Good Girl*, London: Women's Press.

Gurevitch, M., Bennett, T., Curran, J. and Woollacott, J. (eds) (1982), *Culture, Society and the Media*, London: Methuen.

Heaven, P. and Rowe, D. (1991), 'Gender Sport and Body Image', unpublished paper.

Hendry, L. (1978), *School, Sport and Leisure*, London: Lepus Books.

Henley, N. (1977), *Body Politics: Power, Sex and Nonverbal Communication*, Englewood Cliffs, NJ: Prentice Hall.

Hollander, A. (1980), *Seeing Through Clothes*, New York: Avon Books.

Horne, J. (1988), 'Generalist Sports Magazines in the USA and UK: Researching Representations of Sport', paper presented at the NASSS Conference, Cincinnati, USA.

Horne, J. and Bentley, C. (1989), '"Fitness Chic" and the Construction of Lifestyles', paper presented at the LSA Conference, 'Leisure, Health and Well Being'.

Humberstone, B. (1986), 'A Study of Gender and Schooling in Outdoor Education', in J. Evans (ed.), *Physical Education, Sport and Schooling*, Lewes: Falmer Press.

ILEA (1984), *Providing Equal Opportunities for Girls and Boys in Physical Education*, London: Physical Education Teachers Centre.

Kelly, J. (1983), 'The Doubled Vision of Feminist Theory', in J. Newton, M. P. Ryan and J. R. Walkowitz (eds), *Sex and Class in Women's History*, London: Routledge & Kegan Paul.

Kennard, J. (1977), 'The History of Physical Education', in *Signs: Journal for Women in Culture and Society*, Vol. 2, Pt 4: 835-42.

Kimmel, M. (1987), 'Rethinking "Masculinity": New Directions in Research', in M. Kimmel, *Changing Men*, London: Sage Publications.

Klein, M.-L. (1988), 'Women in the Discourse of Sports Reports', in *International Review for the Sociology of Sport*, Vol. 23, No. 1: 139-51.

Kuhn, A. (1985), *The Power of the Image: Essays on Representation and Sexuality*, London: Routledge & Kegan Paul.

Leaman, O. (1984), *Sit on the Sidelines and Watch the Boys Play: Sex Differentiation in Physical Education*, York: Longman.

Lenskyj, H. (1986), *Out of Bounds: Women, Sport and Sexuality*, Toronto: Women's Press.

Lodziak, C. (1986), *The Power of Television: A Critical Appraisal*, London: Frances Pinter.

McKay, J. and Rowe, D. (1987), 'Ideology, the Media, and Australian Sport', in *Sociology of Sport Journal*, Vol. 4: 58-73.

MacNeill, M. (1988), 'Active Women, Media Representations, and Ideology', in J. Harvey and H. Cantelon (eds) *Not Just a Game: Essays in Canadian Sport Sociology*, Ottawa: University of Ottawa: 195–213.

McRobbie, A. (1978), 'Working Class Girls and the Culture of Femininity', in *Contemporary Cultural Studies II: Women Take Issue*, London: Hutchinson.

McRobbie, A. (1991), *Feminism and Youth Culture: From Jackie to Just Seventeen*, London: Macmillan.

McRobbie, A. and Garber, J. (1976), 'Girls and Subcultures', in S. Hall and T. Jefferson (eds), *Resistance Through Rituals*, London: Hutchinson.

Mahony, P. (1985), *Schools for the Boys? Co-education reassessed*, London: Hutchinson.

Messner, M. (1988) 'Sports and Male Domination: The Female Athlete as Contested Ideological Terrain', in *Sociology of Sport Journal*, No. 5: 197–211.

Messner, M. and Sabo, D. (1990), 'Toward a Critical Feminist Reappraisal of Sport, Men, and the Gender Order', in M. Messner and D. Sabo (eds), *Sport, Men, and the Gender Order: Critical Feminist Perspectives*, Champaign, Ill.: Human Kinetics.

Messner, M., Duncan, M. and Jensen, K. (1993), 'Separating the Men from the Girls: The Gendered Language of Televised Sports', in *Gender and Society*, Vol. 7, No. 1: 120–38.

Miles, S. and Middleton, C. (1990), 'Girls' Education in the Balance: The ERA and Inequality', in M. Flude and M. Hammer (eds), *The Education Reform Act 1988: Its Origins and Implications*, Lewes: Falmer Press.

Navratilova, M. with Vecsey, G. (1985), *Being Myself*, Glasgow: Collins.

Okeley, J. (1979), 'Privileged, Schooled and Finished: Boarding School for Girls', in S. Ardener (ed.), *Defining Females*, London: Croom Helm.

Pronger, B. (1990), *The Arena of Masculinity: Sports, Homosexuality, and the Meaning of Sex*, London: GMP Publishers.

Reid, I. and Stratta, E. (1989), 'Sex and Gender Differences and this Book', in I. Reid and E. Stratta (eds), *Sex Differences in Britain*, 2nd edn, Aldershot: Gower.

Ryan, T. (1985), 'Roots of Masculinity', in A. Metcalf and M. Humphries (eds), *The Sexuality of Men*, London: Pluto Press.

Scraton, S. (1986), 'Images of Femininity and the Teaching of Girls' Physical Education', in J. Evans (ed.), *Physical Education, Sport and Schooling*, Lewes: Falmer Press.

Scraton, S. (1987), '"Boys Muscle in Where Angels Fear to Tread" – Girls' Sub-cultures and Physical Activities', in J. Horne, D. Jary and A. Tomlinson (eds), *Sport, Leisure and Social Relations*, London: Routledge & Kegan Paul.

Scraton, S. (1992), *Shaping Up to Womanhood: Gender and Girls' Physical Education*, Buckingham: Open University Press.

Seton, F. (1989) 'An Investigation into the Selection and Presentation Values of Sports News and the Differences between the Popular and Serious Press, with regard to the 1988 Seoul Olympics', unpublished BSc dissertation, Roehampton Institute, University of Surrey.

Sharpe, S. (1976), *Just Like a Girl: How Girls Learn to be Women*, Harmondsworth: Pelican.

Sparkes, R. (1988), 'Ways of Seeing Differently', in *Sociology of Sport Journal*, Vol. 5: 155–68.

Sports Council (1992) *Women and Sport: A Consultation Document*, London: Sports Council; reformulated (1993) as *Women and Sport: Policy and Frameworks for Action*.

Talbot, M. (1986), 'Gender and Physical Education', in *British Journal of Physical Education*, Vol. 17, No. 4.

Talbot, M. (1990), 'Gender – a Cross-Curricular Dimension', unpublished paper presented at the NATFHE Dance Section Conference, 'Cross-Curricular Opportunities', London, 15 December.

Tomlinson, A. (ed.) (1990), *Consumption, Identity and Style: Marketing, Meanings, and the Packaging of Pleasure*, London: Routledge.

Turner, B. (1991), 'Recent Developments in the Theory of the Body', in M. Featherstone, M. Hepworth and B. Turner (eds), *The Body: Social Process and Cultural Theory*, London: Sage Publications.

Whannel, G. (1992), *Fields in Vision: Television Sport and Cultural Transformation*, London: Routledge.

Whitson, D. (1990), 'Sport in the Social Construction of Masculinity', in M. Messner and D. Sabo (eds), *Sport, Men, and the Gender Order: Critical Feminist Perspectives*, Champaign, Ill.: Human Kinetics.

Whyld, J. (ed.) (1983), *Sexism in the Secondary Curriculum*, London: Harper & Row.

Williams, A. (1989), 'Equal Opportunities and Primary School Physical Education', in *British Journal of Physical Education*, Vol. 20.

Williams, C., Lawrence, G. and Rowe, D. (1986), 'Patriarchy, Media and Sport', in G. Lawrence and D. Rowe (eds), *Power Play*, Sydney: Hale & Iremonger.

Williams, L. (1990), *Hard Core: Power, Pleasure and the 'Frenzy of the Visible'*, London: Virago.

Willis, P. (1977), *Learning to Labour*, Farnborough: Saxon House.

Willis, P. (1978), *Profane Culture*, London: Routledge & Kegan Paul.

Winship, J. (1980), 'Sexuality for Sale', in S. Hall, D. Hobson, A. Lowe and P. Willis (eds), *Culture, Media, Language*, London: Hutchinson.

Wolpe, A.-M. (1977), *Some Processes in Sexist Education*, London: WRRC.

Young, I. (1990), *Throwing Like a Girl and Other Essays in Philosophy and Social Theory*, Bloomington and Indianapolis: Indiana University Press.

8 GENDER RELATIONS OF POWER: INSTITUTIONALIZED DISCRIMINATION

Baird, V. (1992), 'We've Only Just Begun', in *The New International*, No. 227: 4–7.

Barraclough, L. (1991) 'Discrimination against Women in Golf', unpublished BSc dissertation, Roehampton Institute, University of Surrey.

Beechey, V. (1982), 'Some Notes on Female Wage Labour in Capitalist Production', in M. Evans (ed.), *The Woman Question*, Oxford: Fontana.

Benston, M. (1982), 'The Political Economy of Women's Liberation', in M. Evans (ed.), *The Woman Question*, Oxford: Fontana.

Berlioux, M. (1981), 'Women in the Promotion and Administration of Sport', in *FIEP Bulletin*, Vol. 51, No. 2: 22–7.

Blinde, E., Greendorfer, S. and Shanker, R. (1992), 'Differential Media Coverage of Men's and Women's Intercollegiate Basketball: Reflection of Gender Ideology', in *Journal of Sport and Social Issues*, Vol. 15, No. 2: 98–115.

Blue, A. (1987), *Grace Under Pressure: The Emergence of Women in Sport*, London: Sidgwick & Jackson.

Boutilier, M. and San Giovanni, L. (1983), *The Sporting Woman*, Champaign, Ill.: Human Kinetics.

Brackenridge, C. (1990), 'Myth, Drama or Crisis? Cross-Gender Coaching Relationships', *Coaching Focus* (Summer).

Brackenridge, C. (1992), 'Sexual Abuse of Children in Sport: A Comparative Exploration of Research Methodologies and Professional Practice', paper presented at the Olympic Scientific Congress, Malaga, Spain.

Brown, J. (1984), 'Outcomes for Women in Sport', paper presented at the International Conference on Women and Competitive Sport, Sydney, Australia.

Carrington, B. and Leaman, O. (1986), 'Equal Opportunities and Physical Education', in J. Evans (ed.), *Physical Education, Sport and Schooling*, Lewes: Falmer Press.

Cary, L. (1990), 'The Representation of Men and Particularly Women in the Sports Sections of Daily Newspapers with special reference to Tennis', unpublished BSc Dissertation, Roehampton Institute, University of Surrey.

Council of Europe (1976), *European Sport for All Charter*, Strasbourg: Council of Europe.

Council of Europe (1989), *Women and Sport: Taking the Lead*, Brussels: Council of Europe.

Council of Europe (1992), *Political Declaration on the New European Sports Charter*, Brussels: Council of Europe.

Crosset, T. (1986), 'Male Coach/Female Athlete Relationships', paper presented at the Norwegian Confederation of Sport Conference, 'Coaching Female Top Level Athletes', Norway, 15–16 November.

Deem, R. (1978), *Women and School*, London: Routledge & Kegan Paul.

Deem, R. (1984), 'Paid Work, Leisure and Non-employment: Shifting Boundaries and Gender Differences', paper presented at the BSA Annual Conference, University of Bradford, UK.

Deem, R. (1986), *All Work and No Play? The Sociology of Women and Leisure*, Milton Keynes: Open University Press.

Delamont, S. (1980), *Sex Roles and the School*, London: Methuen.

Department of Education and Science (1991a), *Physical Education for ages 5 to 16*, London: HMSO.

Department of Education and Science (1991b), *Sport and Active Recreation*, London: HMSO.

Department of Education and Science (1992), *Physical Education in the National Curriculum*, London: HMSO.

Equal Opportunities Commission (1976), *Guide to the Sex Discrimination Act* (1975), London: HMSO.

European Sports Conference Charter (1989), IX European Sports Conference, Sofia.

European Sports Conference Working Group (1991), *Women in Sport*, report to the X European Sports Conference, Oslo.

Evans, J. (ed.) (1988), *Teachers, Teaching and Control in Physical Education*, Lewes: Falmer Press.

Fasting, K. (1989), 'Women's Leadership in Sport', in Council of Europe, *Women and Sport: Taking the Lead*, Brussels: Council of Europe.

Fasting, K. and Tangen, J. (1983), 'Gender and Sport in Norwegian Mass Media', in *International Review for the Sociology of Sport*, Vol. 1, No. 18: 61–71.

Flintoff, A. (1990a), 'Physical Education, Equal Opportunities and the National Curriculum: Crisis or Challenge', in *Physical Education Review*, Vol. 13, No. 2: 85–100.

Flintoff, A. (1990b), 'Women in Physical Education', in *Recman 90 Seminar Report: Sports Development*, London: Sports Council.

Gaccione, L. (1991), 'Where is the "progression" for women athletic's?', in *CSSS Digest* (Centre for the Study of Sport in Society, Northeastern University), Vol. 3, No. 2 (Summer): 11.

Gilroy, S. (1989), 'The EmBodyment of Power: Gender and Physical Activity', in *Leisure Studies*, Vol. 8, No. 2: 163–73.

Government of Canada (1992a), *Women in Sport: Update*.

Government of Canada (1992b), *Women in Sport*.

Green, E., Hebron, S. and Woodward, D. (1987), *Leisure and Gender: A Study of Sheffield Women's Leisure Experiences*, final report to the ESRC/Sports Council Joint Panel of Leisure Research, London: Sports Council/ESRC.

Hall, A., Cullen, D. and Slack, T. (1990) 'The Gender Structure of National Sport Organizations', *Sport Canada*, Vol. 2, No. 1.

Hall, S. (1986), 'Media Power and Class Power', in J. Curran *et al.*, *Bending Reality: The State of the Media*, London: Pluto Press.

Hammond, B. (1991), 'Sexism in Athletics: A Personal Exploration', unpublished paper.

Hargreaves, J. A. (1989), 'The Promise and Problems of Women's Leisure and Sport', in C. Rojek (ed.), *Leisure for Leisure*, London: Macmillan.

Heaven, P. and Rowe, D. (1991), 'Gender Sport and Body Image', unpublished paper.

Henley, N. (1977), *Body Politics: Power, Sex and Nonverbal Communication*, Englewood Cliffs, NJ: Prentice Hall.

Houlihan, B. (1991), *The Government and Politics of Sport*, London: Routledge.

Hult, J. (1989), 'Women's Struggle for Governance in US Amateur Athletics', in *International Review for the Sociology of Sport*, Vol. 24, No. 3: 249–64.

ILEA (1984), *Providing Equal Opportunities for Girls and Boys in Physical Education*, London: Physical Education Teachers Centre.

ITF News (1992), August, London: ITF.

Kidane, F. (1987), 'Women in the Olympic Movement', in *Continental Sports*, No. 36 (August–October).

Klein, M.-L. (1988), 'Women in the Discourse of Sports Reports', in *International Review for the Sociology of Sport*, Vol. 23, No. 2: 139–51.

Klein, M.-L. (1989), 'The Discourse in the Sports Media: Strategies to Improve Women's Role and Image', in Council of Europe (1989), *Women and Sport: Taking the Lead*, Brussels: Council of Europe.

Labour Party (1991), *Charter for Sport*, London: Labour Party.

Leath, V. and Lumpkin, A. (1992), 'An Analysis of Sportswomen on the Covers and in the Feature Articles of Women's Sports and Fitness Magazines, 1975–1989', in *Journal of Sport and Social Issues*, Vol. 16, No. 2.

Lee, J. (1992), 'Media Portrayals of Male and Female Athletes: Analysis of Newspaper Accounts of the 1984 and 1988 Summer Games', in *International Review for the Sociology of Sport*, Vol. 27, No. 3.

Lelliott, J. (1991), 'Grant News', in *Sports News* (Summer).

Lenskyj, H. (1986), *Out of Bounds: Women, Sport and Sexuality*, Toronto: Women's Press.

Lucas, I. (1990), 'A Career in Leisure', in *Sport and Leisure* (July/August).

McKay, J. and Rowe, D. (1987), 'Ideology, the Media, and Australian Sport', in *Sociology of Sport Journal*, Vol. 4: 258–73.

MacKinnon, C. (1989), *Toward a Feminist Theory of the State*, London: Harvard University Press.

Mahony, P. (1985), *Schools for the Boys?*, London: Hutchinson.

Messner, M., Duncan, M. and Jensen, K. (1993), 'Separating the Men from the Girls: The Gendered Language of Televised Sports', in *Gender and Society*, Vol. 7, No. 1.

Pannick, D. (1983), *Sex Discrimination in Sport*, Manchester: Equal Opportunities Commission.

Pronger, B. (1990), *The Arena of Masculinity: Sports, Homosexuality, and the Meaning of Sex*, London: GMP Publishers.

Robinson, L. (1993), 'Images of Women Athletes: A Content Analysis of the British Media', in *Working Papers in Sport and Society*, University of Warwick, Coventry.

Schofield, S. (1992), 'A Sociological Study of Women's Professional Golf in Europe', unpublished BSc dissertation, Roehampton Institute, University of Surrey.

Scraton, S. (1992), *Shaping Up to Womanhood: Gender and Girls' Physical Education*, Buckingham: Open University Press.

Seton, F. (1989), 'Selection and Presentation Values of Sports News', unpublished BSc dissertation, Roehampton Institute, University of Surrey.

Sports Council (1982), *Sport in the Community: The Next Ten Years*, London: Sports Council.

Sports Council (1988), *Sport in the Community: Into the Nineties: A Strategy for Sport 1988–1993*, London: Sports Council.

Sports Council (1992), *Women and Sport: A Consultation Document*, London: Sports Council; reformulated (1993) as *Women and Sport: Policy and Frameworks for Action*.

Streather, J. (1979), 'One Parent Families and Leisure', in Z. Strelitz (ed.), *Leisure and Family Diversity*, London: Leisure Studies Association.

Sunday Observer (1991), six-week series entitled 'Teach Your Children Sport' (14, 21, 28 July, 4, 11, 18 August).

Talbot, M. (1987), 'The Contribution of Comparative Studies in Understanding the Relationships Between Women and Sports Structures', paper presented at the congress on 'Movement and Sport in Women's Life', University of Jyvaskyla, Finland.

Talbot, M. (1988), '"Their Own Worst Enemy?" Women and Leisure Provision', in E. Wimbush and M. Talbot, *Relative Freedoms*, Milton Keynes: Open University Press.

Talbot, M. (1989), 'Family Diversity: Women, Physical Activity and Family Life', keynote paper presented at the Eleventh Congress of the International Association of Physical Education and Sport for Girls and Women, Bali, Indonesia, 22–9 July.

Talbot, M. (1990), 'Gender – a Cross-Curricular Dimension', paper presented at the NATFHE Dance Section Conference, 'Cross-Curricular Opportunities', London, 15 December.

Thompson, S. (1988), 'Challenging the Hegemony: New Zealand Women's Opposition to Rugby and the Reproduction of a Capitalist Patriarchy', in *International Review for the Sociology of Sport*, Vol. 23, No. 3: 205–12.

White, A. (1987), 'Women Coaches: Problems and Issues', in *Coaching Focus*, No. 6.

White, A. (1989), 'Family Influences on the Sports Participation of Young Women in Britain', paper presented at the Eleventh Congress of the International Association of PE in Sport for Girls and Women, Bali, Indonesia, 22–9 July.

White, A. (1991a), 'Women in Top Level Sport', paper presented at the Second IOC Congress on Sport Sciences.

White, A. (1991b), 'Sports Equity: A New Concept?', paper presented at the Sport and Leisure Scotland Conference '91, 25–7 November.

White, A. and Brackenridge, C. (1985), 'Who Rules Sport? Gender Divisions in the Power Structure of British Sports Organisations from 1960', in *International Review for the Sociology of Sport*, Vol. 20, No. 1/2.

White, A., Maygothling, R. and Carr, C. (1989), *The Dedicated Few: the Social World of Women Coaches in Britain in the 80s*, Centre for the Study and Promotion of Sport and Recreation for Women and Girls, West Sussex Institute of Higher Education.

White, J. (1988), 'Women in Leisure Service Management', in E. Wimbush and M. Talbot (eds), *Relative Freedoms*, Milton Keynes: Open University Press.

White, J. (1990), 'Helping Themselves to Power: the Burgeoning of Women in Leisure Management', paper presented at the World Congress of Sociology, Madrid, Spain.

Whitson, D. and MacIntosh, D. (1989), 'Gender and Power: Explanations of Gender Inequalities in Canadian Sport Organisations', in *International Review for the Sociology of Sport*, Vol. 24, No. 2: 137–50.

Williams, C., Lawrence, G. and Rowe, D. (1986), 'Patriarchy, Media and Sport', in G. Lawrence and D. Rowe (eds), *Power Play*, Sydney: Hale & Iremonger.

Williams, J. and Woodhouse, J. (1991), 'Can Play, Will Play? Women and Football in Britain', Sir Norman Chester Centre for Football Research, Department of Sociology, University of Leicester, in J. Williams and S. Wagg (eds), *Going into Europe: British Football and Social Change*, Leicester: Leicester University Press.

Wilson, J. (1988), *Politics and Leisure*, London: Unwin Hyman.

Wimbush, E. (1986), *Women, Leisure and Well-Being*, Edinburgh: Centre for Leisure Research, Dunfermline College.

Yorganci, I. (1992), 'Gender, Power and Sexual Harassment in Sport', unpublished paper, University of Brighton.

9 OLYMPIC WOMEN: A STRUGGLE FOR RECOGNITION

Adedeji, J. (1982), 'Social Change and Women in African Sport', *International Social Science Journal*, Vol. 34, No. 2: 209–18.

Arnold, P. (1983), *The Olympic Games: Athens 1896 to Los Angeles 1984*, London: Hamlyn.

Berck, P. (1993), 'The Challenge of Gender Equity in Non-Racial South Africa', in *Action*, the Canadian Association for the Advancement of Women and Sport and Physical Activity.

Blue, A. (1988), *Faster, Higher, Further: Women's Triumphs and Disasters at the Olympics*, London: Virago.

Boutilier, M. and San Giovanni, L. (1983), *The Sporting Woman*, Champaign, Ill.: Human Kinetics.

Dyer, K. (1982), *Catching Up the Men: Women in Sport*, London: Junction Books.

Eliott-Lynn, S. (1925), *Athletics for Women and Girls: How to be an Athlete and Why*, London: Robert Scott.

Ferris, E. (1991), 'Gender Verification in Sport: the Need for Change?', in *British Journal of Sports Medicine*, Vol. 25, No. 1: 17–20.

Gerber, E. (ed.) (1974), *The American Woman in Sport*, New York: Addison Wesley.

Gerber, E. (1975), 'The Controlled Development of Collegiate Sport for Women, 1929–1936', in *Journal of Sport History*, Vol. 2, No. 1: 1–28.

Hargreaves, J. A. (1984a), 'Women and the Olympic Phenomenon', in A. Tomlinson and G. Whannel (eds), *The Five Ring Circus: Money, Power and Politics at the Olympic Games*, London: Pluto Press.

Hargreaves, J. A. (1984b), 'Taking Men on at their Games', in *Marxism Today* (August).

Hargreaves, J. A. (1990), 'Gender on the Sports Agenda', in *International Review for the Sociology of Sport*, Vol. 25, No. 4: 287–309.

Hijris, S. (1993), 'Sport for Women in Bahrain', in *Relay*, No. 8, London: Sports Council.

Hult, J. (1989), 'Women's Struggle for Governance in US Amateur Athletics', in *International Review for the Sociology of Sport*, Vol. 24, No. 3: 249–64.

IOC (1991) *Olympic Charter*, Lausanne: IOC.

Kennard, J. (1977), 'The History of Physical Education', in *Signs: Journal for Women in Culture and Society*, Vol. 2, Pt 4: 835–42.

Leigh, M. (1974), 'The Evolution of Women's Participation in the Summer Olympic Games, 1900–1948', PhD dissertation, Ohio State University; quoted in J. Kennard

(1977), 'The History of Physical Education', in *Signs: Journal for Women in Culture and Society*, Vol. 2, Pt 4: 835–42.

Lenskyj, H. (1986), *Out of Bounds: Women, Sport and Sexuality*, Toronto: Women's Press.

Lovesey, P. (1980), *The Official Centenary of the Amateur Athletic Association*, Enfield: Guinness Superlatives.

Mikan, V. (1993), 'From Command Economy to Free Market', in *Relay*, No. 8, London: Sports Council.

Mitchell, S. (1977), 'Women's Participation in the Olympic Games, 1900–1926', in *Journal of Sport History*, Vol. 4, No. 2: 208–28.

Nichols, P. (1993), 'Ethiopia's Leading Lady Slips Silently into Durham', *Guardian*, 18 January.

Riordan, J. (1984), 'The Worker's Olympics', in A. Tomlinson and G. Whannel (eds) (1984), *The Five Ring Circus: Money, Politics and Power at the Olympic Games*, London: Pluto Press.

Riordan, J. (1985), 'Some Comparisons of Women's Sport in East and West', in *International Review for the Sociology of Sport*, Vol. 20, Nos 1–2: 117–26.

Riordan, J. (1986), 'State and Sport in Developing Societies', *International Review for Sociology of Sport*, Vol. 21, No. 4: 287–303.

Segrave, J. and Chu, D. (eds) (1981), *Olympism*, Champaign, Ill: Human Kinetics.

Simri, U. (1979), *Women at the Olympic Games*, Wingate Monograph Series No. 7, Netanya (Israel): Wingate Institute for Physical Education and Sport.

Talbot, M. (1989), 'Family Diversity: Women. Physical Activity and Family Life', paper presented at the Eleventh Congress of the International Association of Physical Education and Sport for Girls and Women, Bali, Indonesia, 22–9 July.

Tordoff, W. (1992), *Government and Politics in Africa*, 2nd edn, London: Macmillan.

Wilkinson, T. (1984), 'Marathon Mentality – the risks sportsmen run', *The Listener* (May).

Williams, C., Lawrence, G. and Rowe, D. (1986), 'Patriarchy, Media and Sport', in G. Lawrence and D. Rowe (eds), *Power Play*, Sydney: Hale & Iremonger.

10 SPORTS FOR ALL WOMEN: PROBLEMS AND PROGRESS

AENA (1991), *Annual Report and Accounts 1990–91*, Hertfordshire: AENA.

AENA (1993), *Netball*, Hertfordshire: AENA.

Birrell, S. (1989), 'Racial Relations Theories and Sport: Suggestions for a More Critical Analysis', *Sociology of Sport*, Vol. 6: 212–17.

Carrington, B., Chivers, T. and Williams, T. (1987), 'Gender, Leisure and Sport: A Case Study of Young People of South Asian Descent', in *Leisure Studies*, Vol. 6, No. 3: 265–79.

Carrington, B. and Williams, T. (1988), 'Patriarchy and Ethnicity: The Link between School Physical Education and Community Leisure Activities', in J. Evans (ed.), *Teachers, Teaching and Control in Physical Education*, London: Falmer Press: 83–96.

Cashmore, E. (1982), *Black Sportsmen*, London: Routledge & Kegan Paul.

Crum, B. (1988), 'A Critical Analysis of Korfball as a "Non-Sexist Sport"', in *International Review for the Sociology of Sport*, Vol. 23, No. 3: 233–43.

David, D. (1991), 'Success in the Long Term', *Sport and Leisure* (November/December).

Dewar, A. (1991), 'Incorporation or Resistance?: Towards an Analysis of Women's Responses to Sexual Oppression in Sport', in *International Review for the Sociology of Sport*, Vol. 26, No. 1.

Dixey, R. (1982), 'Asian Women and Sport', in *British Journal of Physical Education*, Vol. 13, No. 4: 108, 114.

Featherstone, M. (1982), 'The Body in Consumer Culture', in M. Featherstone, M. Hepworth and B. Turner (eds) (1991), *The Body: Social Process and Cultural Theory*, London: Sage Publications.

Featherstone, M. and Hepworth, M. (1988) 'The Mask of Ageing and the Postmodern Life Course', in M. Featherstone, M. Hepworth and B. Turner (eds) (1991), *The Body: Social Process and Cultural Theory*, London: Sage Publications.

Fleming, S. (1988), 'Asian Lifestyles and Sports Participation', paper presented at the Leisure Studies Association Second International Conference, 'Leisure, Labour and Lifestyles: International Comparisons', University of Sussex, Brighton, England.

Fluegelman, A. (ed.) (1976), *The New Games Book*, New York: Doubleday.

Frank, A. (1991), 'For a Sociology of the Body: An Analytic Review', in M. Featherstone, M. Hepworth and B. Turner (eds), *The Body: Social Process and Cultural Theory*, London: Sage Publications.

Fuller, M. (1990), 'A Whole New Ballgame', in *Magazine of the NL*, Vol. 25, No. 11.

Grayson, E. (1987), 'The Law and Women in Sport', in *Coaching Focus*, No 6.

Griffin, P. and Genasci, J. (1990), 'Addressing Homophobia in Physical Education: Responsibilities for Teachers and Researchers', in M. Messner and D. Sabo (eds) *Sport, Men and the Gender Order*, Champaign, Ill.: Human Kinetics.

Grimes, P. and French, L. (1987), 'Barriers to Disabled Women's Participation in Sports', in *Journal of Physical Education, Recreation and Dance*, Vol. 50, No. 3.

Hargreaves, J. A. (1990), 'Gender on the Sports Agenda', in *International Review for the Sociology of Sport*, Vol. 25, No. 4: 287–309.

Hargreaves, J. A. (1991), 'Running Gay', in *Sport and Leisure* (November–December).

Hargreaves, J. A. (1992), 'Women and Sport: Alternative Values and Practices', paper presented at the Olympic Scientific Congress, 'Sport and Quality of Life', Malaga, Spain.

ITF News (1992), No. 46.

James, B. (1990), 'Sport and Disability in Britain Today', unpublished BSc dissertation, Roehampton Institute, University of Surrey.

Jarvie, G. (1991), 'Sport, Racism and Ethnicity: Introduction', in G. Jarvie (ed.), *Sport, Racism and Ethnicity*, London: Falmer Press.

Kidd, D. (1983), 'Getting Physical: Compulsory Heterosexuality and Sport', in *Canadian Woman Studies*, Vol. 4, No. 3: 62–5.

Lashley, H. (1991), 'Promoting Anti-racist Policy and Practice', in *Sport and Leisure* (November/December).

Lenskyj, H. (1986), *Out of Bounds: Women, Sport and Sexuality*, Toronto: Women's Press.

Lenskyj, H. (1990), 'Power and Play: Gender and Sexuality Issues in Sport and Physical Activity', *International Review for the Sociology of Sport*, Vol. 25, No. 3: 235–43.

Leonard, G. (1979) 'Winning Isn't Everything. It's Nothing', in A. Yiannakis (ed.), *Sports Sociology*, Dubuque, Iowa: Kendall Hunt.

Lightbown, C. (1987), *Millwall in the Community*, London: Saint Clair Press.

Lovell, T. (1991), 'Sport, Racism and Young Women', in G. Jarvie (ed.), *Sport, Racism and Ethnicity*, London: Falmer Press.

Lyons, A. (1988), *Asian Women and Sport*, West Midlands: Sports Council.

MacNeill, M. (1988), 'Active Women, Media Representations, and Ideology', in J. Harvey and H. Cantelon (eds), *Not Just a Game: Essays in Canadian Sport Sociology*, Ottawa: University of Ottawa.

Marshall, T. (1991), 'Building on Ability', in *Sport and Leisure* (May/June).

Messner, M. (1990), 'Masculinities and Athletic Careers: Bonding and Status Differences', in M. Messner and D. Sabo (eds), *Sport, Men, and the Gender Order: Critical Feminist Perspectives*, Champaign, Ill.: Human Kinetics.

Messner, M. and Sabo, D. (eds) (1990), *Sport, Men, and the Gender Order: Critical Feminist Perspectives*, Champaign, Ill.: Human Kinetics.

Minister of Sport (1989), Review Group Report, 'Building on Ability', London: HMSO.

Moucha, S. (1991), 'The Disabled Female Athlete as Role Model', in *Journal of Physical Education, Recreation and Dance*, Vol. 62, No. 3.

Nelson, M. Burton (1991a), 'A Silence so Loud it Screams', in *Sports Illustrated*, (May).

Nelson, M. Burton (1991b), *Are We Winning Yet? How Women are Changing Sports and Sports are Changing Women*, New York: Random House.

North West Council for Sport and Recreation (1991), *Women and Sport in the North West*, Sports Council (North West).

Oliver, M. (1990), *The Politics of Disablement*, London: Macmillan.

Orlick, T. (1978), *The Co-operative Sports and Games Book*, New York: Pantheon Books.

Palzkill, B. (1990), 'Between Gymshoes and Highheels – the Development of a Lesbian Identity and Existence in Top Class Sport', in *International Review for the Sociology of Sport*, Vol. 25, No. 3.

Popplewell, O. (1986), *Crowd Safety and Control at Sportgrounds: Final Report*, London: HMSO.

Pronger, B. (1990), *The Arena of Masculinity: Sports, Homosexuality and the Meaning of Sex*, London: GMP Publishers.

Rail, G. (1990), 'Women's Sport in the Post-War Period', paper presented at the Thirtieth Session of the International Olympic Academy.

Raval, S. (1989), 'Gender, Leisure and Sport: a Case Study of Young People of Asian Descent – a Response', *Leisure Studies*, Vol. 8: 237–40.

Reid, I. (1989), 'Vital Statistics', in I. Reid and E. Stratta (eds), *Sex Differences in Britain*, 2nd edn, Aldershot: Gower.

Reid, I. and Stratta, E. (1989), 'Sex and Gender Differences and this Book', in I. Reid and E. Stratta (eds), *Sex Differences in Britain*, 2nd edn, Aldershot: Gower.

Romney, J. (1991), 'The Big Chill', *Weekend Guardian*, 10–11 August.

Schofield, S. (1992), 'A Sociological Study of Women's Professional Golf in Europe', unpublished BSc dissertation, Roehampton Institute, University of Surrey.

Sfeir, L. (1985), 'The Status of Muslim Women in Sport: Conflict between Cultural Tradition and Modernization', in *International Review for the Sociology of Sport*, Vol. 20, No. 4: 283–305.

Sparkes, A. (1992), 'Identity Management Strategies in Shifting Contexts: A Life History Analysis of a Lesbian Physical Education Teacher', unpublished paper, University of Exeter.

Sports Council (1982), *Sport in the Community: The Next Ten Years*, London: Sports Council.

Sports Council (1988a), *Sport in the Community: Into the Nineties: A Strategy for Sport 1988–1993*, London: Sports Council.

Sports Council (1988b), *Women and Sport: A Regional Strategy*, Birmingham: Sports Council.

Sports Council (1990), *People in Sport* (fact sheet), London: Sports Council.

Sports Council (1992a), *Women and Sport: A Consultation Document*, London: Sports Council; reformulated (1993) as *Women and Sport: Policy and Frameworks for Action*.

Sports Council (1992b), *Sport in the Nineties – New Horizons: a Draft for Consultation*, London: Sports Council; reissued (1993) as *Sport in the Nineties – New Horizons*.

Stempel, G., Mills, A., Goldberg, A. and Bell, R. (1990) *A Report on the Millwall Community Sports Scheme Exchange Visit to Football Clubs in West Germany*, London: Millwall Football Club.

Summerfield, K. and White, A. (1989), 'Korfball: A Model of Egalitarianism?', in *Sociology of Sport Journal*, Vol. 6: 144–51.

Talbot, M. (1981) 'Managing Sport for All', paper presented at the Panhellenic Physical Education Association Conference, 'Sport for All and Physical Education', Athens, Greece.

Talbot, M. (1982), 'Women's Leisure: Bingo, Boredom or Badminton', in I. Glaister (ed.), *Physical Education, Sport and Leisure: Sociological Perspectives*, Oxford: Evenlode Press.

Turnbull, A. (1985), *Running Together*, London: Allen & Unwin.

Turner, B. (1991), 'Recent Developments in the Theory of the Body', and 'The Discourse of Diet', in M. Featherstone, M. Hepworth and B. Turner (eds), *The Body: Social Process and Cultural Theory*, London: Sage Publications.

Unity '94, a 1994 Gay Games publication.

White, A. (1991), 'Sports Equity: A New Concept?', paper presented at the Sport and Leisure Scotland Conference '91, 25–7 November.

Williams, J. and Woodhouse, J. (1991), 'Can Play? Will Play? Women and Football in Britain', Sir Norman Chester Centre for Football Research, Department of Sociology, University of Leicester; in J. Williams and S. Wagg (eds), *Going into Europe: British Football and Social Change*, Leicester: Leicester University Press.

Wimbush, E. and Talbot, M. (1988), *Relative Freedoms: Women and Leisure*, Milton Keynes: Open University Press.

Women's Equality Unit (1984), *Being Together: Southwark Women Talking about Leisure*, London: Women's Equality Unit.

Women's Sports Foundation (1990), *Front Runners: Examples of New Initiatives and Good Practice in the Provision of Sport and Leisure for Women and Girls*, London: Printing Tower Print.

11 INTO THE TWENTY-FIRST CENTURY: DIVERSITY AND EMPOWERMENT

Barraclough, L. (1991), 'Discrimination Against Women in Golf', unpublished BSc dissertation, Roehampton Institute, University of Surrey.

Combes, A. (1991), 'This One Will Run and Run', in *Weekend Guardian* (2–3 March).

Dewar, A. (1991), 'Incorporation or Resistance?: Towards an Analysis of Women's Responses to Sexual Oppression in Sport', in *International Review for the Sociology of Sport*, Vol. 26, No. 1.

Dyer, K. (1982), *Catching Up the Men: Women in Sport*, London: Junction Books.

Dyer, K. (ed.) (1989), *Sportswomen Towards 2000: A Celebration*, South Australia: Hyde Park Press.

Grayson, E. (1987), 'The Law and Women in Sport', in *Coaching Focus*, No. 6.

Hammond D. (1991), 'Sexism in Athletics: A Personal Exploration', unpublished.

Hargreaves, J. A. (1984), 'Action Replay: Looking at Women in Sport', In J. Holland (ed.), *Feminist Action*, Hounslow: Battle Axe Books.

Lenskyj, H. (1986), *Out of Bounds: Women, Sport and Sexuality*, Toronto: Women's Press.

Martin, A. (1979), *The Equestrian Woman*, London: Paddington Press.

Ramsden, C. (1973), *Ladies in Racing*, London: Stanley Paul.

Thompson, A. (1992), 'Women in League', in *Sport and Leisure*, January/February.

Author index

This index is not a comprehensive list of all the authors referenced in every chapter, but a selection of those considered to be most helpful to the reader. There are very few authors of nineteenth century texts listed here. Organizations and bodies such as the AENA, the Board of Education and the Sports Council, which have produced their own publications, are featured in the subject index.

Subject index

Adams, Eleanor 284–5
administration: women's involvement in 183, 184, 198, 200, 249, 260
adolesence 156–8; class differences 157
advertising: and gender 148, 158; and sexuality 161, 166, 167, 195, 206
aerobics 160-1, 239, 240, 242, 246, 247; in schools 156
African countries 226–7, 229, 230, 232–3; African Games 230
Afro-Caribbean women; *see* black women
age 165, 181, 239, 246, 264–8; and class 21; and disability 264, 266
agency: of women in sports 127, 130, 286, 288; and structure 7, 12, 37–8, 272; *see also* autonomy; freedom
aggression: aggressive masculinity 38, 171; in boys' PE 190; gender differences 111, 145–7, 149, 152, 163; in male sports 7, 31, 43, 108, 149, 237; opposition to 40, 240, 248–9
All England Netball Association (AENA) 124, 250; *see also* netball
angling 126
anorexia nervosa 161
Anstey College 49, 56, 74, 75, 79, 82
Anstey, Rhoda 49, 85
Arabic women in sports 231
archery 66, 88, 98–9, 210
Arnold, Matthew 60
Asia 227; Asian Games 230; Asian women 28, 181, 243, 245, 254, 255–60
athleticism: in women's sports 117, 130, 163, 167–8, 196, 261; cult of 43, 60, 83, 108, 209
athletics 95, 129–34, 201, 211–14, 218, 279–80; Amateur Athletic Association

131, 280; British Athletic Federation 200, 283; International Amateur Athletic Federation (IAAF) 212, 213, 218, 223, 280; and sponsorship 204, 206; Women's Amateur Athletic Association 280; Women's Athletic Association 130, 131, 133
Atkins, Sue 282
Australia 184, 186, 249, 250
autonomy: and control 271–2; *see also* agency; freedom
aviation 118

badminton 53, 64, 100, 103, 117, 201
Bagot Stack, Mary 134, 135
bandy 98
baseball 116, 195
basketball 66, 103, 165; NCAA Women's Basketball Championships 197
Beale, Dorothea 56, 57, 63–4, 74
Beauvoir, Simone de 148
Bedford College 56, 74, 75, 82
Bergman Österberg, *see* Österberg
Berlioux, Monique 221
bicycling; *see* cycling
billiards 11
biology: biological differences between the sexes 7, 30, 31, 43–7, 222, 282–4; biological explanations about women's sports 105–7, 125, 133–4, 177, 212–13, 214, 217; biological reductionism 43, 62; biologism 146, 155–6
black sportswomen 232–3, 250, 251, 255–60
Blankers-Koen, Fanny 216
body-building 168-9, 275

body maintenance 160-2
Boulmerka, Hassiba 231, 232
bowls 66, 126, 137, 176, 203, 250, 266
boxing 30, 114, 143, 195, 217, 218, 282-3
British Workers' Sports Federation 138, 140
British Empire Games 134
British Olympic Association; see Olympics
Bruce, Honorary Mrs Victor 11
bulimia 161
Burton, Beryl 285
Buss, Frances Mary 56, 63-5, 74

calisthenics 48, 55, 57, 58, 63, 64, 103, 104
Canada 183-4, 200, 201, 204, 230, 246, 262, 263; Canadian Association for the Advancement of Women and Sport 287
canoe slalom 218
capitalist relations and gender relations 23, 24, 34-6
car-racing 118
Central Council of Physical Recreation (CCPR) 235; Central Council of Physical Training and Recreation (CCPTR) 137
Chambers, Mrs Lambert 116
chauvinism: in sports 19, 29, 43, 209; male chauvinism 30, 123;
Chelsea College 74, 79
China 164, 227
civilizing process 13, 16
Clarke, Dr Edward 44
class: class differences in female leisure and sports 20, 107, 109-11, 113, 118-20, 120, 178, 185, 235-6; class relations and female sports 79-81, 235-6; and gender 21, 23, 35-6, 179; middle-class PE 55-62, 63-8, 120-1; middle-class women and sports 47-55, 108, 118-20, 246; ruling-class patronage of female sports 71-2, 104-5, 124, 135; upper-class women and sports 88-91, 118-19; working-class PE 68-74, 121-2; working-class women and sports 110-11, 124, 138-144, 250-3
climbing 118, 119; rock-climbing 239, 247
clubs: girls' club movement 79-80, 110-11, 138; see also Polytechnics

coaching 198-9; 200-3, 239; see also National Coaching Foundation
Cobbe, Frances P. 108
comics: sports in 149-50
commercialization: of the female body 158-60, 245; of female sports 236-7; of sports 17, 113; of sportswomen 162-3, 207, 226
Commonwealth Games 162, 195, 198, 230, 269
communist sports 141, 224-5, 226
competitiveness: and masculinity 31, 38, 63, 108, 149; in boys' PE 190
Compulsory Competitive Tendering (CCT) 177-8
Comte, Auguste 44
conservation of energy: theory of 45, 48, 59, 60, 83, 123, 134; see also constitutional overstrain
constitutional overstrain 213; see also conservation of energy
Coubertin, Baron Pierre de 209, 211, 213
Coulson, Phyllis 137
Council of Europe 184
cricket 84, 98, 102, 121, 123-4, 276-7; International Women's Cricket Council 276; Women's Cricket Association 124, 276; Women's Cricket World Cup 276-7
croquet 53, 57, 63, 98-9; All England Croquet Club 98
Crowther Report 152
culture: adolescent culture 156-8; consumer culture 156, 160-3; definition of 12, 36; and nature 34, 43
Curtis Cup 125
cycling 91, 92-3, 94-5, 139; cycle racing 114; Cyclists Touring Club 94; long distance cycling 284

dance 203; disco dance 156; in higher education 192-3; in the National Curriculum 11, 152, 153, 154, 189-90
Dartford College 49, 56, 74, 78, 79, 82, 84, 85
darts 114
Darwinism 44-6, 70, 77, 83, 90, 91, 106, 111, 133
Davies, Emily 84
Davies, Sharron 162
Decker, Mary 170
developing countries 223, 226, 227-34